D=169
D1226512

# THE GENIUS OF THE GERMAN LYRIC

*By the same author:*

WELTLOHN, TEUFELSBEICHTE, WALDBRUDER
(DAME WORLD, MEDIEVAL EXEMPLA)

THE GENIUS OF THE GERMAN LYRIC. An Historical Survey Of Its Formal And Metaphysical Values

GERMAN LYRICS OF THE SEVENTEENTH CENTURY
(with W. F. Mainland)

HÖLDERLIN, poems

TRISTAN UND ISOLT, a poem by Gottfried von Strassburg

DIE FREIEN RHYTHMEN IN DER DEUTSCHEN LYRIK

DIE NEUERE DEUTSCHE LYRIK VOM BAROCK BIS ZUR GEGENWART (in W. Stammler's *Aufriss*), 2nd enlarged edition

THE HARRAP ANTHOLOGY OF GERMAN POETRY
(with P. Williams)

MEDUSA'S MIRROR. Studies in German Literature

GOETHE, 1779

*Portrait by H. Pfenninger, Zürich Stadtbibliothek*

# THE GENIUS OF THE GERMAN LYRIC

*An Historical Survey of its Formal and Metaphysical Values*

*by*

A. Closs, M.A., D.Phil.

*Professor of German,*
*University of Bristol*

LONDON

THE CRESSET PRESS

MCMLXII

© 1938, 1962 by August Closs

Published in Great Britain by
The Cresset Press 11 Fitzroy Square London W.1

FIRST PUBLISHED IN 1938

SECOND EDITION REVISED AND ENLARGED 1962

PT
571
.C6

*Printed in Great Britain by*
*The Camelot Press Ltd., London and Southampton*

TO MY WIFE
HANNAH PRIEBSCH CLOSS
(1905–1953)
IN HER UNTIRING QUEST
OF SPIRIT AND FORM

116641

# PREFACE TO THE SECOND EDITION

It is almost a quarter of a century since the First Edition of this book on the formal and metaphysical values of German lyric poetry was published. Its appeal to a scholarly and wider cultural circle found such keen response here and abroad, that it became urgently necessary to issue a Second Edition, which is not only a revision of the previous one but which also offers a much needed and entirely new section on the development of the German lyric from the last war to 1960. The other chapters remain essentially unaltered.

To avoid expense the additional portion of the book replaces the Bibliography which, when brought up to date, will develop into a separate volume. As regards individual authors, anthologies, general criticism, aesthetic theory and translations, etc., I should like to refer to the selected lists of reference-books in my '*Medusa's Mirror*' (Cresset Press, 1957) and in '*The Harrap Anthology of German Poetry*' (1957), in Josef Körner's '*Bibliographisches Handbuch des deutschen Schrifttums*,' Bern, 1949, and also in Professor Angel Flores's '*Anthology of German Poetry from Hölderlin to Rilke in English Translations*,' New York, 1960.

It gives me profound satisfaction that even after almost a generation the fundamental substance of this comprehensive study can stand. I have, however, been sincerely grateful for all detailed criticisms, friendly as well as adverse, and wherever justified I have carefully checked and corrected points of interpretation and analysis, always trying to keep a balance between these two approaches to literature. It is my fervent hope that this Second Edition will help to deepen the understanding and appreciation of the creative forces in German lyric poetry.

To my revered friend and colleague in the U.S.A., Professor Emeritus Bayard Quincy Morgan of Stanford University, I owe special thanks for going through the whole First Edition as to presentation and style, and I have incorporated a number of his valuable suggestions. I am also grateful for the encouragement in my research, which I received from Professor Emeritus E. H. Zeydel (Cincinnati), Professor V. Lange (Princeton), Professor D. J. Enright (now at the University of Malaya, Singapore), Professor W. F. Mainland (Sheffield), J. B. Leishman (Fellow of St. John's, Oxford), and from Professor Emeritus L. A. Willoughby (London) and Professor Emeritus W. E. Collinson (Liverpool), both being most eminent scholars and pupils of the late Professor R. Priebsch to whom I owe the greatest debt as regards integrity of scholarship, research and personal happiness.

I am very grateful to Miss Ursula Codrington for reading the galley-proofs. My colleague Dr. Estelle Morgan most generously helped me in reading the page-proofs and in preparing the word-index.

Finally I wish to thank my daughter, Miss Elizabeth Closs, B.A. (Oxon.) (now at Berkeley, University of California), for help in preparing the MS. for the press.

A. C.

*New Year* 1962

# PREFACE TO THE FIRST EDITION

(SHORTENED)

THIS volume represents the fruit of many years' research into the formal and metaphysical values of the German lyric. The author, who believes this to be the first comprehensive study of its kind in the English language, has laid *especial stress on individual analyses of the poems*, thereby hoping to interpret their individuality as a phenomenon peculiar to itself and to a particular moment in history. He trusts that he has in some ways followed paths hitherto untrodden, as for instance in his evaluation of the lyric during the transition from the sixteenth to the seventeenth century, and the significance of the 'baroque'; likewise in discussing poems by Klopstock, the Romantics, by Austrian poets, Mörike, Dehmel, George, and others. Holz has been dealt with in special detail as an exponent of 'free verse.'

It is not the aim of the book to present in unbroken outline the entire history of the German lyric, nor is it based on any *a priori* or absolute ideal of form. The author has rather used the *object* as a starting-point which, however, he regards as largely determined by intellectual, historic, and social factors (see the minnesong). Any attempt to set up sharply defined categories should, in his estimation, result only from a final summing up of *conclusions drawn from individual analyses*. Thus we shall, for instance, realize that the seventeenth-century lyric is by no means 'baroque' in all its manifestations, even though the 'courtly-baroque' element is predominant.

Each century seeks and finds its own consummation. In the course of this study the author has taken especial care to avoid the mistake of regarding one century merely as the forerunner of its possibly more famous successor. He points to the simultaneous presence of old and new values.

Form and expression are as closely related as skin and bone. It is the intuitive aesthetic conscience of the poet, and also his social, religious, and racial attitude as child of his age, which determine his choice of form (sonnet, ode, hymn, etc.). Where form is no more than formula, a borrowed pattern, or where the school not the individual rules supreme, the lyric too easily becomes but a husk, the toy of empty virtuosity. In such cases stress has been laid on the source of inspiration, e.g. *West-östlicher Divan*, *Phantasus*, rather than on the imitations. The research of German and foreign scholars has not been ignored. But both in regard to criticism and to poetry itself, the author only discusses such works as he has himself read. It is his earnest hope that his own work will be more than superficially scanned and that it may appeal not only to the scholar, but to a wider cultural circle.

In analysing a poem, not every formal weakness has been dragged into the light with the punctiliousness of a Beckmesser. Where, however, as in Hebbel's case, some sudden rift seems to illumine the essential peculiarity of a poet, this ungenerous harping on faults seems justified. The author is only too well aware of the limitations of criticism. Hölderlin's words: 'They only believe in the divine who themselves possess it' mean that *understanding is the result of affinity*. To unveil the secret is to comprehend the inner necessity of a work of art. A comparison of motifs (always remembering that one and the same motif may be a source of new inspiration to various poets) helps our understanding, though the poet's individuality must ever be regarded as the chief problem. Nor must it be forgotten that similar means (metre, caesura, etc.) can often produce very different effects. Moreover, the date or period of a poem is not without significance. Indeed, the lyric did not flourish in every age, for instance in the *Gründerzeit*. As the purest expression of a poet's or a people's individuality the lyric has many advantages over dramatic or narrative art. . . .

The author wishes to express his gratitude to the Colston Research Fund of the University of Bristol for a grant which helped towards the publication of this work.

In pursuing his studies the author has found a constant aid in the unique collection of early editions and incunabula, belonging to the late Professor Robert Priebsch, which has come into his possession through the generosity of his wife.

The author cannot conclude this book without thanking Hannah

Priebsch Closs to whom this book is dedicated, and his colleague Professor J. Crofts (Bristol University), for so generously revising the MS. before it finally went to press. Miss J. Lambdin kindly undertook the arduous task of preparing the word-index.

The choice of illustrations does not necessarily correspond to the author's predilection for certain poets, but was dictated by material circumstances.

A. C.

*Spring* 1938

# CONTENTS

CONTENTS

# ILLUSTRATIONS

# INTRODUCTION

## THE ORIGINS OF THE GERMAN LYRIC

WE still possess traces of lyric verse dating from the Old High German period, although the bulk of the material has, alas, vanished. Measured against the wealth of scaldic song inherited from Norway and Iceland, the loss of its German counterpart is all the more bitter. Whereas ancient Norse literature can offer a variety of types: children's songs, love-songs, derisive songs, jesting songs (which may be compared to the German *Schnadahüpfl*) no vestige of them remains in Anglo-Saxon and Old High German literature. A favourite form of scaldic song is the long *Preislied* (laudatory poem) with its complex construction in which the hero's deeds are extolled. The *kenning* (e.g. battle = the storm of the Valkyrie, gold = the dragon's bed) is typical of these songs as is also a peculiar disintegration of syntax which reminds one of the convulsions of Nordic linear ornament. But apart from Caedmon's hymn or the Old English poem on Athelstan's victory at Brunanburh, and references in *Beowulf* and historical accounts, the Old High German *Ludwigslied* is the only remaining parallel to the *Preislied.*

The Norse lays abound with legends of gods and heroes. In Old High German on the other hand, only the *Hildebrandslied* is preserved, which in style bears resemblance to the *Finnesburh Lay.* Like this Anglo-Saxon poem it is but a fragment, a lump of ore from the treasure-trove of Germanic history, full of the rugged force that belongs only to the heroic lay with its vehement alliterative rhythm.

It was at the time of the 'migration of the peoples,' from the third to the sixth century A.D., that such Germanic heroic poetry developed in praise of the intrepid leaders whom men could look up to with proud faith. The Old High German *Hildebrandslied* was entered in a Latin MS. during the second decade of the ninth century by two monks of the monastery of Fulda, which was founded by the Anglo-Saxon missionary St. Boniface, later Archbishop of Mainz. The *Hildebrandslied* possesses the essentially dramatic character of the Germanic heroic lay, its terseness of expression (foreshadowing the later ballads) and its avoidance of mere description. There is no trace of the comic or grotesque. Its theme is that of the tragic conflict between father and son, so popular in modern psychological literature.

Had the Codex in which Charlemagne preserved the *barbara et antiquissima carmina* which dealt with the deeds and wars of ancient kings not been destroyed, we might still possess more lays of this type. For instance, we hear of Bernlêf, a blind Frisian poet of the eighth century, who sang of the feuds of heroes to the accompaniment of the harp.

The Anglo-Saxon elegies bear witness to the existence of love-lyrics. Old High German literature also contains elegiac effusions, as we learn from certain passages of Otfrid's, who wanted to put an end to heathen song with his Gospels. The prohibitive laws levelled by the Church against the singing of *amatoria cantica, orationes amatoriae, seculares cantilenae, cantica rustica et inepta, chori foeminei*, etc., again point to erotic literature. Old High German contains the word *winileod*, which is glossed as *psalmi plebei*. From Charlemagne's *Capitularium* (789) we learn that certain nuns are subject to the following law: *ut nullatenus ibi uuinoleodos scribere vel mittere praesumant*. Possibly the nuns themselves were the authors of such songs.

We may also take it for granted that, though so far we have not come across any, dancing-songs did exist. Other types of short poems such as magic spells and charms, however, remain; also riddles, as is proved by a Latin version of one on 'the featherless bird.' It was indeed in the Latin tongue that during the ninth century Godescalc wrote hymns of great lyric power.

The earliest extant example of German lyric poetry may be found in the Bavarian *Ruodlieb* (about 1050) which is also written in Latin (tr. into English by E. H. Zeydel, cf. *Germanistik* I.1, pp. 42/43), but incorporates two German rhymes:

> *tantumdem* liebes, *veniat quantum modo* loubes,
> *et volucrum* wunna *quot sint, tot dic sibi* minna.

The twelfth century gave birth to that precious jewel:

*Dû bist mîn, ich bin dîn:*
*des solt dû gewis sîn.*
*dû bist beslozzen*
*in mînem herzen;*
*verlorn ist daz slüzzelîn:*
*dû muost och immer darinne sîn.*

It appears at the end of a Latin letter addressed to a cleric by a learned lady. The lines are not those of a folk-song, but a touchingly simple confession recalling the betrothal formula: *Vivam tuus, vive mea* and *Solomon: Song* (2/16): 'My beloved is mine, and I am his.' . . . It was not until the *Minnesangs Frühling* (about 1170) that German lyric poetry suddenly put forth blossoms so exquisite that at its finest moments with Walther, Wolfram, and Heinrich von Morungen, it can in its own particular way rival the lyrics of Goethe.

# I
# THE GERMAN MINNESINGERS

*Revived interest in the Middle Ages*

German minnesong—the word conjures up a visionary world of knights and minstrels, of romanticism buried beneath the dust of seven hundred years. But if the legacy of medieval lyric verse is to mean more to us than an object of mere sentimental infatuation or a dead text mutilated and dissected by philological zeal, we must investigate its origins and development, its ethic and æsthetic code, and endeavour to understand something of the history of those social conditions that gave it birth. Our first step, in approaching these problems, must be to ask what significance this literary phenomenon of the Middle Ages has for our present age, which witnessed Stefan George invoking a 'third humanism' with his vision of 'Sparta's steel-bound courage wedded to Ionia's grace.' How remote George's attitude is from that of the true Middle Ages is proved by his *Sagen und Sänge*, in which a solemn *Parzivalstimmung*, the love-cult (*Minnedienst*), or the prowess of the Knight Templar, are treated without any attempt to regain their local colour. They mainly represent stages of the poet's own spiritual development. But the dawn of the twentieth century also gave birth to Rilke's *Stunden-Buch*, the *memento mori* of the modern *Gottsucher*, singing of the monastic life and pilgrimage, of poverty and death:

> *We are only the husk and the leaf.*
> *The great death which lives in each of us,*
> *That is the fruit round which all turns.*

A gulf separates such mysticism, with its meditations on death and the *vita contemplativa*, from the heritage of Goethe's classicism or even George's steel-tempered vision of Christianity. In deep gratitude to the Worpswede painter Heinrich Vogeler, Rilke, the poet of the *Marienleben*, turns from the beguilements of *Dame World* to set out on his quest of *Gottesminne*. Not that the medieval poet despised life.

In the field of research many a treatise published during recent years testifies that here too interest in the Middle Ages is by no means exhausted, although the vast production of medieval texts and *Monumenta Germaniae Historica* are inevitably resulting in a diminished output. The popularity enjoyed by Hefele's essays, Schmalenbach's *Das Mittelalter* and Landsberg's *Die Welt des Mittelalters und wir* is characteristic of our present-day attitude, whilst a revived enthusiasm for medieval art was furthered by Dvořak, Worringer, Strzygowski, Dehio, Pinder, and others. Research on the cultural history of the Middle Ages pointed out the importance of transcendental gradualism, for instance in Walter's '*Ich saz ûf eime steine*,' where asceticism and earthly joy seek reconciliation. *Utile et Honestum* are allotted their special positions in the moral scale leading towards *Summum Bonum*. We see therefore that the Middle Ages are by no means dead. Improving on Eiken's *Geschichte und System der mittelalterlichen Weltanschauung*, H. Brinkmann and A. v. Martin based their studies on Troeltsch, who denied the purely ascetic character of medieval thought and pointed to its organic unity in which the spirit of classicism yet lingered. There is no longer any doubt that the antique age itself knew pessimism, asceticism, and mysticism (through Plotinus, the Stoics, and Orphism), and that harmony is not only to be found in the culture of Greece and Rome but in the Middle Ages, for instance in the cult of the holy Virgin (*Marienideal*). Likewise medieval literature and art are not lacking in the profane element. The classic grandeur of the carven figures at Naumburg and the Bamberg *Rider*, that symbol of *hôher muot* and *mâze*, afford parallels to the Staufen ideal in the field of art.

### *Social and Political Conditions*

More than seven hundred years have passed since German art and song put forth their first incomparable blossom. In 1227 Walther von der Vogelweide composed his moving elegy:

*Owê war sint verswunden alliu mîniu jâr? . . .*

Half religious, half political, it is at once a confession and meditation on his own life, tinged with something of the spirit of Parzival. A few years later—Wolfram and Heinrich von Morungen having already preceded him—he bade farewell to this world. Walther's fresh and powerful gift of song, his unique personality which burst the conventions of contemporary lyric poetry, or transfused them with new vitality, his intimate yet proudly noble tone, would in themselves suffice to render the German minnesong immortal. Certainly it may be difficult to feel at ease amidst the constrained forms which bound the chivalric ideal, but Walther and his somewhat older contemporary Reinmar, Wolfram, with his verse pent with volcanic fire, Heinrich von Morungen, the poet of the swinging rhythm: '*Ich hôrte ûf der heide . . .*,' or the darkly passionate dawn-song: '*Owê, sol aber mir iemer mê . . .*,' and many another throng to join their exquisite lyric note to the glory of epic verse which triumphed in Hartmann, Gottfried, Wolfram, and that mighty unknown writer of the *Nibelungenlied*.

We shall understand the birth, development, and decay of the minnesong far better if we try to obtain a picture of the social and political circumstances which gave it birth, at the time when the proud walls of the Wartburg, near Eisenach in the heart of the Thuringian forests, resounded with the fervour of the *Sängerstreit*. Here Landgraf Hermann, famed for the hospitality he offered to many an unruly company of minstrels, enriched his court with the song of Walther and Wolfram.

This period, and that shortly preceding it, recognized three social classes of poets, the wandering scholar, the cleric, and the knight. The fourth class of poets, the 'burgher-scholar,' though represented in this early period by Gottfried of Strassburg, did not reach full development until the age of chivalry had passed. The so-called vagantes, wandering professional minstrels, were not always clerics. They sang their own songs and others as a means of livelihood. We must thus differentiate between worldly cleric verse, professional poetry (Walther), and the so-called lower orders of song (*niedere Trink-, Spiel- und Betteldichtung*).

The clerics, for the most part monks who until about 1150 had held sway over literary activity, now gradually lost their influence, although they continued even till a far later date to embellish their sermons with German poetry and use it as a means of popularizing their ascetic and ecclesiastic *Weltanschauung*. From the pulpit there reverberated ever and again, in prose and rhyme, the sombre admonition to reject *Frau Welt*, whose seductive power was decried even by laymen, both of the knightly and bourgeois class. Thus Walther in his valediction to the earth sings:

*Frô Werlt, ich hân ze vil gesogen:*
*Ich wil entwonen, des ist zît. . . .*

Lyric and epic effusions poured forth in praise of the Trinity, of Mary, the saints, and martyrs. Not only subjects from the Old and New Testaments, but also those of worldly origin (*Alexanderlied*, *Rolandslied*) were recited by clerics as an instrument of edification. They paled when chivalry, developing its own artistic code, gave birth in the minnesong to a form of lyric poetry which was the pure expression of its social cult. For the knights not only encouraged worldly poetry but were also well acquainted with spiritual themes, such as crusading songs, legends, and poetry in praise of the Virgin Mary.

Thus the minnesong reached its perfection in the thirteenth century when knighthood was at its zenith. The clergy had likewise secured a privileged position for themselves, for the mitred shepherds of the soul were simultaneously lords of the realm. Jeopardized by the inexorable struggle for power between church and state, the emperor's sovereign authority threatened to collapse. Henry IV was forced to suffer humiliation at Canossa in order to regain his kingdom. Gregory VII (Hildebrand) summoned Christendom to fight the paynim, thereby (as Scherer rightly recognized) enabling his successors to weld all the chivalric ideals and ambitions of the West into one great weapon and place it in the hand of the church, where it was soon found useful for other purposes, besides that of subduing the paynim. That same Gregory, as wily a statesman as he was pope, summoned the sovereignty of the people against the emperor.

Then once again the Staufen, Frederick Barbarossa († 1190), Henry VI († 1197), and his son Frederick II († 1250), the most illustrious of his line, who in his indefatigable struggle against a succession of popes (Innocent III, Honorius III, Gregory IX, and Innocent IV) led the Holy Roman empire to the last climax of its glory under the Staufen reign, laughed defiance in the face of Rome. He who fostered both the Italian canzona and German minnesong stands as a glorious symbol of cultural relations which flourished between different lands.

Chivalry, a European phenomenon, was, for all its exclusive class-consciousness, cosmopolitan in character, a fact to which education, social forms and organization all bear witness. Until he had reached his seventh year the knight-to-be remained under the care of his mother, after which the child (*kint* or *kindelîn*) was sent to another court to receive his education. At the age of fifteen the young noble (*junchêrre*) was initiated yet further into the rules of the court, of the chase and the tournament. At twenty he was usually dubbed knight, after he had been well versed in courtly etiquette—*wol gebâren und wider die frouwen sprechen, gotes hulde und der werlde vröude mêren.* One is tempted to compare this harmonious social upbringing with that of Castiglione's Cortegiano, who represents the social ideal of the Italian renaissance with its emphasis on self-control, knightly games, duelling, riding, dancing, swimming, knowledge of several languages and belles-lettres, æsthetic taste, musical talent, etc., or we may see something of the same spirit still reflected in the 'gentleman' of the present day. The knight was supposed to be *magnanimus, ingenuus, largifluus, egregius,* and *strenuus,* according to the favourite formula, the first letters of these adjectives spelling the word *m-i-l-e-s.* The dubbing entitled the young knight to carry his shield in the service of God, of his liege lord and of love (*minne*). The court festival, particularly the opening of the court by Frederick Barbarossa at Mainz in 1184, heightened the glory of knighthood; both German and Romance singers attended to pay homage to the emperor. Other factors too tended to render chivalric culture international —the yearning of the Northern emperors for the South, their repeated journeys and long sojourns in Italy, the influx of German scholars to the University of Paris (founded about 1200), where a few decades earlier Peter Abélard (1079–1142) in his controversy with William of Champeaux had known triumph and defeat, or again the Eastern world opened up by the crusades, with strange lore and sensuous fantasy, likewise jousts, feasts, and dynastic relationships. At Whitsun 1156, Frederick I married Beatrice of Burgundy, the latter state and that of Provence thus accruing to him as family property. The frequent French expressions in medieval German literature point to the close inter-relationships existing between the two countries; *tjoste*, *schanze*, *âventiure*, *harnisch*, *buhurt* may serve as a few examples.

Round about the year 1168, Gautier of Arras who lived at the court of Thibaut of Blois presented his epic poem *Ille et Galéron* to the empress Beatrice. The romance treats of subject-matter recounted in Marie de France's last lay. In 1196–1197 the Provençal troubadour Peire Vidal lodged with King Emmerich of Hungary, who had married the daughter of Alphonso II of Aragon, so that one may accept the probability of Vidal's influence on Walther. Also Flemish forms, e.g. *ritter*, *dörper*, *wâpen*, *ors*, *bluemekin*, *schapellekîn*, and others, found their way into Middle High German language and literature. But inspiration did not alone come from without. The German minnesong was also able to draw rich sources of creative strength from out its own soil. Without them it could have been no more than a pale imitation of alien forms, and we must not on any account forget that the *Minnesangs Frühling*, which we shall soon consider, had created its own independent lyric verse before a far-reaching or direct contact between German and Romance poetry had taken place.

### *The Moral Concept of Chivalry*

The cultural influences already discussed were not the only factors contributing to the development of the minnesong. Amongst others we remember the high-hearted, noble ethos which illumined the path of knighthood vesting its representative with the significance of a *miles Christianus*. Nevertheless it is the æsthetic rather than the religious element (in Wolfram's sense) which we find stressed in lyric poetry. The perfect knight approaches the ideal of spiritual-physical harmony, of seriousness wedded to gaiety, nobility enhanced by beauty, more nearly than any dream of man since the days of classic Greece. Gottfried von Strassburg's *Tristan*, or the Bamberg *Rider*, bear witness to the fact. Spiritualized beauty, valour, and self-control unite to create that picture of grace and dignity which we find in the description of Isolde herself when she enters the hall at the side of her mother. Perfect manners, delight in beauty and grace, in the glamour of the court, in exquisite form, subtle mannerisms and polished speech provided a balance to the virile defiance of the fighter.

Often the knight not only revelled in passive enjoyment of art, but played an active part as exponent of music and song within his aristocratic circle. Knighthood demanded deeds not only in battle (in *schimpf und ernst*) but also in song, as we read in *Tristan* and *Parzival*. Yet it is not in Wolfram's epic, the most powerful expression of Middle High German literature, that the *æsthetic* ideal of chivalry finds its purest expression, but in Gottfried's immortal eulogy on love, where joy and sorrow intermingle to a rare formal perfection, which for all its virtuosity escaped the platitudes of superficial rhetoric.

The strict code of morals and virtue of the period embodied an æsthetic ideal founded on Platonic, Aristotelean and Stoic concepts which had been transfused by the spirit of Christianity. Plato's and Cicero's *Virtutes* appear ennobled by Christian moral philosophy and imbued with transcendental principles. To serve God is man's highest aim. It is only through self-realization and in his heartfelt search for God that Parzival is cleansed of thoughtless sin and finds his way to God, the *Summum Bonum*. He wins the crown of all knightly questing. The worldly Gawain achieves only the *Honestum* through his prowess as fighter. Base lust of pleasure pursues the *Utile*, mere worldly possessions. How often duty, heart's desire, and honour bitterly oppose one another: cf. Friedrich von Hûsen's: *Mîn herze und mîn lîp diu wellent scheiden*. This yearning to discover a graduated system of life, a union between monkish asceticism and earthly ambitions, *der werlte lop, der sêle heil* (Hartmann), or *lop und êre und dar zuo gotes hulde* (Reinmar) found pregnant expression in Walther's aphorism:

*Dekeinen rât kond ich gegeben,*
*wie man driu dinc erwürbe,*
*der keines niht verdürbe.*
*diu zwei sint êre und varnde guot,*
*daz dicke ein ander schaden tuot:*
*daz dritte ist gotes hulde,*
*der zweier übergulde.*

The reconciliation of these antithetical ideas is the desired goal which almost drives Walther in his old age to flee the pleasures of this earthly life: *Frou Werlt . . . dîn zart hât mich vil nâch betrogen. . . .* Soul-tormented abnegation of the world re-echoes through Hartmann's crusading song: *Diu werlt mich lachet triegent an . . .* or Kolmas's: *Ditze leben smilzt als ein zin. . . .* We see therefore that a dualism, felt to exist between earthly and spiritual life, casts its shadow over the minnesong. In this respect the inclination towards an æsthetically harmonious form of life as expressed in the words *Got und der werlt wol gevallen* appears doubly significant. The virtues recommended for this balanced attitude towards life are continually reflected in the dream-picture of the chivalrous hero of Middle High German literature.

The culture peculiar to court life during the Staufen period thus appears not as a vain and empty *formula*, but as something born of a fervent yearning, a vital *necessity*. Ideals and customs that belong to the sacred duties of knighthood include the admonition to shun sybaritic idleness (*sich verligen*), to act honourably in the face of the enemy and towards women. This essentially *static* form of culture seeks to avoid all excess of passion. Even the paths pursued by the heroes of the medieval German romances are hedged in by *a formal code*.

The system of virtue advocated in the teachings of Plato Aristotle, and Cicero, mitigated by Christian concepts, provides in some measure the basis of medieval morality.

In his *Nicomachean Ethics*, Aristotle developed the Platonic theory of life to a complete system, and it was principally through Cicero's *De Officiis* that Platonic-Aristotelean ethics were transmuted into our Christian moral code. St. Augustine invests the creed of *Summum Bonum, Honestum, Utile* with Christian meaning. Worldly pleasures fade to dust before the glory of the heavenly state. The four cardinal virtues are subordinated to God, the highest Good.

During the first quarter of the sixth century Boethius in his *De consolatione philosophiae* also rejects worldly possessions in favour of the highest Good, God, beneath whose sovereignty the virtues are ranged in a graduated scale.

A certain frequently copied and printed treatise, *Moralis Philosophia de honesto et utili* is particularly saturated with Cicero's ethic principle of *honestum*, cf. Migne 171.

The moral treatise of Thomasin of Zerclaere's Middle High German work: *Der Welsche Gast*, composed 1215–1216, derives to a great extent from the *Moralis Philosophia*, although the former exceeds its limits by recognizing the foundation of all virtue in *staete* which simultaneously represents the realization of all good. Only through *staete* can the moral structure of society and the divine order prevailing in everything be secured. *Mâze* (moderation) appears as the sister of *staete*. The former is analogous to Aristotle's μεσότης, *mediocritas*, *medietas*. She guards the golden mean (μηδὲν ἄγαν).

The term *zuht*, i.e. good breeding, forms a parallel to Cicero's *decorum* (*De Officiis*, I.27) and is an attribute of *temperentia*, *modestia*. Thomasin enlarges its meaning by applying it also to courtly and social *tugent*, good manners. *Tugent* represents spiritual perfection and belongs to the category *honestum*.

A moral code of equal scope to Thomasin's will *not* be found amongst the minnesingers, but the quasi-antique, quasi-Christian character of their conception of life is undeniable, *even though direct contact with classic learning and medieval moral philosophy be lacking*, as for instance in Walther's meditations on *Gotes hulde*, *êre*, *varnde guot* = *bona corporis et bona fortunae*. Walther struggles to reconcile earthly love and divine salvation, and God Himself is conceived, particularly in the crusading songs, as liege lord.

The term *êre* is enveloped in subtle ambiguity. As seen from a subjective point of view it represents a feeling of honour, honourable action and also love of honour, and is thus an attribute of *honestum*. Considered objectively it appears as the bestowal of honour, recognition, and corresponds to the Middle High German *wirde* and to the *utile* of classic ethics.

In the *hohe Minne* the virtues are invested with fresh vitality. *Fortitudo* in its Christian sense and *justitia* lead to patient contentment which Reinmar considers the guerdon of yearning love; cf. the poem beginning:

> *Ez tuot ein leit nâch liebe wê.*
> *Sô tuot ouch lîhte ein liep nâch leide wol. . . .*

The command of *mâze* (self-mastery) assuages the violent lust of conquest. With chivalrous clemency (*erbermde*) the triumphant hero demands only *sicherheit* instead of slaying his victim. Tolerance advocated by the Church rules when even the pagan knight Feirefiz casts his sword aside seeing that his combatant Parzival stands unarmed. Nevertheless the tolerance thus praised in medieval minnesong and epic must not be confused with its modern counterpart, nor is it the fruit of 'enlightened' rationalism, but flows from dauntless knightly courage, from that magnanimity to which we so often referred as one of the significant forms of culture which ruled society during the Staufen era. Much may doubtless be accredited to the influence of Christian thought, for the Church was in many respects the tutor of knighthood, as we see by the countless parallels which can be drawn between the ethical terms employed in both institutions: thus *amor*, *caritas*, service of women, service of God, *arbeit* for love, *arbeit* for the kingdom of heaven. The virtue of humility may be traced back to Christian categorical values, not to the antique. The conflict between *humilitas* and *superbia* is found in Prudentius's *Psychomachia*. In courtly morals humility is mitigated to modesty. *Minne* is as stated above also an ennobling motive power.

Minnesong and love-cult (*Minnedienst*), in so far as they are born of alien influence, will be discussed in the next chapter. Here we may remark that Old Germanic literature itself knows nothing of love service devoted in a similar way to married women of noble birth, and that the only characteristic Germanic feature of this strange custom is suggested by the relations of the vassal to his liege lord, i.e. *Gefolgschaftstreue*.

*Hohe Minne*

We must imagine ourselves in the midst of the courtly world as it flourished at the end of the romanesque period and on the threshold of the gothic, that we may procure a picture of the minnesinger as member of the *familia* or as a welcome guest whiling away the tedium of long winter evenings in the baronial hall. His was an art not naïvely spontaneous but highly formal, and intended for aristocratic society. The poetry of *hohe Minne* is comprehensible only as the product of an exclusive class, the limited community of the noblesse and the ecclesiastical court. Singer, patron, and public belonged to the same circle. The Hohenstaufen themselves composed minnesongs or fostered music and song at their court. Hence the poetry of the period is lacking neither in praise of prince or peer, nor in blame, as we see from the *schelte* or reproof which meets a stinting hand that knows too little of *milte*; thus Walther's *Spruch* against Otto—or his challenge to Philip: *Philippes künec, die nâhe spehenden zîhent dich. . . . Denk an den milten Salatîn . . . gedenke an den von Engellant . .* ; whilst on the other hand where *milte* swells to reckless extravagance as at the Thuringian court he recommends it might well be tempered with *mâze.*

The knights were the exponents of the minnesong which reached its full flowering time between the last decades of the twelfth century and second or third of the thirteenth, the period of the *höfische Sonderkultur*. German and Romance singers met at the festival held by the emperor Frederick I at Mainz in the year 1184. His son, Henry VI, was himself a minnesinger and did much to foster poetry and song among members of his circle, to which belonged Rheingraf Friedrich von Hûsen, Bernger von Horheim, and Bligger von Steinach. Henry VI's son, the great Frederick II himself, has been credited with the authorship of three canzone:

(a) *De la mia disianza. . . .*
(b) *Poi ke ti piace, amore . . .*
(c) *Oi lasso, non pensai. . . .*

Though none of them exceeds mediocrity they are of literary and historical importance in that they bear as strong an affinity to the minne-lyric as to that of the troubadours. In contrast to the above the canzone *Dolce meo drudo* betrays true creative power. It was perhaps written by Frederick's son Frederick of Antiochia (re Frederigo). Another son of the Stupor Mundi, the rebellious king Henry VII, composed songs in the manner of Gottfried von Neifen (Nîfen), who himself, together with his pupil Ulrich von Winterstetten, was connected with the poetic circle surrounding the king, a circle embracing such names as Burkart von Hohenfels, the East Frankish Count Otto von Botenlauben, the Swabian Hiltbolt von Schwangau and perhaps the Schenk von Limburg and the Swabian Taler. But to the singers of Hohenstaufen blood we must add also the names of those other two sons of Frederick II, Manfred whom Dante encountered in the *Purgatorio*, and Enzio, whose long imprisonment in Bologna was solaced by music and song, likewise Konradin, *der junge Konrad* of the Manesse Codex, who is believed to have been the son of Konrad IV, not, as was formerly supposed, the latter himself.

But other courts held no mean place as rivals of the Hohenstaufen, for instance that of the Babenbergers at Vienna, or the Landgraf Hermann in Thuringia; the courts of Meissen, Anhalt, Bavaria, and Bohemia; and those established by the nobles of Durn, Wertheim, Zähringer, Abenberg, Leiningen, and Henneberg, or of Bishop Wolfger von Passau (later Patriarch of Aquileja); above all, the grim court of the Guelphs. The Staufen appear gay and light-hearted by the side of the latter. Repeated court festivals at Worms, Speyer, Mainz, Würzburg, Nymwegen, Gelnhausen, connections with Burgundy and Provence through Barbarossa's wife Beatrice, cast glamour and power on the Staufen dynasty. They revelled in splendour, were tolerant (Frederick II) towards the pagans, and were captivated by the sensuous lure of the East. The *Literatur-Sprache* of the Rhine was fostered at their court.

The court of the Guelphs gathered at Regensburg, the residence of Henry the Proud. Pious and passionately devoted to German tradition and the national cause, though in its very conservatism adhering to the Latin tongue, it presented a strong contrast to that of the Ghibellines. To the Guelph court belong both the *Rolandslied* (composed in the reign of Henry the Proud) and the *Kaiserchronik*, the *Lucidarius* being especially composed at the command of Henry the Lion at the end of the twelfth century. The lay of *König Rother* and the Frankish romance *Herzog Ernst* also betray friendship towards the Guelphs.

Through court and castle re-echoed the strains of the minnesong, for the pleasure of high-born society and in homage to some lady whose name remained unrevealed. The oft-repeated expressions: *tougen minne*, *rüemen*, *huote*, accentuate the secret nature of love (*minne*), though Walther may sing:

*Mînes herzen tiefiu wunde*
*diu muoz iemer offen stên*
*sin werde heil von Hiltegunde*

on which occasion Walther may be using the name Hiltegunde in connection with his own as a play on the names of the Hiltegund saga.

The singer is loyal to his lady, as is the vassal to his lord. The *vrouwe* (*Herrin*) is mistress, the singer, as we have seen above, her servant *dienest* (*Diener*), her *eigen man*, bondman. He is her subject, *undertân.* He knows that his yearning can never be fulfilled; hence mourning and lament (*trûren, klagen*) is the keynote of his songs. *Minne* is merely an illusion, *ein wân.* In return for his song of praise the poet expects *lôn in der nôt*, a guerdon for his sorrow, i.e. her favour (*genâde unde hulde*). Thus faithfulness (*triuwe*) finds recompense; perhaps there is some truth in the suggestion that the love-cult (*Minnedienst*) belonged to the duties of the ministeriales, although not enjoined amongst the feudal laws.

In contrast to the *Minnesangs Frühling* only the wedded lady is worshipped, not the lowly or even high-born maiden, who, like Kriemhild in the *Nibelungenlied*, was forced to live in virginal confinement at court or castle. But Walther's *Mädchenlieder* are clearly inspired by young girls of low rank. Hence Reinmar's *hohe Minne*, in which melancholy yearning is embellished with melodious versification and subtle dialects, is transfused by Walther with fresh vitality. Here, as in his powerful political and spiritually edifying poetry and crusading songs, Walther frees the German minnesong from plagiarism of French conventions and endows it with a poignantly human note.

Already Reinmar of Hagenau, whom Gottfried in his *Tristan* calls the nightingale of Hagenau:

> *Hagenouwe . . . diu aller doene houbetlist*
> *versigelt in ir zungen truoc,*

sang before the court of Vienna a *rede* on woman's worth:

> *Sô wol dir, wîp, wie reine ein nam!*

Walther praises these verses in his manly elegy on Reinmar. He too speaks of

> *frouwen und guotes wîbes siten.*

He sings of the

> *edeliu schoene frouwe reine. . . .*

Here *frouwe* still remains the dream for which Walther then substitutes his *wîp* ideal. The strict tone of courtly etiquette is thus violated; the generic term usurps the privileges of class-concepts:

*Wîp muoz iemer sîn der wîbe hôhste name*
*und tiuret baz denn vrowe, als ichz erkenne . . .*

The nobility of the soul is here placed above social rank, thus expressing a decisive revolt against a purely formal poetry of fashion. A note of national pride rings through Walther's eulogy on German women:

*Ir sult sprechen willekomen. . . .*

Here Walther does not only worship woman but seeks to instruct her in *tugent*. Already Dietmar of Aist and Ulrich of Guotenburg sing of the soothing power of love. This initiation into the ethical values of Cortesia plays an essential part in the concept of ideal woman (*frouwe*) who is honoured with the traditional attributes: *guote, schoene, reine*, and is moreover in the German minnesong compared to the highest possession, *Gotes hulde und êre*.

*Ob aber ich des sunde sule hân,*
*zwû schûf er sie sô rehte wol getân,*

cries Friedrich von Hûsen, and Albrecht von Jôhansdorf calls true *minne* a prayer to God.

The greatest happiness that the singer could hope to gain as reward for his homage was *der hôhe muot*.

One cannot deny that if the jewels are not separated from the dross the general tone of the *hohe Minnelyrik* is monotonous. The same theme is repeated in unending conventional variations. *Trûren* remains the constant keynote of these songs. Love is described as a malady whose suffering must be tempered to gaiety by the self-control (*mâze*) demanded by court etiquette.

The researches of F. Gennrich have done much to increase our knowledge of the music of the minnesong. He believes the formal structure of its verses to have been based on the following types to which the singers of the period could have had recourse: the litany, rondeau, sequence, and the hymn.

From these four basic types and a few variations Gennrich attempts to reconstruct the formal problems of the minnesong and the verse structure of the medieval lyric. Three of these are dependent on church music (litany, sequence, hymn), and thus point to the close relationship between the minnesong and the older ecclesiastic and Latin lyric. That Gennrich founds his theory on songs of the troubadours of Provence, of the trouvères of Northern France and later medieval songs is comprehensible since the melodies of the Middle High German minnesongs have, alas, nearly all been lost. But we must never forget that also the Middle High German singer was poet and composer at the same time. He had to find a new melody (*dôn, wîse*), for his text, because he was accounted a thief (*doene-diep*) if he used another's melody for his own verse. Also music for several voices was apparently not unknown during the period.

Typical motifs are provided by parallels and contrasts drawn between nature and love. The *Minnesangs Frühling* is again particularly rich in such examples. The spring and autumntide of the German landscape are reflected in its songs.

Here we may also mention some similes which in the *Minnesangs Frühling* are largely inspired by nature:

Anonymous: *As a precious stone embedded in gold the lover rests in the heart of his beloved.*

Der von Kürenberg: *As the rose blossoms on the thorn are the blushes of my beloved.*

*Like a dark star my lady must hide her love.*

Burggraf von Rietenburg: *Like gold in a crucible is proven the singer's love.*

Dietmar von Ast: *Beautiful as the sun is my beloved.*

*Even as the ship obeys the steersman the singer is slave of his mistress.*

H. v. Veldeke: *Tin and gold = Young and old.*

Der von Kolmas: *Life melts like tin.*
(The theme of the *Weltlohn* is heard here.)

Ulrich von Guotenburg: *As the hot sun bids the trees blossom in the dew, so sight of the beloved inspires the singer.*

*To plough the sand = to do something useless.*

R. von Fenis: *Even as the sun gives the moon radiance, the beloved fills the heart of the poet with joy.*

Der von Kolmas: *Gall is hidden in honey, and in life also.*

H. v. Morungen: *To cause a tree to bend its branches at one's bidding is easier than to win a woman's heart.*

*As the sun shines in the face of the morning, so radiant is the beloved in the eyes of the poet.*

*White as lilies, red as roses is the colour of my lady, radiant is she as the full moon.*

*Like gay spring and an Easter day is my beloved.*

*Just as the sun breaks through glass, she penetrates the heart.*

Reinmar v. H.: *Like the falcon and eagle, the courage of the singer mounts to heaven.*

The song with *Stollen* and *Abgesang* (two equal verses with a third of a different type attached) and the *Leich* (song with irregular lines) are the favourite forms of the Middle High German lyric. 'Reinmar the Fiddler' is probably author of the *Spruch* on Liutolt von Savene through which the names of several types of minnesong have been handed down to us:

*Tageliet klageliet hügeliet zügeliet tanzliet leich er kan,*
*er singet kriuzliet twingliet schimpfliet lobeliet rüegliet.*

To these may be added the *pastourelle*, the song of the beautiful peasant girl and her gallant knight. With the help of native dance music Neidhardt developed the former song-type to a 'courtly village lyric' (*Dorflyrik*). Further we should mention religious songs, amongst which are included crusading songs (discussed above), also discourses on the vanity of Dame World, and particularly the *Spruchdichtungen* which are so often found in Middle High German poetry, and part of which must be sharply distinguished from the true lyric type, whilst the other part bears close relationship to the minnesong.

*Origins*

What are the origins of the German minnesong? Even today this question has still received no thoroughly convincing answer, although it has given rise to most lively controversy amongst scholars of both German and Romance literature. *Rudello*, the first ballad in Uhland's cycle '*Sängerliebe*,' begins with the words:

*In den Thalen der Provence*
*ist der Minnesang entsprossen*

and it can now be accepted as certainty that the *hohe Minnesang*, though not its springtide in Austria and Germany, was born in that sun-kissed Southern land, in the Provence with its ancient Roman heritage.

In spite of having to admit external influences, we must not underestimate the peculiarities of the European minne-lyric, nor must we under any circumstances lose sight of its unique qualities as a formal historical phenomenon.

In regard to the question of its origins the works of F. Gennrich, H. Brinkmann, K. Burdach, and J. Schwietering call for attention. These authors together with many others are exponents of the well-known theories of imitation as to literary themes and influences: (1) the medieval Latin love-poetry; (2) the Arabian court-poetry of Andalusian rulers; (3) Ovid; (4) *Mariendienst*, i.e. service in honour of Mary as the interceder between God and man; (5) the Cathar heresy; (6) the analogies to Bernhard von Clairvaux's mystic conception of a divine love (cf. the three degrees of love).

A synthesis of these various theories will probably bring us nearest the truth, whilst the influence of the crusades (cf. the poems and life of William of Poitou) must also be taken into consideration in regard to such problems.

In the opinion of F. Gennrich, the songs of the Provençal troubadour Marcabrun, composed in honour of the lady *Emperairiz* that she in recompense might petition the 'emperor of Spain', Alfonso VII, on his behalf, betray the influence of the cult of the holy Virgin (*Mariendienst*). The latter, in particular through its conception of intercession, is considered by Gennrich to have proved a model for the troubadour's song. Thus Marcabrun's

*Emperairiz, pregaz per mei*
*qu'eu farai vostre prez richir*

appears to find a striking parallel in the song:

*O Maria, Deu maire, Deus t'es e fils e paire,*
*Domna preia per nos to fil.*

K. Burdach and S. Singer seek for traces of Arabian songs of homage in troubadour poetry inaugurated in the Provence during the twelfth century. Bodmer, and Herder in his *Humanitätsbriefe*, had already pointed to the possibility of such interrelations.

D. Scheludko (*Archivum Roman.* vol. 12) rejects Burdach's theory by maintaining that not a single linguistic Arabic expression appears in the minne-lyric. Nevertheless we may well admit the presence of certain affinities on a spiritual plane, a fact of which R. Erckmann (in *DVj*, 1931) has been fully able to convince us in drawing carefully considered parallels with certain aspects of Eastern thought. Relying on Burdach's researches and subsequently augmenting and correcting them, Erckmann came to regard the *hohe Minne* as a purely Western art but recognized in the proud egocentric attitude of Hispano-Moorish culture an element that might be called a *formal anticipation* of all that the Occident was ultimately to develop though filling it with different spiritual content. In the course of centuries and notwithstanding the impediments afforded by language and religion, formal analogies between European chivalry and the Western caliphates (which began to reach the height of their splendour under Abd-er-Rahmân I) were gradually strengthened. Cultural relationships between France and Spain and conflicts between Berbers and Moors favoured the survival of the West Goths in the North of Spain. Thus was established the kingdom of Leon, whilst Barcelona grew to a margravate from Charlemagne's Spanish realm. In the ninth century Navarre became a separate country in the land of the Basques and later in the tenth century rose even to the dignity of a kingdom. This period witnessed the glorious reign of Abd-er-Rahmân III (912-961). His successors, in particular the lord chamberlain Ibn Abî 'Amir, Almansor († 1002), likewise ruled as insatiable despots to whom the courts of Northern Spain were forced to pay homage. Christian soldiers in the Moorish army encouraged the exchange of culture. In the eleventh century the caliphate fell, whilst in the middle of the same century the North united, first under Ferdinand I, King of Castile, who brought Leon and Navarre beneath his sway. It is this king and others who prove themselves inheritors of Arabian culture, chivalry, honour, and gallantry. The Pyrenees did not afford an obstacle to yet wider transmission of Oriental thought. Ecclesiastical and political links between Northern Spain and France were forged still tighter during the course of the eleventh century.

Burdach's investigations, principally inspired by Count Schack's *Poesie und Kunst in Spanien und Sizilien*, revealed unexpected parallels between Moorish court-poetry and that of the Provence: worship of woman, and service for her sake (courtship), the part played by married women, secrecy regarding their names, amorous yearning, spies, and the hopelessness of courtship, etc. Even traces of the *Tagelied* (*alba*, dawn-song) are discoverable amongst the Moorish court lyrics of the Andalusian rulers. The origin of the *Tagelied* is, however, considered to be the pseudo-Ovidian letter of Leander to Hero. The story of Hero and Leander is itself probably of Persian origin. The Moors were only too ready to borrow literary social forms from their subjugated Persian neighbours.

Another important source of material is the classic novel—the Latin version of the Greek Alexander romance, the late Roman Apollonius romance, the Latin version of the Greek Trojan romance and the legend of Amor and Psyche, a tale of Oriental origin. Burdach is well aware of the fact that these offer but historic points of contact and parallels to the minnesong. That spiritual change which alone could give birth to the minnesong is not yet present here.

Since Burdach, two attempts have been made to discover the origins of the German minnesongs not only on Latin but also on German soil, and whilst rejecting Burdach's hypothesis they simultaneously shed light on the influence of classic and medieval Latin literature. J. Schwietering believes in the *Einwirkung der Antike auf die Entstehung des frühen deutschen Minnesangs* (1924). The so-called *Wechsel* (alternation) found in the minnesong is considered to be due to the influence of Ovid's *Heroides*. H. v. Morungen's invectives against *huote* may be traced to Ovid's *Amores*. Also that unforgettable dialogue of H. v. Morungen's *Tagelied*: '*Owê, sol aber mir iemer mê . . .*' may bear some connection with the Latin example. The wandering scholars may have played some part in transmitting Ovid's verses, but Latin influence must not be considered the one and only source of the minne-lyric. Schwietering limits his far-reaching enquiry into such relationships by a careful reference to 'conscious narrowness.' Moreover, one must realize once and for all that not everything depends on influence; for affinity of emotions may surely independently create similar imagery.

Nevertheless, though maintaining every possible reservation, we cannot shut our eyes to amazing resemblances, particularly to the works of Ovid: Schwietering points to the love-monologue (Pyramus), the warning against the spies (Paris-Helena), the swan song (Dido), swallow and nightingale (Procne-Philomela), Narcissus, and epitaph, etc. Walther's '*Under der linden*' is connected with Ovid's Sappho epistle '*Invenio silvam, quae saepe cubilia nobis praebuit—agnovi pressas . . . caespitis herbas.*' Above all the figure of Dido, the languishing forsaken queen, which was handed down through countless literary generations, may well have inspired medieval poets such as the knight of Kürenberg, whose falcon song again recalls reminiscences of Herkules and Omphale. The theme of adultery is already to be found in the legend of Venus and Mars. The closest approach to classic models is, however, less recognizable in the reappearance of isolated literary motifs than in an affinity of *Stimmung*, created by a balanced attitude towards life, and affirmation of earthly existence.

Yet another attempt to unravel the tangled problems relating to the minnesong has been made by H. Brinkmann in his intriguing and well-founded researches on the dependence of German minne-lyric on medieval Latin poetry. But proofs of Ovid's influence on certain amorous and epistolary poetry of the eleventh century in Angers will not suffice, alas, to explain the origins of the minnesong, though we here clearly observe medieval Latin inspiration in Anjou, from whence it spread North and South to Mainz, Normandy, England, Poitou, Aquitaine. Sentimental correspondence between clerics and nuns certainly furthered the influx of medieval Latin forms. For reasons relating both to time and space, Brinkmann rejects not only the Maysong theory of Gaston Paris and Bielschowky's explanation of the Hymn on Spring, but also Burdach's Arabian hypothesis. In his *Geschichte der lateinischen Liebesdichtung im Mittelalter* and *Entstehungsgeschichte des Minnesangs* he traces the development of literary correspondence back to Merovingian and Carolingian times (Apollonius Sidonius, Venantius, Aldhelm, Boniface, Alkuin, and others).

Marbode of Rennes (born in Angers in 1035), his pupil Balderich of Bourgueil (born in 1046), and Hildebert of Tours (born about 1056) exerted a particularly strong influence on the literary circles of the eleventh-century period through their epistles.

Hence from Angers threads were spun in England, and Hildebert exalts Adela the daughter of William the Conqueror and wife of the Count of Blois as *prima dearum.* Matilda, too, the wife of Henry I and daughter of Malcolm III of Scotland, is praised by Hildebert and Marbode. The love-cult (*Frauendienst*) thus appears to have been foreshadowed by this ecclesiastically flavoured tradition in Angers. Earthly love had in the meantime been praised by the dissolute vagantes. Both sources, the Angevin literary tradition and the songs of the wandering scholars, contributed, according to Brinkmann, to the development of *minne.* To these may be added the influence of hymnal verse, from which Brinkmann believes the references to nature were derived:

> *Noctis tempus iam praeterit,*
> *iam gallus canit viribus*
> (*Analecta Hymnica*),

or the holy hymn:

> *lux clara surgens rutilat,*
> *quae dulce festum nuntiat*
> (*Analecta Hymnica*).

Thus here, as with Burdach and others, essential elements of the minnesong are represented as offshoots of an earlier foreign tradition, so that the minnesong, which in many ways contradicts the spirit of chivalry, appears as an alien growth. Its native roots, however, we shall seek to discover in the *Minnesangs Frühling.*

*Des Minnesangs Frühling*

(*a*)

The bulk of the minnesongs known to us through MSS. may be divided into two classes: firstly, the original knightly love-song (*ritterliches Liebeslied*) which developed at any rate to a great extent independently of the traditional occidental minnesongs; secondly, the courtly panegyrical lyric in praise of *my lady* which may largely be traced to Romance and perhaps Arabian-Persian influence, and whose artifices caused Walther and others to turn rebelliously towards the *niedere Minne* (uncourtly love).

The first of the above two great groups of minnesong is entitled

*Des Minnesangs Frühling*, and embraces the names of the knightly singers who preceded Walther: Der von Kürenberg, Meinlôh von Sevelingen, Burggraf von Regensburg, Burggraf von Rietenburg, Spervogel, Dietmar von Aist, Friedrich von Hûsen, Heinrich von Veldeke, Ulrich von Guotenburg, Graf Rudolf von Fenis, Albrecht von Jôhansdorf, Heinrich von Rugge, Bernger von Horheim, Hartwic von Rute, Bligger von Steinach, Der von Kolmas, Heinrich von Morungen, Engelhart von Adelnburg, Reinmar, and Hartmann von Aue.

The term *Minnesangs Frühling* should, however, only be applied to them with reservations, for here again we meet with at least three distinct groups. Thus the *South-Eastern* region gave birth to its specific type of song—the *knightly lyric of the Danube valley*, which differs both in its concept of love and its poetic form from the minnesongs of *Swabia-Franconia*, and *Thuringia*. To the last-mentioned group we may add the name of Heinrich von Veldeke who, though a Netherlander by birth, stood in close contact with the Thuringian court. We shall for the moment be concerned with the first group, that of the Danube valley, since it provides particularly lucid evidence of the difference between the knightly love-lyric and the artificial courtly minnesong.

High on the banks of the Danube above a sea of cherry blossom and sun-steeped vineyard, the ruins of medieval castles alternate with the proud façades of baroque monasteries, whose redundant curves seem re-echoed in the swinging breadth of the Danube. Here it was that the defiant Nibelungen pressed on towards their doom. Between Vienna and the granite precipices of the monastery of Melk, near that most exquisite monument of Northern baroque, the monastic church of Dürnstein, stand the crumbling walls of the castle in which Richard Lionheart was held captive by the Austrian duke until, according to legend, he was liberated by the singer Blondel.

It is from amidst these regions that we receive literary proofs of the existence of knightly love-songs, so-called *trûtliet*, dating as far back as 1160. In '*Des tôdes gehügede*' Heinrich von Melk speaks of a *trûtliet* which his dead hero can never entune again in woman's praise.

At this period such *trûtliet*, sung at court, were regarded as a new custom. They did not yet pretend to the significance of the panegyric minne-lyric, but were songs which the knight composed in homage to woman and which provided entertainment at the dances:

*wâ sint die fûze dâ mit er gie*
*höfslîchen mit den frowen?*

We shall find an absence of any direct Romance or Arabian-Persian influence on the Danubian lyric. *Minne-ethos*, style and rhythm of these poems are in fact so remote from the main European tradition that we must seek their source rather in the *trûtliet*, in traditional communal German folk-lyrics and in verses such as: '*Dû bist mîn. . . .*' We must not forget that more than a hundred years earlier (and likewise in the district of the Tegernsee) German rhymes: *liebes . . . loubes*, *wunna . . . minna* had been incorporated in the *Ruodlieb* romance, and that these may also with all probability be traced to a folk-song origin. During the middle of the twelfth century Regensburg on the Danube witnessed the production of the *Kaiserchronik*, the work of a Bavarian cleric. Here Totila worships mighty love:

*Umbe di minne ist iz aver sô getân*
*dâ nemac nicht lebentiges vor gestân . . .*

—love which heals and rejuvenates, which inspires chivalry and courage. Through woman men may attain such joy.

Of the singers belonging to this Danubian group we know but a few by name: the knight of Kürenberg, probably of 'ministerial' lineage and from the neighbourhood of Linz, Meinlôh of Sevelingen, the Burggraf of Regensburg, and the Burggraf of Rietenburg. The last two may possibly be regarded either as father and son or as two brothers, for the Burggrafschaft of Regensburg was a heritage of the Rietenburg family until 1184. To this company of singers who flourished during the second half of the twelfth century belongs also Dietmar of Aist (Eist), whose ancestral home lay in Upper Austria by the little River Agast or Agist. Dietmar has left us our earliest and very simple example of the *Tagelied*, which at this stage had not yet introduced the idea of the watchman sounding his warning. Thus four or five singers are known to us as representatives of the so-called knightly love-song of the South-Eastern Danube.

The *minne-ethos* of these poems—the singer's attitude towards his surroundings and man's relations to woman, whether married or maiden—differs fundamentally from that proclaimed in the *hohe Minnesang*. In the *Minnesangs Frühling*, woman or maiden is treated not only as recipient, but herself appears caught in the meshes of passion whose yearning is given expression in the poem. Woman is conceived as lover, not as the beloved. We must, however, not be misled into thinking that man is not represented as courting her love. The difference between the *Minnesangs Frühling* and the *hohe Minne* is not caused by endowing the two sexes with opposite rôles but by the peculiar love-cult of the *Frauendienst* (homage to women), which the *hohe Minnesang* identified with the poet's hopeless love for his liege lady or a married woman of noble birth. That this relationship did not in actual life always remain on a platonic basis is beside the point in this discussion, which is concerned primarily with ideas and their formal equivalent. In the *Minnesangs Frühling*, however, this concept of passion which harbours no hopes of fulfilment does not yet supply the keynote of its lyric verse.

We have already stated that in the latter woman herself appears as supplicant. She begs her lover:

*daz er mir holt sî,*
*als er hie vor was.*

(Der von Kürenberg.)

She complains that envious spies robbed her of her chivalrous knight:

*daz mir den benomen hân*
*die merker und ir nît.*

In another poem, which like the last was composed by Der von Kürenberg, the lovesick lady stands on the battlements and hears the song of the warrior, who scorns her, ring through the night:

*Ich stuont mir nehtint spâte an einer zinnen:*
*dô hôrt ich einen ritter vil wol singen*
*in Kürenberges wîse al ûz der menigîn.*
*er muoz mir diu lant rûmen, ald ich geniete mich sîn.*

I KÚNIG CHŮNRAT DER JUNGE
*(Manesse Codex, Heidelberg)*

# Zwey ſchöne ne we Lieder / Das erſt / Es ſteht ein Lind in jenem Thal/ꝛc. in ſeiner eygnen Me lodey.

# Das ander / ich můß von hinnen ſcheiden /ꝛc. In ſeiner eygnen weiß zů ſingen.

II ZWEY SCHOͤNE NEWE LIEDER
Printed in Strassburg about 1560
*(From Könnecke's 'Bilderatlas'; Elwert'scher Verlag, Marburg)*

*Nu brinc mir her vil balde mîn ros, mîn îsengwant.*
*wan ich muoz einer frouwen rûmen diu lant.*
*diu wil mich des betwingen, daz ich ir holt sî.*
*si muoz der mîner minne iemer darbende sîn.*

Such passionate abandonment provides a strong contrast to Burkart of Hohenfels's inviolable damsel who cries:

*Jô mües er mich niunstunt toeten*
*ê ich würde im undertân.*

The narrative type used by Der von Kürenberg in the above poem is also characteristic of his song about the falcon which a lady tames over the space of a year, until, trimming the feathers with gold, and tying a silk ribbon around its claws, she bids it fly to far-off lands:

*Ich zôh mir einen valken mêre danne ein jâr;*
*dô ich in gezamete als ich in wolte hân*
*und ich im sîn gevidere mit golde wol bewant,*
*er huop sich ûf vil hôhe und floug in anderiu lant.*

*Sît sah ich den valken schône vliegen:*
*er fuorte an sînem fuoze sîdîne riemen*
*und was im sîn gevidere alrôt guldîn.*
*got sende si zesamene die gerne geliebe wellen sîn.*

Something of the spirit of that lovely song seems still to linger on after the decline of knighthood; as for instance in the fourteenth-century song of Heinrich of Mugelin, who spent many years at Prag under the patronage of Karl IV:

*Ein frouwe sprach: mîn falke ist mir enphlogen.*

Shadowed by envious courtiers, spies and jealous women, love still endures:

*staechens ûz ir ougen,*
*mir râtent mîne sinne*
*an deheinen andern man. . . .*

These verses of Meinlôh of Sevelingen, who sang of love's triumph over death, find their counterpart in a poem of the Burggraf of Regensburg:

*und laegen si vor leide tôt,*
*ich wil im iemer wesen holt.*

The first lines bear witness to ideas absolutely opposed to those of the panegyrical minne-lyric. Whereas in the *hohe Minne* the knight is his lady's vassal, the woman is here obedient to his will, tireless in winning his love.

Thus in the *Minnesangs Frühling*, knight and noble lady appear anxious and disquieted. A faithful messenger is often the bearer of their amorous tidings which the poet presents as a dialogue. In a poem of this type by Dietmar of Aist which also opens with descriptive verses:

*Ez stuont ein frouwe alleine*
*und warte uber heide*
*und warte ir liebes.*
*sô gesach si valken fliegen . . .*

a lady once again appears torn with longing and desire. Traces of the minnesong's courtly manner may be discernible in his dawn-song: *Slâfest dû, mîn friedel ziere?* especially in the following line:

*swaz dû gebiutst, daz leiste ich, friundin mîn . . .*

though it is not the watchman but a little bird who warns the lovers of the approach of day. According to A. Romain and W. de Gruyter the song is an original *Tagelied*, and represents a species of lyric which had sprung from popular sources and here celebrates the first stage of its transmutation into the courtly convention. The characteristic form of the dawn-song is already apparent in that the woman is here the first to wake and warn her knight.

Friedrich von Hûsen (Hausen), of Rhineland nobility in the neighbourhood of Worms, inaugurates a different concept of love, redolent of the courtly ideals of the Provence. A sharp boundary divides his verse from that of the South-Eastern poets of the Danubian valley, although vestiges of French influence may be discovered now and again even in the latter.

The singer complains and suffers torment for love of his lady:

*Einer frowen was ich zam,*
*diu âne lôn mîn dienest nam*

though even the songs of H. v. Morungen and Reinmar still contain a woman's lovesick lamentations.

Spies, those 'villainous knaves' (the *huoter* and *merker*) and many another envious traitor, now proved frequent material for the love-poem. Heinrich von Veldeke points to the evil influence which such *huote* may exert on morality, although the Danubian poets also knew spies and enviers and liars. In the Danubian group we further find that the relation of a vassal to his lord is only occasionally transferred to the courtly mode of *minne*:

*Ich bin holt einer frouwen.*

This song by Meinlôh of Sevelingen ends with a vow to maintain love even beyond the grave:

*sturbe ich nâch ir minne,*
*und wurde ich danne lebende,*
*sô wurbe ich aber umb daz wîp* . . .

In Friedrich von Hûsen's poems, however, we often meet with the typical concept of liege love. Thus the ideal of love-cult provides a measure by which we may gauge those graduated differences separating anonymous popular songs such as '*Dû bist mîn*,' and their derivatives, the love-songs, from the Western minnelyric in which Romance influence began to prevail.

The line of development starts with the knight of Kürenberg. Dietmar of Aist follows, whilst the Burggraf of Rietenburg brings up the rear; for in him we may clearly perceive a connecting link with the poetry of the *hohe Minne* and of the troubadours. But Der von Kürenberg, Dietmar von Aist, Meinlôh of Sevelingen (*wie wol er frowen dienen kan*) and the Burggraf of Regensburg may by no means be designated writers of folk-songs, they are true poets of chivalry whose simplicity and sense of terse reality seem however to bear closer affinity to the folk-song and the early Middle High German epic than to the *hohe Minnesang*. That they also absorbed something of the latter's tone was but the natural outcome of their rank and of the atmosphere which surrounded them.

A certain simplicity of form is equally characteristic of the verse of these five poets. Purity of rhyme is not yet regarded as essential. Plays upon rhymes and repetition of one and the same rhyme at the close of a poem are found amongst the later verse of the Danubian group; particularly in that of the Burggraf of Rietenburg, who clearly betrays signs of Romance influence. Apart from a few such examples simple rhymes are used, rhyme-couplets, further crossed rhymes and *Reimumklammerung* of unrhymed lines; cf. Meinlôh von Sevelingen's '*Ez mac niht heizen minne.*' Sounding rhymes with masculine syllables (*minnè : singèn*), the rhymeless short line called *die Waise*, originally formed from the first half of the 'long line,' appear fairly frequently. The Swabian-Franconian and the Thuringian groups show a more complicated form of verse structure and poetic technique; thus Heinrich von Veldeke (*In dem aberellen* . . .) or the *Wechsel* of Heinrich von Morungen, in the dialogue of whose dawn-song the man's utterances are echoed by the woman's '*Owê*' (*Ich hân si für alliu wîp*).

In the *Minnesangs Frühling*, the verses of Dietmar of Aist betray a particular taste for the *Frauenstrophen*: songs which are sung by a woman and express her womanly sentiment now in the form of a monologue (cf. *Ez stuont ein frouwe alleine* . . .) or an admonition to her lover (cf. *Sô wol dir, summerwunne* . . .), now as a message which is to be borne to her knight:

*Nu sage dem ritter edele*
*daz er sich wol behuote. . . .*

That girls and women themselves composed love-lyrics cannot be denied, for we have already pointed to that precious gem: *Dû bist mîn* . . . Other poems too, such as *Diu linde ist an dem ende* . . ., were made by women, although the authorship of the majority of poems must be accredited to men, as is suggested by the opening lines of Dietmar von Aist's poem, *Ez stuont* . . . and the narrative remarks, *sprach ein wîp* . . ., etc. That men were the authors of the following verses is certain:

*Wîp unde vederspil*
*die werdent lîhte zam.*
*swer si ze rehte lucket,*
*sô suochent sî den man*
(Der von Kürenberg),

or

*Ich lebe stolzlîche* . . .
(Meinlôh of Sevelingen).

F. Vogt has applied the term *doppelseitiges Minnelied* to poems in which the dialogue between man and woman is not differentiated by narrative, thus Der von Kürenberg's song which consists of one verse:

*Jô stuont ich nehtint spâte*
*vor dînem bette:*
*dô getorst ich dich, frouwe,*
*niwet wecken.*
*. . . daz gehazze*
*got den dînen lîp.*

The two-sided type of *doppelseitiges Minnelied* is also represented by those dialogues and *Botenlieder* in which the messenger acts as go-between for knight or lady; cf. Dietmar von Aist's:

*Seneder friundinne bote,*
*nu sage dem schoenen wîbe . . .*

An essentially German characteristic to which we can find no real parallel in Romance poetry is the use of the *Wechsel*, in which parted lovers speak of each other—as though some kind of telepathy inspired them to recite their feelings in the form of a monologue: cf. *Ich lac den winter eine* (Burggraf von Regensburg). The close relationship between the verses sometimes suggests a spoken dialogue: cf. *Ich stuont mir nehtint spâte . . .* (Der von Kürenberg).

How far this style is dependent on alien form cannot be fully ascertained. Influence from the West may be accepted up to a point even in the *Minnesangs Frühling*. Crusaders journeyed through the valley of the Danube. In July 1147 the French crusading troops encamped in Regensburg. Ladies accompanied the crusading army. Germans and Frenchmen fought side by side against the paynim. How strongly the difference between earthly and divine service was felt at the beginning of the crusades is proved by Hartmann's crusade song:

*Dem kriuze zimt wol reiner muot*
*und kiusche site. . . .*

The *Sinnspruch* of the wandering scholars, the erotic poetry of the 'goliards,' vagantes, medieval Latin epistolary verse and Ovid's *Heroides*, may have played some part in the evolution of the *Minnesangs Frühling*. A general anticipation of the *Frauendienst* and possibly the part played by the spies (*merker*) suggest that even the Danubian group of singers, whose verses seem so remote from the panegyric minne-lyric, may have caught a breath of Provençal song. Through indirect contact, possibly only by hearsay, something of Western refinement may have penetrated even to them. Fundamentally, however, the love-song of the Danubian country remains a thing apart, rooted in the soil which gave it birth, a prelude to the *hohe Minnesang*. Its natural freshness, its reminiscence of popular folk-song, its very name, spell magic —*Des Minnesangs Frühling*.

(*b*)

In addition to the lyrics of the Danubian valley, those earliest relics of the German minnesong, we find a vast number of other songs which at first betray indisputable Provençal influence. Amongst these we may discover many a pearl. The brusque freshness of Heinrich von Veldeke's songs breaks the monotony of the minnesong convention. His light vein of humour is far removed from the seriousness of Friedrich von Hûsen, yet the latter has left songs that cannot fail to move us with their deep-felt sincerity. Morality and heart's desire should be reconciled, he sings:

*Swenn ich vor gote getar,*
*sô gedenke ich ir. . . .*

Such beauty in woman is divine! On the eve of the crusade of 1189 he composes a song on the discord of body and soul, a theme which continues throughout the history of the minnesong:

*Mîn herze und mîn lîp die wellent scheiden.*

It was perhaps on this same crusade that Hartmann von Aue sang the lines mentioned above:

*Dem kriuze zimt wol reiner muot.*

To attain the world's praise, the soul's salvation—*der werlte lôp, der sele heil*—should be man's aim. Illusion blinds his life on earth; love of God (*Gottesminne*) alone can bring him the peace he yearns for.

The poems of Hartwic von Rute contain powerful imagery. The Bavarian singer Albrecht von Jôhansdorf, who meets with such eulogy in the pages of G. Freytag's '*Bilder aus deutscher Vergangenheit*,' dreams like Friedrich von Hûsen of the divine nature of love: *si* (minne) *tiuret unde ist guot*. His verses are full of tenderness: *Ine erwache nimer ezn sî mîn êrste segen daz got ir êren müeze phlegen.* . . . True love, he sings, endures beyond the grave: *Mich mac der tôt von ir minnen wol scheiden; anders nieman.* . . . Earthly and divine love spring from the same root.

Heinrich von Morungen is the greatest poet of the *Minnesangs Frühling*. In his imaginative richness, the originality and daring of his poetic idiom, he transcends all poets preceding Walther save one, Wolfram von Eschenbach. Happily we possess more facts about H. v. Morungen's life than Walther's. The castle of Morungen bei Sangerhausen in Thuringia was most likely his ancestral home. Between 1197–1202, when he was about fifty years of age, he is supposed to have set out on a long journey which led him through the Holy Land to 'India' (probably Persia). In the chronicle *Urkundenbuch der Stadt Leipzig* we read that about the year 1217, at any rate before 1221, the Markgraf Dietrich von Meissen, son-in-law of Hermann of Thuringia, handed over a yearly contribution of ten talents to the monastery of St. Thomas in Leipzig, a donation which, as we hear further, had till then been enjoyed by Henricus de Morungen *miles emeritus*, who now, however, voluntarily placed it at Dietrich's service. Records again render sure proof of Morungen's death in 1222.

The songs of Provence deeply inspired this poet. Close parallels may be drawn between his verses and those of Bernart de Ventadorn or we may discover in them certain affinities with songs by the Count of Poitiers, Jaufré Rudel, Peire Vidal, Guillaume de Cabestaing.

At times he uses motifs strongly reminiscent of Ovid (cf. the fable of the nymph Echo, *Metam.* III):

*Der sô vil geriefe in einen toubin walt,*
*iz antwurt ime dar ûz eteswenne*
(DLD, p. 49),

or compare again Ovid's *Amores* II, Elegy 6, and H. v. Morungen's:

*Wêr ein sitich odir ein star, die mohtin sît*
*gelernit hân daz sie sprêchin: 'Minne.'* . . .

or Ovid, *Metam.* VI (*Procne and Philomela*), and H. v. Morungen's:

*Iz ist site der nahtegale.*
*swenn sie ir liet volendit, so geswînit sie.*
*durch daz volge ab ich der swale.*

Yet just these parallels disclose at the same time H. v. Morungen's creative power, which sorrow and joy alike rouse to poignant expression and crystallize to such pregnant form, for instance, in his dawn-song, which may well be called one of the greatest love-lyrics in European literature of all time:

*Owê sol aber mir iemer mê . . .*,

or

*Ich hôrte ûf der heide. . . .*

H. von Morungen often borrows imagery from nature in gentle or in solemn mood. His beloved is *des liehten meien schîn*, and the poet's *ôsterlîcher tac*, a *paschale gaudium.* The form of his verse is quickened by passion, now teeming with joy, now rent in torment. In dark rancour he determines that his heart's misery shall be avenged by his son, whose beauty shall one day vanquish the woman who now rejects him. The old primitive lust for *Blutrache* glows in his song:

*Mîme kinde wil ich erbin dise nôt. . . .*

Bitter is the torment of hopeless passion which finds but dreams for guerdon. Hard it is to serve a lady who harries the land of her vassal like a robber. Love triumphs over life—indeed beyond death itself, for love is not bound to the body:

*daz's iuwerr sêle dienet dort*
*als einem reinen wîbe.*

Wolfram von Eschenbach, a contemporary of H. von Morungen, excels him in rugged force of personality. His passionate brooding spirit creates strangely intense imagery, as when in one of his dawn-songs he speaks of the sun:

*Sîne klawen durh die wolken sint geslagen.*
*er stîget ûf mit grôzer kraft.*
*Ich sih in grâwen tägelîch als er wil tagen.*

Only eight of his songs have come down to us, and they are largely *Tagelieder*, for which he was famed.

His fearless individuality is reflected in the praise he bestows on the love of husband and wife:

*Swer phliget odr ie gephlac,*
*daz er bî lieben wîbe lac*
*den merkern unverborgen. . . .*

—a poem which was evidently composed at the time of his marriage, and certainly not later than 1202.

The height of Wolfram's achievement as a lyric poet seems to have been attained about 1200, that is to say, before his sojourn at the Thuringian court, where he enjoyed Landgraf Hermann's patronage from 1203 until the latter's death in 1217, after which the poet returned to his Bavarian home.

Of great importance in the history of the dawn-song is Wolfram's use of the figure of the watchman. It is the minnesong's storm and stress and hate that fills such songs as:

*Si beide luste, daz er kuste si genuoc:*
*gevluochet wart dem tage. . . .*

The proud full-hearted consciousness of his creative strength causes him to say of himself in *Parzival*:

*Ich bin Wolfram von Eschenbach*
*und kan ein teil mit sange.*

After the boundless force and vigour of Wolfram's verse the songs of Herr Reinmar von Hagenau in Alsatia (Reinmar der Alte as distinct from Reinmar von Zweter) appear refined and attenuated both in form and variety of theme. In discussing the 'ethical code' we already referred to him as a typical representative of courtly-tempered yearning:

*Ez tuot ein leit nâch liebe wê.*

Reinmar's eulogy of women, *Sô wol dir, wîp, wie reine ein nam,* was welcomed joyfully by his famous rival Walther von der Vogelweide.

As Reinmar's melodies have been lost it is difficult to do full justice to the virtuosity of his harmonious verse-composition and his hair-splitting dialectics, and although his songs may lack Wolfram's passion and Walther's fresh charm they won full measure of praise both from Walther and Gottfried von Strassburg. At the same time Walther by no means hushes up the quarrel between Reinmar and himself:

> *dich selben wolt ich lützel klagen;*
> *ich klage dîn edelen kunst daz sist verdorben.*

Carl von Kraus gives a detailed account of Walther's polemics against Reinmar, and when the latter lets his full scorn fall upon Walther, as one who being less suited to the vocation of love should modestly retire into the background:

> *dâ er niht zu tuonne hât*

a ruthless literary feud results, from which Reinmar's somewhat younger rival was ultimately to emerge with flying colours.

*Walther von der Vogelweide*

Gottfried von Strassburg's high opinion of Walther is well known through those famous lines in *Tristan*:

> *Wer leitet nû die lieben schar?*
> *. . . diu von der Vogelweide. . . .*

To this elaborate eulogy may be added the simple homage of Hugo von Trimberg, the humble schoolmaster of Bamberg:

> *Herr Walther von der Vogelweid*
> *swer des vergäz der tät mir leid.*

Nearly all our knowledge of Walther's genius and life must be drawn from his songs and from such of his sayings as have been recorded in MSS. Here he proves himself a master of word, with a strong sense of melodic values. His sensitive spirit touches an endless scale of emotions from simple human sentiment and delicate intimacy to fierce manly passion and glowing enthusiasm.

His sanguine temperament betrays his Austrian blood. Easily offended, he is carried away by the violence of his feelings only to sink back into dark brooding, yet immediately he emerges again bubbling over with high spirits and humour. This waywardness of spirit, reflected in his songs by continuous vacillation between merriment and melancholy, by lavish praise of generous patrons alternating with venomous attacks on the enemy, by gratitude giving place to creative pride, captivated contemporary society as it still has power to fascinate us today:

> *Lât mich an eime stabe gân*
> *und werben umbe werdekeit*
> *mit unverzageter arebeit,*
> *als ich von kinde habe getân.*

As pious defender of the faith in its struggle against the greed of the pope, as champion of patriotism and the rights of the state against papal aggrandizement, Walther towers above all other singers of his era, greatest of all Middle High German poets in the sphere of politics and humanity. His lofty ideal of brotherhood educates man to self-control (*mâze*):

> *Wer sleht den lewen? wer sleht den risen?. . . .*
> *daz tuot jener, der sich selber twinget.*
> cf. Herder's poem: *Tapfer ist der Löwensieger.*

Apart from the eulogies of Hugo von Trimberg and Gottfried and one by Thomasin von Zerclaere we possess few contemporary records of Walther's life. The sole documentary evidence is an inventory of travel expenses incurred by Wolfger von Ellenbrechtskirchen, Bishop of Passau, in which we read that a present of five soldi was accorded to *Walthero cantori de Vogelweide* at Zeiselmauer to purchase him a fur robe. It is therefore on Walther's poems that we must rely to gain a picture of his personality, a picture which K. Burdach has outlined for us against the wide horizon of political and ecclesiastical warfare that shook the Staufen era. A. Schönbach's *Walther von der Vogelweide* (revised by H. Schneider) conjures up a lively portrait of the poet and includes interesting observations on medieval court life and *Minnedienst*.

Those well-known lines: '*Ze Ôsterrîche lernt ich singen unde sagen,*' give us a clue which may now, in spite of A. Wallner's hypothesis, be definitely regarded as referring, not to Walther's tuition under Reinmar, but to the existence of an older tradition of Austrian lyric verse. On the other hand, no more than legend underlies the story of Walther's participation in the competitive singing (*Sängerkrieg*) on the Wartburg, his studies at Paris and Constantinople, or his enduring love for a Saracen lady. To the world of myth belongs also the mastersingers' claim to regard Walther as one of their twelve illustrious ancestors, whilst it is equally vain to hail Walther as a forerunner of Luther or of modern enlightenment.

We cannot yet even point to Walther's birthplace with any degree of certainty, for families bearing the name of Vogelweide existed at that period in Switzerland, Franconia, Lower Austria and the districts of Passau, Tirol, and Bohemia. We cannot, moreover, discover any official records of a noble house of this name, and though the market-place of Bozen (Bolzano) boasts a proud memorial to Walther by Heinrich Natter, even the Vogelweidehof in the Eisacktal cannot rightly claim the poet as its own.

Pseudonyms such as Spervogel, Falchelinus, der wilde Mann, Regenbogen, Rûmzlant, and others cause one to suspect that Walther's name also contains some sort of symbolic significance. It is also uncertain whether Walther was ever dubbed knight, although his songs, and the fact that he was addressed as *hêr*, would point to his knightly birth. Walther indeed refers to himself as *hêr*. On the other hand we must not disregard the somewhat distant tone in which he incites the knights to set out on a crusade, although even this by no means excludes the possibility of his being of impoverished knightly ancestry, which, as we noted before, often led to the ranks of minstrelsy:

*Dar an gedenkent, ritter: ez ist iuwer dinc.*
*ir tragent die liehten helme und manegen herten rinc,*
*dar zuo die vesten schilte und diu gewîhten swert.*

In the Heidelberg Manesse Codex Walther is numbered amongst the ministeriales, though we must again not forget that the order of precedence given here is hardly to be relied on, and that the Spielmann Geltâr for instance receives the title of *hêr*.

Certain it is that Walther passed many years at the famous court of the Babenberger in Vienna under the patronage of the Duke Leopold V († 1194) and his son Frederick, who found an early death in 1198, victim of the crusades. His successor Leopold VI cared little for the frivolities of song, and Walther was forced to roam the land until at last he found a generous host in the person of the Staufen King Philip. Thus he was able to take part in the

Christmas festival held at Magdeburg in 1199, whence he probably set out for the Wartburg.

In spite of his *spilmans nôt* Walther's purse was not quite empty. He appears to have possessed both squire and steed, and although he did not refuse the gift of a fur coat from Wolfger his pride forbade him to accept worn clothing:

*Getragene wât ich nie genan.*

The years 1198–1220 saw Walther wandering from place to place. At one time he visited the court of the avaricious Landgraf Hermann of Thuringia who, as we know through Heinrich von Veldeke, Wolfram von Eschenbach, Heinrich von Morungen, Herbort von Fritzlar and A. von Halberstadt, was famed as a patron of the arts. On his journeys Walther must also have come to the court of the Markgraf Dietrich von Meissen, and as a member of the *familia* in Thuringia Walther repeatedly found hearth and home, though no pecuniary benefit. A note of bitterness runs through Walther's account of affairs of state into which he received deep insight on his travels.

What age the poet had reached on his death we cannot tell. In one of his last songs:

*Ir reiniu wîp, ir werden man . . .*

he says that he has sung of *minne* for forty years and more, so that we may consider his career as singer to have begun about 1188, and the date of his birth to have been somewhere near 1170.

K. Halbach in his study on Walther proves that the young poet Walther in his early work shows knowledge of Hartmann von Aue's minnesongs of 1195. This date provides a clue for ascertaining about what year Walther came to Vienna.

On the threshold of the new century he composed his great political song:

*Ich sach mit mînen ougen*
*man unde wîbe tougen*

which deals with the conflict between state and church, emperor and pope (at that time Innocent III, who was crowned ecclesiastical sovereign in 1198 at the age of thirty-seven).

As singer of this epoch-making struggle between Guelph and Ghibelline (Welf and Waibling) Walther excels all the poets of his time by the burning splendour and moral force of his speech. He holds an intermediate position between the imperial realm and the hierarchy. For a short space of time he seems to vacillate between Guelph and Staufen, who represented respectively the church and state parties, without losing his own ground. It is true that Walther wandered from one liege lord to another, but he remained ever true to the cause of the Reich, defending it with dauntless candour against the intrigues of the Curia.

The circumstances were briefly as follows: Walther first supported the Staufen Philip against the Guelph claimant Otto. His fiery patriotic spirit yearned to see order and discipline quell the bickerings of the German realm (*tiuschiu zunge*=the German people), which reminded him of a menagerie. In his first *Spruch*, *pax et justitia*, those primary concepts of German kingship are personified as living creatures suffering betrayal and violation in the midst of political chaos. Vehemently Walther inveighs against the influence of Rome which sowed the seeds of disruption over the German empire. Yet in spite of his faith towards Philip, whose candidature for the throne he had furthered in his songs, he never received the fiefdom which he had dreamed might be his recompense. Once more Walther was faced with the life of wandering minstrelsy.

At this period his political opinions underwent a decided change. His wanderings brought him to Thuringia, where, probably under the influence of the Landgraf Hermann and his son-in-law Dietrich von Meissen, he turned against Philip. For a time he seems to have revisited Austria. In the autumn of 1203 his name appears in the archives of a former champion of the Staufen and lover of the arts, Wolfger, Bishop of Passau, who was raised to the dignity of Patriarch of Aquileja in 1204, after which he retired from Staufen politics. It was probably in the train of this pillar of the church that Walther attended the marriage celebrations of Duke Leopold and the Byzantine princess Theodora Komnena, and possibly it was on this occasion that he sang his immortal *Deutschland, Deutschland über alles* to the circle of knights and noble dames:

*Ir sult sprechen willekomen:*
*der iu mære bringet, daz bin ich . . .*
*Tiusche man sint wol gezogen,*
*rehte als engel sint diu wîp getân.*
*Swer sie schildet, derst betrogen:*
*ich enkan sîn anders niht verstân.*
*Tugent und reine minne, swer die suochen wil,*
*der sol komen in unser lant: dâ ist wünne vil:*
*lange müeze ich leben dar inne!*

His activities during the following years are veiled in mystery Through Dietrich von Meissen Walther must have come into contact with Heinrich von Morungen, the court-poet of the Markgraf.

On the assassination of Philip Walther sings the praises of the Guelph emperor Otto at the court festivals held in Frankfurt in March 1212. He hails the empire and hurls contumely at the Roman Curia and the corrupt clergy, above all at Innocent, who in the year 1213 had caused alms boxes to be put up for his benefit in the German realm. Otto promised Walther rewards which, however, never materialized. Deeply offended in view of all he had done to support the emperor's cause against Rome, Walther once more returned to the Staufen, this time to Frederick II. How far the Landgraf of Thuringia's persuasions caused him to take this step is open to speculation.

This period inaugurates the third stage of Walther's career as a political partisan. His confession:

*Wie solt ich den geminnen der mir übele tuot . . .*

is deeply moving in its honesty. Again he pleads for a home and fiefdom, which Frederick at last grants him in 1220. Gratitude and rejoicing fill his song:

*Ich hân mîn lêhen, al diu werlt, ich hân mîn lêhen.*

In all probability this boon was granted him on the coronation of Frederick's son Henry as German king, which Walther celebrated in song.

The consciousness of his waning years seems to have inspired those lines of sorrowful weariness: '*Owê war sint verswunden alliu mîniu jâr!*'

Is it possible that Walther took part in the crusade which his song glorifies in the summer of 1227? We cannot tell. Nothing is known of his life or his verse after that date. Death may have found him out on his estate in or near Würzburg. All traces of its exact whereabouts have faded with his name. We at any rate rest happy in the possession of his matchless song which had already won the renown and praise of his greatest contemporaries, Wolfram and Gottfried. Speaking generally we should say that Walther's didactic muse exerted most influence on the singers of Middle and Northern Germany, whilst his lyric note was more often caught by the poets of the South.

We saw that Walther's art represents the climax of the German medieval lyric. We know him as the poet of *Minne-*, *Spruch-* and *Kreuzlieder*, as an unrivalled composer of patriotic, political, and religious epigrams, as the champion of the Staufen and the Guelph realm, and defender of true Christianity against ecclesiastical aggression. Before Walther no poets had found such inspiration for their song in politics. He appears fully conscious of his high mission, nor must we forget that he remained true to his ideals even when his career in Vienna was wrecked. It was indeed his life amongst the wandering scholars which freed him inwardly and outwardly from the trammels of court conventions. The somewhat bloodless vein of his earlier contemplative lyrics in the style of Reinmar was soon transfused with fresh life. Yet in his heart Walther ever cherished the courtly chivalric ideal of: '*êre, fuoge, mâze, staete, hôhe minne.*'

Walther is a typical poet of society as it flourished on the threshold of the thirteenth century, also his religious songs were dictated by circumstances then prevailing. Walther's verses were definitely intended for a polished public whose idealistic sensibility they express, whilst he rejoices and mourns with his courtly world, or chastises it in his endeavour to imbue it with a noble and tempered attitude towards life. *Mâze* remains for him the ideal of all human aspiration, and only fiery indignation at some injustice causes Walther now and again to break the laws of that code. Even his erotic songs are governed by *mâze*: cf.

*Si wunder wol gemachet wîp,*
*daz mir noch werde ir habedanc! . . .*

and the enchanting poem:

*Under der linden*
*an der heide. . . .*

We saw that Walther began his career as minnesinger in the Viennese School, but he soon freed himself from the bonds of traditional *courtoisie*. Zest for life and a love of nature in spring's gladness or winter's grief, moreover a sensuous appreciation of real life, soon rendered his songs more dramatic and vital than had been their wont during the *Wiener Lehrjahre*. Overwrought spirituality and abstract meditations on the nature of love are replaced by warmer and more full-blooded imagery. The life-giving spring of that Latin-German poetry of the vagantes quickened his genius to rich maturity. Walther's contact with those true minstrels of the earth, whose love-lyrics and gnomic sayings we find in Spervogel's and others' verse, came as a blessing to German poetry. The courtly minne-lyric was thereby rendered more human, whilst Walther deems the love of a simple peasant girl as praiseworthy a token of womanhood as the gracious favour of some noble dame. This popular note is echoed in his songs: '*Under der linden . . .*,' '*Herzeliebez frouwelîn . . .*,' '*Nemt, frouwe, disen kranz . . .*,' etc. These verses which form the most charming part of Walther's poetic legacy are however not quite *volkstümlich* in the true sense, for they are clearly stylized.

What the attitude of the court was towards these poems of 'uncourtly' love (*niedere Minne*) can only be surmised. Evidently they found comparatively little favour:

*Sie verwîzent mir daz ich*
*sô nidere wende mînen sanc. . . .*

On the other hand this *niedere* minne-lyric may well have been relished by those who were weary of the monotony of courtly songs. Walther, however, did not howl with the wolves! He did not allow his poetry to be dragged down to the level of Neidhart's *Unfuoge*, whose growing popularity filled his spirit with rancour:

*Owê, hovelîchez singen,*
*daz dich ungefüege doene*
*solten ie ze hove verdringen. . . .*

For Walther remained true to the *hohe Minne*, although his poems in praise of ladies of birth lack the exquisite charm of his unique songs of simple love. Yet even the former often possess a freshness of perception seldom found amongst the rank and file of minnesong compositions—thus those beautiful lines in praise of some high-born lady: '*Sô die bluomen ûz dem grase dringent*...', already referred to. The sculptured figures of Naumburg seem to rise before our eyes in all their noble grandeur as we read some of Walther's descriptions of women.

Walther had by this time far outgrown the one-sided convention of his youth. He demanded reciprocal devotion:

*Minne ist zweier herzen wünne:*
*teilent sie gelîche, sost diu minne dâ.*
(cf. *Carmina Burana*, 51, 4.)

Walther betrays himself as a connoisseur of love in:

*Ich wil daz wol zürnen müeze*
*liep mit liebe*. . . .

Reconciliation of love and God is his highest aim: *gotes hulde und mîner frowen minne* (*Summum Bonum et Honestum*).

How far Walther's love-poems are founded on fact cannot be ascertained. To spy into private secrets is but a misuse of time, particularly in the case of medieval lyric poets of whose lives we know so little. Their concept of *wân* and reality appears so entangled, and may be inspired by a spiritual attitude so different from our own, that any speculations on the subject may lead us into gravest misrepresentations of their intention. One fact, however, seems to remain clear, namely that Walther was himself aware of the contradictory character of the *Minnedienst*. But at the end, he turns like Wolfram to sing the praise of matrimonial joys.

### *Aftermath and Decline*

After the death of Walther, and even during his own lifetime, the minnesong begins to betray the crudities of so-called courtly village poetry (*höfische Dorfpoesie*) or it lives on as a worn-out mannerism, shining only with the pale light of reflected glory, though Ulrich von Lichtenstein (of Styrian ancestry) and a few others gifted with formal talent brighten its decadence for a fleeting moment. Coarse realism, a popular vein favoured especially by Gottfried von Neifen, and courtly refinement are incongruously intermingled by the poets of this period such as Der Tannhäuser, Herr Burkart von Hohenfels, and others.

Herr Neidhart von Reuenthal, who belonged to the Bavarian *Dienstadel*, is considered the creator and hero of courtly village poetry. Fair spring that follows full of reckless glee in winter's mournful path, girls dancing amidst the green clover around the linden tree, the small bird's song—all these rouse Neidhart's peasants to merry ribaldry. Even death seems vanquished:

*Ein altiu mit dem tôde vaht*
*beide tac und ouch die naht.*
*diu sprang sider*
*als ein wider. . . .*

Many of his songs give us a palpably real picture of the social life of the peasant, particularly in Austria:

*Rûmet ûz die schämel und die stüele!*
*heiz die schragen*
*vürder tragen!*
*hiute sul wir tanzens werden müeder,*
*werfet ûf die stuben, sô ist ez küele . . .*
(*DLD*, p. 150).

But just as six hundred years later, after Goethe's death, creative impulse relaxed, decay now gnawed at the mask of an empty convention. The flower of minnesong degenerated to formal virtuosity.

We have already heard that great lords, even kings (Wenzel of Bohemia), princes (Anhalt), dukes (Heinrich von Breslau) and counts still composed minnesongs during the middle of the thirteenth century, and some like Hugo von Montfort and Oswald von Wolkenstein even later. But gradually the aristocrat as poet and singer ceded to the wandering burgher class, though the latter on the whole took more kindly to the *Spruchdichtung*. Petty artifices, crumbs of learning, formal tricks foreshadow the style of the mastersong. We find them in the poetry of Konrad von Würzburg and Heinrich von Meissen (Frauenlob, † 1318 in

Mainz), who in contrast to Walther's and Regenbogen's praise of *wîp* pays tribute to the *frouwe*, while his verses literally brim over with conceit.

Ulrich von Lichtenstein's '*Frauendienst*' may rank as the earliest example of autobiography in German literature. R. Bechstein has called it the most peculiar and informative story of the Middle Ages which at the same time provides a principal source of research in cultural history. How careful we must nevertheless be in accepting such fantastic anecdotes as facts we pointed out before. As a proof of faith to his lady-love Lichtenstein cuts off his finger:

> *Dô nam ich sâ daz mezer sîn*
> *und satzt ez ûf den vinger mîn. . . .*
> *. . . Er sluoc: der vinger der spranc dan . . .*

whilst to win her grace he claims to have ridden from Venice to Vienna clad as *frou Venus*, in which guise we may behold him mounted on his armoured horse in the Manesse Codex. The decline of the *Minnedienst* was by this time far advanced.

Hugo von Montfort (born 1357) is a peculiar phenomenon in this transitional period after the minnesong, planted like some rugged immovable rock in the midst of predatory knighthood (*Raubritter*), *Faustrecht*, and poetic decay. He was twenty years older than his countryman Oswald von Wolkenstein, of noble birth and noble spirit. As a boy of fourteen he rode out into the world. Two years later he suddenly won considerable possessions through marriage, though his passionate heart ever fell a prey to others' charms. Even a crusade to Prussia that brought him outward fame, but was in reality a failure, could not tame his wild nature, and only the death of his father awakened his latent force of character. He thereupon proves himself a fine singer in praise of noble ladies, and a dauntless combatant of ecclesiastical avarice and the shame of the schism, turning from the wiles of *Frou Werlt* to *Gottes Minne*. This change in moral outlook was brought about through the influence of his faithful wife. On her death he married yet twice again, whilst fortune smiled on him, bringing him renown at the court of Duke Leopold where he held the office of *Hofmeister* and steward. But on the threshold of the fifteenth century the house of Montfort was threatened by the revolt of the Swiss Confederations and the peasants. Not only Bregenz and its environs, but also their Styrian possessions stood in jeopardy of destruction by troops and marauders, but Hugo von Montfort stood firm, doggedly defending the ancient privileges of his class. In 1423 he died and was laid to rest in the Church of the Minorites in Bruck an der Mur (Styria).

As poet and as human being alike, H. v. Montfort wore his heart on his sleeve. His language abounds with living imagery, but is by no means free of rhythmic and metric carelessness and word-padding. He never succeeded in welding his material to convincing form. Thus the doom which was fast closing in on aristocratic culture fastened on the poetic art itself. The age of chivalry had reached its end. The formal boundaries of the arts were dissolved even in the lyric, in which long-winded narrative and rhetorical pedagogy intermingle. Its degeneration is also evident in the fact that Montfort left the musical composition of his poems to his true servant Bürk Mangolt. This division between poet and composer now became the fashion.

Oswald von Wolkenstein, who was born in 1377, was also the scion of Tirolese nobility. At the age of ten he set out in the world and spent thirteen years in travel, visiting North and East Europe, the Mediterranean, the Black Sea, and even Persia:

*In Frankereich,*
*Ispanien, Arragun, Castilie, Engelant,*
*Tenmark, Sweden, Pehem, Ungern dort,*
*in Püllen und Afferen,*
*in Cippern und Cecilie,*
*in Portigal, Granaten, Soldans kron,*
*Die sechzen künigreich*
*hab ich umbvaren. . . .*

On these wanderings he probably hired himself as squire to some lord and learned ten languages:

*Franzoisch, mörisch, katlonisch und kastilian,*
*teutsch, latein, windisch, lampertisch, reuschisch und roman. . . .*
*auch kund ich vidlen, trummen, pauken, pfeiffen. . . .*

In 1401 he is again found in Tirol. A few years later he began waging ruthless feuds in order to add to his estates. The year 1415 inaugurated a new stage in his career and he appears as retainer of Sigismund at Constance, in which capacity he visits Spain and

France. In 1417 he married and proved himself a practical husband and father of many children, stolidly defending his illegally augmented estate. In 1421 he was betrayed, lured into imprisonment and put to torture. In 1423 he was at last liberated only to be thrown into captivity once more until the feud was settled to his own advantage in 1427. His death must in all probability have occurred in 1445. The rich strain of adventures which accompanied the life of this late minnesinger overflowed in the unbridled stream of his song which no *hôhe zuht* or *mâze* ever tempered.

## *THE MASTERSINGERS*

The origins of the mastersong must be sought in the minnesong, especially in its proverbial verse from which the masters borrowed many features of metre and syntax, such for instance as enjambement and parenthesis. But folksongs and religious literature also offered models on which to work and many a *Meisterton* recalls a Gregorian chant. The members of the school of mastersingers were divided into different ranks: the poet who *carmen fingit*, the singer who *instrumentis agit*, and the *Merker* who *instrumentorum opus carmenque diiudicat*. According to Stammler these categories are found described in St. Victor's *Eruditio didascalica* (II. cap. 13, Migne 176, 757). David was the patron of the masters, who particularly favoured biblical themes as a means of edifying themselves and their audience. The seven *artes liberales* provided the basis of their vocal art, which soon succumbed to the atrophy of erudition. The mastersingers included scholars amongst their ranks, for instance the philologist and notary Johann Spreng who, born in Augsburg in 1524, translated Ovid, Virgil, and Homer. Although the habit of awarding a garland as prize to the best singer was perhaps adopted from some humbler folk-custom (itself originally derived from courtly manners), the mastersong gradually lost all contact with life and degenerated to mechanical craftsmanship that hid sterility beneath a panoply of intricate rules and formulas; cf. A. Taylor: *The Literary History of Meistergesang*, 1937, New York.

The Flemish versifiers (Rederijkers) show a similar choice of subjects, but have really no connection with the German movement. Poor honest Adam Puschmann's handbook of rules for poets, *Gründlicher Bericht des deutschen Meistergesangs*, 1571, is the earliest document of importance concerning the mastersongs in our possession. It was intended to rescue the art from the decay into which it was so fast declining. Its author was born in 1532 in Görlitz, and at first pursued a tailor's trade till he was made cantor. He was a Lutheran and pupil of Hans Sachs, on whose death he published his famous *Elogium reverendi viri Johannis Sachsen Norinbergensis*. In 1600 he followed Hans Sachs to the grave. The dedication of the *Bericht* refers to the mastersong's dependence on the minne-lyric, and hails its twelve glorious ancestors as seven noblemen [Walther, Wolffgangus Rohn (Wolfram?), Marner, Frauenlob, Mügeling, Klingsohr, Starcke Popp (Boppe)], and five burghers [Regenbogen, Römer, Kantzler, Stolle, Konrad von Würzburg]. No less a personage than Otto I, it maintains, summoned these twelve patrons to Paris in 962 and proclaimed them masters of their art.

Puschmann's treatise differentiates between different types of rhyme, namely, masculine, feminine, etc. The line must not contain more than thirteen syllables, because one could not manage more in one breath (*auff einmahl*). The second treatise explains the table of rules and enumerates its twenty-four *Strafartikel* and eleven *Strafartikel in die Scherffe*: e.g.

> The songs must be composed and sung in High German, i.e. in the language of the imperial chancellory and the Wittenberg, Nürnberg and Frankfurt Bibles;
> false *Meinung*, i.e. superstitious doctrines must be eschewed;
> likewise Latin that defies the laws of grammar. . . .

Though great freedom obtained regarding the choice of themes, the form is constrained by the red tape of pedantic decrees.

The following are also accounted offences:

> *blinde Meinung*, i.e. an unclear sentence;
> *blindes Wort*, i.e. an unclear word;

etc.

Puschmann's third treatise deals with the length of the tune; no tune must have less than seven rhymes or lines, and must not exceed a hundred. The tune must be the master's own invention. This amendment was due to Folz, the barber of Worms, before whose day it was customary to sing only the melodies of the twelve ancestors.

The members of the mastersinger school were, as stated, divided into categories. The pupil novice must memorize every detail of the tables of rules. The *singer* must be acquainted with every existing tune. The *poet* must compose new words to old melodies. The *master* (the highest rank attainable) must invent a new tune. Mainz is praised as the *alma mater* of the schools. Strassburg, Nürnberg (where a mastersinger school persisted as late as 1770), Worms, and other towns follow. But they never penetrated to North Germany, although the minnesong had found its way thither, to wit with Wizlâv von Rügen and Herman der Damen.

Johann Christophorus Wagenseil, born in Nürnberg in 1633, was appointed professor of law and Oriental languages. In 1697, as an appendix to his description of Nürnberg (*De civitate . . . Norinbergensi*), he published his *Buch von der Meistersinger holdseligen Kunst, Anfang, Fortübung, Nutzbarkeiten und Lehrsätzen.* He distinctly betrays the influence of Puschmann and to some extent inspired R. Wagner's opera *Die Meistersinger*. Wagenseil mentioned two hundred and twenty-one master-tunes under their quaint names—the *black-ink-air* of Ambrosius Metzger, the *short-monkey-air* of Georg Hager, the *striped saffron-flower-air* of Hans Findeisen, the *rose-tone-air* of Hans Sachs, the *cupid's-bow-air*, the *green-lime-flower-air*, the *all-too-short-sunset-air*, etc. Wagenseil's account of the singers' customs and habits, coloured, now by the solemn atmosphere of the church which brooded over their gatherings, now by the ribald gaiety of the inns whither they afterwards dispersed, makes good reading.

But praise of God and edification were looked upon as the noblest aim of the mastersong or *Meisterlied* (a bar built up of verses with two *Stollen* and one *Abgesang*), particularly during the earlier period of its existence. Profane but serious themes borrowed from legend and history (Tell, Charlemagne, Luther, etc.), also found their way into the general store of subject-matter. Towards the end of the fifteenth century the mastersong entered the period of its final downfall. In vain did H. Folz attempt to reform it; it remained alien to the æsthetic ideals of the new age. Even in musical and technical respects the mastersongs were soon outclassed. Instrumental music was rapidly developing new forms of expression whilst the mastersingers remained sterile, hidebound by local jealousy and the narrowness of the guilds. The difference between *Lied* and *Spruch*, which the minnesong had never lost sight of, now counted for nothing. The sense of any profound relationship between content and form was lost.

A fifteenth-century manuscript at Colmar presents the most extensive collection of mastersongs in our possession. It commences with the songs of Frauenlob, who indeed was estimated the most prolific of the composers. Frauenlob's *langer Ton* was particularly popular. The greater part of the collection is assigned to religious songs, to the praise of Mary, the Holy Trinity, the death of the Redeemer, and similar themes. The *Straflieder*, too, are well to the fore. These are songs in which clumsy poetasters are derided on account of their not infrequent allusions to the *termini technici* of the mastersingers. The Colmar manuscript, moreover, clearly shows to what minnesingers the mastersingers were most indebted. It is also interesting to note that the scribe who wrote this manuscript himself appears here as a mastersinger, the inventor of an original air.

# II
# THE GERMAN FOLK-SONG

---

(A)

By now the glory of the German minnesong had degenerated into the pedantry of the mastersingers. But in the meantime in the fourteenth and fifteenth centuries the folk-song—that fair flower of true German *Gemüt*—had enriched the realm of poetry. The heart of the entire nation lives in its folk-songs. They are its solace in sorrow and solitude. Inciting heroic deed, they enhance present reality with the glamour of an immortal past. To the emigrant old songs such as '*Es waren zwei Königskinder*' and others provide a bond between him and the fatherland. When all other links appear broken a German folk-song sung beneath an American Christmas-tree or in a sailors' tavern in some alien port fills him with nostalgia for German woods and the German Rhine. Thus language and song may provide ties more intimate than economic relations.

In the folk-song (a term all too vague) we may more clearly than in any other poetic genre observe a nation's power to regenerate itself. Pessimistic allegations to the effect that the caged bird loses its voice, the *Salontiroler* sings abominably, or that a popular ragtime like *Donna Clara* wins the heart of the people, are but half-truths. Great epochs or revolutionary movements such as the age of Luther, Hutten's struggle against Rome, King Frederick II's and Napoleon's campaigns, and the Great War itself, revived many a slumbering source of inspiration. The 'folk' must not be confused with the 'masses.' One cannot deny that, like the latter, it also is not averse to a ribald joke, though in many cases the dubious tone of some phrase is more due to its rendering into the literary language than to anything else. The 'folk' embraces the highest and lowest strata of the nation. The view that the folk-song was born of some vague community that once happily existed, or even persists to the present day, must now, however, be dismissed as a romantic dream. The creative faculty belongs to the individual alone, though maintaining no individual prerogative, and the poet's consciousness is inwoven with that of his people. The 'folk' does not create poetry; it selects, reproduces and adapts material to its own use, thereby dissolving the subjective elements of the prototype. If it lacks such unconscious participation in the life of a nation, a poem but seldom becomes a folk-song. We refer here to the 'folk' (particularly the peasants) who share certain traditions of language, custom, mentality, and action. Nevertheless we should include also the civic proletarian community—the workers. Thus the term 'folk' has a definite meaning only where the higher and lower classes of society are not estranged by differing concepts of culture, and where churchman and layman can join whole-heartedly in a song. Such happy conditions seem to have passed away, and their disappearance may be used as an argument by those who foretell the decline of European civilization. But under the stress of universal calamity, as for instance in war-time, individual emotion attains universal significance, the nation regains something of that lost sense of unity, till not only families but whole countries are knit together in a vast sort of brotherhood. Thus even the present day has witnessed the birth and revival of songs which could become folk-songs.

In enquiring into the essential qualities of the folk-song we can either pursue the objective method of J. Meier, who compares songs in their various extant forms, or we can deal with them subjectively. The latter attitude is that adopted by J. Schwietering and his school, who regard the folk-song as the expression of a community (*Gemeinschaft*), and thus suggest the existence of a *Dorfkultur*. A wise synthesis of the two methods can be said to produce the best results.

The term *Volkslied* itself is not old. It was coined by Herder and appeared in his '*Von deutscher Art und Kunst*' in 1773, a period which witnessed the bitterest tension between literary poetry and popular feeling. Before Herder's time it was customary to speak of *Gesellenlied*, *Buhl-*, *Landsknecht-* (*Schwartenhals-*), *Trink-*, *Reuter-*, *Soldaten-*, *Natur-*, *Studenten-*, *Liebes-*, *Marsch-*, *Schelmen-*, *Kinder-*, *Fastnachts-*, *Kriegs-*, *Jäger-*, *Heuer-* (*Berg-*

*knappen-*), *Gras-*, *Historien-*, *Strassenlied*, *Bauerngesang*, *Bergreihen*, *carmen vulgare*,—*triviale*,—*rusticum*,—*barbarum*, *etc.*

In the Third Realm there was a marked tendency to identify the German folk-song with the German song itself, an attitude reminiscent of certain words of Goethe declaring that only one type of poetry exists, namely that which flows alike from the lips of artisan and noble, provided they are gifted with the divine spirit.

(B)

It is indeed difficult to approach folk-songs with strict definitions, for as '*the true folk-song*' does not exist we cannot say that it possesses a particular style. Uhland attempted to rediscover its true form, and consequently gave his own songs and ballads a uniformity which cannot be considered characteristic of the folk-song itself, for the latter is subject to external change. Nevertheless in the fourteenth, fifteenth, and sixteenth centuries the folk-song achieved such importance that it really seems to present certain typical features which might up to a point justify the use of the term *Volksliedstil*. We may here point to the following characteristics: a love of simple melodies, simple rhythm and verse construction, verses of four to eight lines or infrequently two lines, with four lifts, and freedom concerning the use of dips (though the metre is, generally speaking, iambic). In contrast to the minnesong, the rhymes are seldom pure. Masculine and feminine rhymes alternate at random. Often there is no rhyme at all. Expression is untrammelled by pedantry whilst any word which in the literary prototype defeats the comprehension of the popular mind is naïvely exchanged for one affiliated in sound or meaning, though often utterly deprived of its original significance. We here speak of the text being *zersungen*, e.g. *Schöneberg* > *schönste Burg*, *Ural* > *Urwald*, *Diana* > *Die Anna*, *Ça ira* > *Sairassa*, *Marlborough* > *Marlbröck*. Childlike expressions such as *ri-ra-rauschen*, *Schwi- Schwa-Schwalbe*, are equally typical. Corruptions of words based on association naturally give rise to abundant variation, due partly to inaccurate hearing: *Im Spiele der Waffen* > *in spielender Waffe*, partly to simplification as regards meaning and analogy: *Reiher* > *Geier*: '*Ein Reiher kreist über dem Rohre*' > '*der Geier steigt über die Berge,*' or '*der Geier streicht über die Berge,*' or '*der Adler kreist über die Berge,*' or '*der Adler rauscht über die Lüfte.*'

We see therefore that in the folk-song not only material and motif but form itself are mutable quantities. The 'folk' knows nothing of individual values but corrupts the songs it meets with, at the same time endowing them with its own local colouring. Local variations of this type are presented by:

*Zu Strassburg auf der Schanz* > *Zu Ratzeburg. . . .*

or

*O Strassburg, O Strassburg, du wunderschöne Stadt* >
*Ach Rendsburg, Ach Rendsburg. . . .*

The substitution of 'lady' for 'wench':

*Es spielte ein Graf mit einer Magd* > *Es ritt ein Ritter mit einer Magd* >
*Es spielte ein Ritter mit einer Madam . . .*

effects not only an alteration in verbal quantity but in social significance. On the other hand the original may suffer an opposite fate and the courtly vein be humbled to the level of the bourgeois, as in the ballad of the knight and the maiden (*EB*, I, 41).

Through this process of *zersingen* the 'folk-song' developed a sort of formula—a skeleton around whose bare bones fancy could ever weave new variations. The structure remains unchanged, but place, persons and landscape are adapted to the milieu of the singer. To this vital variability and pristine strength the folk-song owes a great part of its charm.

Another characteristic element is presented by the frequent insertion of the word *und* or *es*, which on the other hand is often suppressed: '*Sah ein Knab*' . . .; also *Ich* can be dropped: '*Weiss mir ein Blümlein blau. . . .*' Formulas such as: '*Ich weiss ein Blum,*' '*Ich weiss ein hübsches Freuelein . . .,*' alliteration, internal rhyme, onomatopoeia, parallels and crescendos are all typical of the folk-song. The peculiar juxtaposition of lines seemingly complete in themselves must not be confused with modern verse technique, with its intellectual conceits and conscious associative and suggestive power. The folk-song's strength lies in its power to convey emotion with poignant directness through language simple and devoid of bombast. Its formal structure is loose and allows of great freedom in syntax and verbal arrangement. Thus the adjective often follows the noun instead of preceding it: '*Röslein rot*,' '*Mägdlein fein. . . .*' The refrain and other forms of repetition are naturally enough a frequent occurrence. The meaning should only be suggested:

*Ich hort ein sichellin rauschen,*
*wol rauschen durch das korn,*
*ich hort ein feine magt klagen:*
*sie het ir lieb verlorn.*

'*La rauschen, lieb, la rauschen!*
*ich acht nit wie es ge;*
*ich hab mir ein bulen erworben*
*in feiel und grünen kle.*'

'*Hast du ein bulen erworben*
*in feiel und grünen kle,*
*so ste ich hie alleine,*
*tut meinem herzen we.*'

or:

*Dört hoch auf jenem berge*
*da get ein mülerad,*
*das malet nichts denn liebe*
*die nacht biss an den tag;*
*die müle ist zerbrochen,*
*die liebe hat ein end,*
*so gsegen dich got, mein feines lieb!*
*iez far ich ins ellend.*

or:

*Es warb ein schöner jüngling*
*über ein braiten see*
*umb eines königs tochter,*
*nach leid geschach im wee.*

*Ach Elslein, holder bule,*
*wie gern wer ich bei dir!*
*so flieszen zwei tiefe wasser*
*wol zwischen dir und mir.*

and : *Ach Elslein, liebes Elselein,*
*wie gern wär ich bei dir!*
*so sein zwei tiefe wasser*
*wol zwischen dir und mir.*

*'Das bringt mir groszen schmerzen,*
*herzallerliebster gsell!*
*red ich von ganzem herzen,*
*habs für grosz ungefell.'*

*'Hoff, zeit werd es wol enden,*
*hoff, glück werd kummen drein,*
*sich in als guts verwenden,*
*herzliebstes Elselein!'*

The author of a folk-song is thinking not so much of its æsthetic value as of its subject-matter. The folk-song aims at straightforward description, especially in the historic songs which provided an excellent means of distributing news, before the newspapers of the *Fugger* and the letters of the humanists came into vogue. Whilst the historic song—echo of the ancient heroic poem and *Preislied*—was enjoying utmost popularity and being carried far and wide, another type of song also developed whose burden was of a gentler, more melancholy vein, telling of lovers' parting, of wanderlust, of joy and pain, true love and faithlessness. In both cases the use of parable and symbol appears as a typical feature of the folk-song, e.g. flower = virgin, rose-garden = love's guerdon, lover = barrel of wine (cf. '*Den liebsten Buhlen, den ich han . . .*'), cuckoo = rival, innocence = love, forget-me-not = faithfulness, falcon (borrowed from the minnesong) = beloved.

Characteristic of the folk-song is a certain disjointed, bounding quality in its narrative. It is true that the hasty condensed style of the ballad is not always due to the process of *zersingen*, for, to take the case of the historic songs, the poet presupposes some knowledge of events on the hearer's part and by pretermitting them leaves whole gaps in his story. But these the 'folk' revelled in filling with its own phantasies. Moreover, we must not ignore the fact that the oldest readings were continually being improved upon, with the result that the text was much corrupted and the gaps became incomprehensible. The main point is that the lack of continuity and the naïve nonsense of such songs should *not* be considered as *necessarily* belonging to the original version.

If at the beginning of this chapter we admitted that no definite style could be assigned to the folk-song, we have nevertheless, in the course of the argument, been able to point to many peculiarities that withstand the many changes to which the folk-song is naturally subject. Changing times, changing taste, the mutability of man's attitude towards life leave their mark on these songs, which nevertheless retain their character as true expression of German popular feeling. Not one but many laws govern the folk-song, so that the term *Vielgesetzlichkeit* is here preferable to that of *Eingesetzlichkeit*. An excellent example of its use is provided by Ittenbach's analysis of the ballad *Graf und Nonne*. He dissects the various elements that constitute the form of this poem. The above song was compounded from single verses taken from a ballad (*Count and Nun*), a tavern-song or *Reuterlied* or *Landsknechtlied* and a wandering-song. The introduction of the dragoon served as a means of blending these many heterogeneous elements to some sort of unity. Thus we see that the terse vigour of the folk-song style is not due to such romantic reasons as is generally supposed.

Even the *formalistic quality* of these songs can to some extent be traced to their conglomerate nature. Here again Ittenbach in discussing the ballad of the *Mordwirtin* has proved convincingly that the folk-song is no *Kunstlied*, and must not be treated as such. Clichés such as a *snow-white hand* or *black-brown eyes* must not lightly be thought to betray any deeper emotional significance in relation to the chief character in the song (as though, for instance the black-brown eyes had here been used to suggest the bad conscience of the murderous innkeeper!) These, like the more commonplace *white hands*, *rose-red mouth*, are merely conventional equipment of *mein feins Liebchen*, my bonny lass.

The song was intended to be sung. The melody must therefore be taken into account when examining the text. The metric form of the verses is known as *Weise*. The word 'tune' applies to the melody. F. M. Böhme has greatly enlightened us on the melodies of the folk-song. His immortal treasure-trove of old German songs supplies us with an astonishing number of melodies, many of which have long been silent in the public ear. But since then, many worldly tunes were borrowed by the catholic and evangelical churches and even incorporated in the Mass, whilst inversely many spiritual songs (particularly those of the fifteenth and sixteenth centuries) were parodied and translated for mundane purposes, a very large number of tunes have been preserved till the present day.

Thus in religious songs such as:

*Es ist ein Schloss Sion genant. . . .*

*Ich weiss mir ein ewigs Himmelreich,*
*das ist gantz schön gebawet*

(*B*. p. 100)

we clearly see that they owe their origin to a certain folk-song:

*Es ligt ein Schloss in Österreich,*
*das ist gar wol erbawet. . . .*

The rhythm of the folk-song is usually moderate, though not too slow. The leisured measure of the dance was often followed by somewhat livelier strains, the so-called after-dance. The vocal melody followed a distinct beat, though the latter often changed during the course of the song: a fact which may sound strange to the modern ear (though not to the truly modern!). We also find that the accent is not infrequently shifted from a chief syllable to a subsidiary one, whereby each syllable in the text may demand its own musical note. The German folk-song is intended for a single voice, i.e. men and women joined together singing in octaves. The secondary accompanying voice was a later innovation, which possibly resulted from the fact that the German instruments (the horn and trumpet), in contrast with the guitar or harp, called for a second voice as accompaniment. According to Böhme the principal melody—the *cantus firmus*—was at first given to the tenor, except in such songs as: '*Innsbruck, ich muss dich lassen* . . .,' '*Ach Elslein* . . .,' where the descant led. This was seldom the case in the sixteenth century to which period these melodies belong, but at the close of the century the descant was generally favoured with the chief part.

The age and derivation of the folk-song melody are often quite uncertain, as the oldest documents hardly reach further back than the fourteenth or indeed the fifteenth and sixteenth centuries, where they appear in MSS., prints, and journals. Uhland's collection is chiefly compiled from sixteenth-century material, though the religious songs: '*Christ ist erstanden . . .*' or '*In Gottes Namen fahren wir . . .*' belong to the twelfth and thirteenth centuries. Until lately German scholarship was inclined to regard the folk-song and ballad as, in the main, little more than a corruption of the cultured forms (*herabgesunkenes Kulturgut*) of the courtly period. When dealing with the origins of the minnesong we pointed to the fallibilities and exaggerations such opinions involve. The heroic maiden of noble birth who features in so many ballads is not borrowed from the world of courtly *Minne*, but suggests agrarian conditions at a period when nobility and peasants were as yet undifferentiated. These traits are still faintly discernible in the German folk-song. Hence we cannot interpret all *volkstümliche* elements as atavisms of a past cultured form. Moreover, we must acknowledge the existence since time immemorial of a so-called minor poetry (*Kleindichtung*) of which we may discover an echo today in the *Schnadahüpfl*, *Tschumperlieder*, *Trutzlieder*, *Neck-*, *Wiegenlieder*, etc. There is, in fact, every likelihood that a great body of folk-songs existed long before any of them were written down.

(c)

The German folk-song, as we have seen, draws its life from the community of peasants, huntsmen, millers, soldiers, and others. In regard to context and rank, the songs might well be ranged under various categories, for instance *historical songs*, or better, *songs* termed *political* on account of their propagandist nature. These provide us with most valuable material concerning the history of culture and custom. Such songs are usually lacking in æsthetic quality and they may be said to fill the part played by journalism at the present day. It would on the whole be more satisfactory to speak of historical songs than of historical folk-songs. One of the most popular songs of this type is '*Epple von Geilingen*,' which dates from the fourteenth century and consists of forty-three rhymed couplets. The first verses describe Epple's predatory raids on Nürnberg. Then follow the adventures of the boots under the Frauentor, Epple's flight across the river Main, the attack on the merchant, the cruelty meted out to the peasants and, lastly, the capture of Epple at Farnbach, his defence, his last message to his mother and his execution on the Rabenstein. The actual facts as recounted in the Nürnberg chronicles and local legend are freely treated and embellished. The story of Epple's leap into the Main was probably a coarsened adaptation of Epple's leap from the ramparts of Nürnberg. The finale in particular has but little connection with historical tradition.

Historic legend of great age is provided above all by the later *Hildebrandslied* dating from the fifteenth century. A comparison with the old High German *Hildebrandslied* betrays a decided weakening of the tragic element and the introduction of the *Spielmann's* (gleeman's) tone. The story is based on the conflict between father and son, a theme which finds a counterpart in the Persian tale of Rustem and Sohrab, the Greek of Odysseus and Telegonus, the Russian of Ilya of Murom, the Irish of Cuchullain and Conlaoch, the South Hessian of Johan ûz dem Vergiere, but the late version of the *Hildebrandslied* has lost the heroic austerity of the ancient poem.

Heroes, gods, demigods, and characters from myth and legend such as Siegfried provide material for the folk-song.

The Northern world of love and saga which Percy has retrieved from oblivion could never be equalled by that which Herder was able to discover on German soil.

Nevertheless the German folk-song can boast a wealth of love-, wandering-, dance- and nature-songs that no other land possesses. Even traces of the *winileod*, as we have seen, are to be found in monastic prohibitions, or in ancient fragments such as the *Ruodlieb*. With one of the most charming features of these love-songs we are already acquainted through the minnesong, namely the poet's sensibility to the joys of summer and winter's cruelty. The folk-singer's heart responds to the carefree mirth of spring—it mourns with the falling leaves. Roses, violets, and flowery garlands are associated with his beloved. Each flower possesses some symbolic meaning; thus the forget-me-not signifies faithfulness, the stitchwort comfort in heart-sorrow, the daisy precociousness, the sweet-briar the beloved herself, marjoram incitement to joy. The garden is itself a symbol of love.

Colours play an important part in this connection. But colour allegories on green, gold, black, etc., are not favoured until the fourteenth century. Clara Hätzlerin's famous fifteenth century collection introduces purely didactic songs, '*Von allerlei Farben*' or '*Von der grünen Farbe*,' about colour values.

Anthologies often provide poignant proofs of the transitoriness of man's life. How many poets who appear in Hätzlerin's anthology (1471)—Heinrich der Teichner, the Austrian knight Peter Suchenwirt, Suchensinn, Muskatblüt, Hermann von Sachsenheim—would otherwise be forgotten. Thus her collection is of much value to the literary historian. These lyrics were not confined like the minnesong to a privileged class, but intended for the masses. They belong to the epoch opening with Charles IV and closing with Frederick III, the epoch of civic aggrandizement, of the Helvetic confederacy, of the Hussites, the Turkish peril and sword-law. No common cause knit the German people to any political or spiritual unity. No princedom, no city stood out as a vital centre of culture. Aristocracy and burgher engaged each other in deadly feud. The general disruption is reflected in the anthology above-mentioned. Judged by minnesong standards, these songs betray deterioration to a bewildering degree. Religious and all too worldly elements, ribald catches, love-songs and hymns in praise of the Virgin intermingle at random. Even language lacks uniformity. Old forms and new, old content and new, wage irreconcilable war on one another. Hätzlerin's anthology contains simple love-songs, advice on table manners (*Tischzucht*), rules of etiquette, preambles, flowery *Marienlieder* [Mary is the ark of the covenant, Aaron's rod, Ezekiel's porch, a pot of myrrh, a wand of grace], moreover, drolleries by Rosenblüt and others, quodlibets and, strange to say, only one political song. An affectation of the minnetone is often obvious, but it is in the few songs which catch the popular tone that the anthology gives us its best. Love and nature are here perfectly interblended and flow untrammelled from the poet's heart.

Prior to Hätzlerin's collection, the *Limburg Chronicle*, the work of a cleric, Tilemann Elhen von Wolfhagen († 1402), gives some quotations and information (very fragmentary, alas) regarding folk-songs. It tells us of *flagellation* and *supplication songs* of the time of the Black Death. The learned author of the *Chronicle*, who preens himself with maxims from Aristotle, Cato, and the Bible, warns the reader against the emotional extravagance of the flagellants. Our chief source of knowledge concerning these songs is the hexametric *Chronicon Hugonis sacerdotis Rutelinga* of 1349. The flagellation songs, which are related to the songs of pilgrimage and chants (*misericordia*, *kyrie*, etc.), must be studied with circumspection as far as their appearance in the *Limburg Chronicle* is concerned, for by Tilemann's time they had died out and were known to him only by hearsay. The *Chronicle* also tells us something of popular love-songs of the period. Thus we hear that the following songs were in vogue; in 1361:

*Miden, scheiden, daz dut werlich we . . .*

and in 1374:

*Gepuret reine und suberlich*
*weiss ich ein wip gar minniclich. . . .*

In a later chapter, dedicated to the religious songs of the following period, we shall consider the question of formative influences affecting both the Catholic and Protestant parties respectively. As already mentioned, printed specimens of folk-songs did not flourish until the sixteenth century.

Songs of parting and *Wanderlust* are largely connected with the love-song type. The same applies to the dance-songs, the dawn-songs, and the watchman's warnings. The latter were of course originally not *volkstümlich*, but in the course of time they were incorporated in the treasury of folk-themes and ultimately even exerted some influence over the evangelical church-song.

The *Riddle-songs* form a special category. In a song of the twelfth century the newly arrived guest Meister Tragemund, who has visited seventy-two countries, finds a ready answer to the questions put to him, e.g.:

What tree produces fruit without flowers ? (juniper)
What bird suckles its young ? (the bat)
What bird has no tongue ? (stork)
What bird has no stomach ? (diving duck)
What is whiter than the snow ? (sun)
What is quicker than the deer ? (wind)
What is higher than the hill ? (tree)
What is darker than the night ? (raven), etc.

A German riddle-song in Latin guise has probably come down to us in the song so well known to us through the *Carmina Burana: Stetit puella* ('A girl stood in her dress so red. If anyone touched her, her dress rustled'). Verse 3 was apparently once independent, verse 1 was perhaps a riddle-song, or it was connected with the so-called *Perhtenlaufen.*

The custom of *garland singing* also favoured the introduction of the riddle. A lover is forced to answer questions demanded of him by his girl. The garland as guerdon reminds one of the master-singers, but in reality it possesses a deeper significance, for virginity was forfeited with the garland. The origin of the riddle-song is to be discovered in Icelandic and Anglo-Saxon literature. Unfortunately the German songs retain but a faint echo of that reciprocal riddle-making between a host and his divine guest (a motif so popular in the story of Odin). Themes dealing with *rival contests* between summer and winter (cf. *Altercatio ecclesiae et synagogue . . .*) are closely related to the latter species. Impossible adventures, the wonders of a fool's paradise, are presented in the *Schlaraffenland*: Doors and walls are built of cake. Each house is surrounded by a fence of sausages. Wine gushes from the fountains, fish, fried and ready to eat, disport themselves in the waters, roasted birds fly straight into one's mouth. Hans Sachs's description of this Utopia is renowned. But such absurd fictions are not limited to the *Schlaraffenland* alone. Walther von der Vogelweide's song:

*Genuoge hêrren sînt gelîch den gougelaeren. . . .*

and the Latin lay *modus florum,* which probably dates from the tenth century, are early examples of similar phantasies. To the category of convivial music belong also the wish-songs (*Wunschlieder*) and curse-songs, blessings and spells borrowed from the fairy-tale.

How strong an influence the fairy-tale element exerted over the German folk-song is shown by Uhland in his comparative studies of *fable-songs,* the wild man of the wood and his wife, the giant and the genii of the hills, and in his enquiry into the rôles allotted to the various animals. Thus we find Ursus the bear as merry-maker (cf. Siegfried's adventure); then the wild boar as symbolic image of the hero (cf. Nibelungen: Siegfried, Volker); the wolf as Isegrim, versed in legend or as denouncer of heartless mankind (cf. the wolf's complaint by Hans Sachs); likewise the hare or the swan on the spit laments over man's ingratitude. The animals' wedding (frog and mouse) and their funeral processions are favourite topics frequently seasoned with a satiric vein. Of all such themes the bird-tale seems most popular. The cuckoo is not only a cunning rival, but above all a herald of the spring. But the chief rôle amongst the birds was assigned to *Dame Nightingale*. The minnesinger had already honoured her with the title *frouwe* (lady). Her sweet song, her message and advice also move the heart of the simple folk-singer to profound sorrow and rich joy. In an exquisite song of the sixteenth century the nightingale is love's messenger:

*Es steht ein Lind in jenem Tal,*
*ist oben breit und unten schmal,*

*Ist oben breit und unten schmal,*
*darauf da sitzt Frau Nachtigal. . . .*

In addition to the numerous classifications already made in regard to context, the folk-song might also be ordered according to social rank. For the peasant, mountain dweller, student, monk, wanderer, burgher, huntsman, miller, tailor, weaver, and the rest, each endowed it with the particular stamp of his own class, or the song makes fun of his peculiarities, as for instance those of the tailor. The *children's songs* often suffer through the would-be *naïveté* of the pedagogue. The craftsman's and worker's songs affect a more universal note. The so-called *mowing-song* may refer to the act of mowing, but need not necessarily re-echo the rhythm of mowing. In his book on *Das deutsche Arbeitslied* (1936), J. Schopp differentiates clearly between a true work-song which very likely was actually improvised during worktime, and the false work-song in which a folk-song was adapted to the rhythm of the work in hand.

### *The 'Working-song'*

The German *working-song* has a double origin. On the one hand it developed from corruption of other folk-songs, charms and flax-gathering songs (they themselves having been partly

May-dance songs and 'girl-auction' songs), or it can also have been composed at actual work. In the latter case the working rhythm is of great importance, as K. Bücher shows in his book on *Arbeit und Rhythmus*. Nevertheless the rhythm of many working songs, e.g. *Arbeitsruflieder*, is not always dependent on the working rhythm, but rhythm in song and work are somehow adapted to each other. According to Schopp we may differentiate four types of working-song:

1. Working-songs expressing a *command* or an encouraging cry generally from the foreman, e.g.

*Hii-o-ruck!*
*Hiioo-ruck!*

or so-called *Rammer-songs* sung whilst lifting and sinking wooden posts into the ground or into a wall (in West Prussia):

*Hi-hopp!*
*Auf'n Kopp!*
*noch einmal*
*op en dal.*

or a song heard during the Great War:

*Einmal auf,*
*nochmal drauf!*
*der muss hinein,*
*dann hält er fein,*
*dann hält er stand*
*fürs Vaterland*

or again songs containing a symbolic meaning. In the *Rammer-song* we may also find traces of other types of song, in particular the loosely strung verses of *children's sermons*:

*Der Weinstock hat Reben,*
*Reben hat der Weinstock,*
*das Kalb ist kein Ziegenbock . . .*

2. Another group of working-songs is represented by the so-called *Arbeitstakt songs* which follow the rhythm of the work in hand, e.g. when plucking or treading millet-pap, gathering hops, bringing in the harvest, threshing, flax-pulling, treading the vine,

milking, churning, spinning, knitting, or pasturing the cattle. Although the introduction of the threshing-machine did much to destroy communal labour, the rhythmic song is still much used, particularly by country people when working either in company or alone. Motifs from ancient charms often make their appearance:

*Bodder, Bodder, rehre dich,*
*ahlt Häx ich krie dich . . .*

The *Jodler* is a particularly popular form of working-song, with its characteristic jumpy alternative of chest-tone and head-tone; especially in the Alps where the herdsman's (*Senne*) song is heard reverberating from hill to hill:

*Hå-i-å-i-å-ä-i, hå-i-å-i-ä-i-å* . . . (Upper Austria).

3. The third group represents the so-called *Arbeitszähl* songs. They differ from the group last mentioned in that they do not determine the rhythm of the work, though to a certain extent they regulate the rhythmless tempo of the work in hand. They constitute rhymes which, originally used for counting purposes, were later changed into working-songs, e.g. the song of the days of the week:

*Mantg giht dä Woch â,*
*Dienstg ho mr wuhlgetâ,*
*Mîtewoch is dä Woch halb aus,*
*Donnerstag sei ka Borten in Haus,*
*Freitg schlat dä Mutte aus,*
*Sunnômd wiede ein,*
*Doss mr Sunntg beisamme sei*
*bei ân guten Hîrschbrei.*

4. A fourth group must be mentioned, the so-called rhythmical *Merkreime* which develop as imitations of sounds produced by the work itself. Thus the noise of threshing or weaving is copied by the voice. For instance, in threshing, the accompaniment to the double beat runs *Tipp-tåpp*, to the six-beat *Tippadi, tåppadi.* Or we have a rather longer rhyme from Büdesheim near Bingen which mocks at the labourer's ravenous appetite:

*Drei Drescher*
*sechs Fresser. . . .*

Carters' and drovers' songs, etc., may also develop from mere cries, such for instance as the shepherd uses to gather in his flocks. Cows are lured by their nicknames:

*die Gflecket, Gschegget, d'Langbeneri.*

From the shepherd's cries, e.g. *Loba*, songs of real sense often developed.

We have now traced the circle of *Volkslieder*, and shall leave the question of its further development until we discuss the work of Herder, who raised the *Volkslied* from the humble position to which it had sunk to a literary category of momentous importance. In the meantime external and internal circumstance combined to change the character of the German people and with it its most natural form of expression, the song. How deeply the change in fashion affected the remaining bulk of the folk-song is shown by the great decrease in historical songs and traditional motifs under the influx of songs inspired by the last two centuries.

# III

# DECLINE AND REBIRTH

*Deutschorden—the Teutonic Order of Knighthood*

The strange short-lived Indian summer of Middle High German literature, which had developed under the influence of the Teutonic Order of Knighthood in the Eastern marches whilst in the South chivalry was fast falling into decay, derived inspiration largely from historic and religious themes: Judith, the Maccabees, Job, Daniel, etc.

German song gathered no fresh impulse thereby, for the maintenance of a patriotic militant spirit was considered by the Teutonic Order to be the chief duty of its brotherhood, whose members indeed were monk and knight, priest and general (like the Maccabees) at one and the same time. Their aim was to set out as Knights of Christ on their Eastern crusade and there conquer and colonize new territory for the fatherland. Thus Prussia began to play a part in European history. The Teutonic Order could boast many a princely patron, such for instance as Frederick II and Ottokar of Bohemia, and had by the end of the thirteenth century secured rule over Prussia. In 1309, the seat of the High Master was removed from Venice to Marienburg. But towards the close of the thirteenth century religious fervour had already begun to abate, so that Heinrich der Teichner bitterly railed at the corruption that abounded on these Prussian expeditions. The adventurous element in knighthood had on the whole too little in common with a more lofty mission to allow of its absorbing the first vague indications of a religious revival, although the knights nevertheless gained some knowledge of the mystic thought of the period through Johannes von Marienwerder's *Leben der seligen Vrouwen Dorothee von Montau* († 1394), etc., whilst already in the thirteenth century they had come into contact with Jutta von Sangerhausen, a compatriot of Mechthild von Magdeburg, and with Christina Ebner from Engeltal near Nürnberg.

*Mysticism*

Three works—the *Vita Christi* of the Carthusian monk Ludolf von Sachsen, Seuse's popular *Büchlein von der ewigen Weisheit* and the *Meditationes de vita Christi* of Thomas à Kempis—encouraged a growing desire for a more contemplative attitude towards life. Meditation on death and asceticism opened up the way for *mysticism* which, seeking to break down all barriers between man and God, celebrates the *unio mystica*, the nuptials of the soul with its bridegroom Christ. 'I' and 'thou' as correlatives of nature and God merge with one another. According to whether stress is laid on the mystic's volitional, speculative or emotional quality, we differentiate between speculative mysticism and so-called nun's mysticism (cf. Hildegard von Bingen's *Sci vias Domini* and Mechthild von Magdeburg's *Das fliessende Licht*). The latter owes much to the influence of Bernhard of Clairvaux, who through his will-power and imitation of Christ sought to achieve a mystic union with God. Mysticism was greatly furthered through the founding of the Franciscan Order in 1210 and that of the Dominicans (Thomists) in 1220, as also by the copious literature pertaining to the lives of the saints. But the concept of the nun (as distinct from Holy Church) being the bride of Christ appears already in the *Trudperter Hohelied*, the first book of German mysticism, which dates from the twelfth century. When the right of *cura monialium* was bestowed on the *fratres docti* of the German Dominican order, the latter were endowed with a first-rate means of working on popular sentiment through their sermons, and whipping the audience to ecstatic fervour.

*Speculative mysticism* seeks to fathom the divine essence through rational thought, beholding therein *lûter wesen* (*actus purus*). But few could follow the metaphysical flights of Eckhart († 1327). Tauler's († 1361) moral counsels were more comprehensible, but it was Seuse († 1366) the minnesinger of divine love who won the hearts of these rapt 'friends of God.' The three paths of mysticism were—the *via purgativa—illuminativa—unitiva*, or *reinunge—*

*erluhtunge—vereinunge* in the words of the so-called Frankfurter (about 1400) who won Luther's praise. Of these the two former naturally played a more important part in the world of everyday existence, initiating the postulant into the mystery of *Entbilden* (dematerialization) and the negation of the *Dingwelt* (material world). A vision of ultimate reward beckons the true believer and faithful bride. It is the fatherland, the eternal city of God, which, conjured up before modern eyes by Gerhart Hauptmann in *Hanneles Himmelfahrt*, owes its origin to Seuse's *Ewige Weisheit*: 'The city of the blessed gleams from a distance interwoven with gold, shimmering with rare pearls, inlaid with costly gems, translucent as crystal, burning with roses and lilies and all manner of flowers. Now look out on to the heavenly moor! Oh, the joy of summer, the woods of laughing May, the vale of true joy! Here loving glances fly apace, here are harps, viols, singing, tripping, dancing, and merry music.' From the spring's gushing streams the heart can drink at will and with rapt eye gaze into the mirror of the eternal Godhead. In this contemplative surrender to God the mystic soul finds its reward. Such blessedness is won only through God's grace.

In the meantime mysticism had degenerated into *speculative sophistry*. Nicolaus Cusanus or Cues († 1464), who issued from the Windesheimer Congregation founded by Geert Groot, was the first to strive once more towards the heights of Eckhart's ideal, though now by the help of advanced mathematics. But ultimate enlightenment was never granted him.

Intellectual vision is imageless. This process of 'unforming' life must needs lead to the death of all æsthetic activity. But a glance at the Christian art of this period (the Pietà, the Man of many Sorrows, the Stations of the Cross, St. John reclining on the breast of our Lord) reveals the fact that the very pursuit of the *imitation of Christ*, of the εἰκὼν τοῦ θεοῦ, inspired its particular imagery.

The expressive vocabulary used by late medieval mystic writers proves no less that human imagination was aroused to wild flights of phantasy by yearning for mystic experience, e.g. *înbilden* = to impress, *ûfquellen* = to well up, *abeval* = the shedding of the mortal coil, *entmenschet* = released from the relativity of human existence, *însehen* = to look into oneself, *înslac* = God's invasion of man, etc.

Thus mysticism created its own world of imagery and its own language in order to express man's union with the absolute, the so-called *cognitio Dei experimentalis* which takes place in the secret depths of the soul (*profundo centro*), and of which St. John of the Cross was to write later in his *Living Flame of Love* (1584). From out such sublimated *Seelenstimmung* were born many a heartfelt prayer and the mystic lyric.

The waning of the Middle Ages witnessed an increasing yearning for death. The Black Death of 1348 lay like a pall on all joy. Nevertheless before the actual renaissance in Germany a growing consciousness of human significance asserted itself against such morbid inclination. Johannes von Tepl, the *Ploughman of Bohemia*, broods on the subject of death's significance and the equilibrium of the soul. This treatise, which is both linguistically and morally of exceptional value, bears affinity to Petrarch's more lyrical *De remediis utriusque fortunae* as also to Seneca's Stoic doctrine of being mature for death. In spite of the emancipated views suggested by Johannes's impeachment of death, the 'Ackermann' appears on the whole still bound to medieval pedantry and religious limitation as contrasted with the æsthetic aspirations of Petrarch.

How strongly secular morality impregnates the lyric is evident in Clara Hätzlerin's anthology. In one of the folk-poems for instance a girl defends her right to love in face of the parson, for through their passion she and her lover had become reformed characters. A thing of the past were the ascetic doctrines of Thomas Aquinas who, like St. Augustine, approved of sexual intercourse in marriage only as a means of procreation, and indeed regarded abstinence in marriage as far preferable to bodily union.

The Germany of the Middle Ages was fast disappearing. The towns were attaining importance as centres of culture in place of the monasteries. Laymen were becoming the rivals of the monks in administration. This new light-hearted spirit is reflected in the pages of Boccaccio's *Decameron*. But to say that woman here appears for the first time as an individual, capable of holding her own by the side of the man, would be to forget Brunhilde and Isolde. The Italian renaissance and humanism found their way to the North, at first through the mediation of the early German humanists and translators: Albrecht von Eyb, Gregor von Heimburg, Niclas von Wyle, H. Steinhöwel, etc.

*Augsburg* opened its gates to cultural and economic inter-relations with Venice. The city of Holbein the Elder and the papist Fugger was also the home of the latter's friend K. Peutinger (a relative of the Welser) who did much to encourage renaissance ideals in the North. Through the emperor Charles IV (of the Luxembourg line) and his chancellor Johannes von Neumarkt, *Prag* had enjoyed immediate contact with Petrarch and Rienzi, and had likewise absorbed much Italian influence by way of Avignon, thus becoming a hotbed of modern culture. At the beginning of the sixteenth century *Cologne*, the citadel of Dominican erudition that once had harboured Albertus Magnus, Thomas Aquinas, Duns Scotus, and Master Eckhart himself within its walls, was swept by the annihilating scorn of that masterpiece of German wit and satire, the *Epistolae obscurorum virorum. Basel, Erfurt, Nürnberg* and many another town fostered the new spirit.

Yearning for the South drove many a German to Italy, on the other hand the Council of Basel (1431–1449) brought many an Italian scholar to Germany, and thus propagated the growth of humanist erudition. In 1459 a university was founded at Basel itself, receiving formal recognition from the humanist pope, Pius II (Aeneas Sylvius, the author of *Euryalus and Lucretia*). The famous printing houses of Amerbach and Froben provided beautiful and costly editions of the classics. It was Froben who published Erasmus's Greek version of the New Testament.

It is not surprising that Erasmus's conservative catholic humanism found a particularly favourable milieu in Basel. Here, on the threshold of the reformation, many a scholar and author sought a haven in which he could quietly pursue his speculations on medieval 'realist' philosophy, which, though in its death-throes, cleverly succeeded in turning modern discoveries in the field of humanism to its own ends.

A factor of historical significance in the development of this movement was the introduction of 'realist' philosophy into Basel University, by Johann Heynlin à Lapide in 1473. This former rector of the Sorbonne soon gathered round him an important literary circle which included Peter Schott, Agricola, Tritheim, Sebastian Brant, J. Geiler von Keisersberg, and Wimpfeling.

The three last writers have been cited as forerunners of the reformation. It is due to a misapprehension, for they were didactic moralists who remained faithful to the church's authority. Sebastian Brant's *Narrenschiff* represents the most important product of this circle. He was a paragon of civic burgher mentality. The learned author, who had been educated only on German soil, proves himself a master of rhetoric, not a lyric poet, with his quantitative syllabled verse. Intoxicated by a plethora of themes, the century was less interested in formal values than in subject matter. Brant possesses an unending stock of German idioms and proverbs, popular jokes and morality. The *Narrenschiff* is in reality a compilation of extracts from the Bible, Plutarch, Ovid, and the fathers of the church (from the *Corpus iuris canonici*). Virgil, his particular favourite, does not play much part in this extraordinary work whose thematic form (the jester's boat) exerted such influence on subsequent generations, in particular on J. Locher (who translated it into Latin—*Stultifera Navis*), Murner, H. Sachs, Fischart, etc.

The political indifference and weary resignation of these moralists in Basel and Strassburg (whither Brant had been summoned as civic clerk through the influence of Geiler) proved at length too boring to the younger generation. Much to their annoyance J. Locher levelled violent attacks against scholastic theology. By the time Reuchlin, who had also resided for a short time at Basel, kindled the flame that should destroy Dominican-ridden Cologne, the North was ready for the advent of Luther, who was to proclaim Germany's reformation in deed and word. We see, however, that the reformation and the renaissance do not on their first appearance stand at enmity with each other.

The literary circle at *Erfurt* could boast amongst its members Eobanus Hessus, Euricius Cordus (the pupil of Nik. Marschalk, author of the first Greek grammar in Germany), Mutianus Rufus, and particularly Crotus Rubeanus, the bitterest opponent of the *Cologne Dunkelmänner*. In 1521 the same city welcomed Luther who lodged there on his way to Worms. The uncertainty of social and political conditions, however, caused many a humanist to shake in his shoes and turn his back on Luther. *Ingolstadt's* university, which had only been founded in 1472, was enriched by Celtes's short sojourn, and his lectures on rhetoric, poetics,

Cicero, Ovid, etc. *Heidelberg*, the oldest university inside Germany (founded in 1386), also enjoyed a visit from Celtes, who had fled thither to escape the plague. Though the learned doctors here as in other places still clung tenaciously to the outmoded doctrines of Alexander de Villadieu's *Doctrinale*, the influence of the great wanderer-poet Celtes and his gloriously independent-minded contemporary, the Frisian Rudolf Agricula, was ultimately not to be withstood. Thus through them and that friend of humanism, the Pfalzgräfin Mechthild, classic thought and classic sensibility blossomed anew. *Strassburg* harboured not only such enterprising publishers as Hüpfuff (who edited works by Brant, Murner and Knoblauch), but also sturdy patriots like Wimpfeling, the author of *Germania*. In *Mainz*, Archbishop Berthold of Henneberg founded the *Sodalitas Rhenana*. *Vienna*, where Celtes also taught rhetoric and poetics, was the sanctuary of the *Sodalitas litteraria Danubiana*. Here, too, Maximilian I founded the *Collegium* for poetics and rhetoric, and under his guardianship humanism became a vital force.

Vienna, a hundred years after the foundation of its university in 1365, was consumed by the conflict between the tyrannical Albrecht VI and his weak brother and liege lord, the emperor Frederick III. We read of the rebellious attitude of the citizens in Michael Behaim's detailed chronicle: *Buch von den Wienern* (1462–1465). Both author and work stand between two epochs. This simply told chronicle intermixes old and new words. Behaim possesses a rich store of idioms and proverbial expressions which he adds to by his own invention. Even *North Germany* (Münster i.W., Rostock, Hamburg, and other towns) was transfused by the new ideals. But above all, mention must be made of *Nürnberg*, the home of Albrecht Dürer, the geographer Regiomontanus, the watchmaker Henle, Hartmann Schedel, the doctor of medicine and author of the *Weltchronik*, the astronomer Martin Behaim, and W. Pirkheimer, patron of art.

In the meantime, that restless wanderer Paracelsus († 1541), forsaking the paths of mysticism and scepticism alike, pursued his quest of the arcanum, nature's secret remedies. His unfailing belief in the healing powers of divine nature and human charity came as a blessing to science. A few years after his death Nostradamus, born at St. Rémy in Provence, published his prophecies

(*Centurien*) of the Golden Age to come. One year earlier there appeared in Geneva the *Apologe* (1554) of the refugee Bernardino Ochino, former head of the Capuchin order. Spiced with many a scurrilous anecdote, it hurled contumely at priesthood and church. We have thus penetrated far into the sixteenth century, which in Germany might well be termed the age not of the renaissance but of the reformation.

*Hans Sachs* (1494-1576) is the most versatile and most productive poet of the age, but as the most noteworthy of the mastersingers he still represents an early tradition. In his poems he lays too much stress on the quantitative value of the syllables. His verse is alternative (although certain scholars, e.g. Goedeke, would vainly deny this fact). Forced verbal contractions such as *errett* (*errettet*) or elongations such as *sahe*, *ein traume*, arbitrary accentuation of words: *éinigér*, *géwurm*; or the poetic licence which Sachs allows himself for the sake of rhyme—all these limitations make it only too obvious that the German lyric had to free itself from its formal paralysis and linguistic chaos before it could attain pregnant expression. The literary and historical significance of Opitz could serve as a model here. In the meantime forces were gradually being assembled to promote a new High German lyric poetry worthy of the name.

*Humanistic Latin verse* prepared the way by introducing a new æsthetic criterion and elegance of style. Anacreon, Horace, Propertius, Tibullus, Ovid, Martial, Catullus were amongst the poets whom the humanist pedants most favoured as models. We would here refer, though only in passing, to their panegyrics, their songs of friendship, of love, of travel, and good fortune. The most important of these poets are Celtes with his enticing love-songs and his hymn in praise of Nürnberg, and Petrus Lotichius Secundus who was moved to heartfelt song by the death of his beloved. Of Ovid's works the *Heroides* possessed a particular appeal for the humanist poets, and were first adopted as a model by Eobanus Hessus. He also acquainted the world with bucolic verse, which he composed, not according to the sentimental pastoral manner later so fashionable, but often as a mere means of disguising contemporary events, or as scenic background to some royal panegyric.

S. Lemnius praises the beauty of nature, even of the Alps—a taste rare enough at the time! Bold von Hutten cultivated historical poetry. He also excelled in satire such as we find in his *Niemand.* We could add the name of many a worthy poet to this list. The following short survey will suffice to prove how valuable, from the formal point of view, this Latin verse was to the new High German poetry that began to flourish towards the end of the sixteenth century. The influence of Latin was still strong in Germany. About the year 1600 roughly 66 per cent of books appeared in Latin.

### *Conrad Celtes and Other Neo-Latin Humanists*

Under Conrad Celtes (1459–1508) Neo-Latin humanism in Germany reached its first high level of merit. Celtes (Konrad Pickel) came from Franconia. His craving for knowledge and wanderlust lured him from one European country to another, until he finally settled in Vienna, where he passed the last eleven years of his life, revered as scholar and poet. His erotic elegies in four books (*Amores*, 1502) provide a lively portrait of the man in spite of their literary artifice. At various periods of his restless existence he fell prey to the charms of Venus. In Krakau she took on the form of a seductive Polish girl and in Nürnberg that of an equally vain creature Elsula. In the Rhineland the light-of-love Ursula captured his heart, yet only to be torn from him by the plague. Finally in the last book of *Amores* he sings praises of a fair Lübeck maid, Barbara.

The odes of C. Celtes likewise appeared in four volumes, and again it is love which here inspires his pen to Horatian stanzas, though patriotic sentiments, dreams of Utopian reforms to be fulfilled by humanism, and the proud conviction of his poetic genius, enflame his soul.

Ulrich von Hutten (1488–1523) belongs to the next generation —a militant poet in whom inspiration was kindled ever anew through his fervent love of the fatherland. His passionate temperament drove him, stricken as he was by poverty and ill-health, into repeated misfortune. Such for instance was his quarrel with a former patron, Professor Lötze in Greifswald, who on a journey to Rostock in the midst of winter had the poet robbed of his last penny and literally stripped to the skin—an affront which Hutten was later to avenge by his elegies.

Hutten's relation to the poets of his home may be studied in the well-known tenth elegy of the second book. But only his passionate reaction to the patriotic cause aroused the full sonorous chords of his rhetoric. Singing of Maximilian's wars with Venice he incites Germany to rally against the false foe. Reuchlin's struggle with the Cologne Dominicans offered a new opportunity for a patriotic panegyric. Ultimately, when Luther's works were burned at the instigation of Charles V, Hutten's fury was kindled not only to deeds in words but in arms. Sickingen's refusal to help him, however, once again plunged him into doubt which only his heroic attitude towards life was able to conquer. Hutten's lines:

*Ich habs gewagt mit sinnen*
*und trag des noch kein rew.*
*Mag ich nit dran gewinnen,*
*noch muss man spüren trew.*
*Dar mit ich main;*
*nit aim allein,*
*wen man es wolt erkennen,*
*dem land zu gut,*
*wie wol man tut*
*ein pfaffenfeint mich nennen*

became a German maxim.

The Erfurt circle played an important part in the development of the new Latin lyric of the sixteenth century. Eobanus Koch (Hessus) from Hesse stood at its head. Hessus, who died early, composed eleven cycles of pastoral poems (*Bucolicon*) as far back as 1509. They consist of eclogues, through which he was enabled to inspire his German contemporaries to the writing of bucolic lyrics, a form of poetry with which they had already become acquainted through Bebel. Hessus often made this form of song a pretext for veiled personal allusions to the Erfurt humanist circle. Mutianus's *beata tranquillitas* in particular won the praise of the poet whose storm-tossed existence failed to quell his carefree spirit. The *Christian Heroides* by Hessus appeared in 1514, inspired perhaps by Parcellius's work whose own *Heroides* were, however, published later. The primal source of this type of poetry, which in the seventeenth century was to adopt an erotic tone, was Ovid. Amongst other poetic inventions termed *Epistles of the Saints*, Eobanus composed a letter from Mary Magdalene to the Saviour after His resurrection, and another from the Virgin Mary to St. John in Patmos.

Eobanus's dirges reflect a fashion of the day and of Neo-Latin occasional verse (*Epicedium*). Where sorrow inspires him, as in his poem on Hutten or Albrecht Dürer, many of his poems are not without depth of feeling. Also those of his contemporaries who were yet living received eulogy from his pen, in particular Luther, who passed three days in Erfurt on his way to Worms. That visit was commemorated by Eobanus in certain elegies on the 'reformer of Germany.' But the cultural decline of scholarship which set in as a result of the political upheaval marred the humanist's enthusiasm for Luther's work. Thus Eobanus's gay spirits soon gave way to utmost dejection. Nevertheless he still retained much of his debonair grace of manner. Amongst the new Latin lyric poets he stands out as the foremost exponent of occasional verse.

Hesse too gave birth to that coiner of epigrams, Euricius Cordus (*Heinrich Solde*?). In his eclogues he fell under the influence of his friend Eobanus, whom he, however, excels in power of vivid description.

Another and probably the greatest of the new Latin poets whom we shall shortly discuss, Petrus Lotichius, was related to the Wittenberg circle. A university had been founded in the latter town in 1502, but this wave of humanist learning soon yielded to the might of the Lutheran Bible. Whilst at Wittenberg Melanchthon first fell under the spell of Luther, but later managed to reconcile classicism and the church. His ambitious son-in-law Georg Sabinus, who afterwards became the rector of Königsberg University and professor in Frankfurt a. d. Oder, is much more facile in form, though he lacks Melanchthon's sincerity. The fame and influence of Sabinus spread far beyond the pale of Wittenberg. Amongst his followers should be mentioned Simon Lemnius from Graubünden (Grisons), who coming to Wittenberg temporarily associated with the Neo-Latin circle there. His epigrams, which abound in flattering eulogies on the Archbishop Albrecht von Mainz, brought him into ill-favour with Luther (an enemy of the archbishop), and ended in Lemnius retaliating with his satires, in particular the *Monachopornomachia* (1540). The passionate nature of the poet then burst forth in the unbridled vehemence of his love-songs, whose crass realism may in spite of true sincerity alienate the reader. Lemnius also turns to the beauties of nature, even to those of the Alps, though he intermingles his descriptions of the latter not only with biographical experiences but Neo-Latin pedantry. His language was in some measure freed by his emotional fervour. His poetic power, however, remains bound by the formalisms of the Neo-Latin convention.

Petrus Lotichius Secundus (1528–1560) from Hesse must rank as the most outstanding of the German Neo-Latin poets of the sixteenth century. As a boy of seventeen he volunteered for the Schmalkaldian war, only to repent too late of his impetuousness. The rough-and-tumble tone of the Landsknecht's life wounded his sensitive spirit. His father's death dealt him another blow. The news reached him in the midst of the horrors of the siege of Magdeburg, which was surrounded by Duke Maurice of Saxony's army. We see from his first book of elegies that his yearning for home and the gentle art of poetry grew intensely. On the expiration of his military duties, Petrus Lotichius Secundus returned to Wittenberg and afterwards (1550), in the capacity of companion to wealthy patricians, made a journey to France where he passed three years at Paris and Montpellier studying medicine and law. Bitter experience in the shape of robbery on land and sea, the joys and sorrows of love, the terror of the inquisition, wrought havoc on his soul. An overpowering longing for his beloved Claudia and his home in Wittenberg, moreover, fears aroused on her behalf by the perils of war, left him no peace. The second book of Lotichius's elegies tells of these sufferings. Across the dreams of his *domina puella*, his all too haughty Claudia, flits the gentle form of another young girl; but the poet remained faithful to his Claudia and woos her once again.

His joy and melancholy find utterance amidst landscape scenes. True poetic intuition kindled his spirit. Profoundly moving in their simplicity and their passionate sincerity, his songs alternate between nature and human experience.

These and the elegies that followed them far excel the Neo-Latin products of his German contemporaries. When after four years Petrus Lotichius Secundus returned from France to Germany he was greeted by further misfortunes. His patron Daniel

Stibar lay near to death, his mother was no more, his fatherland rent by wars. Restless, he fled to Italy, to Padua and then to Bologna, where he attained his doctorate. Even here ill-fortune followed in his wake, for all unwillingly he quaffed a poisoned love-philtre, and thereafter for the rest of his life was troubled by a malignant recurring fever. His poetic powers, however, remained unscathed. In his third book of elegies, which contains a lament on the death of his French *puella tunicata* (an experience dating from his sojourn in France), he reaches the zenith of his poetic power. G. Ellinger calls it *Lebensbeichte*, a poetic confession unrivalled by anything that the sixteenth century in Germany can present.

Once more Petrus Lotichius Secundus returned to his native land. He became professor of botany and medicine at Heidelberg. From his biography (1585), the work of his friend Johannes Hagen (Hagius), we may obtain a picture of the last years of his short life. The poems written during his Heidelberg period return for the most part to the traditional tone of Neo-Latin occasional verse. In 1560 Petrus Lotichius Secundus died. His works prove that true genius could quicken even the stereotyped forms of Neo-Latin verse. It was not the heroics of life, but the tender subtle moods of nature and yearning for his fatherland that moved him to song. In moments of divine inspiration he sometimes discovered a harmony between the external and spiritual aspect of life, a gift that was known to but few German lyric poets before Goethe's time. In his eclogues warm emotion pulsates beneath the bleak scheme of the Neo-Latin formula. Especially where fate dealt him the hardest blows, his spirit finds an expressive medium which never falls into the world-laden rhetoric of his satellites. Certainly we should not, like G. Ellinger, consider P. Lotichius Secundus superior to the most famous of the New High German lyric poets preceding Klopstock, for Gryphius, Fleming, Paul Gerhardt, and Günther find a language for their emotional experiences which in spite of tradition and religious dogma does not in regard to sincerity rank beneath that of Petrus Lotichius Secundus. Nevertheless we may hail him as a forerunner of the most important exponents of 'occasional' verse in German.

*Albrecht von Eyb*

Albrecht von Eyb (1420–1475), *not* Wyle, as Baechtold believed, deserves recognition as the first German humanist, though many modern critics would divide that honour between the two poets. Through his connections with Pavia and Bologna, Eyb, a Franconian by birth, became a champion of classic erudition in Germany even before he met Aeneas Sylvius, who influenced Wyle and is too often recognized as the one and only source of German humanism. During his first visit to Italy Eyb bought a manuscript of Terence, copied one of Valerius Maximus and personally collected a book of quotations: *Liber multorum Poetarum*. Returning to the North, he was the first to try his hand at the humanist style in the land of the *barbarians*. It may well be that his passionate *Tractatus* was in some measure inspired by the *Euryalus and Lucretia*, but it was only on his second visit to Italy that he came into contact with Pope Pius II (Aeneas Sylvius). Eyb can hardly be called a German Petrarch or Boccaccio, nor is he the initiator of a new formalistic movement like Heinrich von Veldeke or later Opitz. It must not be forgotten that humanism was not natural to the Northern peoples, as it was to the descendants of Rome, and that it therefore remained the privilege of a narrow erudite class who had little contact with the people. Nevertheless Eyb not only proved himself a fine Latin stylist but managed to give his writings a distinctly German flavour. After he had presented his fatherland with a book on humanist rhetoric he actually at the age of fifty-two published a work, namely, his famous *Ehebüchlein*, in his native tongue. The author, who here as elsewhere refrains from polemics against the church, writes in praise of marriage with serene classic worldliness untroubled by Christian asceticism. His library, which, thanks to Hartmann Schedel's transcriptions, was preserved at any rate in part up to the present day, proves Eyb's importance in the history of German culture.

We should (as in the case of Hutten) take the opportunity of refuting certain critics' sweeping allegations concerning the Italianization of German literature. For Eyb's literary work is thoroughly rooted in German soil. He translates, or better, germanizes classic dramas, makes the German tongue acquainted with antique concepts and tries to find a German synonym for alien expressions.

Certainly this humanism is much fettered by Latin syntax (Eyb knew no Greek). A breath of patriotic air blew from Tübingen and invigorated the work of Reuchlin, Bebel, Frischlin, and others, whilst later in the seventeenth century one of the late humanists, F. H. Flayder (often named *Frischlinus secundus*), based his Latin dramas on typically German themes.

Above all we must not forget that German literature, having fallen into stylistic degeneration, stood in dire need of the new will to form which humanism inspired. After Eyb, but before the birth of Petrus Lotichius Secundus, there developed a new form of song which influenced the poets of his circle—the protestant hymn.

## *THE HYMN*

### (*a*) *The Evangelical Hymn*

The evangelical hymn did not develop from formal tradition but owed its origin to Luther's creative genius. It was born in 1523, when Luther published twenty-five hymns in the Erfurt *Enchiridion*, eighteen of which were his own. This *Enchiridion* may be called the first evangelical hymnal, and contains Luther's song about the martyrdom of two Lutheran Augustinian monks in Brussels:

> *Ein neues lied wir heben an,*
> *das walt Gott unser Herre. . . .*

In the name of his militant cause, Luther let this his first song ring out over the triumphant dawn of the reformation. In the year 1524 there appeared also an enlarged edition of thirty-two evangelical hymns in the *Geystliches Gesangk Buchleyn* (Wittenberg), Luther being the author of twenty-five of these songs and of the preface, in which he discusses the significance of the hymn in the religious service and in what manner it is pleasing to Our Lord. Word and song, he says, should in future serve God:

'that religious songs are good and pleasing to God, should be known to every Christian, and are therefore composed in four parts, for no other reason than that I should like youth, which shall and must be educated in music and other religious arts, to have something to tear it away from love-songs and other fleshly allurements and in their place learn something of benefit to its soul, so that Good should fill it with joy, as it should young people.'

*Musica* is in Luther's eyes one of the most beautiful of God's gifts. She drives away the devil, rescues man from pride, rage, and vice. '*Next to theology I should give the highest place and honour to music.*' Thus communal singing became an essential part of religious service. In songs which (in the name of the community) reveal not merely personal emotion or scholastic subtleties, the community may really take a part in divine celebration. Luther's followers: Paul Speratus, Paul Eber, and others, likewise adopt the same impersonal tone.

The content of the Lutheran hymn is derived largely from the communal biblical creed and the catechism, from Latin sequences and old German songs, hymns, and psalms, as for instance in that mighty clarion call of the year 1529:

> *Ein feste Burg ist unser Gott,*
> *ein gute Wehr und Waffen.*
> *Er hilft uns frei aus aller Not. . . .*

(cf. Psalm xlvi: *Deus noster refugium et virtus*), in the psalm of 1524: *Aus tiefer Not schrei ich zu dir* (cf. Psalm cxxx), in the hymn: *Herr Gott dich loben wir* (cf. the Ambrosian *Te Deum laudamus*), or in the song: *Mitten wir im Leben . . .* (cf. Notker Balbulus's antiphony: *Media vita in morte sumus*). Luther's predilection for psalms (which were imitated and added to by N. Selneccer, the friend of Melanchthon, and by B. Waldis, the reviser of Aesop's Fables) by no means arises from any special preference for the Old Testament. Nor did Luther dream of the harsh dogma to which his ideas were ultimately to petrify in the hands of his disciples: E. Alberus, J. Mathesius, N. Herman, and others.

With a few exceptions Luther's songs must have sounded familiar to German ears with their strong reminiscences of the folk-songs: e.g. '*Vom Himmel hoch, da komm ich her, ich bring euch gute neue Mär. . . .*' The immediate source of this charming Christmas song is to be found in the second chapter of the Gospel according to St. Luke. Even here Luther does not give vent to merely personal feeling. Just as his poetic gift was only developed in his struggles with the enemies of the reformation, so his songs remain true to his cause. The humanists took *words* themselves so seriously that grammatical mistakes were considered by them not only a lack of education but of ethic degeneration, for the cultivation of languages and culture in general afforded in their eyes a basis of human life. To Luther *words* only had value in so far as they served the proclamation of the Truth. He looked upon the Saviour, not as a wise *doctor doctissimus*, but as the *Logos*, the Second Person of the Holy Trinity, who through His sacrifice and death had brought salvation to sinful man. The reformation was to appeal also to the poor in spirit for whom many a proud humanist had coined the name of *Beanus* = (b) *bestia*, (e) *equalis*, (a) *asino*, (n) *nihil*, (v) *vere*, (s) *sciens*.

But Luther in spite of his essentially German character was not the true representative of the patriotic wing of the reformation. His sallies were directed principally against the Roman priesthood, not against the foreigner and alien-minded German, for it was his will that one and all should join in praise of God.

The religious songs of the *reformers* began to show signs of deviation from the evangelical hymn proper when Zwingli and his followers gradually pushed the communal song into the background and, instead, adhered ever more strictly to the words of the psalms. A. Lobwasser's rather dry but influential translation of the psalms (printed in 1573, though actually written before Schede's version, 1572) strengthened the reformers' partiality for the psalms yet further.

It seems that the *Gesellschaftslied*, which (both before and after Regnart) was in full process of development at the same time, provides no bridge to the religious song of the sixteenth century, and yet, quite apart from any superficial social affinity, interrelationships continually suggest themselves between the two. The *Kontrafakturen*, i.e. religious songs derived from mundane songs, clearly point to such influence as H. J. Moser convincingly proves in examining G. Rhaw's collection of motets: *Gesenge fur die gemeinen Schulen* (1544). Here certain courtly melodies are turned to religious use, e.g. Senfl's lyric: *The married state is mostly called a sacrament* was originally a wedding-lay now to be sung by the evangelical community at the marriage service.

Adaptations of worldly folk-song melodies to religious purposes (both protestant and catholic) are moreover frequently found; e.g. *Der Lindenschmid*:

> *Was wöllen wir singen und heben an?*
> *Das Beste, das wir gelernet han . . .*

and

> *In Jesus Namen heben wir an,*
> *das Beste, das wir gelernet han . . .*

The melody of Gerhardt's famous lyric, *O Häupt voll Blut und Wunden*, is no other than that of a love-song: *Mein Gmüth ist mir verwirret*, and a close comparison may be drawn between *Den liebsten Herren, den ich han . . .* and the well-known drinking song: *Den liebsten Buhlen, den ich han. . . .*

### (*b*) *The Catholic Hymn*

Through Luther, who, it must be remembered, was not the father of the religious song as such but of the evangelical hymn, the catholic hymn was reformed and stimulated. To this fact the episcopal authorized hymnal song-books of the sixteenth century, by M. Vehe (1537); J. Leisentritt (1567); Christoph Hecyrus (Schweher), (1581); K. Ulenberg (1582), etc., clearly bear witness.

As the Catholic church has until the present day obstinately and carefully preserved its Latin liturgy, the German song could be included only as an exception even in the High Mass. The German song could under no condition whatever replace the chorals: *Gloria in excelsis*, the Creed, or the Offertory, etc., but was sometimes sung simultaneously with or after these. It most easily found a place before and after the sermon, or at mass shortly before or after the Transubstantiation and at Holy Communion. It even happened as an act of special consideration, and then only by the bishop's permission, that the Latin choral might sometimes be replaced by one in the German tongue, if for instance some zealous divine scented therein a means of luring an erring protestant sheep back to the Catholic fold. In the seventeenth century similar aims caused the Jesuits to compile a religious book of songs, the *Harmony of David* (1659), derived from Protestant sources.

Catholic processions, pilgrimages, the introduction in the

thirteenth century of the Corpus Christi festival, holy days in honour of the Virgin Mary, the Angelus, Easter, Christmas, and Whitsuntide celebrations, all provided material for the development of the German Catholic song. Its origins may probably be traced back to elaboration of the Litany refrain, *kyrie eleison* in the Gregorian chant. The earliest existing *leis* (abbreviation of *kyrie eleison*) is considered to be the song of St. Peter, composed during the ninth to the tenth century—*Unsar trohtîn hât farsalt sancte Petre giuualt.* That still popular Easter hymn: *Christ ist erstanden,* and the Whitsuntide *leis*: *Nu bitten wir den heiligen Geist,* date back to the twelfth century. A song in praise of the Ascension: *Christ fuor gen himele,* has been handed down to us as a religious folk-song from the fourteenth century. During the fifteenth century the German church song was enriched by Heinrich von Laufenberg († 1460), who translated Latin hymns and invented religious words of his own for worldly melodies, e.g. *Ich wölt, dass ich doheime wär. . . .* Mysticism seems to have exerted scarcely any far-reaching influence on the development of the German hymn, though it has sometimes left a few traces in songs such as: *Wer sich des Maien wölle. . . .*

*The Gesellschaftslied*

*Formal values of the German lyric on the threshold of the baroque.*—At the time when the post-Lutheran evangelical hymn was rapidly developing, the so-called Italianate *Gesellschaftslied* enjoyed a short-lived period of glory which reached its zenith on the threshold of the seventeenth century. It was immediately preceded by the lyric style of the renaissance which, as a legacy of courtly medieval poetry, forms a bridge between the *Minne-* and *Meisterlied* and the German renaissance.

The cultured lyric or *Renaissancelyrik deutscher Musiker,* in vogue about the year 1500, is not without its merit, though it was all too soon cast in the shade by the contemporary folk-song. Today such volumes as those printed in Öglin in Augsburg 1512, (the oldest German printed song-book), P. Schöffer in Mainz in 1513, or Arnt von Aachen (Köln, 1515) are treasured because they not only reflect the spirit of the age but present an example of the linguistic influence of humanism on the German lyric of the early renaissance. More formal in tone than the folk-song and certainly more elegant in expression than the *Meisterlied*, they point in retrospect to the minne-lyric and as forerunners of Opitz herald in the future.

The poems in Georg Forster's *Frische Teutsche Liedlein in fünf Teilen* (1539 ff.) are largely culled from various collections of the period, in particular from Öglin, P. Schöffer, Ott, and others. Forster tampers with his sources in a truly dilettante manner. Words are sacrificed for the sake of the melody. See Forster's references to his own methods: '*Die weil wir aber nicht der Text, sondern der Composition halben, die Liedlein in truck gegeben. . . .*' The collection is rich in both themes and forms. The folk-song element (*Innsbruck, ich muss dich lassen*) alternates with verbal virtuosity, didactic phrases and purely foreign (e.g. *vitrum nostrum*) or mongrel expressions:

> *Es ritt ein jeger hetzen auss*
> *Bene venertis domine . . .*

or '*Wir zogen in das feldt . . .*' with a foreign refrain: '*Strampedemi, alami presente al vostra signori.*'

According to Böhme the latter was composed during the first two decades of the sixteenth century. The refrain '*Strombetta mi-a-la-mi, presenti alla mostra, Signori*' really means in German: '*Trompetet mi-a-la-mi, erscheint zur Musterung, ihr Herren.*'

In spite of its untrustworthy philological renderings, Forster's song-book is of the utmost importance in providing examples of songs popular shortly before and after Luther's death. In addition to the Italian elements mentioned above, we may discover signs of influence from the Netherlands: cf. II. 26:

> *Ich weet ein Vrauken amorues*
> *di ic van herten minne. . . .*

Towards the end of the sixteenth century the Italianate form of the German *Gesellschaftslied* suddenly burst into full blossom. Its origin may be traced to a definite occasion, i.e. to the appearance in 1574 (1576) of the Netherlandish poet Jacob Regnart's collection of *Villanelles*, the first in the German tongue. Hence Regnart (1540-1599) was one of the first to stimulate the growth of the German *Kunstlied*, which thus originally seems to have been inspired by musical inclinations. This, however, does not imply that Italian influence only reached German lyric poetry through the agency of music. At first the text was considered of second-rate importance. Italian music ruled the market. Since Petrucci had inaugurated the printing of music in 1502 Italy had gained a monopoly over the music of Europe. The introduction of the chromatic scale and the development of a new type of song resulted in the gradual disappearance of the *cantus firmus*, which had enjoyed popularity in Germany and particularly in the Netherlands. The fact that the individual voices now began to gain independence gave the Italian song a character peculiarly its own. As mentioned above Germany first made its acquaintance through Regnart's *Villanelles*. These are mostly three-part folk-songs which the Italian peasants and labourers sang at work. The German folk-song is indeed usually regarded as a three-part song (two *Stollen* and one *Abgesang*), though it is in reality but two-part, for its two *Stollen* are not so sharply divided according to verses as in the case of the *villanelle*. On the other hand the German folk-song often uses the popular octosyllabic verse, whilst Italian virtuosity is inclined to favour the more melodious form of seven or eleven syllables.

Regnart adopted the metre of the *villanelle*, and at first also adhered to its content. Afterwards he composed German words to fit the new verse-form. That the text retained an Italianate flavour is not surprising. Velten in '*Das Ältere Deutsche Gesellschaftslied*,' 1914 points out that the typical *villanelle* beginning 𝅗𝅥 𝅗𝅥 𝅗𝅥 caused Regnart to accentuate the first syllable of his German verses. Thus *form* and *content* of the German lyric were much enriched. The song:

*Venus, du und dein Kind*
*seit alle beyde blind . . .*

derived from an Italianate verse pattern (cf. *Chi mi consolera, chi vita mi dara . . .*) and became the prototype for many a German song; cf. Val. Haussmann's

*Venus, du und dein Kind,*
*macht manchen sehend blind . . .*

or the satirical poem on the Winterkönig (*Fliegendes Blatt*, 1621):

*Fritz, du verwehntes Kind,*
*wie bistu worden so blind. . . .*

It is also found for instance in Paul van der Aelst's famous compilation of songs and pastorals *Blum und Ausbund allerhand auserlesener weltlicher, züchtiger Lieder und Reime* (1602). The latter incidentally presents a gold-mine of Italian, French, German, and Netherlandish songs of the period, many being taken from Forster's collection. An example of adherence to Italian *themes* is afforded by Regnart's popular *Brunnenlied*:

*Wer sehen wil zwen lebendige Brunnen,*
*der sol mein zwey betrübte Augen sehen . . .*

cf.

*Chi vuol veder duo fonti d'aqua viva,*
*venga a veder questi occhi egri e dolenti.*

(R. Velten, pp. 30 f.)

In the course of time, however, Regnart emancipated himself even more from Romance influence and, instead, took up the tradition of the German folk-song, as may be proved by a comparison between various *villanelle* collections. By 1580, the sudden influx of Italian renaissance forms had ebbed. Regnart's followers: Lechner, Harnisch, Gregorius Lange, Brechtl, and others, poured old wine into new bottles whose labels bore the name of *villanelle*. Among that company only Pinello escaped the styleless irregularities of the plagiarists.

In the last decade of the sixteenth century the German *Gesellschaftslied* burgeoned to new and lovelier blossom. Again Italian music and visits to Venice provided a source of inspiration to Northern poets, chief amongst whom was Christoph von Schallenberg. Interest was now primarily concentrated on the Italianate text. It was now not so much the *villanelle* as the *canzonetta* in four- or five-line verses that fascinated the German composers. Whilst Cesare Zacharia's *Suave et dillettevole canzonette* (1590) with their German and Italian text failed to exert any great influence on German collections (excepting of course V. Haussmann's additions to Zacharia's songs), Christoph von Schallenberg's works must rightly rank as the glory of the Italianate

German *Gesellschaftslied*. Through his ability to transfuse Italian texts with truly German feeling, new Southern themes were often fitted harmoniously into Northern songs.

The madrigal seems to have made its first appearance under H. L. Hassler: *Newe teutsche Gesang nach Art der Welschen Madrigalien und Canzonetten* (1596). His contemporary, Valentin Haussmann, whom we had occasion to mention above, was not blessed with the good fortune that enabled Hassler and Schallenberg to experience Italian music on Southern soil. Thus Haussmann, especially in the early stages of his career, though in no way claiming to originate new melodies is more inclined to affect the folk-song tone. Here indeed he was far more successful than in his later attempts to achieve that reconciliation of German and Italian elements in which Hassler so often excelled. Haussmann's strength lies rather in the comparatively individual quality of his texts, which he shapes to an alien musical form. But true æsthetic harmony can scarcely be achieved where the pattern is but fitted on the theme like a fashionable dress on a rustic body. The discrepancies between Southern and Northern elements in the Italianate German song of the early seventeenth century, whether in the form of *villanelle*, *canzonetta*, or madrigal, could of necessity lead only to speedy decay.

The *quodlibets* that provide an amusing pastime for idle hours were more to the public taste. The Italian *Gesellschaftslied* was moreover doomed to oblivion on the appearance of Opitz, who rejected the *villanelle*, the *canzonetta*, and eleven-syllable verse in favour of the alexandrine, and generally speaking proved more susceptible to French influence, though by this roundabout path Italian elements found a new means of entry into the German lyric.

Shortly before this transitory though intensive cultivation of the Italian song ceased, a more patriotically inclined genius arose in the shape of J. H. Schein (1586–1630). In spite of reminiscences of Hassler, his *Venuskräntzlein oder Neue weltliche Lieder zu fünf Stimmen, Instrumental-Tänze und Kanzonen* (1609) already intimates a rebirth of the native tradition, e.g.:

*Lasst uns freuen und fröhlich sein!*

Thus the folk-song had in the meantime not suffered complete eclipse. Schein's *Musica boscareccia oder Waldliederlein* (1621 ff.) is of a great interest from the point of view of musical history, offering one of the earliest examples of the introduction of the Italian symphonic accompaniment or 'concert style.' The *basso continuo* is here used according to the Italian manner, though retaining certain peculiarities of style. The accusations made against Schein's use of foreign words are scarcely merited, for the full-blooded *Landsknecht-song* ('*Wir zogen in das feldt*') itself contains similar transgressions. Nor do they suffer from the preciosity and *raffinement* of Stefan George's tonal verses which are based on no existing language. Of Schein's *woodland songs*, one at least, *Frau Nachtigall*, was rescued from oblivion by Hoffmann von Fallersleben. It offers a marked instance of Schein's propensities towards the folk-song, whilst the poet's individuality appears most marked in his short collection *Studentenschmaus*. One song: '*Frisch auf, ihr Klosterbrüder mein*,' with its alternative solo and chorus, contains the refrain '*Sa sa ! sa sa !*' still popular in student songs of the present day (see Erck I, 176). Another: '*So da, mein liebes Brüderlein*' creates a moist and merry (*feucht-fröhliche*) *Stimmung* with its metrical use of diminutives: *Brüderlein*, *Trünkelein*, *Gläslein*. Inspired by Claudio Monteverdi's madrigals, Schein also tried his hand at *Diletti pastorali* (*Hirtenlust*), and also composed instrumental suites: *Banchetto musicale*, in which appear the *Pavane* and its after-dance, the *Galliarde*, the vivacious *Courante* and the *Allemande*.

J. H. Schein thus belongs to the tail-end of the movement, though he reached heights which the majority of other *Gesellschaftslieder* poets scarcely rivalled. Not only was Paul Fleming a great admirer of Schein, but the vast quantity of imitations which his works inspired bears witness to the influence Schein exerted on the following period. The baroque elaboration to which the *Gesellschaftslied* succumbed under the influence of the Petrarchan manner will be discussed later. In the meantime we must cast a glance at those absurd *pastoral conceits* which were already referred to in the collections of Paul van der Aelst. Though Italian songs may have introduced such themes into the German song, the pastoral only attained real popularity after the appearance of the Latin rendering of Tasso's *Aminta* and after Guarini's *Pastor Fido* had been translated into German.

Altus

Discantus

Tenor

Bassus

Aus sonderer kūstlicher art/ vnd mit höchstem fleiss seind diß gesangkbücher/mit Tenor Discant Bass vñ Alt Corgiert worden/ jn d Kayserlichen vnnd dess hailigen reichs Stat Augspurg/vñ durch Erhart öglin getruckt vnd volendt/ am newzehenden tag des Monats July von der geburt xpi vnnsers liebñ herrn/ jn dem xv hunndertesten vnnd zwelften jare

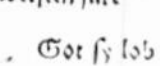

Zwischen perg vnd tieffe tal/da ligt ain freie strassen/ wer seinen püll nit haben mag/ der müß yn faren lassen.
A iij

III ÖGLIN'S LIEDERBUCH (1512)
*(From Könnecke's 'Bilderatlas'; Elwert'scher Verlag, Marburg)*

IV MARTINI OPITII ACHT BÜCHER DEUTSCHER POEMATUM (1625)

# IV

# MARTIN OPITZ

(1597–1639)

---

FROM the previous chapter we shall have gathered how far we may accept the statement that modern German poetry begins with the year 1624, even though Opitz does not derive his style from the Italian lyric. The above year witnessed the publication of J. W. Zincgref's selection of German poetry, containing also Opitz's *Aristarchus* and Zincgref's own poems. The collection proudly boasted a new era in German poetry. However, it was not Zincgref but Opitz who became its critic and formal arbiter. His *Buch von der deutschen Poeterey* (Breslau, 1624) may be considered a landmark in the history of German literature. It offers no æsthetic philosophy but is a handbook of prosody, providing a criterion by which to judge both the past and the future. The work breathes the influence of Ronsard and Scaliger, but originality in the sense demanded later by the 'storm and stress' was here not intended. It sought rather to draw up a comprehensible system of poetic forms. The immediate forerunners of Opitz were T. Hübner and Diederich von dem Werder, but Opitz's fame and title as creator of forms—*princeps poetarum Germaniae*—which cast all the German intelligentsia in the shade, continued throughout the seventeenth century well into Gottsched's era. The latter's fanatic classicism, which Opitz on the whole carefully avoided both in regard to form and content, finally led to the pitfalls of formalism. World-wide vision and cosmic emotion only found true expression through the classic poet whose verse appears at once so supremely individual and yet of universal significance, whereas Opitz's relation to nature and mankind and to his friends remains hidebound by humanistic social forms and pedantic accuracy. One must here, however, beware of drawing imaginary pictures of a special intellectual class, existing as a sort of parallel to the chivalry of the minnesingers.

German literature was thus forced to pass through Opitz's school of discipline in order to recover from the plethora of subject-matter that had flooded the sixteenth century. Thus it subjected itself to a rigorous training in both German and foreign verse construction and added polish to expression and form by the practice of translation. In his capacity as remoulder of language and form Opitz appears as a highlight in German literature. The fact, however, that he turned to alien models whose spirit was in many cases remote from native ideals was certainly a means of making Germany (which could not boast a Paris!) acquainted with foreign culture, but it retarded the process of versification and simultaneously laid bare a gulf between Opitz's learned, quotation-ridden works and the genius of the German people which his fervent patriotism failed to bridge over. It must not be thought that Opitz was ever aware of his lack of mystic and 'folk-bound' powers. He remained isolated in his intellectual world in which however, as Protestant Silesian, he discovered many an aristocratic patron (including indeed not a few of the anti-Protestant party), and thus became a European celebrity. The Netherlandish poets Daniel Heinsius, in Holland, and Hugo Grotius, in Paris, were amongst his illustrious friends. In 1628 he was knighted by Kaiser Ferdinand. Political embassies and panegyrics in honour of his patrons gave glamour to his learning. It was Opitz's aim to rival the foreign humanists.

Already in his Latin article *Aristarchus sive de contemptu linguae teutonicae*, Martin Opitz at the age of twenty-one appears fully aware of his own worth as champion of German poetry. But, as the very title indicates, he steps into the ranks as a humanistically-minded patriot, or better, as a patriotic humanist. Certainly Opitz's finest German verses in the well-known '*Trostgedicht in Widerwärtigkeit des Krieges*' written during the early years of the disastrous Thirty Years War, though bearing a later dedication (1633), were inspired by profound love of the fatherland. His words are full of warm-hearted faith:

*Wir sind ja deutsch geboren,*
*ein Volk, das nimmer sein Herz hat verloren.*
(*Geistliche Poemata.*)

Yet how little of the spirit of Gryphius and Grimmelshausen seems to move in this long poem in four books and rhymed six-foot lines with its tone of pedantry.

In the hours of approaching death, words of deeper emotion seem to spring from the poet's heart, but even here they fade beneath the veneer of cold rhetoric. The poet knows that evil threatens to be the conqueror. Death ends all pain and at the same time glorifies the patient endurer who suffers God's will to be done, and whom Our Lord will recompense in the life to come. Edified by reason man's courage should be steeled to stoic serenity (*constantia, firmitas animi*). Emotion gives way to didactics.

Opitz was also the author of '*Lob des Krieges Gottes*' (with a Latin dedication dating from the year 1628) containing the characteristically humanistic introductory hymn:

> *O Mars, ich singe dich, du starker Gott der Kriege,*
> *du Schutz der Billigkeit, du Geber aller Siege. . . .*

A divine genealogy is divulged, Juno and Jupiter presented as the parents of Mars and the latter's descent from Sparta explained, whilst the variability of his name according to different races and localities, as also his divine attributes and heroic deeds, his amours and offspring, his favourites amongst the nations, are duly accounted for. The patriotic note is not missing in that Mars appears as the deity of a valorous Germany.

War with its tumultuous passion is affirmed by Opitz. Mars incites and seeks out the enemy. He kindles the spirit of man. Fame hastens on before him; his two steeds, terror and fear, accompany him. The poem reaches its zenith in the horrible vision of Bellona, the wife of Mars, with her blood-coloured hair and firebrand held aloft; rape, poverty, hunger, thirst, envy, pestilence and solitude at last yield to palm-crowned victory. Burdened by mythological allegorical reference, and excessive in length, the verses enter on a catalogue of man's discoveries and inventions to end with a survey of the German fatherland, which is threatened by the Turks and must at last escape from the blood-stained hands of the war-god. Thereupon follow yet further expositions on the praise of Mars with certain quotations and allusions.

This poem gives sure proof of the fact that pedantic German

poetry of the seventeenth century is not so remote from life as is often supposed. Topical events are, however, most sharply reflected by the dramas of the period, as we see in Gryphius's views on the divine right of kings, e.g. in his drama *Carolus Stuardus*.

Opitz's patriotic sentiments are again passionately expressed in the *Vorrede* of his '*Weltliche Poemata.*' In his dedication (1628) to Fürst Ludwig zu Anhalt, Graf von Ascanien und Ballenstadt, he sings the praises of Augustinian Rome, when the art of poetry flourished under the protection of noble patrons. The court of Charlemagne and of the Staufen, the renaissance of Italy and France, should likewise offer an example to the wise and virtuous regent whom German poetry will render immortal. Just as Alexander ever bore a dagger and a 'Homer' at his side, the German prince should ever keep his poet at hand. The latter, however, must uphold the purity of language, as once the patriotic Roman had craved pardon for using a foreign word when lacking the necessary expression in the mother-tongue.

The *autonomy* of the poet in regard to the world is more marked in the *Buch von der deutschen Poeterey* (1624). As Opitz well knew, genius cannot be born of method and laws and he was therefore chary in the matter of influence and inspiration. The importance he laid on the intellect nevertheless betrays his affinity with the *Aufklärung* which would have set reason itself on the throne of poesy at the time when German verse had lost all dignity through formal confusion. Style now became a symbol of conscience. Hence the refined scholar Opitz in the sixth chapter of the *Poeterey* demands primarily elegance and grace of words which must be pure (i.e. good High German) and lucid. Mixed languages, padding and impurity of rhyme, lack of clarity in the syntax (such as ambiguity regarding nominative and accusative in the neuter) are tabooed. The seventh chapter, *Von den Reimen*, is full of schoolmasterly rules against the hiatus, and acclaims the iambic alexandrine, with a pedantic *caesura masculinae terminationis* following the sixth syllable, as the model of heroic verse. The characteristically German accentuation of stress as compared with the quantitative reckoning of syllables in the classics provides a rare and refreshingly homely note in this handbook of rules for German poets.

For the sonnet (which a hundred years later was banned by Gottsched) Opitz likewise recommends the alexandrine or alternatively the French *vers common.* The sonnet, which reached Germany from Italy by way of France, is restricted to an exact scheme—fourteen lines of which the first, fourth, fifth, and eighth are rhymed, and again the second, third, sixth, and seventh, whereby feminine or, as the case may be, masculine endings in each group are interchanged with masculine or feminine ones in the second. The last six lines (two tercets) can be treated at will, though the rhyming of the ninth and tenth, the eleventh and fourteenth, the twelfth and thirteenth lines is advised.

How deeply Opitz, though foreshadowing a new style, is rooted in renaissance tradition not only as theoretician but as versemaker may be proved by analytical contrasts based on the following sonnet:

*Dies wunderliche Werk, das Gott hat aufgericht,*
*Die Erde, Luft und See, des Himmels hohe Thronen,*
*Das alles, was man kann und auch nicht kann bewohnen,*
*Hätt' es kein', oder auch zwo Sonnen, stünd es nicht.*

*Ich arm betrübtes Tier muss zweier Sonnen Licht*
*Vertragen, die mir arg für meine Liebe lohnen,*
*Ja, die bei Tag und Nacht auch meiner nicht verschonen;*
*Doch ärger ist die Pein, wann mir der Glanz gebricht.*

*Was Wunder ist es dann, dass ihr mich sehet sterben*
*Mehr als zehntausendmal, eh kaum hingeht ein Tag,*
*Und immer wiederumb belebt zur neuen Plag?*

*Ist Sie mir allzunah, muss ich durch Sie verderben:*
*Ist Sie denn ganz hinweg, so hab ich lauter Nacht;*
*Doch wähl ich mir den Tod, den mir die Hitze macht.*

It is a product of reason built up with a virtuosity in crescendo, deduction and concluding *pointe* that defies every harmonious canon of classic verse. The first verse introduces the theme: Nature is nothing without its sun (the two suns represent the eyes of the beloved).

The second verse brings the crescendo: 'I, wretched wight,

bear the light of two suns.' Day and night are thereby treated as antithesis and as such related to the ego. Third verse: The author suffers death by day more than ten thousand times: '*Ever new pain.*'

The fourth verse brings the *pointe*: near—far = day—night; concluding *pointe*: '*rather I choose death near the sun which inflames me.*'

How serene by contrast G. Keller's lines in his precious poem: '*Augen, meine lieben Fensterlein*' ring in one's ears. Sensuous joy and contemplation balance each other when the poet turns to the thought of life's light extinguished. On the other hand what erotic frivolity is reflected by Philipp von Zesen's musical '*Das achte Lied auf die der überirdischen Rosemund liebes-reizende Augen!*' The latter indulges in exquisite variations on the word *lieb* which appears in every single line, three times in fact in the last but one, though only once in the last, but here it achieves an effective crisis in the midst of three verbs which all end with the syllable *lob*:

*Und lass mich, trautes Lieb, dein liebster Liebling sein!*
*Dann dich erhöb ich, lieb ich, lob ich nur allein.*

We are no less tempted to contrast Opitz's poem with that of Weckherlin's *Von ihren überschönen Augen*:

*Ihr Augen, die ihr mich mit einem Blick und Plitz*
*Scharpf oder süss nach Lust könnt strafen und belohnen;*
*O liebliches Gestirn, Stern', deren Licht und Hitz*
*Kann, züchtigend den Stolz, der Züchtigen verschonen;*

*Und ihr, der Lieb Werkzeug, Kundschafter unsrer Witz,*
*Augbrauen, ja vielmehr Triumphbogen, nein, Kronen,*
*Darunder Lieb und Zucht in überschönem Sitz,*
*Mit brauner Klarheit Schmuck erleuchtet, leuchtend wohnen!*

*Wer recht kann eure Form, Farb, Wesen, Würkung, Kraft,*
*Der kann der Engeln Stand, Schein, Schönheit, Tun und Gehen,*
*Der kann der wahren Lieb Gewalt und Aigenschaft,*

*Der Schönheit Schönheit selbs, der Seelen Freud und Flehen,*
*Und der Glückseligkeit und Tugenden Freindschaft*
*In Euch (der Natur Kunst besehend) wohl verstehen.*

This sonnet is also a piece of virtuosity but of a type more reminiscent of Opitz's. It begins with rhetoric and works with antitheses. First verse: eyes can punish, reward and chastise; further the antithesis: *scharf—süss*; the second verse brings the crescendo: the tool of love, of our wit, triumphal arches, crowns; the third verse abounds with alliterations, assonances, enumerations, which are concluded by the final verse with its parenthetically pointed antithesis: *nature—art*, but it lacks the force of Opitz's sonnet. The inner tension between supposition and deduction, expectant confusion and final conclusion appears both with Opitz and Weckherlin happily wedded to the sonnet form.

With reference to popular and much imitated forms, see also Opitz's *Ihr schwarzen Augen*:

> *Ihr schwarzen Augen ihr und du auch schwarzes Haar*
> *Der frischen Flavien, die vor mein Herze war,*
> *Auff die ich pflag zu richten*
> *Mehr als ein Weiser soll*
> *Mein Schreiben, Tun und Dichten,*
> *Gehabt euch jetzund wol. . . .*

The structure of this poem inspired many poets to imitations: cf. Stieler's '*Die Nacht, die sonst den Buhlern fügt und süsse Hoffnung macht*'; Chr. Weise's '*So geht das liebste Kind von euren Augen aus*'; Angelus Silesius's '*Ihr keuschen Augen ihr, mein allerliebstes Licht*'; Schirmer's '*Ihr Augen voller Brunst und du, du Purpur-Mund*'; Fleming's '*Aurora schlummre noch,*' etc. The formalistic tendency of such poetry colours and simultaneously veils the poet's attitude towards *nature*. She is not sufficient in herself, the poet does not submerge his identity in hers. She is but a decorative background, the painted scene in which the poet himself plays an actor's part or gives this rôle to his hero. We would here mention in particular Opitz's sonnet '*Vom Wolffesbrunnen bey Heydelberg,*' as it treats of a definite object in a neighbourhood well known to us. The comparison appearing in the first verse: *fountain-prince* is an external invention, the words *land, crown and head* and *life* (nymph) a pale abstraction, whilst the concluding line finally brings its cumbrous *pointe*. The intellectual conceit, not emotion aroused by nature, creates the *Stimmung* here.

Contrasted with Opitz's poem Sigmund (Betulius) von

Birken's '*Fountain Song*' betrays unexpectedly rhythmic, sensuous power:

*Du edler Brunnen du, mit Ruh und Lust umbgeben,*
*Mit Bergen hier und da, als einer Burg umbringt,*
*Prinz aller schönen Quell', aus welchem Wasser dringt*
*Anmutiger dann Milch und köstlicher dann Reben;*

*Da unsres Landes Kron und Häupt mit seinem Leben,*
*Der werten Nymph, die lange Zeit verbringt,*
*Da das Geflügel ihr zu Ehren lieblich singt,*
*Da nur Ergetzlichkeit und keusche Wollust schweben:*

*Vergeblich bist du nicht in dieses grüne Tal*
*Beschlossen von Gebirg und Klippen überall;*
*Die künstliche Natur hat darumb dich umbfangen*

*Mit Felsen und Gepüsch, auf dass man wissen soll,*
*Dass alle Fröhlichkeit sei Müh und Arbeit voll,*
*Und dass auch nichts so schön, es sei schwer zu erlangen.*

(Martin Opitz.)

*Hellglänzendes Silber! mit welchem sich gatten*
*Der astigen Linden weitstreifende Schatten!*
*Deine sanftkühlend-geruhige Lust*
*Ist jedem bewusst!*

*Wie sollten kunst-ahmende Pinsel bemalen*
*Die Blätter, die schirmen vor brennenden Strahlen?*
*Keiner der Stämme, so grünlich beziert,*
*Die Ordnung verführt.*

*Es lispeln und wispeln die schlüpfrige Brunnen,*
*Von ihnen ist diese Begrünung gerunnen.*
*Sie schauren, betrauren und fürchten bereit*
*Die schneiichte Zeit.*

(Sigmund von Birken.)
Pseudonym: Betulius

The awakened senses are here in the first verse almost attuned to impressionist concepts, e.g. silvery lights and the broad shadows of the many-branched lime tree, though they do not indulge in vague synaesthesia. The second verse with its rhetorical question is still closely bound to the impression though tending towards abstraction. The third verse betrays the poet of the seventeenth century with his *pointe* fixed on winter, decay, and death. The metric formula is clearly maintained throughout.

The '*Sauerbronnen—Liedlein*,' by J. W. Zincgref and other fountain-songs by G. Finckelthaus or H. Assmann Frh. von Abschatz also fall within the tradition of the period, when the romantic nature-worship of stifled city masses had not as yet replaced the fashionable sojourn at the spa. Nature is but a foil to the actors. How must society have revelled in the description of the fountain, which the author intended as a parallel to the fate of Argenis and Poliarchus! C. F. Meyer's sensuous architectonic vision (*Aufsteigt der Strahl*) and Rilke's magic objectivity in the '*Römische Fontäne*' are unknown to seventeenth-century poets and novelists.

Of great importance is Opitz's song '*Ach, Liebste, lass uns eilen*' in the tone of Ronsard's '*Ma belle je vous prie*.' The *carpe diem* motif here takes on a peculiar form which may be described as *haptic*, a dance-like tripping over the surface, lacking all sense of depth, whilst emotion flees before an intellectual virtuosity that plays with the transitoriness of life (a favourite motif in the seventeenth century). Any individual note is obscured by traditional abstraction: the gift of beauty, the cheek's embellishment, etc. Homburg, a poet of Upper Saxony, in his rendering of the Ronsard-Opitz song accentuates rather the landscape element: flora, clover, heath, than characteristic human allusions.

Simon Dach's may-song, '*Komm, Dorinde, lass uns eilen*,' appears when compared to Opitz and Homburg almost coarse in its simplicity. Nature and the human heart are at harmony. Tree speaks to tree, bough entwines with bough. Nature reflects itself in the springtide of love, though expression appears sometimes in the form of reflection. Where Dach, however, gives free vent to poetic intuition, his freshness and the directness of his vision raise him above the level of Opitz and Homburg.

Opitz's store of themes was by no means limited to those mentioned above. Amongst his verses '*Vielguet*' as an occasional poem in rhymed couplets and alexandrines describes the royal farm of his lord, Heinrich Wentzel von Münsterberg. The author, who asserts that that which is famed good often engenders evil, employs learnedness and wit above a religious undertone. Apparent dignity is but illusion:

*Die Ähre beugt sich, worinnen Körner sind,*
*die aufrecht steht, ist Sprew und fleuget in den Wind.*

Amidst the ocean of man's unrest, the prince's '*Vielguet*' appears as a harbour of peace where one may dwell in merriment though with temperance—a wish-phantasy. Beneath the erotic pastoral mask lies a deep yearning for joy and serenity.

Opitz's version (put to music by H. Schütz in 1627) of Rinuccini's '*Daphne*' cast the very heavens at the feet of an amazed audience. Ovid, connoisseur in the art of love, speaks the prologue. Naked little Cupid breaks the proud will of the python-slayer Apollo who is now inflamed with passion for Daphne and pines and smarts for love. Everything in life must yield to Amor's power which is here not presented as an affair of state as in John Barclay's *Argenis* which, thanks to the translation by Opitz, became a model for German seventeenth-century novels. At last Fortuna requites the indefatigable hero with her favours. The significance given to Eros in the Petrarchan mannerisms of the European love-poems will, I trust, become clear in the course of the following section.

*Fleming, Dach, and others*

*Petrarchism.* The noun *petrarchism* was coined by Ronsard and was often used by Opitz himself, having been distorted to the verb *petrarquiser*. One of Opitz's earliest sonnets (a translation from the Netherlandish) betrays Petrarchan conventions:

*Die Lippen sind Corall, die Wangen sind Rubin,*
*die zarten Brüste sind die schönsten Chrysoliten,*
*O were nicht Demant ihr Herz und zarter Sinn!*

Paul Fleming (1609–1640), who hails Schein and Opitz as his models, having learned the Petrarchan manner from the latter, excels his master in preciosity of style. H. Pyritz in his systematic study of Fleming discovers the source of all the German's stock of metaphors and mythological references in Petrarch (1304–1374) himself. The gold of Petrarch's love-lyrics had tarnished to the rusty coinage of hackneyed similes: e.g. cheeks like roses or rubies, lips like coral gates, hair like gold, a countenance like diamond, breasts like marble balls, hands like jewels, rose-red mouth, eyes like crystal or the stars, etc. Name and motif were thus derived from Petrarch, the cliché itself, however, must fall to the account of his followers and satellites. These were represented in Italy by Pietro Bembo († 1547), in France by the Pléjade, in England by Surrey and Wyatt, in Spain by Montemayor, in Holland by D. Heinsius whose petrarchism cast its influence on Opitz even before he became acquainted with Montemayor. Especial attention must be paid to the new Latin poetry of Europe as a transmitter of Petrarchan forms, for from this international platform the allure of such preciosities penetrated even to the seventeenth-century German song.

In the mouth of the Petrarchans their master's passionate antithetical utterances were petrified to a formula, a virtuoso's cadenzas on love's joy and love's defeat, embellished with a surfeit of hyperbole. Petrarch himself had already praised his beloved's golden hair, her rose-red mouth, had scolded Amor, sighed and pined under his mistress's wayward tricks. Tears gush from his death-entreating eyes. He therein approaches the mannered idealisms of the troubadours and the *dolce stil nuovo* which raised Amor to the rank of a virtue. The thirteenth-century poets Guido Cavalcanti and Guido Guinizelli, and Dante himself in his *Vita Nuova*, are the greatest exponents of the tender style which afterwards declined into the coarsened virtuosity of Cino da Pistoia.

It would exceed the scope of this book to enter more deeply into the question of the Petrarchan sources, such for instance as their anacreontic-sapphic prototype. The Platonic concept of man's relation to the Universe (in *Timaeus*) and the treatises on Eros whom the Italian renaissance writers Pico della Mirandola, Ficino, and others regarded as a cosmic, life-giving power fertilized the anthropomorphic attitude of the period. Such interrelationships have as yet scarcely been dealt with in any detail—least of all those references to the *microcosmos* and *macrocosmos* or Paracelsian concepts which frequently crop up in the German lyric.

At present we would examine the range of formulas (e.g. flame of love—praise of love—sickness in love) which, already discernible in Opitz's poetry, now flood the German lyric, although Paul Fleming refrains from endowing them with that steely cynicism in which the 'second' Silesian school rejoiced. An anacreontic flavour is scarcely noticeable. Fleming delights in genuinely Petrarchan eroticism. Thus his starting-point is the late renaissance and Opitz whose formalized type of song appears to have an especial appeal for him. Later on he adopts an impassioned Petrarchan manner and without borrowing directly from Petrarch himself, raises it to a place of primary importance in the seventeenth-century German lyric. Nevertheless it hardly deserves the name of baroque. Such a designation would hardly fit here, for Fleming's later development clearly betrays an antibaroque attitude. His poetic intuition was far profounder than Opitz's and eventually far surpassed the latter's love-lyrics, in particular the odes, though not his religious songs. Fleming's epitaph on Opitz contains the following eulogy:

*Du Pindar*
*du Homer*
*du Maro unsrer Zeiten. . . .*

But his Reval (Tallinn) period and a journey to Persia had the effect of freeing Fleming from the influence of Opitz and his verbal conventions. A work of truly poignant expression hardly came from his pen, nevertheless we may thank him for many a song of tender charm, both simple and frolicsome, e.g. '*Wie er wolle geküsset seyn . . .*'

A playful tone runs through this bridal song '*Braut-Liedt*' with its sweet alternating refrain: *Amaryllis—Mirtyllus*. This fifth book of *Odes* is a store of melodious rhymes abounding in assonance and alliteration: e.g. '*Aurora schlummre noch*,' . . . or '*O liebliche Wangen, Ihr macht mir Verlangen*,' . . . or the beautiful love-poem '*An Anemonen*.'

Fleming's religious verse is less compelling, though not without a certain individuality. Certainly Ode I. 4: '*In allen meinen Taten*' (*Nach des* 6. *Psalms Weise*), still has power to admonish our conscience. But the Christian sentiments expressed in Ode I, 1: '*Lass dich nur nichts nicht tauren*,' may easily be unmasked as the stoic creed of Fleming's self-discipline (cf. his '*Sey dennoch unverzagt*'). By its side Storm's '*Oktoberlied*,' which was born of actual experience, only shows how dependent on purely typical values is Fleming's poem, whose concluding line reminds us of

Augustine's maxim: *In te ipsum redi, noli foras ire.* Yet in comparison with other poetic reflections of the period, excepting Gryphius's verse, Fleming appears pleasingly simple. Thus T. Hoeck's '*Der Autor beweint das Leben*' is burdened by humanistic pedantry. The opening lines, which remind us of Hans Sachs, match the clumsily learned style of the remaining verses. H. v. Hofmannswaldau's '*Gedanken bei Antretung des fünfzigsten Jahres*' on the other hand betrays the wit of the verbal juggler.

The Silesian Friedrich von Logau (1604–1655) learned much from Opitz and Paul Fleming. He published his rhymes under the transparent pseudonym of Solomon von Golaw.

Although hardly noticed by his own generation, his fame was revived by Lessing, since when he enjoys the reputation of a German Martial, and as such can hardly fall within the pale of the present work. There is, however, a fundamental difference between Logau's rather dry wit and Martial's fanciful satires. Logau's verses, which uphold the purity of German language and culture, caused him to be particularly popular in Germany since Lessing.

Amongst the less brilliant but painstaking of Opitz's followers was Andreas Tscherning (1611–1659). Reduced to poverty and unemployment by the wars, he was rescued by Opitz, until a professorship at the university of Rostock secured him a tolerable income at a time when the muse's grace had long since forsaken the Breslau of J. Heermann and August Buchner. These and Opitz had urged Tscherning to try his hand at verse-making. It is to his credit to have been the first to translate the Arabic apophthegms (Ali) into German. Nor must one forget to give his comprehensive book on prosody its due, though it can scarcely claim originality. It is based above all on Opitz's *Poeterey*, on Schottelius and Buchner, the latter having successfully reintroduced the dactyl into German verse. As poet Tscherning was dependent on the encouragement of his friends. No sooner did the latter fail him than his creative powers flagged. Chance ruled his art as it did his life. Tscherning was related to Opitz and, like the latter, a native of Bunzlau, a town which suffered much under the Thirty Years War. The tragic fate of the short-lived Winterkönig, followed a decade later by the ruthless vengeance of the counter-reformation party, left indelible scars upon its history.

The German songs in praise of the Winterkönig, Frederick V, Elector Palatine, can be mentioned here only in passing. For the most part political parodies, they offer excellent examples of popular satirical pseudonyms. Thus the *Jesuiten* become the *Saviten*, *Prag*—*Plag*, *Scultetus*—*Stultetus*, etc. They moreover reveal another instance of the habit of attaching a wordly text to a religious melody, or the coining of suggestive introductory lines by means of association, thus: '*O Herr, ich schrey auss tieffer Noth . . .*' or '*Fritz, du verwehntes Kind, wie bistu worden so blind . . .*', based on a melody popularized by Regnart's compositions (1574, *Kurtzweilige Teutsche Liedlein*), cf. *B*. p. 302.

Another of Opitz's followers, and a relation of Tscherning, was Andreas Scultetus, a Silesian whom the world soon forgot. As a schoolboy he participated in the memorial service held in honour of Opitz's death. J. Scheffler was a fellow-pupil of Scultetus and like him a convert to the Catholic faith. Scultetus must be included here only on account of Lessing, who rescued him from oblivion and praised his religious hymn: '*Österliche Triumphposaune*.' Scultetus's language is exaggerated and distorted by bombast and pedantry. If anywhere his strength lay in the direction of the epic. Indeed, one of his poems, '*Blutt-schwitzend-Tods-ringender Jesus*' (about 1643), may be said to inaugurate the New High German epic, and thus precedes the epic of W. H. von Hohberg, '*Habspurgischer Ottobert*' (1664).

The works of George Rudolf Weckherlin, a Swabian, boast certain peculiarities of poetic diction that appear far removed from that of Opitz. A preoccupation with verbal accent, apparent in certain improvements to which Weckherlin submitted his own works, perhaps suggests the influence of Opitz's *Poeterey*. Nevertheless the hiatus sometimes remains a conscious revolt against the law (e.g. *meine Ehr*, *deine Ohren*). Weckherlin, it is true, calls Opitz the most excellent of German poets, but in his preface to the *Geistliche und Weltliche Gedichte* he turns against him, possibly because he feared his own work might be eclipsed by the Opitz school.

Whilst the arbiter Opitz restored the German lyric to rhythmic and grammatic law and order, Weckherlin (1584–1653) arose as a new rebel against the æsthetic canon. He deliberately ignored accent, e.g. *Nátur* (!), *lébendig* (!), etc., and even dared to pollute

Opitz's pure German with the Swabian dialect! (e.g. *lützel*, *Predig*, or *die süsse Blick*). Schiller was scarcely to prove less of a sinner in this respect. Carefree and irresponsible in his genius Weckherlin cared nothing for inaccuracies. Yet the above characteristics justify no conclusion other than that Weckherlin's works afford a stylistic antithesis to the polished manner of Opitz. Weckherlin's supposed use of anglicisms is denied by H. Fischer, and has certainly been much exaggerated. It is true that Weckherlin, first as Under-Secretary of State, then as secretary for foreign tongues, and finally as Milton's assistant, spent many years in England and a few in Paris. Yet these sojourns abroad gave but greater ease to his native tongue. He ever maintained close contact with his fatherland. Even the fact that Weckherlin composed poems in English and translated his own German verse into that language (e.g. '*Triumf, or Triumphall shews, set forth lately at Stuttgart, written first in German and now in English,*' *Stuttgart*, 1616) provides no convincing proof of a marked dependence on English conventions.

The odes of Ronsard seem to have had a special attraction for Weckherlin, both in regard to content and form. Other foreign poets whose works may be said to have provided models for certain of Weckherlin's verses are Ovid, Virgil, Horace, Martial, Petrarch, Tasso, Ariosto, Guarini, J. du Bellay, Malherbe, Rémy Belleau, Drummond, Donne, Wotton, and Thomas Morus. According to Vietor, Weckherlin may be called the founder of the *Gesellige Ode*.

The question of claims of precedence between Opitz and Weckherlin is a debatable point. Borinski refuses to rank Weckherlin first, either in regard to period or quality. On the other hand we must give some consideration to Weckherlin's own assertions in his *Geistliche und Weltliche Gedichte*, 1648: 'Nevertheless I can say that many of my poetic works . . . were composed before aught was known of the wisdom and art which they [Opitz's circle] now boast.' Weckherlin's *Oden und Gesänge*, vol. i (1618), doubtless appeared *before* Zincgref's, but he can hardly be called the leader of modern German poetry. Weckherlin's rhetoric excels Opitz's in redundancy and panache. An inexhaustible mine of verbal virtuosity offered ample material for an elegy of a hundred and one verses in six-line alexandrines on the death of

Gustav Adolf. It is possible, though not actually proved, that this poem is but a veiled *captatio benevolentiae*, a would-be means of winning Sweden's special favour, which however failed to materialize.

Weckherlin's verbal skill leads him (for instance in his translation of the Psalms) to attempt a closer relationship between music and the spoken word; see Weckherlin's and Luther's renderings of the twenty-third Psalm. Instead of Luther's terse mode of expression Weckherlin uses ten verses, each containing twelve lines rhymed crossways. Verbal multiplication, crescendos and accumulation now enrich, now spoil his style.

Antithesis was a favourite device of Weckherlin's and often gives his work an epigrammatic bite. His sentences frequently have that perpendicular finality which was to become so characteristic of Stefan George's early style. In a few acrimonious sentences Weckherlin can deliver a deadly thrust at an opponent.

*Königsberg*

Opitz's fame cast poor Weckherlin in the shade. We can hardly read any German anthology of seventeenth-century German verse whose preface or dedication does not boast the name of Opitz. He was the hero of the *Königsberg school* of poets. In their mourning-songs, drinking-songs, their hymns and pastorals, we may ever hear a monotonous undertone of jaded Petrarchan sentiments:

*Ihre Lippen wie Corallen,*
*ihrer Wangen Milch und Blut. . . .*

cf. *Gedichte des Königsberger Dichterkreises aus Heinrich Alberts Arien und musikalischer Kürbishütte*, 1638-1650 (edited by J. H. Fischer, Halle, 1883). Yet generally speaking this group of *East German poets* does not so much indulge in bombastic pedantry as re-echo Simon Dach's cry: '*Memento mori.*'—'*Parcere non didicit mors ulli, est omnibus aequa*,' or revel grimly in the dance of death:

*Kommet Schritt bey Schritt heran*
*der verseelte Todes-mann,*
*raffet von uns was wir haben. . . .*

The tone of their poems with the pastoral pseudonyms: H.

Albert = *Damon*, S. Dach = *Chasmindo*, R. Roberthin = *Berrintho*, Kaldenbach = *Celadon*, etc., tends to be simpler and more heartfelt than that of their revered model, Opitz. But this gentle company of poets, who sat in Albert's summer-house singing the songs they had engraved on the rind of gourds, remains hidebound by the limits of bourgeois morality. In 1638 was published the first part of the *Arien und Melodeyen*. Its editor, the musician and composer Heinrich Albert (nephew of the famous Dresden musician Heinrich Schütz) deemed it necessary to offer excuses for the love-songs: '*Da auch Jemanden der Bulenlieder Nahme schrecken wolte, lebe ich in der Hoffnung, . . . werde sich erweisen, dass sie mehr auff Tugendt und Sittsamkeit als Geilheit zielen.*'

Opitz's Ronsardian ode on *Vivere* received its counterpart in Albert's *Discere*:

*Ich empfinde gar ein Grawen,*
*Bachus, dass ich für und für*
*bin gesessen neben dir. . . .*

The good things of life, however, were by no means disdained by that much travelled linguist Robert Roberthin. He was a hospitable patron of our circle of poets whose most lyrically gifted member was doubtless Simon Dach. The latter's death (1659) resulted in the final disruption of the group, their social comradeship having actually ended with Roberthin and Albert († 1651). That well-known song *Ännchen von Tharau*, with its quaint philistine inscription: '*Trewe Lieb' ist jederzeit zu gehorsamen bereit*,' is wrongly attributed to Dach, though its motto is borrowed from the latter's poem *Nymphe*. It was more probably written by Albert himself, as W. Ziesemer points out fairly convincingly in the *Altpreussische Forschungen* (1924) basing his argument on Robert Priebsch's valuable discovery of Dach's *Bauer-Lied:*

*Grethke, war umb heffstu mi*
*doch so sehr bedrövet?*

As the metre and linguistic peculiarity of *Ännchen* betray deviations from the usual East Prussian *Platt*: *öm* for *man*, *däch* for *doch*, etc., we must conclude that the *Ännchen* song is certainly not by Dach, even though we may not admit Albert as its author.

Dach's powers of lyric expression are not really as versatile as they appear. An uncouth, peasant-like quality reminiscent of

Neidhart, though lacking any suggestion of lasciviousness, alternates with simple pious songs: his moods range from a humble religious acceptance of death to affirmation of life. In reality his was a simple soul that eschewed all pathos and rhetoric in life as in art, and followed its own course untrammelled by tradition. He lives in memory not as the vociferant of ecclesiastic dogma, nor as the fervent prophet of war-stricken Germany, but as a gentle lyric poet singing his songs amidst his circle of friends in the far-off marches of Prussia, which on the whole escaped the ravages of the Thirty Years War. There is an intimate quality in his work that enhances daily life and seems to waken reminiscences of the folk-song. Yet his sentiments are still a little too commonplace and hardly spring from truly poetic intuition.

## *FURTHER DEVELOPMENTS OF THE BAROQUE LYRIC*

### *Religious Meditation and La Vie Galante—The Path of Faith*

During the heyday of literary activity in Königsberg, the East Frankish regions of Germany produced their own school of poets, the Nürnberg circle, whose speciality was the pastoral. Their æsthetic doctrine bears close resemblance to Opitz's linguistic reforms and those of the German *Sprachgesellschaften*. The latter were composed for the most part of patriotic aristocrats, of poets and scholars who united to combat the verbal trickery and corruption that was ravaging literature like a fashionable plague. It is true that their fervour sometimes led to absurd exaggeration, but the cultural value of their activity cannot be denied. Their ideas were influenced by religious and political events and they were in particular inspired by J. Böhme, in whose eyes man appeared a prophet of God (cf. Böhme's *Aurora*, cap. 18, § 48 ff.).

The first of these German linguistic societies *Die fruchtbringende Gesellschaft*, or *Der Palmenorden* (Weimar, 1617), was founded by the Prince of Anhalt-Köthen, a member of the Accademia della Crusca in Florence. The brotherhood regarded it their bounden duty to lead a life of moral integrity and uphold the purity of their native tongue. Those initiated into the mysteries of the society received a pseudonym. Prince Ludwig bore the title *nurturer*. His chamberlain, Kaspar von Teutleben, who had actually been the instigator of the movement, was called *the man rich in flour*; Opitz, the *crowned head* (a title not adopted until 1629). G. Ph. Harsdörffer (known as *the player*) and J. G. Schottelius (*the seeker*) only became members in 1642, to be followed by J. M. Moscherosch (*the dreamer*), Philipp von Zesen (*the poet of the well-tempered phrase*), and others.

In 1633 Strassburg gave birth to the 'Honourable Company of Fir-trees,' i.e. *Aufrichtige Gesellschaft von der Tannen*, whose very emblem the fir was intended as a patriotic protest to the *Order of the Palm*. Better known to posterity is the patriotic society in Hamburg, which was founded almost a decade later by that overzealous purist Philipp von Zesen. Nürnberg poets, such as G. P. Harsdörffer and J. Klai (*the stranger*), and even Dutchmen—J. van den Vondel (*the treasure-trove*)—were numbered amongst its elect. In Lübeck, J. Rist inaugurated the short-lived *Order of the Elbeswan*, whose rules forbade the inclusion of foreigners. Amongst the remaining societies we should mention the *Poetic Society of Leipzig*, which was later under Gottsched to develop into the *German Society*. Today the *General German Linguistic Society*, founded in 1886, forms the central cell of linguistic reform.

The most important seventeenth-century contribution to the study of the German language, is J. G. Schottelius's *Opus de lingua Germanica* (1663). In his dedication to the Duke of Braunschweig and Lübeck he cites the Celtic language as the primal source of the German tongue, one of many outlived theories found in this lengthy, rambling work. And yet the writer's patriotic enthusiasm cannot but galvanize even the present-day readers. Schottelius investigates the origin of words, thereby paying special attention to the relationship between object and expression. The mystic doctrine of the *natural language* (possibly attributable to J. Böhme) seems to have had some influence here. Schottelius is evidently acquainted with the Stoic theory of *φύσει* and *θέσει*. He regards stem-words as the foundations of a language. They derive from nature and symbolize objects. He proudly commends the descriptive tonal colour of the German tongue which, in comparison with the Greek, is so rich in imitation of animal and natural sounds. Schottelius also examines *image rhymes*, i.e. rhymes which offer typographic representation of the object in question—an egg, a pyramid, a grave, a goblet, a cross—and thus theoretically justify their right to live.

This affords a departure from Opitz's ideas. In the *Haubtsprache* considerable space is devoted to the discussion of the pictorial lyric in Schottelius's *Art of German verse and rhyme*, though Scaliger had already approached the subject in his prosody in anticipation of the modern lyric! This decorative arrangement of lines in seventeenth-century verse bears a superficial resemblance to the form of Holz's *Phantasus*, but the anapaests and dactyls were brusquely rejected by Holz. On the other hand certain logical unities reminiscent of those in *Phantasus* may sometimes be detected in Schottelius's quotations of pictorial rhymes. In the seventeenth century this mannerism was put an end to by the classic ideologies of Boileau, but pictorial lyrics still appear in textbooks of the eighteenth century, e.g. in M. Gottfried Ludwig's *Teutsche Poesie, vor die in Gymnasiis und Schulen studirende Jugend . . . mit einem hierzu gehörigen Reim-Register versehen*' (Leipzig, 1745). In traversing the pages of Schottelius's *Teutsche Haubtsprache* we often meet with the name of Harsdörffer, whose works and opinions are there cited with profound esteem.

G. P. Harsdörffer (1607–1658) was not only one of the founders of the Nürnberg *Pegnesischer Blumenorden*, but also furthered its activities in many directions. Harsdörffer (*Strephon*) himself was the master of the order. His young friend J. Klai, S. von Birken, Schottelius and Rist were members. Their vows were consecrated to the honour of God and their beloved native tongue. Harsdörffer's *Frauenzimmergesprächspiele* (1641 ff.), and his handbook, *Der Nürnberger Trichter* (1647 ff.) advocate a union of painting and poetry, picture and word. The Nürnberg school thereby became not only an influence in German literature of the period but foreshadowed the tonal imagery and symbolism of Brentano's musical 'lyric of the soul.' Harsdörffer attempts exact acoustic reproduction of the impression aroused, of an idea or some experience (e.g. war, tempest). A surfeit of merely jingling sound and poverty of imaginative vision prevent him, however, from attaining anything like the verbal richness of the modern 'naturalistic' school. The tyranny of pure rhyme, formal rhythm, assonance, and repetition outweigh all expressive values. Harsdörffer's style of *tonal painting* probably achieved the fame it did because he was one of the first German poets to work in this direction. Nevertheless, the assertion made by some critics that German literature could reap but little benefit from such innovations is unjust, and moreover due to an inability to appreciate the musical values of the language. Such critics are evidently too much influenced by the purely rational significance of word and content, as exemplified by the work of Fischart, Hans Sachs, etc. The excellent survey of and reference guide to *The Archives of the Pegnesischer Blumenorden* by Professor Blake Lee Spahr (University of California Press, Berkeley, 1960) gives most valuable information on German baroque literature in general and the Nürnberg poets in particular.

In his tonal paintings Harsdöffer was primarily influenced by the pastorals and marinistic foibles of Italian fashion. Spain (Montemayor's *Diana*), France (Pléjade), and the Netherlands doubtless also left their impression on his work. In the course of his struggles against the bombast and exaggerated imitations of his own style, Harsdörffer was eventually forced to retreat into the background. His aims were forgotten until with the rise of romanticism, German poetry set out once more on paths somewhat similar to those he had trodden.

Philipp von Zesen's (1619–1689) melodious may-song: '*Glimmert ihr Sterne . . .*' is born of sheer joy of musical expression, making one dream of Brentano and Tieck, though form and content are not yet perfectly fused as in Goethe's '*Wie herrlich leuchtet mir die Natur.*' Zesen's melodious tones resound from rhyme to rhyme, one word being caught up from another as later in Holz's *Phantasus*. This verbal virtuosity aroused Rist's protest. The same mellifluence characterizes even the antithetical style of his sonnets. The single line no longer corresponds with the integer of sense. Alliteration loses its expressive power and degenerates to mere frippery. What a contrast is afforded by the bluntness of B. H. Brockes's eulogy of spring ('*Willkommen, liebster Mai! Wie lieblich und wie schön*'), in which those useful vegetables, spinach, asparagus, hops and lettuce are catalogued for the glory of God—a veritable product of the age of enlightenment! His pedantic conceit spares us no detail of all his knowledge concerning wheat, millet, hemp, and linseed, whilst he painstakingly invents a new calendar to fit the rustic occupations of the year. Nevertheless, one must admit that in spite of his pedantry Brockes possessed an eye for nature and thus laid the foundations on which a later generation could build.

In 1656 appeared one of the most popular song-books of the middle of the seventeenth century, the *Venus-Gärtlein: oder viel schöne, ausserlesene weltliche Lieder, allen züchtigen Jungfrawen und Jung-Gesellen zu Ehren, und durch Vermehrung etlicher newer Lieder zum andernmahl in Druck verfertigt*. Many folk-songs and bawdy lays, scarcely prized at the time, and many a famous *Gesellschaftslied* are contained in this volume, e.g. songs or versions of songs by Rist, J. K. Göring, Dach, Zesen, H. Albert, Finckelthaus, Voigtländer; also drinking-songs, acrostics, pastorals, and the later *Hildebrandslied*. Especial favourites were such pieces as '*Daphnis wolte Blumen brechen*,' whose melody offered a prototype for many another song; further, '*O Magdeburg halt dich feste*,' the *Lindenschmidt*, and perhaps most popular of all, '*Daphnis gieng vor wenig Tagen*,' which may be traced back to J. Rist.

The *Geharnischte Venus* (1660), the work of an Erfurter poet, K. Stieler, excels in formal virtuosity. Rollicking vivacity is bridled by an incredible lightness of touch. More impetuous than Opitz he nevertheless still adheres to the latter's technical formality. One of his most rhythmically effective lyrics, '*Nacht-last, Tages-lust*,' was produced by the thematic development of the first verse of Opitz's poem '*Ihr schwarzen Augen*.' The beautifully constructed serenade '*Willkommen Fürstinn aller Nächte*' ends on a note of dramatic suspense. The scene unveils itself in calculated gradations:—First verse: The princess and the prince. Second verse: Heavenly lamps. Third verse: *Zephyr* and *Pomonenäste*. Fourth verse: Yearning and hesitation. Fifth verse: Flora and Venus. The theatrical concluding line: '*Still, Lauten-klang, mein Liebchen ist schon dar*,' puts an abrupt end to all imaginative flights.

Such virtuosity of form and melody appears the result of definite literary influence, namely that of J. Plavius, a member of the Danzig circle (*Plauen* circle). The latter's tonal poems have been somewhat unjustly ignored to the advantage of Opitz's logic. From 1657 on K. Stieler himself spent some years at Danzig. The town was at that time under Polish authority, but more as a matter of form than in reality. Its dependence seems on the whole to have consisted in little more than the payment of tribute to the Polish king. The poetry of this mighty Hansa port on the Baltic remained German in language and spirit. It was here that Opitz edited the *Annolied* shortly before his death. During the

Thirty Years War this city of venerable burghers enjoyed a comparative period of calm, blossoming forth in poetry and song, *Weichselschäferei*. The Thuringian poet, Joh. Plavius (Plauen), M. Albinus, J. P. Titz, an imitator of Opitz's *Poeterey*, all resided at Danzig, J. Plavius reaching the town before Opitz himself. But Titz's lyric poetry has little to do with that of Opitz. Plavius's importance depends largely on the influence he exerted over Gryphius and Hofmannswaldau in their youth.

The virtuosity of the seventeenth-century German lyric leads in a direct line to the *galanteries* of Hofmannswaldau. At the same time, however, a wave of religious fervour awakened expressions of profounder sentiment (above all in Gryphius) in protest against the frivolities of current literature. The Silesian poet Daniel von Czepko (1605–1660) represents as it were a bridge between the early baroque humanisms of Opitz and the mystic death-yearning of Gryphius. From the speculations of Tauler, Eckhart, Böhme, Paracelsus, and others, D. v. Czepko constructed an eclectic scientific doctrine which he imparted to the public in the form of learned pious prose and religious songs. In his '*Trostschrift an Charisius*' he ponders on the mystery of death which he interprets as the cross-roads between damnation and heavenly bliss, as a passage to a new birth which conquers death. But in the course of his intellectual development the problem of death appears to him in an ever-changing light. '*Parentatio*' (1660), a work written shortly before his death, differentiates between *Magia*, the doctrine of the saving influence of grace, and revelation through the *Cabbala* and *Alchymia*, the art of material composition.

Here again spirit triumphs over matter. Pansophy, the doctrine of the realization of God through an understanding of nature, did not appear to D. v. Czepko the only means of salvation. He was a Protestant. As such and as a servant of the crown he struggled valiantly between free thought and loyalty. But his religious songs are not burdened by polemics but give sincere expression to his experience of death and of the divine.

D. v. Czepko's influence on his contemporaries has hitherto been underestimated. In his '*Sexcenta Monodisticha Sapientium*' he actually foreshadows the '*Cherubinischer Wandersmann*.' His worldly pastoral epic, '*Coridon und Phyllis*,' which he continually revised, is notable on account of its *anti-courtly* views, its scorn of mere fashion and its autobiographical interest. Its form, however, adheres to the courtly-pastoral manner. D. v. Czepko's dependence on tradition and Opitz is particularly evident in the following sonnet, a prize example of the proto-baroque alexandrine sonnet form:

*Der Frühling stellt sich ein, des Jahres Blüt' und Glanz:*
*Mein Sinn, schau, was geschieht, hab acht auf deine Schanz.*
*Itzt steigt die Sonn' empor: erwecke dein Gemüte!*
*Das Vieh verlässt den Stall: geh aus des Leibes Hütte!*

*Das Dorf kommt auf das Feld: zeuch in die Sinnen ein!*
*Das Gras verlässt der Reif: verlass' der Wollust Schein!*
*Die Vögel stimmen an: du sollst die Zungen binden.*
*Die Berge schlei'rn sich ab vom Schnee: du von den Sünden.*

*Im Fall du dieses tust und zierst, was in dir ist,*
*Und hast der Seelen Lenz in diesem auserkiest,*
*Dass Sonne, Vieh und Dorf, Gras, Vogel, Berg, ingleichen*

*Gemüte, Leib und Sinn, Lust, Zung und Lenz erweichen,*
*So ist es wohl getan. Was wohl vor Gaben Schar*
*Bringt solcher Frühling nicht in unser Lebensjahr!*

All too obvious in its construction it abounds in antitheses and parallels. Verses three and four unite cause and issue, strange to relate, from outwards inwards, the last line of the third verse affording an exact parallel to the first line of the fourth, the word *Lust* being counted as a 'dip' on account of the metre (sun, beasts, village, grass, bird, mountain-sentiment, body, sense, joy, tongue, spring).

The most individual of these poets was the Silesian Andreas Gryphius (Greif) (1616–1664). His language is rough-hewn, his rhythm unmelodious. The high-baroque ideal is apparent only in the content, not in the form of his poems. Some hidden impulse urges him onward without rest, his heart cries out in agony. His fancy conjures up terrible images of suffering. Yet he too derives from Opitz's school, only that his song seems born of deeper sincerity. In his poem '*An Eugenie*' antithesis is happily blended with the characteristic sonnet pattern.

Nevertheless dependence on Opitz's lyric style (not the latter's drama) with its teutonized humanism often produces an unbearable tension between rhetoric and emotion even in Gryphius's work. All the same he does not fall a prey to mere talk. We suggest not that Opitz and his imitators lack any depth of feeling, but that the emotional element is certainly more pronounced in the case of Fleming, Dach, Albert, and in particular Gryphius. When the latter uses the traditional sonnet form with its *pointe* to give vent to the swelling tide of his soul's torment, even the formula seems born of inner necessity. Nor does language then fail to create unity from the chaos of appearance.

In the course of this book, and particularly in discussing Opitz, whose work inclines essentially to classicist ideals, we have, on the whole, deliberately refrained from using the term *baroque*. Much that is often included under this heading should, as we saw, more deservedly bear the title *petrarchism*. We must, indeed, be most circumspect in speaking of baroque in relation to rationalistic and subjective tendencies of the period. The adjective *subjective* does not correspond with an effusion of private sentiment but reveals the ego that has formed its own concept of the universe, whilst the virtuosity of much so-called baroque poetry reflects merely personal foibles resting on a purely accidental basis. The lyric poets of seventeenth-century Germany appear therefore to lack that universal vision and the spiritual freedom associated with the truly great poets.

On the other hand the irrational element exerted an all too powerful influence on the period. Hence, although the rational quality is so blatant in the construction of seventeenth-century verse, it must not be regarded as the *essence* of such poetry. We may go so far as to call it a characteristic trait of the baroque. Death casts its shadow over these worldly frivolities. Dread of the judgement day rescues Gryphius's anguished soul from sin. The exhortation of his ode *Vanitas vanitatum vanitas* penetrated to the Protestant hymnal. Visual images are here transfigured to spiritual utterance and afford a striking contrast to the traditional similes of Hoeck or Kongehl, or particularly those of Schmolcke, who hammers the word *eitel* into the reader's ear in every single line.

Attempts to render emotional tumult by an accumulation of details end, particularly in Gryphius's case, in a deadly duel between expression and word. Quantity rules, unending enumeration of detail, tricks of antithesis are used as a means of breaking down the rigid formula or, on the other hand, quelling the emotional flood. Poetic images crystallize themselves to uncannily palpable form. To illustrate this point we should contrast P. Fleming's *An sich* ('*Sey dennoch unverzagt*') with Gryphius's '*An sich selbst*' and '*Was sind wir Menschen doch?*' In Gryphius's poems the ego is not robbed of its significance. In spite of this massing of material the subjective element often emerges at the end of a poem. It represents more than a technical means of achieving the desired *pointe*. Rather it affords a goal from which by retrospect the apparent chaos of bleak symbolism and metaphor resolves itself to a harmonious and heartfelt image of the poet's vision. The interrelationship of single details, which a lesser talent could form to no more than a catalogue, thus attains some sort of unity, though even Gryphius lacks Goethe's power to give his personal concepts universal significance. The reason for this limitation, which is felt throughout German seventeenth-century poetry, was amply demonstrated in the case of Opitz and his followers. Gradually, by such men as Gryphius, German poetry was prepared to receive the inspiration which rained from heaven on the supreme poet of the classic era. The organic whole replaces the sum-total of detail, a fact which may be accepted quite literally.

Thus for instance in Gryphius's moving lament on his *living death*, each object is as it were separately described and labelled: limbs, eyes, breath, tongue, veins, arms, body. The unity of the image is thus destroyed:

> *Der Atem will nicht fort, die Zunge steht gebunden.*
> *Wer sieht nicht, wenn er sieht die Adern sonder Maus,*
> *die Armen sonder Fleisch. . . .*

We only see the details and yet they are transfused with the glow of the poet's sincere religious fervour. Faith in the Resurrection shall triumph over the sufferings of a Germany torn by conflict and intellectual strife. Not only humanism versus the Middle Ages but also the reformation's struggle with the papal hierarchy, and the gulf separating the learned caste from the simple people, brought about ever new disruption. To see therein only symptoms of degeneration is as short-sighted as to indulge in oracular phrases about the doom of modern Europe.

In any history of the ode Gryphius must hold an outstanding place amongst German seventeenth-century poets. Pindar rather than Horace was his model, though at that period the Greek poet enjoyed by no means the same fame as his Latin successor. Ronsard derived largely from Horace and Weckherlin from Ronsard. Opitz did little to develop the ode, but Gryphius was the first to breathe new fire into its outworn shell until under Klopstock the German lyric attained its own great hymnal form. Hölderlin's translations from Pindar revealed yet more deeply the affinity between the German and the Greek.

Like Opitz, Gryphius adopts the trilogy: *thesis*, *antithesis*, *conclusion*, but a far mightier wind sweeps through the verses of his odes. They abound in strangely compelling phantasies, dramatic and variable rhythms. Their content often indulges in paraphrases from the Psalms, cf. Psalm cxvi. 7 f. with Gryphius's *Ode* I. 10 (see Vietor's '*Geschichte der Ode*'):

1. Thesis—the aftermath of pain.
2. Antithesis—Comfort.
3. Conclusion—Relief.
4. New thesis—New hope.
5. Antithesis—The Lord be praised.
6. Conclusion—Promise of Thanksgiving.

Amongst Gryphius's imitators Johann Heermann (1585–1647), the Poeta Laureatus Caesareus of Brieg, deserves some praise, not as a poet but because of the influence which he exercised on some of his contemporaries. Heermann was also an admirer of his compatriot Opitz. In his religious poems he closely follows the text of his theological sources, e.g. his *Flores ex odoriforo* (1609) which appeared in an enlarged edition of 1644: *Exercitium pietatis*.

The renaissance had established the supremacy of man. The words which Pico della Mirandola puts into the mouth of God: *Medium te mundi posui*, express the new attitude towards life, though still maintaining an ecclesiastic flavour. The conflict between life and the after life, past and present, which had never abated since the Middle Ages reached a climax in German baroque. In Gryphius's case, as we saw, the metaphysical aspect triumphs whilst in Hofmann von Hofmannswaldau (1617–1679) the sensual-erotic element and its attendant *galanteries* hold the field, though even here the very violence of passion seems almost sublimated to a mystic note. He ranks as the most characteristic exponent of the baroque movement in German literature, although no less a representative of the Indian summer of German humanism. C. v. Lohenstein (1635–1683), on the other hand, may be called a late baroque perfector of Gryphius's tradition. Art afforded but a plaything for his wit, as it did for Hofmannswaldau's pleasantries. Any topical, trifling, or sad event provided inspiration for their pen, as we may see by such frequently recurring titles as funeral elegies, wedding celebrations, *divertimenti*, and the inevitable love-song. For both of them life had little to do with art, unless we regard the ease and virtuosity of their poetic technique as the artistic counterpart of their elegant cultured existence. Hofmannswaldau's poems enjoyed widespread circulation. Pastorals from his translation of Guarini's *Pastor Fido*, epigrams, etc., were discussed far and wide. Nearly all his works were published posthumously. The jovial social life of Breslau provided a fitting stage for his poetic activities. His compatriot Opitz's name had here lost nothing of its fame. H. v. Hofmannswaldau himself, who at the age of sixty was honoured with the high title of a Praeses of the Council in the Silesian town, may as a boy very probably have met the great doyen whose poetic conventions (in particular the sonnet) he afterwards adopted. H. v. Hofmannswaldau's path was thus smoothed. He cherishes Opitz's legacy and seeks to preserve the purity of the language and beauty of form. The tempestuous violence of Gryphius's or Zesen's verse yields once more to the steady pace of the alexandrine; the dactyl is rejected. With calculated precision Hofmannswaldau leads his audience to some incredibly bewildering *pointe*, before which the fragile construction of his poem dwindles to a mere illusion; see *Galante Gedichte*, '*Auff ihre Ohren-gehänge*,' or '*Auff ihre Schultern*.' Its various parts with their similes are interchangeable, the children of a mere whim.

Parallels are afforded by art; for instance, in the baroque church in Rohr in Lower Bavaria an angel propels the Virgin Mary skyward above a marble tomb that resembles more closely some pagan bath, a sculptural analogy by the brothers Asam to the *pointe* in literature! Without this drama in stone, the church would appear barren as a festive hall from which the guests had departed. Similarly the exquisite frivolous church of *Vierzehn Heiligen*, near Bamberg, is dominated by its absurd altar that stands planted in the centre like some gilded ceremonial coach; cf. *Art and Life*, by Hannah Priebsch Closs, Oxford, 1936, pp. 86 ff.

Even H. v. Hofmannswaldau's poetic tribute to love and honour is but a gesture by which he clothes fleshly vanities with the veil of virtue. Of his famous heroic epistles, *Heldenbriefe*, all except the tenth and fourteenth, which describe the love of Graf Friedenheim and Fräulein Sittenoren, of Abélard and Héloïse, sing the praises of pure erotic lust, or of the 'love-stricken things' as the author himself calls them. As a rule the masculine point of view is presented, man's love to which the servant girl yields like a willing slave, and which consumes the wife long parted from her husband with shameless yearning. Hofmannswaldau's overcharged phantasy revels in grim horrors. Algerthe's feet dabble in a corpse's blood. D. von Liliencron's *Feudal* appears foreshadowed!

Brilliant paradoxical witticisms flash through his brain. Hyperbole spices the formality of his verse: '*Ein Blick von mir der steckte Dörffer an,*' (*Rudolf an Ermegarden.*) . . . But lucidity is sacrificed: '*Dein Mündlein ist ein Ort von tausend Nachtigalen,*' (*Siegerich an Rosemunden*). His metaphors try to combine warm sensual images with icy antitheses: '*Der Schultern warmer Schnee. . . .*' He knows nothing of the beauty of a woman's love, but enters only on a detailed catalogue of her body's charms.

A comic element is often aroused quite unintentionally by his very rhymes: '*Ich bin ein Erdenkloss . . . ich falle nirgends hin als nur in deine Schooss.*' The frivolous conceits and erotic obsession of these rhymed heroic epistles are characteristic of all his poetry. The introductory words of the murderous tale of *Graf Holdenreich und Adelinde* offer a prototype of his work in general. He says: 'I am here concerned with love and not with stringent laws of morality, and find my pen as easily under the briar-hedge as among the lily-stems. But he who would demand of me more spiritual themes shall have them too. . . .'

These heroic epistles overflow with sentiment, but it is merely lust that wails or exults; he cares nothing for faithful love in wedlock or moral law. Man's duties as a member of the state play second fiddle to his amours. The Count of Gleichen offers his bed and his heart both to a Mohammedan beauty and to his wife. Even the Agnes Bernauer problem (cf. the twelfth letter) is hardly fought out as a spiritual conflict between the burgher and the aristocratic class. On the contrary, Agnes of her own accord tells her beloved to follow the call of youth and abandon himself to his pleasures. The form of these letters, which represent the zenith of H. v. Hofmannswaldau's love poems, betrays the same veil of *galanteries*. His alexandrines even outrival those of Opitz in polish. His verses nevertheless throb with baroque sensuality, flash with ironical wit, yet retain frequently so light a grace that we may hunt in vain throughout German seventeenth-century literature for so exquisite a blending of reason and eroticism, of Opitzian formality and baroque feeling. Bombast was not his only *métier*. The perfection of his formal synthesis, which was a true product of his nature, is his most deserved claim to immortality.

In a panegyric delivered at his burial, C. v. Lohenstein mourns him as the *great Pan* who passed and departed this life as a blessed Christian. Paradoxical as it may seem, this is no empty phrase, for the 'Pan' of Breslau was no faun. As 'Pan' H. v. Hofmannswaldau experienced life too keenly not to lament its transitoriness, which he depicts in a lengthy chain of lines: *Die Welt*. On the other hand, his wit causes him to rebound in the opposite direction. His *Poetic Tombstone Inscriptions* often have biting force.

In the preface of *B. N.'s* (*Neukirch*) *anthology* of seventeenth-century verse, C. v. Lohenstein, Gryphius, Hans von Assig, H. Mühlpfort, H. A. von Abschatz, etc., are discussed from a historical and critical point of view. The said B. N. was no other than the political poet who round about the year 1700 turned against the Silesians to make them, in particular H. v. Hofmannswaldau, the butt of his satire: '*Auf unverständige Poeten*' (about 1713).

To the same generation belongs the malicious and undaunted author of the '*Überschriften*,' Chr. Wernicke (or Warnecke), who not only rebelled against authority on principle (he boasted *nullius in verba iurare magistri* as his motto) but consciously attacked the sickly style of the Pegnitz shepherds and the preciosities of the Silesian school, C. F. Hunold (Menantes) being his especial target. He did not deny the talent of C. v. Lohenstein and H. v. Hofmannswaldau though he did not in the least hesitate in lashing at their weak points (cf. Wernicke's '*Furor poeticus*').

R. L. Freiherr von Canitz, the author of a once famous ode on the death of his wife Doris, also displayed a talent for satire ('*Von der Poesie*') in which he incites the poets to return to nature. His biting couplet:

> *Ein Teutscher ist gelehrt, wenn er solches Teutsch versteht,*
> *Kein Wort kommt vor den Tag, das nicht auf Stelzen geht,*

might well be printed as a motto above the present chapter.

*The meaning of baroque*

We have already admitted that we have rejected an *a priori* use of the term 'baroque'. In discussing H. v. Hofmannswaldau, who is often described as characteristically high baroque, the title was in some ways found to be apposite, though his style cannot be designated as pure baroque, and reveals itself rather as a synthesis of renaissance and modern ideals. H. v. Hofmannswaldau lacks both the ecstatic vein of Quirinus Kuhlmann and the religious fervour of Gryphius. Baroque in the true sense is Grimmelshausen, who as an epic writer lies outside the pale of our argument. We shall, however, have to use 'baroque' as a touchstone for the lyric, as the term has attained such significance not only in German but European literary criticism. We shall here not be concerned with it in its timeless aspect as a recurrent æsthetic ideal, but as an historical phenomenon limited to a definite period.

The term 'baroque' first found popular use in the domain of art criticism. Regarded from the renaissance point of view, baroque was rejected as a positive stylistic phenomenon by Burckhardt and Nietzsche, as also by Benedetto Croce. Riegl won deeper insight into the problem by explaining its appearance as the development of an *optic* concept of art compared to the *haptic* ideals of the renaissance. Dagobert Frey traced the gradual conquest of a *simultaneous* by a *successive* type of vision. To Pinder the beauty of baroque is the expression of a young, virile race.

Spengler, on the other hand, sees in baroque the Faustian death-struggle of a doomed Europe. Worringer regards baroque as the *gothic* principle of style, the irreconcilable enemy of all *classic* aspiration, and a characteristically *Northern* or *German* concept. Dehio also applies timeless, racial values to the term. To Hausenstein, baroque is synonymous with restless momentum and highly strung nerves. In spite of this tempting variety of interpretations not one of them can find a strict analogy in literary criticism.

The subject-matter, style and type of a German seventeenth-century poem are subject to their own special laws. Wölfflin's categories, *open—closed*, etc., do not cover any baroque phenomena in literature. Nor is baroque, as Strich wrongly tries to prove, akin to old Germanic form. German baroque was born under different conditions from those that produced the baroque architecture of Bernini or Borromini, or even the paintings of Rubens, Rembrandt, Van Dyck, Hals, and others. In Germany human lives and fashions alike reflect the horror and upheaval of the Thirty Years War, the vacillations of an economic and æsthetic subservience to foreign influence until gradually racial individuality emerges triumphant over the ruins.

In the field of the German lyric, the conflict, as our enquiry proved, was largely fought out between *paganism* and *Christianity*. A true synthesis, with which H. v. Hofmannswaldau's playful harmonies but toyed, was not achieved before Goethe. Viewed from this angle the German lyric of the baroque period appears as a vain attempt on the part of the German genius to revive the spirit of pagan classicism. The point of extreme tension—the high baroque—would in this case possess a negative value. Moreover, mystics like Gryphius and Spee (to say nothing of Jacob Böhme) remain a class apart.

Ermatinger believes the essential quality of the baroque to lie in the culmination of a struggle between the joys of the flesh and the dream of an after-life. But such a concept remains equally one-sided, ignoring as it does many undeniable historical phenomena of the baroque. Nevertheless, it is useless to seek (like Strich) a unified lyric style of the seventeenth century. That characteristic alluring quality of movement which Strich finds lacking in the sixteenth century fails to appear even in many seventeenth-century poems, as do those insistent variations on a theme which appeared to us important features of seventeenth-century German verse. It is still more dangerous indeed to try and gather the entire phenomena of the period under an *a priori* conceived general denominator entitled *high baroque*.

A study of *single* aspects of the question, such as the consciousness of the ego, the antithesis between art and nature, the concept of man's mortality, or his attitude towards life as reflected in the rich metaphors of seventeenth-century poetry, is more likely to bring enlightenment on the significance of baroque than a general historical survey.

Contrasted with the profound serenity of Goethe's classic *Weltanschauung*, that of the seventeenth century appears dictated by accident, as though history were but the whim of fortune. The seventeenth-century poet is little interested in the description of character but revels in heroics and fame, in courtly manners and pleasures of the flesh, in short, adventures in the name of the sword or amour. His hero aspires to no harmony of body and soul but struts and swaggers with *bravura* gestures. He lives but in the present. Dafnis (*Carpe diem*) remained till Holz's time an assuaging sop to our dread of mortality, though restrained through consciousness of death. Just as the baroque painter registers the fleeting impression in the flash and gleam of colour, so the seventeenth-century poet catches the whim of the moment. His temperament is too restless to render nature eternal. *Emotion* is chained in the fetters of reason. A *plethora of words* and *abundance of material* often render images more intense, but produce simultaneously a general impression of turgid redundancy or violent tension, a state of affairs accentuated by a mania for *synaesthesia*. The writers of the renaissance period also sometimes rendered light by sound, optic by acoustic effects (cf. Kepler's *Harmonice Mundi* (1619), and before him Leonardo da Vinci, Giordano Bruno, etc.). In the philosophy and poetry of the seventeenth century (cf. Athanasius Kircher's *Ars magna lucis et umbrae* or Harsdörffer, etc.), *pictura-poesis* is attempted by a blending of the senses of sight, sound, touch, taste and scent, whilst rational and irrational elements stand side by side in unbearable tension.

The seventeenth-century metaphor is surcharged with such *synaesthesia*, added to an ornate verbosity that springs alike from the intellect and a *pathos* of sentiment, suffocating all sense of form. The emotional value of the theme thereby becomes disseminated in a chaos of sensual and intellectual atoms. Where, however, true æsthetic feeling exists as in Fleming's or Gryphius's verse, the emotional element also remains, whilst with the weaker talents rhetoric turns all to mere formula, personal expression yielding to type.

The *rhetorical* element is a characteristic trait of the seventeenth-century poet's dependence on the court and on publicity. The drama mirrors the fate of dynasties. Class feeling guides personal sentiment. Learned men fawn at the feet of their rulers and patrons. On the other hand the voice of revolt is heard not only in the lower but also in the upper strata of society. Thus on the threshold of the sixteenth century we have Heinrich Julius von Braunschweig's drama *Vincentius Ladislaus*, followed by J. Böhme's unrhetorical mysticism, and the works of D. v. Czepko and Grimmelshausen added to folk-songs and religious songs, etc.

At the same time, the etiquette of the Habsburg court in Vienna extended its influence particularly to South German culture, and it is certainly right to question the universal importance of Versailles in the development of German baroque literature, for the palace was only completed three years after H. v. Hofmannswaldau's death (1679), and Louis XIV entered into residence there as late as 1682. Racine's theatre was not established until 1667. On this account G. Müller calls the seventeenth century the *Habsburg period*, though this universal title is scarcely justified to the same extent as the designation *Stauferzeit* in regard to the twelfth and thirteenth centuries, for the Austrian court hardly exerted a powerful influence on the Lutheran districts. The humanist's proud scorn of the *profanum vulgus* prepared the way for courtly literature. The Jesuits then amalgamated aristocratic absolutism with the ecclesiastic ideal in their spectacular festivities and dramas depicting heavenly and profane love. Even the baroque novel became a stage for history, statecraft, and intrigue. Barclay's novel *Argenis* provides a model for the court manners of the subsequent period. Form and wit are the fashion of the day. The anecdote tends to become epigrammatic.

A *mania for quotations* reflects the overpowering influence of culture on literature. The *isolation of the object* from its cosmic relationship to the universe was but the natural outcome of an artificial attitude towards life. The mask, however, is dropped in the face of death. A study of the problem of death provides F. W. Wentzlaff-Eggebert with a new interpretation of seventeenth-century poetry, in which he differentiates the writers of the period according to whether they tend to exalt this life or the next. Stoic resistance (Gryphius) and mystic yearning (Spee, Scheffler, Kuhlmann) each finds its own way of rising triumphant over the transitoriness of existence. At the close of the century, like some percursor of our modern age, stands J. Christian Günther (1695–1723) staring into the face of death undaunted, steeled by faith in himself and in the dawn of a new world. cf. G. C. Schoolfield: *The German Lyric of the Baroque in Engl. translation*, 1961.

*The influx of mysticism on the eve of pietism*

The birth of the Jesuit father Friedrich Spee (1591–1635) still falls within the sixteenth century. As father-confessor to witches he drew up the *Cautio criminalis, seu de processibus contra sagas* (1631, *auctore incerto theologo Romano*). His *Trutznachtigall* only appeared as a posthumous work in 1649. Even when Spee clothes his muse in pastoral garb he often paints natural scenes of charming sincerity. On the whole, however, he tends to tasteless sentimentalities.

His '*Konterfei des menschlichen Lebens*,' which reminds one slightly of '*Heidenröslein*,' reveals Spee's sensitive feeling for nature. Jesus is the soul's spouse, courting her with words of love, cf. the poem:

*Der trübe Winter ist vorbei,*
*die Kranich wiederkehren. . . .*

In such a setting, the mythological element in verse three ('*Die Jägerin Diana stolz . . .*') appears as surprising as the unexpected ending. This mixture of paganism and Christianity was, however, not new, as Milton's poetry proves. The sixth verse introduces the joys of life as a contrast to its sorrows.

Friedrich Spee's *Güldenes Tugent-Buch* (1649) belongs to the tradition of the period. In his '*Liebreiches Gebet zu Jesus*,' a preparation for the Holy Communion, he prays to the various parts of the body: head, hair, face, eyes, cheeks, mouth, neck, hands, breast, feet, and to the body as a whole. Herein he reflects that typical seventeenth-century trick of isolating and abstracting objects instead of inspiring the totality with spiritual breath. The petrarchisms and metaphors to which we have referred on an earlier page are thus rendered into prose: '*Seyd gegrüsset ihr wunsame Augen meines Herren Jesu Christi, O ihr brinnende Demanten, O ihr glänzende Cristallen. . . .*'

Pompous metaphors obscure the lucidity of the whole, particularly in his prayer to the breast of Christ: '*Sey gegrüsst, O ehrwürdige Brust . . . du veste Burg der ewigen Weisheit, du unerschöpfflicher Schatz Gottes. . . .*'

Spee's religious attitude is strictly catholic. To him all the world's voluptuous beauty rests in God. The three virtues, faith, hope, and charity, are His ways. Spiritual exercises, parables, and pious counsels should guide the erring soul which must first of all humble itself to mere nothingness by virtuous deeds till it is no more than a beggar, a *trodden worm*, a *stinking bat* clinging to the carrion of earthy lust, at which the angelic hosts shudder in horror. Only so can the soul at last attain salvation and divine love.

Spee's spiritual exercises are usually interspersed with verses of eight lines each, whose full value can only be estimated in relation to the doctrinaire prose which they accompany.

Not Cupid, but divine Eros, the *Jesusminne*, should quicken the heart:

*O Venus Kind, Du blinder Knab,*
*leg hin die Pfeil und Bogen. . . .*

This sacred song is based on a profane pattern. Its burden has been transferred to the person of Jesus, but without doing much to diminish the frivolous tone of the first three verses of the poem. As in the *Trutznachtigall*, the soul yearns for its bridegroom with long-drawn sighs; see the poem with twenty-nine verses:

*Ey dass nun jemand sagen köndt!*
*Auf welchem Weg und Strassen*
*Ich meinen liebsten Jesum fünd! . . .*

The *Jesusminne* is based on the mystic love and the *Compassio* of Bernhard of Clairvaux. In his *Eighty-six Sermones in Cantica Canticorum*, he speaks of the *unio mystica*, the *connubium spirituale.*

These were partly inspired by the Song of Songs, which since the days of Origen in the third century had been interpreted as the mystic love of the church (the bride) for God (the bridegroom). The seven songs of Arnulf von Löwen, which were once attributed to Bernhard, likewise prove another source of Spee's passion-lyrics.

It was not due to mere accident that seventeenth-century poets seem often to have turned to the Song of Songs. It had already played some part in the mysticism of the late Middle Ages as an expression of divine desire inhabiting the human soul. The age which laid so much stress on the Apocalypse also paraphrased the Song of Songs as the Virgin Mary's yearning for God, especially as Ambrose (fourth century) had beheld in Sulamit the Queen of Heaven. During the reformation, as for instance in Luther's *Brevis enarratio in Cantica Canticorum*, the *unio mystica* was given political sense. Here, in apparent imitation of St. Augustine's *De civitate Dei*, Sulamit is the embodiment of the flourishing state of Israel.

An influence of the Song of Songs on the profane German lyric can only be traced back as far as the seventeenth century, although the symbolic colours of rose and lily (cf. the Songs of Songs ii. 1: '*I am the rose of Sharon, and the lily of the valleys*') already attain importance in the poetry of courtly love and the folk-song. Even that love-poem, '*Dû bist mîn, ich bin dîn,*' recalls the Song of Songs (ii. 16, vi. 3: '*My beloved is mine, and I am his; he feedeth among the lilies*'). But a far-reaching interrelationship between the sacred and profane lyric is not noticeable before Opitz, or at any rate only shortly before him.

It was Opitz's aim to render his translation even more intelligible than its biblical prototype. Zesen's version was intended as melo-drama; Finckelthaus's, which appeared twenty years before Zesen's, attempted to reform the original in German alexandrines. Rinckart's *Alternating Choruses*, Quirinus Kuhlmann's ecstasies (*Liebesküsse*), and G. Arnold's *Lob- und Liebes-Sprüche* (1700) in which Sophia figures as the mystic bride of the Spirit, one and all contain motifs borrowed from the Song of Songs.

Through repeated treatment of the theme by these and by other poets (e.g. Sudermann, Dilherr, Harsdörffer, Beccau) the Cantica Canticorum attained great influence both over the spiritually edifying and the profane erotic poetry of the period. It is characteristic that the pastoral element (Psyche as shepherdess) is stressed where the tone is not expressly erudite or governed by the mannerisms of a verbal alchemy, such as Abraham von Franckenberg or Quirinus Kuhlmann in particular were wont to affect.

In an article on the '*Geheimnisvolles Triumph-Lied*' (printed in G. Arnold's *Göttlicher Liebesfuncken*, but actually the work of an unknown pupil of Jacob Böhme), E. Benz points to this peculiar verbal alchemy which arranges alphabetical letters and syllables in strange sequence according to a mystic code. Quirinus Kuhlmann's anagrams and his mystic interpretation of his own name are well known: *Kuhlmann*=*Kühlmann* (God who cools the evil-inflamed world), or *Kuhlmann* himself, who in his *Kühlpsalmen* quenches the satanic fire of the Kohlmann (the pope). The print itself plays an important part. Thus alphabetical letters may be transformed to numbers: *ex*=e*X*, or isolated they are shown to contain some strange significance, e.g. in Abraham von Franckenberg's work, *arcano* becomes *ArcanO*, with obvious reference to *A*(*lpha*) and *O*(*mega*).

The lyric poetry of Angelus Silesius (Johann Scheffler, 1624–1677) bears marked affinity to bridal mysticism and to the hymns on the Passion and Wounds of the Saviour. Scheffler came of a Breslau family which in the course of history had become Polish, but was now once more German. Scheffler's father had at the late age of sixty-two married a girl thirty-eight years younger than himself. Both parents died not very long after. The young poet made friends with Scultetus and Colerus (Köler), Opitz's first biographer, afterwards visiting Strassburg and Holland, the stronghold of the mystic sects of the Mennonites and the 'Collegiantes' and also of many a fervent religious freethinker. In 1647 Scheffler set out for Italy, a year later receiving the degree of doctor of medicine at the University of Padua. On his return to Silesia in 1649 the mystic writings of Jacob Böhme became his chief inspiration. The accidental values of life retreated before his ever-growing realization of the essential, to which he gave proverbial expression in the alexandrine couplets of the '*Cherubinischer Wandersmann*':

*Zufall und Wesen*:

*Mensch werde wesentlich; denn wann die Welt vergeht,*
*So fällt der Zufall weg, das Wesen das besteht.*

or *Du selbst musst Sonne sein*:

*Ich selbst muss Sonne sein, ich muss mit meinen Strahlen*
*Das farbenlose Meer der ganzen Gottheit malen.*

Scheffler's mystic inclinations were strengthened by the study of Eckhart, Tauler, Valentin Weigel, D. v. Czepko's *Monodisticha* and particularly Abraham von Franckenberg († 1652) who had been personally acquainted with Böhme. In 1653 Scheffler became a convert to the Roman Catholic church, an action comprehensible enough on the part of one whose faith felt trammelled by the rigid letter and biblical puritanism of the Protestant faith, and found kinship rather with the language of the Catholic mystics. A year later Ferdinand III awarded him the post of *kaiserlich-königlicher Hofmedikus* and in 1661 he was ordained priest, thereupon becoming so fanatic a persecutor of all heresy that even the official exponents of the counter-reformation recoiled at the violence of his zeal, which bore many a point in common with that of the Jesuits.

Scheffler's literary activity, however, dates from the time previous to his conversion. In 1657, the year in which the 1st edition of '*Cherubinischer Wandersmann*' was published, appeared also the '*Heilige Seelen-Lust oder . . . verliebte Psyche*,' a collection of poems not yet influenced by the Catholic church, but which give vent to a passionate yearning for the soul's union with God. Any direct dependence on Spee or above all on the *Pegnitz-Schäfer* has as yet not been traced, although a certain resemblance to the form and content of that tradition is remarkable:

*Cupido, blindes Kind,*
*Pack dich hinweg geschwind*
*Mit deinen Narrenpfeilen. . . .*

*Ich bin von Jesu wund*
*Und fühle noch zur Stund*
*Sein Feuer in mir brennen. . . .*

Scheffler's importance lies in the fact that as author of pious proverbs and songs he provides a bridge between the mysticism of the past and that of the coming pietism. The poems of this former Protestant now found a way into the Catholic hymnal, e.g. '*O Ewigkeit, O Ewigkeit . . .*'

The greatest of the Protestant hymn-writers was Paul Gerhardt (1607–1676), a native of Gräfenhainichen. His famous song: '*O Häupt voll Blut und Wunden . . .*' derives from a Latin source: *Salve caput cruentatum, totum spinis coronatum* by B. Claravallensis (twelfth century), and is simultaneously a spiritualized rendering of Hassler's song: '*Mein Gemüt ist mir verwirret*' (see *Kontrafakturen*). Gerhardt's poem, which contains ten verses, has two or rather three parts. Verses 1–4 describe the Passion and Death of Our Lord, verses 5–7 form the transition to the last two verses, which crave God's mercy for us poor sinners in the hour of our death. Although the poem is subjective in feeling it must be regarded rather as a communal hymn than an individualistic lyric. Duplicated expressions such as: *Blut-Wunden*, *Schmerz-Hohn*, *Ehr-Zier*, *schrickt-scheut*, give the song rhetorical breadth, but its decisive character is fashioned by the syntax which employs, particularly in verse 9, the triple repetition of *wann*. The intellectual conceits of verse 7 with their play on the word *Leben* betray the introspective, brooding nature of this poet, in whom passion, however, is restrained by formal parallels and a steady rhythm. Compare for instance Spee's restless crescendo of the words *lass ab*, repeated three times on top of each other, in his poem '*Ein kurzes poetisch Christgesang*.'

Paul Gerhardt knows how to combine his *subjective* emotions with the *objective* though unorthodox church-hymn. Of the latter baroque *Auflockerung* we had cause to speak when discussing the work of Gryphius.

Yet another product of Gerhardt's sojourn in Mittenwald, where for a few years he held the post of *Probst* previous to his appointment as deacon to the church of St. Nikolai in Berlin, is his '*Trostlied*' with its acrostic title: *Befiehl dem Herrn deine Wege, und hoff auf ihn. Er wird's wohl machen.* Its model was evidently provided by the fifth verse of the thirty-seventh psalm, which inspired religious poetry both before and after Paul Gerhardt's time; for instance, the songs of the Baron von Winnenburg, B. Schmolcke, or J. Olearius, though none of these attained Gerhardt's profundity.

Less long-winded and simpler in tone is the tranquil song on the peace of night which ends in that heartfelt prayer:

*Nun ruhen alle Wälder,*
*Vieh, Menschen, Städt und Felder,*
*Es schläft die ganze Welt;*
*Ihr aber meine Sinnen,*
*Auf, auf! Ihr sollt beginnen. . . .*

The horrors of death shall not trouble him who, absorbed in his faith in man's salvation through Jesus Christ, can care but little for earthly pleasures. The '*Fürstinn aller Nächte*' does not appear to Gerhardt, as she had to Stieler amidst alluring scenery. Rather she is to him the symbol of death that brings release, the path to the Beyond and to God.

# V

# AUFKLÄRUNG AND PIETISM

*The Aufklärung*

The baroque flauntings of German seventeenth-century literature were followed as we have seen by a reaction. This issued, however, not only from forces innate in the German genius, but was encouraged by foreign influence, namely the so-called *Aufklärung*, i.e. enlightenment, the *émancipation intellectuelle* or *secolo dei lumi*.

This movement was not really German but of alien origin, and derived inspiration particularly from England and France. It upheld reason as the absolute criterion, and in particular levelled its attacks against the privileges and prejudices of medieval orthodoxy. The state, economics, history and human life in general are all subjected to the infallible control of reason. This new philosophy of enlightenment which attained supremacy in Germany about the middle of the eighteenth century may be traced back to two main sources: on the one hand *rationalism*, which had its origin in France and whose system was applied in Germany, on the other *empiricism*, which was based on English philosophy and used the inductive method. The two movements resemble each other in their common repudiation of medieval dogmatic ecclesiastic authority, their exaltation of man's senses and intellect, and their belief in the progress of humanity and individual liberty founded on the idea of equal rights.

*Rationalism*, in contrast to *empiricism*, is not based on actual sense perception, but on rational understanding with the help of logic and mathematics. It demanded that reason should govern emotion and the elemental, incalculable and unconscious powers of life. Blinded by the light of reason men failed to see that an excess of logic lowers existence to a merely mechanical plane.

Moreover an increasing standardization of personality was not only alien both to the ideals set up by the renaissance and to those of the German race, but also to the mystic emotional essence of religion itself.

The German lyric in the age of *Aufklärung* (about 1700–1770) probably failed to reach poetic heights not only because the hour of its glory was yet to come, but because the irrational nature of the German genius was fundamentally opposed to the concepts of enlightenment. The latter over-accentuated the formal values and sought to combine principles historically and essentially opposed to one another, e.g. the law of the three unities (place, time, and action) which actually owed its origin to the conditions of the ancient Greek stage.

The father of enlightenment was Cartesius (Descartes) († 1650), who in his *Meditationes* foreshadowed modern materialism. Spinoza († 1677) had once more reconciled the gulf between spirit and matter which had been torn open by Descartes. This he achieved by accepting the evidence of a unified infinite substance. Descartes does not build his philosophy on facts, i.e. on the senses and corporeal existence, but he pins absolute faith in his doctrine: *Cogito, ergo sum.* He attempts to win to a clear realization of life through mathematics, according to deductive methods. The problem of cause and effect and the 'law of contradiction,' i.e. one and the same idea cannot signify simultaneously one thing and its opposite, are favourite axioms of his rationalistic system whose influence penetrated to Germany.

Whilst French rationalism sought to discover the *vérités de raison*, English empiricism set out in quest of the *vérités de fait*, thereby showing a predilection for science. Its roots may be discovered in Francis Bacon († 1626) and Hobbes († 1679), who by the use of the inductive method arrives at conclusions about sensual perception (*sensualism*) and problems pertaining to corporeal existence (*materialism*), ideas which exerted some little influence on the freemasonry of the period. J. Locke († 1704) derives his philosophy from that of Hobbes. His *Essay concerning human understanding* marks him as the founder of so-called psychological empiricism, which then finds its consummation in Hume. *Experience* supplies the basis of Locke's studies. He describes the inexperienced human soul as a *tabula rasa*, thus denying the

Cartesian concept of 'innate ideas.' His doctrine, *nihil est in intellectu quod non prius fuerit in sensu*, must be interpreted in this sense. Locke's liberal utilitarian attitude towards life, his belief in progress, are typical of this mode of philosophy. Voltaire, Montesquieu, Condillac, Bonnet, and Helvétius developed Locke's ideas yet further.

Shaftesbury († 1713) mitigated the starkness of egoistic materialism by his so-called *moral sensualism*, in which a pleasurable realization of beauty and good should blend with individualism to a harmonious unity. After Shaftesbury, D. Hume († 1776) directed special attention to the problem of instinctive emotion. Psychological questions began to arouse interest. To Hume also experience alone is of worth. According to him consciousness is a sum of perceptions gathered from experience and their relationship. Ideas have their corresponding place in our experience, but where there is any doubt as to this correspondence between impression and idea, as for instance in the problem of cause and effect, science must only speak of probabilities. This predilection for the concrete, for sensual observation strengthened man's sense of reality, as we see not only in the positivist and relativist philosophy of the English and in the European bourgeoisie of the period in general, but in the German *Aufklärungslyrik* itself. The soul's dependence on the body was now scientifically proved, an idea echoed in Diderot's, Fielding's and Smollett's descriptions of manners. A realization of the importance of sensual and emotional forces gradually gave rise to a profounder understanding of the imagination to which the work of the Swiss critics Bodmer and Breitinger bears witness, although it is here combined with the enlightened but obscure demand that the phantastic should appear possible. Further instances of appreciation of the imagination are supplied by the *Spectator*, but may be found already in Shaftesbury. A growing tendency towards clear perception remains supreme both in philosophy and literature. This in the case of lyric poetry may be proved by an inspection of the *Bremer Beiträge*.

A susceptibility to the irrational had been much furthered by G. W. Leibniz (1646–1716). His learning certainly betrays a decidedly logical substructure but simultaneously inclines strongly towards *German idealism*. For the supernatural, which was derided by the school of enlightenment, finds a place in Leibniz's attitude towards life as a superrational element. God, freewill, and other problems remain unsolved mysteries. Thus the irrational quality again plays its part in European philosophy. Knowledge and faith need thus no longer represent opposing forces. According to Leibniz's ideas, as promulgated in a treatise on the *correspondence of faith and reason* which he levelled against Bayle, our reason is a gift of God and a drop of the ocean of divine reason. Beginning with the principle that two truths cannot contradict each other, Leibniz proves a correspondence between cognition and faith. His *Théodicée* (*on the Goodness of God, Man's Liberty of Mind and the Origin of Evil*) is chiefly concerned with the apparent antithesis of faith and cognition. Evil is here displayed as the result of ignorance and prejudice.

Existence was once more held to possess unity. Thus about the middle of the century the bitterest and most enlightened 'enemies of pietism' found some friends amongst their rivals, whilst vice versa the pietists themselves were able to make converts of some of the intellectual free-thinkers.

By reason of his doctrine of the monads and the prestabilized harmony of the universe, Leibniz may be called the founder of a philosophy at once universally acceptable and yet truly German in its idealism. He therewith foreshadows many of the discoveries of his age, and seeks to weld French rationalism and English sensualism to a synthesis. He does not refute Locke's opinion regarding the importance of sensual elements, but he simultaneously acknowledges the existence of an *a priori* intellect. Nor does he believe only in one substance but in many monads, each of which mirrors the macrocosm. For instance, just as the sea is not reflected in the monad *seaman* in the same way as it is in the monad *wanderer* or *philosopher*, the whole world is likewise manifold in its phenomena, the highest monad being God Himself. The world rests at harmony *sub specie aeternitatis*. Not only through the ideas quoted above, but in many another sphere of knowledge, the author of the *Nouveaux essais* exerted a far-reaching influence on the intellectual life of Europe. He was a universal genius, a man of the world and a statesman who not only dedicated himself to philosophy or politics, but cultivated the study of law, physics, mathematics, geology, chemistry, etc., and likewise fought bravely to maintain the purity and dignity of the German language.

His intellectual legacy was, however, never fully appreciated until many years after his death when his works were at last able to appear in complete form. A mind less original yet of tremendous logic and systematic power was that of Christian Wolff († 1754), Leibniz's pupil. He popularized and tabulated his master's ideas, thus robbing them of their soaring flights and problematic intensity, but he thereby provided German *Aufklärung* with a universal philosophic system of purpose and comprehensible and 'sensible thoughts' which even attempted to bring phantasy within its bounds. Johann Christoph Gottsched (1700–1766), a pupil of Wolff, is well known on account of his prescription of morality and his demand of the three unities in *Versuch einer kritischen Dichtkunst vor die Deutschen; darinnen erstlich die allgemeinen Regeln der Poesie, hernach alle besonderen Gattungen der Gedichte, abgehandelt und mit Exempeln erläutert werden. Überall aber gezeigt wird, dass das Wesen der Poesie in einer Nachahmung der Natur bestehe* (1730). Both demands are alarming examples of the sovereignty of reason in the realm of poetry. (See *Krit. Dichtkunst*, IV, p. 21, X, p. 11, IV, p. 28, etc.)

As an instrument of erudition and comedy, the lyric poetry of the enlightened era appears as the true child of its age. But even Gottsched is not altogether lacking in sentiment. As a lyric writer he followed in the footsteps of the poets of the transition—Canitz, Besser, König, and Pietsch, whose praises he was so wont to sing. Gottsched led German verse into the sphere of concrete moral reality, that is to say he abandoned baroque virtuosities for a matter-of-fact description of the object. The contemporary pietist movement, though starting from a very different basis and with another aim in mind, tended likewise towards a more realistic concept of art.

*Pietism*

In contrast to the international nature of the *Aufklärung*, *pietism* may be called an essentially German movement, born already before the age of enlightenment, in fact shortly after the reformation. It, however, bears close relationship to the European religious revivals in general, reaping inspiration from the sentimental literature of England (Richardson, Young, Macpherson) and the French *Comédie larmoyante*. We have already referred to the period of transition from pietism to the *Aufklärung*. Where the lyric is concerned it is indeed not desirable to draw a sharp dividing line between *Aufklärung* and pietism, for reason itself must allow for a comparative emotional accent (*Herzenssprache*) in all poetry. Even the verse of the so-called enlightened is not without some warmth of feeling. It is thus only for the sake of clarity that we have sundered these two movements more sharply than actual fact demands. Leibniz's philosophy in particular proved a means of bridging or mitigating the apparently irreconcilable antithesis.

In his *Collegia pietatis*, P. J. Spener († 1705) gave utterance to a pietistic attitude towards life. With its erudite orisons it offered a strong appeal to the most various types of society. The pietist movement won much ground through the zeal of a theologian of the name of A. H. Francke († 1727), its particular stronghold being Halle, the town in which S. G. Lange and J. I. Pyra studied. Königsberg likewise ranked as a citadel of pietism through the literary activity of H. Lysius and F. A. Schulz.

The characteristically German features in this movement soon became evident. Its source may be found in mysticism and in the courtly minne-lyric. A veneration for the word of the Bible also points to affinities with the reformation, but its accentuation of subjective values inaugurates a new post-reformation world. The language is emotional to the point of ecstasy. Piety is felt to be a quality of the heart. We might almost see therein a revival of St. Augustine's doctrine, *noli foras ire*, but between him and Spener and Francke looms the shadow of Luther. It was in particular the orthodoxy of Luther's followers that drove the pietists to seek a more emotional form of religion. From here it is but a step to the profaner Promethean self-glorification of the 'storm and stress,' for pietism wallows not only in ascetic contemplation of Christ's Passion, but also in sensual ecstasies aroused by realization of divine forces in the human soul. The dead letter of dogma yields to the voice of the heart, which soon found passionate utterance in the *Hainbund* and the young *Stürmer*. Wieland, who belonged to the Swabian circle, was also early in his career influenced by the pietist movement. Profoundly moved by the mysteries and irrational ways of the human spirit, Klopstock was inspired to write the first chapters of his *Messias*. With young Goethe and his circle an affirmation of life, drawn from the roots of the heart, triumphantly bursts the fetters of enlightenment.

Spiritual exercises, communion with God and an expansive literature dealing with sermons and prayer (the latter still providing much scope for research) exerted a far-reaching influence both in the schools and domestic life of many a German province. Sensitive souls like that of the leader of the Herrnhuter, N. L. Graf von Zinzendorf, were thereby led into an extravagance of sickly sentiment. Pietist literature showed a peculiar vacillation between self-adulation and asceticism, between a piquant lust of life and worm-like humility, resulting from the acutely sentimental character of the pietist mentality which when expressing itself in secular form may definitely be termed *sentimentalism.* This apparently illogical dualism, which represents a striking trait of all literature of the period falling under pietist influence, seems to be reconciled only through the newly discovered religion of the heart of which we spoke above.

Much of this spiritual development is echoed in the language of Klopstock, Hamann and Goethe. The senses are now able to apprehend the Divine that moves within and around our being. They rejoice and yearn 'towards' (*entgegen*) the revelation of the mystery. Words such as *entgegen* (particularly in compounds), or *ganz*, *heilig*, which were much favoured by Klopstock, already appear in pietist literature. They point to a profounder spiritual attitude in poetry which rejects form for its own sake. A craving for confession encourages introspection (Hamann, Lavater, Fräulein von Klettenberg, and others). How deeply poetry, which had by now taken on a worldlier æsthetic guise, was rooted in these religious origins is proved by the works of Hamann. In his confessions he treads the path of complete self-negation in order to be ultimately raised from the dust through God's mercy. In a later chapter we shall discuss further developments of the movement. Of far-reaching importance to the lyric poetry on the threshold of the eighteenth century is the fact that a tendency towards spiritualization is simultaneously confronted by a realistic attitude towards the external world, significant of the spirit of enlightenment.

With Christian Weise (1642–1708) rationalism almost approaches banal humdrum actuality. The formal virtuosity of the baroque here gives way to a matter-of-fact sobriety. The only poetry of Weise really worth mentioning is his *Überflüssige Gedanken der grünenden Jugend* (1668), some of the convivial songs contained therein of a refreshingly robust and jovial tone. The second part of this collection and *Notwendige Gedanken der grünenden Jugend* (1675) sink to the level of moral didactic doggerel which often only differs from prose through its metre. Capricious wit, a certain homely humour and simple piety and the healthy rebuff he deals at the bombast and affectations of the Silesian school enable us to bear with Weise's dry schoolmasterly style as represented in the *Curieuse Gedanken von deutschen Versen* or in occasional theoretical expositions on his own verse. Nevertheless he remains the child of his age, and, in spite of his doctrine, betrays vestiges of baroque extravagance in his own poems. Thanks to the music J. S. Bach supplied to Weise's religious texts, such as the Passion according to St. John, the author of the *Bäuerischer Machiavellus*, the Faustian *Unvergnügte Seele*, and political didactic novels remains known to posterity.

Barthold Heinrich Brockes (1680–1747), a councillor of Hamburg, enjoys fame on account of his arias and his oratorio on the Passion (1712) which was set to music by Händel. A work of Brockes that is often mentioned but seldom read is his *Irdisches Vergnügen in Gott*, which consists of scientific and moralizing poems with musical accompaniment by J. K. Bachofen, and appeared periodically from the year 1721 onwards. These reflexions, which are often spread over several pages, suggest Leibniz's philosophy watered down for popular use. The world is thus divided into an infinite number of monads each of which can proudly boast that it contains the universe. Ignorance and ingratitude are the source of all evil:

*Aus unerkenntlichkeit kommt alle bosheit her.*
*Der beste Gottesdienst ist, sonder zweifel, der:*
*Wenn man vergnüget schmeckt, recht fühlt, riecht, sieht und höret,*
*Aus schaam, die laster hasst; aus liebe, Gott verehret.*

(*Die Welt.*)

Divine worship and edifying proofs of the purpose of life both in man and in nature provide the keynote of these poems. They are thus to be regarded as reflections on teleology in which the subjective element plays but little part.

The 'song' in the true sense of the word, i.e. as poetic self-expression, is as yet not found here. That Brockes's contemporaries still connected him with Opitz, Besser, Menantes, and even H. v. Hofmannswaldau, is proved by the anonymous *Sammlung auserlesener Gedichte* (1734), with its copperplate engraving showing a road leading to Parnassus, on whose summit these same poets appear enthroned in sublime bliss as the surest guardians against shame and bombast (*Schwulst*). Nevertheless Brockes's work was of epoch-making importance to the development of the modern German lyric during its gradual emancipation from the baroque style and transition to an as yet shallow descriptive lucidity. Even in Brockes's verse we may sometimes still discover baroque traits, for instance the 'registered' compilations of the names of fishes in his pedantic 'essay' on '*Das Wasser*,' or particularly in '*Die Nelken*.' The characteristic baroque antithesis, its *pointe* and melodious extravagance, are none the less entirely lacking. Brockes does not split the material world into atoms or, according to the manner of baroque verbal virtuosity, revel in an alluring play of relationships till each single attributive quality becomes autonomous and the object (e.g. moon, fountain, sun) loses its reality. His *Irdisches Vergnügen* marks a decided step in the direction of realism, even though nature is not yet fully valued as possessing innate artistic and expressive qualities, but is presented in long reflections on the glory of God. We here suggest a comparison between Rainer Maria Rilke's poem 15 Part I of the *Sonette an Orpheus* and Brockes's '*Die güldnen äpfel der Sinesen*' in his poem on a bowl of fruit. On rare occasions, however, religious fervour kindles his erudite verse, for instance '*Der Wolcken-und Lufthimmel*':

*Es schwingt sich mein geist in die sapphirne höhe,*
*Ich eil' ins firmament, ich fliege wie ein strahl*
*Durchs bodenlose meer . . .*

whilst his apotheosis of the sun, the gleaming ocean of joy, the lord of light, the monarch of all the ages, seems almost to foretell the soaring grandeur of Klopstock's and Schiller's odes.

But the major part of these long-winded verses provides no

more than moralistic and utilitarian information on the greatness and omnipresence of God. For this reason Brockes carefully arranges his material as a series of reflections on the time of the day and the seasons of the year, the individual months, the beauty of the sky, the clouds, sun, moon, air, fire, water, earth, all manner of flowers: hyacinth, lily, carnation, crowsfoot, ranunculus, delphinium, rose, crocus, sunflower, tulip, viola, etc.; fish, trees, grain, birds, and other creatures; and finally on the five senses and the good and evil in humanity itself.

It is these frequently mentioned senses—sight, scent, taste, hearing, feeling—that cause him to affirm nature. Thus the perceptive element did much to further the development of realism at this period, which upheld that our experience is culled through the senses. But on the whole Brockes regards the world from the standpoint of a sensible pious gardener who in reverence to the Creator has an eye even for the smallest of His works. The heroic element is utterly lacking in his fundamentally moralizing verse. Brockes invokes the usefulness of creation, not the hero who set up laws for himself and the world. His style is matter-of-fact and often philistine in its pedantry. He delights in the comfort of his home and praises God's benevolence whilst the icy north wind rages without. He spends endless time and care in trying to explain the significance of fire through which our food is rendered palatable. How contentedly he describes his '*Winter-Vergnügen im Zimmer*' and all that he sees, feels, hears, smells and tastes in nature. In his poem '*Die Luft*' he does not fail to inform us minutely about atmospheric pressure, the weather, the circulation of the air. Astronomical and geological expositions in honour of God betray the 'enlightened' author. He knows all about the habits of man and beasts in spring and other seasons of the year. His exceedingly dry poem '*Majus*' reveals the true pedant:

*Ach schmeckt in kräutern, im spinat,*
*Im spargel, hopfen und salat*
*So mancherley blutreinigende kraft,*
*So manchen angenehmen saft.*

What a vast gulf separates these lines from those of Goethe's '*Mailied*'! His wordy poem '*Der Regen*' is another characteristic example of common-sense verse for the use and edification of the public, to which Arno Holz's naturalistic poem on the rain, '*Draussen die Düne*,' presents the most striking contrast.

How continuously Brockes reminds us that whilst regarding nature pious parables flit into his mind. Flowers in particular suggest symbols to him. The lily's drooping head warns him to avoid excess, the violets of March are an emblem of humanity. He compares the red strawberry to a ruddy cheek. The spirit of a flower does not, as for instance in Weinheber's '*Blumenstrauss*,' become an individual metaphor. It is the relationship of all things to their Creator which forms the burden of Brockes's meditations. Nevertheless he taught the Germans to regard nature once again with open eyes. The exactitude of some of his observations, as for instance the lines in his poem on the moon, '*Der Mond*,' may almost be said to anticipate impressionism.

In contrast to Brockes, the Silesian poet J. Christian Günther (1695–1723) of Striegau causes the German lyric to soar high above the prosaic plane of enlightenment, and at the same time foreshadows Klopstock, and like Brockes frees himself from the baroque, although vestiges of the latter style still appear in his public occasional verse and religious songs. When Günther allows his feelings full play the subjectivity of his emotion outrivals even that of Gryphius, and is indeed unique in the German verse of the period. In his '*Abschied aus seinem Vaterlande*' which he dedicated to his father he proudly exclaims:

*Was die Poesie betrifft, muss ich frey heraus bekennen:*
*Ich empfand schon als Kind ihren Trieb im Herzen brennen.*

His poetic inclination became the supreme passion of his life, the sole means by which existence was rendered endurable. Intrepid of heart he accepts envy's sting and fortune's whim. The rebellious genius of a great personality stirs in his veins. The tragedy of Günther's premature death is enhanced by his heroic struggle against the doom that entangled him, and which he faced with noble fortitude to the end. The legend about his dissipated genius has been proved false by W. Krämer's critical edition of Günther's works. The editor discusses what he considers to have been the guiding forces of the poet's life: Leonore, Ovid, Job, Leibniz, Wolff, and Prince Eugen, or, interpreted as abstract qualities: love, wisdom, God, heroism, and sovereignty. Günther feels like Job beaten by the rod of the Lord. Nevertheless, he raises himself from his dejection through Leibniz's philosophy of the world's harmony; cf. '*Der sich selbst tröstende und befragende Redliche*' and '*Ich lernte nach und nach den Wert des Maro schätzen und frass fast vor Begier, was Wolf und Leibniz setzen.*'

Apparent reminiscences of pietism in his poetry are due to tradition and thus not external to his genius, for his tremendous individualism is not levelled against the world of the senses, but aims rather at self-affirmation. Since Walther's and Wolfram's day no poet had with such faith regarded his art and personality as a mission. This defiance in the face of society, this pride of the true artist as reflected in a poet who belongs neither to the court nor the bourgeoisie, are traits that herald in a new literary era.

He consecrates his work to Heros and Hellas, and not only personal dislike but a sincere antibaroque yearning for Hellenic ideals caused him to hurl barbed words at artistic barbarism and sham. His rival (T. Krause) appeared to him the despicable charlatan whom he often portrays under the name of Crispin in his biting satires. Günther's *Klagelieder*, many of them in rhymed metrical prose, are pitiless in their unsparing revelation of man's weakness, for the poet refuses to howl with the wolves whether at the court or amongst the stolid burghers; cf. '*Bussgedanken über den Zustand der Welt*,' '*Schreiben an Madame* (*Kluge*),' etc. Driven by poverty Gunther was forced to resort to hackwork, but even here he conquered humiliation by adopting the heroic vein, as in his ode on Prince Eugen or in the heart-rending penitence of his '*Bussgedanken*,' written at the close of his life and which end with the words 'a noble death is life's best path.'

The *Eugen Ode*: '*Eugen ist fort. Ihr Musen nach . . .*' is more than an opportune poem written on the occasion of the peace of Passarowitz (1718). It is a sincere liberation of the poet's feelings, and this first truly great heroic ode in the German tongue is rooted in Günther's own spiritual development. Certainly we may discover therein a lack of formal smoothness, but this is largely due to the style of the ode itself, which is modelled on Pindaric and Horatian lines. The classic age, Homer, Ovid, Caesar, the high priests offering in the temple, the Roman army, the Hellenic people, are constantly referred to, now by way of comparison, now as witness or a spur to heroism. Pathos and rhetoric are, however, happily mingled with robust realism and vital description, particularly in such lines as: '*Dort spitzt ein voller Tisch das Ohr. . . .*' This passage concerning *Nachbar Hans* has a striking parallel in Ovid's first heroic epistle: '*Pingit et exiguo Pergama tota mero*,' but its peculiarly natural tone is a rare phenomenon during Günther's period (cf. Krämer's edition IV).

To have proved popular, this ode on the hero whose sword-thrust brings victory at one blow would have had to be decidedly curtailed. Likewise the mixture of epic and lyric would have required purging of its classic trappings and the rhetoric over which Günther with his partiality for anaphora possesses such command. Nevertheless the ode aroused much interest, and certain parts of it still have power to affect the modern reader, particularly the description of the battlefield and the joyful return of the victors. In spite of its passionate context, this long poem of fifty verses numbering ten lines each is clearly constructed, opening significantly with the word *Eugen*. The first part (one hundred and fifty lines) invokes the souls of the classic age and hurls derision at the Turks. The following hundred and fifty lines introduce scenes from contemporary life: the soldier's return and Günther's own joy in nature. The poet's judgment-sentence on the enemy leads to the third part with its vision of coming days and an incitement to new deeds. The conclusion is an apotheosis on Eugen and the emperor Charles VI, ending with the customary poetic *captatio benevolentiae*.

The high-hearted tone, the originality of the language and the *furor poeticus* encased in all too strict a form win Günther the honour of being unquestionably the inaugurator of the 'heroic ode' at the end of the baroque period to which he still partly belongs. Nevertheless we can scarcely follow Krämer in his avowal that Günther was the first to present a woman (Leonore) as an objective personality, for already the works of Paul Fleming not only reveal instances of a similar antibaroque attitude towards woman, but as we have noted Fleming tears aside the veil of fragmentary illusion, and when at his best aims at a unified creative conception of the concrete world; see also p. 70.

Günther, the author of the far-famed students' song:

*Brüder, lasst uns lustig sein,*
*Weil der Frühling währet . . .*

which was inspired by *Gaudeamus igitur*, was renowned as a writer of convivial verse, as his songs of comradeship and less anacreontically flavoured *divertimenti* can well make us believe, but at the same time he remained the champion of the poet's inviolable liberty. Now and again he seems to approach the tone of the youthful Goethe. Promethean defiance resounds through his verses to Leonore. The figure of Günther stands isolated against a background of common faith and tradition. Herein particularly lies one of the greatest differences between him and the typical seventeenth-century poets. Likewise his attitude to death reveals his yearning for the new humanity which will be ruled alone by the dictate of the heart. Günther dedicated his genius first and foremost to life with the passion of one who already feels death in his veins.

Another outstanding personality is the Swiss scholar and poet Albrecht von Haller (1708–1777). He was influenced by Brockes, though a comparison between the two men proves that Haller showed far the greater inclination for profane subjects. In place of Brockes's utilitarian praise of nature, Haller like Günther attacks profound problems, especially those appertaining to culture, to society and the individual city and country life. His contemplative lines, '*Über den Ursprung des Übels*' (1734), suggest reminiscences of Leibniz's *Théodicée.* His earnest mind and poetically passionate treatment of abstract subject-matter carry him far above Brockes's level. In Haller's eyes God created a perfect world, but the path to evil was opened, for He wanted no obedient mechanism, no will-less creatures. Each one of us is of equal value according to his nature. Once upon a time we were all happy and innocent; but, alas, idolatry of the flesh, of gold, lust and ambition, has made us our own hangmen, and we remain oblivious of the fact that our world is but a grain of sand in the ocean of heaven and all creation is due to God's grace.

Thoughts on salvation through Our Lord's death to which these ideas naturally lead were intended as a conclusion to the poem, but much to Haller's regret they were never carried out. Nevertheless his rhetoric touches the sublime and at moments conjures up glorious images, such for instance as that of the sun shining on the mountains:

*Auf jenem Teiche schwimmt der Sonne funkelnd Bild*
*Gleich einem diamanten Schild,*
*Da dort das Urbild selbst vor irdischem Gesichte*
*In einem Strahlenmeer sein flammend Haupt versteckt.*

Five years earlier Haller had sung praises on the beauty of the Alps ('*Alpen,*' first edition 1732) in ten-line alexandrine verses full of finely tempered rhetoric and enthusiasm, inspired by a journey to mountainous regions in the summer of 1728. Till then the Alps had been an undiscovered realm both for sportsman and poet. Meditations on the curse of civilization and the destruction of the peasants' simple bliss, prepared the reader for Rousseau (1712–1778) whom Haller here foreshadows. For, like the Frenchman, the Swiss poet in his '*Alpen*' recalls the Golden Age when abundance, peace, and purity ruled the world. External pleasures can never bring us the contentment which only the dwellers of the Alps can still enjoy. They are denied satiety, but are recompensed by the tranquillity that comes of moderation. They are untouched by class hatred, idleness and ambition. This wistful picture of the life and habits of the communal life of the Alpine people during the various seasons of the year is followed by a eulogy on Switzerland. The finale of this instructive poem awakens faint reminiscences of Horace's '*Beatus ille qui procul negotiis paterna rura bobus exercet suis*':

*O selig, wer wie ihr mit selbst-gezognen Stieren*
*Den angestorbnen Grund von eignen Ackern pflügt. . . .*

Not only Schiller, who perhaps more than any other German classic writer bore some natural affinity to such a contemplative temper, but even Klopstock and Goethe were able to turn to Haller as a prototype. A case in point is provided by a certain passage in Haller's *Falschheit menschlicher Tugenden:* '*Ins Inn're der Natur dringt kein erschaffner Geist, zu glücklich, wann sie noch die äuss're Schale weis't,*' with its anticipation of *Faust* ('*Geheimnisvoll am lichten Tage*').

Notwithstanding its loaded rhetoric Haller's most famous poem is probably an elegiac ode on Mariane ('*Soll ich von deinem Tode singen*') written in 1736, the year which robbed him of his wife. From that time on his muse forsook him almost completely and the poet who had won renown at so early an age dedicated himself to scholarship. His publications on botany, geology, physiology, anatomy and practical medicine, added to countless reviews in the *Göttinger Gelehrten Anzeiger*, brought him universal fame as professor first in Göttingen and later in Bern. The academies of Italy, Denmark, Russia and the Swedish government showered honours upon him. England sought to find favour with him. Shortly before his death he received a visit from the emperor Joseph II. But above all, following Günther, Haller deserves the credit of having enriched the German lyric with noble images.

Friedrich von Hagedorn (1708–1754) appears by contrast as a light-hearted creature who paved the way for the development of German anacreontic verse. Again it is the periphery of the country, Hamburg, which now at the close of the baroque period gives birth to new forces whose influence flows towards central Germany. But even Hagedorn is closely bound to the past, as we can see from his poetry and his introduction to his own odes and songs, in which he spends such praise on Gryphius, Pietsch, König, Besser, and others. His verse (e.g. '*An die Dichtkunst*') is not born of the heart, but is still a playmate in idle hours, though a comforter in sorrow, bringer of joy and the herald of noble thoughts. His rational man-of-the-world character prevented him from abandoning himself to the virtuosities of the anacreontic style, just as it saved him from Haller's melancholy. Poised midway between earnestness and frivolity Hagedorn developed the natural sincere manner, the magically lucid style, so characteristic of his personality. Ease and surety made him a true poet of convivial life who nevertheless by no means lacks depth. His '*Ode an die Freude*':

> '*Freude, Göttin edler Herzen,*
> *Höre mich!*
> *Lass die Lieder, die hier schallen,*
> *Dich vergrössern, dir gefallen!*
> *Was hier tönet, tönt durch dich . . .*'

exults in almost bacchanal recklessness. Its literary prototype may perhaps be found in Weckherlin's '*Drunckenheit.*' But Schiller was to be the first to inebriate the heart with a joy almost divine which rang out beyond the boundaries of class and nationality to swell to a full-throated hymn of brotherhood.

Unforgettable are Hagedorn's fables which exerted so strong an influence on young Gellert. Being a protoform of poetry the fable, as a poetic genre, is closely related to the humorous tale, and anecdote, the riddle, and the proverb. The 'enlightened' writers were particularly addicted to this genre both on account of its *pointe* and its moralistic character. But in their very hands the art of the fable suffered a great decline, as we see in Lessing's theoretic reflections which reduce the fable to a concise intellectual formula. Whereas his frequently dry stories only manage to survive today in dull schoolbooks, Hagedorn's '*Johann der Seifensieder*' or '*Der Fuchs und der Bock*' still live on in the mouth of the people. For here the moral element is clad in a palpable image through which the poet with artistic cunning suddenly reveals the world of human frailty. The fable indeed was Hagedorn's true province, in which he often surpasses the all too elegantly formal wit of his forerunner La Fontaine.

### *Anacreontic Poetry—Gleim, Gellert and their Circle*

The collection of the late Greek anacreontic poems which were first published by Henricus Stephanus under the title Ανακρέοντος Τηΐου μέλη (1554) furthered the so-called anacreontic movement. France, England, and Germany competed in an imitation of this poetry, unconscious of the fact that it was not the work of Anacreon himself. In Germany under Hagedorn it became popular at the beginning of the eighteenth century, but he imitated Horace's *Nil admirari* rather than the Greek bard. Its influence continued until the time of Goethe, whose song '*Kleine Blumen, kleine Blätter*' is the flower of the German anacreontic. It is seldom realized that even the very emotional verses of '*Mignon*' (written before 1784) still show traces of the anacreontic style: gentle breezes, myrtle and laurel, cave and dragon. The poem moreover recalls Thomson's *Seasons*: '*With deep orange glowing through the green.*' However Gleim, not Goethe, was the faithful champion of this poetic manner which exhausted itself in repetition of the same theme.

Twenty years after Klopstock's '*Rosenband*' (1753) there appeared in Halberstadt a small book of one hundred and forty-four pages with the title '*Phantasien nach Petrarkas Manier,*' which can be called one of the most characteristic examples of anacreontic verse, and on this account deserves further notice here. The author, Klamer Eberhard Karl Schmidt, refers to verses which Gleim had inscribed in his copy of Petrarch with a note to the effect that they had inspired him to produce the poems: '*Herr C. Gleim an den Verfasser, in einen geschenkten Petrarch geschrieben*:

> '"*Werd" uns Petrarch, Amintas; es zu werden,*
> *Hast du das Herz, hast du den Geist:*
> *Nur Laura fehlet. . . .*'

But Schmidt assures Gleim that he is content with his humble lot. His talent is very limited and a suspicion of philistinism is occasionally noticeable. The poet asserts his virtue—a feature common to the German anacreontic poets of this circle:

> *Mit behender Zärtlichkeit*
> *Würde Minna dann mich pflücken,*
> *Und an einen Busen drücken,*
> *Den noch nie mein Blick entweiht.*

The *Phantasien* are entitled *Kleine Schwärmereien*, *Kleinigkeiten*, such terms being intended to lay still more stress on the modest pretensions of these short poems. Schmidt probably had in mind the *parva monumenta* of Catullus or Lessing's '*Kleinigkeiten*' (1751) when he called his poetry *klein*. We also find that a great selection of thoughts, images, and figures find the same application in Petrarch's works as in Schmidt's. But it is not always a case of direct borrowing, since the German anacreontic writers often take the same forms from French *salon* poetry, partly from the Italian, and occasionally directly from the old anacreontic writers.

The fifth poem in the *Phantasien*: '*An seine Geliebte, als sie ein Veilchen pflückte*,' forces one almost involuntarily to a comparison with Goethe's '*Veilchen*,' but in Goethe's poem the accidental is raised to a symbol and by this means the poem is endowed with lasting worth. Schmidt is engrossed in personal emotion and cannot raise it to universal significance. All the same this poem is one of his best; it is pervaded by a delicate fragrance, and in part distinguished by pure sentiment unadorned by anacreontic images. But rhyme and language have still a somewhat strange glitter; above all, the closing stanza is very similar in expression to pastoral poetry. There is no trace of any imitation of Petrarch.

In form and frequently in subject-matter Schmidt joins forces with the so-called anacreontic school of Gleim. Prose and verse often alternate. This *genre mêlé* is a favourite device of the anacreontic epistle; as is indeed the accentuation of affected modesty. What impresses us especially is the *kleine Manier* mentioned above, and of which the language of Gleim and Schmidt provides countless examples. The word *zärtlich* is repeated until it becomes a mannerism. *Klein* is an indispensable epithet, *Seufzer* are heavenly blessings, *Tränen* flow ceaselessly. The poet is in a constant state of rapture (*Entzücken*). Likewise we meet with the repeated use of words such as *sanft*, *weich* or *leise* and especially *schön* and *süss*. The *Muse* replaces the poet's *Ego*. Names from mythology and idyllic poetry: Daphne, Diana, Ulysses, etc., are met with frequently. These ancient figures, called into life by the renaissance, are united with the allegory of the Middle Ages and the baroque. Abstractions are personified. Smiles, tears, eyes are introduced in the dialogue. The love motif is dominant. *Cupid* plays an important part as a symbolic figure. He basks in the eyes of the beloved, is mirrored in her tears, lies mockingly in the poet's heart and wounds with his bright arrows. Favourite anacreontic themes in Gleim's poetry, and especially in Schmidt's *Phantasien*, are descriptions of the beloved: 'Death of his beloved,' 'His beloved's eyes,' 'Her feet,' 'The beloved plays the harp,' 'What is love,' and so on.

Anacreontic poetry belongs partly to the pastoral genre. It favours expressions such as: *schäferlich*, *Schäfer*, *Hain*. The boundary between anacreontic and pastoral poetry is often undefined, especially in regard to nature. The poetical use of nature is formal. In descriptions of nature, the small and charming points of a landscape are preferred to the overpoweringly gigantic, e.g. *Quelle*, *Bach*, *Schatten*. The adjective 'silvery' ('silvery clouds, silvery stream') is often used. Cypresses, hills, meadows, fields, 'may-clouds' and stars also belong to the make-up of anacreontic poetry. The images and similes are extravagantly sprinkled with flowers, especially the rose. The animal world is represented by the dove, the lamb, but above all by Philomela, the nightingale.

In many cases the anacreontic poems become pure affectation, devoid of any personal note. This impression of artificiality is increased still more through improbable similes and exaggerated images.

J. W. Gleim (1719–1803) was undoubtedly the most important exponent of this trifling school of poetry in Germany. As secretary to the Chapter, and later as canon, at Halberstadt Cathedral he gathered around him a large circle of anacreontic poets, with whom were associated contributors to the *Bremer Beiträge*, such as Klopstock, Wieland, and indeed most representatives of contemporary German literature. Gleim certainly had a right to pride himself on his *Temple of the muses and of friendship*, the name he bestowed on his spacious reception-room, whose walls he embellished with the portraits of his numerous literary friends and admirers, amongst them several promising poets who were ultimately destined to eclipse him. Today the 'temple' is a museum frequented by student and tourist.

Gleim's thirst for companionship brought him for purely personal reasons a following also amongst political circles and Frederick II actually honoured him with an audience. Gleim had given vent to a eulogy on the Prussian king in his '*Preussische Kriegslieder von einem Grenadier*' (1757 ff.), which were rhythmically based on the pattern of *Chevy Chase*. Patriotic fervour kindles these songs, which may well rank amongst the best poems written in celebration of the Seven Years War, even though they are wanting in æsthetic perfection and lack both the personal and the truly popular tone. Imitations were quick to follow, e.g. C. F. Weisse's tasteless '*Amazonen-Lieder*' and Heinrich Wilhelm von Gerstenberg's '*Kriegslieder eines königlich dänischen Grenadiers*,' Lavater's '*Schweizerlieder*,' etc.

Frederick the Great also found a female encomiast in Anna Luisa Karsch—the 'German Sappho,' a popular rhymestress who is to be numbered amongst Gleim's acquaintances.

From these patriotic and artistic heights, Gleim's poetry all too soon reverted to the frivolous toyings of the anacreontic, which had received a new lease of life through Uz's and Götz's translation of Anacreon's original odes. Of these two friends who had once been fellow students of Gleim in Halle, Uz, as a perusal of his erudite poem '*Théodicée*' must prove, was certainly the more talented. As metaphysical poet he stands midway between Haller and Schiller.

Gleim's friendship also inveigled the Pommeranian aristocrat Ewald Christian von Kleist into the anacreontic mania. Ten years before he was mortally wounded at Kunersdorf appeared the first canto of his epic poem in hexameters '*Der Frühling*' (1749), which won the praises of Herder and Schiller. It was destined to remain a fragment. In addition to the influence of Thomson's *Seasons* which E. von Kleist only knew in Brockes's rather poor translation we may recognize that of Haller, both in regard to Kleist's language and to his ideas. Though himself a friend of Kleist's the incorruptible Lessing did not fail to criticize the *Frühling's* lack of unified action which neither alluring detail nor lyric descriptions of nature could hide. E. von Kleist does not betray the sharp perception that we find, for instance, in Arno Holz's description of spring in '*Phantasus*,' where the words *dort* and *jetzt* produce the illusion of an actual happening in its irrevocable momentary immediacy. Kleist keeps to generalizations. His language is as powerful as his imagery. Horses rove the forest, bulls dash past: '*Aus ihrer Nasen raucht Brunst, sie spalten mit Hörnern das Erdreich, und toben im Nebel von Staub*.'

Another adherent of Gleim's circle was gentle J. Georg Jacobi, to whose journal *Iris* (1774 ff.) Goethe contributed. Jacobi's younger brother Frederick was, on account of his sentimental novel *Woldemar*, forced to suffer the well deserved derision of Goethe.

In 1757, the year in which Gleim first invoked his warlike muse in the '*Preussische Kriegslieder*,' Christian Fürchtegott Gellert (1715–1769) published his '*Geistliche Oden und Lieder*' which in their frequent sentimentality appealed to the pietist inclinations of the age. These religious doctrinal poems have little in common with the fervent utterance of the reformation; likewise they avoid the ecstatic note of the mystic's *Jesusminne*, though Gellert strikes a far warmer tone than the rational-minded Gottsched and his followers. As he himself explains in his foreword, Gellert here attempts to arouse emotion in the reader's heart and steep it in the beauty of the Protestant religion. He had dreamed of transfusing the intellectual burden of these poems with an expressive feeling which his mild bourgeois morality could, alas, never kindle. Fundamentally he still owed much to 'enlightenment.' In the latter sense he drew up a table of rules for the composition of religious verse; 'it must possess a universal comprehensibility that nurtures reason.' Poetry should speak to the heart rather than to the imagination, whose splendid images all too easily lose contact with the common language of life (reason) and the sublime simplicity of the Holy Scriptures. Both from a theoretical and practical point of view the duality, reason and emotion, in the *Oden fürs Herz* and the *Lehroden* is expressed in a strictly intelligible form. Six of these odes were given a pianoforte accompaniment by Beethoven, e.g. '*Gott, deine Güte reicht so weit.*'

In the poetry of Gellert, the ramparts of the *Aufklärung* were certainly undermined, though they still afford a definite boundary soon to be stormed and finally demolished beneath the onslaught of the next generation.

Already, on the publication of Breitinger's *Critische Dichtkunst* and Bodmer's *Critische Abhandlung von dem Wunderbaren in der Poesie* (1740), Gottsched's star began to wane. Nevertheless even these rival forces from Switzerland (notwithstanding their fruitful influence on young German genius) betray their dependence on enlightenment when they demand of the poet sane reason, 'the compass of the imagination,' as a warrant of poetic probability. The weakly, somewhat querulous Gellert had a similar concept of poetry. Yet on the threshold of the 'storm and stress' he ranked as perhaps the most popular force in German literature, and his fame as a writer of fables spread far beyond the limits of his native land. It was moreover with Gellert that German literature began to achieve international fame. His generous-hearted leniency and universally intelligible fables won him many followers. The modest, pampered professor of philosophy at the *alma mater Lipsiensis* was much sought after as mentor and correspondent. His words cast a spell on his readers and on his students, to whom he imparted his knowledge with kindly bearing and in simple terms. Frederick the Great called him the most sensible of all German scholars.

Gellert also enjoyed friendly relations with the Saxon partisans of the *Bremer Beiträge* (1744–1748), though he never broke with Gottsched in the manner of his comrades. Amongst the latter were

K. C. Gärtner, Johann Andreas Cramer, the editor of the weekly journal the *Nordischer Aufseher*, the promising dramatist and critic Johann Elias Schlegel, and Johann Adolf Schlegel, father of the two 'romantic' brothers. Further, Johann Arnold Ebert, who translated Young's *Night Thoughts* in 1751, Justus Friedrich Wilhelm Zachariä, the satirist Gottlieb Wilhelm Rabener, Nikolaus Dietrich Giseke and others. Klopstock also, from whom Gellert became ever more estranged and whose genius put all the others in sudden eclipse, belonged to this literary circle.

VI

# FRIEDRICH GOTTLIEB KLOPSTOCK

(1724–1803)

LOOKING back on the forerunners of the classic era of German literature we must come to the conclusion that it is wrong to suppose that Klopstock was the first to introduce a passionately lyric note and a lofty religious attitude towards nature into German poetry. But in more than one sense Klopstock may certainly be considered the champion of a new epoch. He is the spiritual descendant of Pindar, the poet of the sublime style, and as such he foreshadows Hölderlin and Stefan George. Until Klopstock's day the New High German poet had enjoyed neither rank nor dignity, and could practise his art only as a side-line. The poet who was not blessed with worldly possessions suffered utter destitution. But Klopstock in all the proud surety of his genius held his own against the ruling forces of society. Never since the days of Wolfram von Eschenbach and Walther von der Vogelweide had a German poet (with the exception of Christian Günther) felt so strongly the ennobling glory of creative power. Never before, not even at the time of the minnesong, had a member of bourgeois society felt his poetic talent as a divine mission. Never before had a sublime subject like the '*Messias*' been treated with such poetic fire. Even seen against the horizon of the future, Klopstock's fame remains inviolable, though his epic is to the modern generation little more than a landmark in literary history. For with his birth the hour of Germany's entry into literary glory had struck. Klopstock freed poetry from the straitjacket of convention, from the limitations of the accidental, and endowed it with the sincerity of profound personal experience. If his life's work may be judged in the light of a creative protest to break down the barriers of form and emotional constraint, that of Stefan

George in the '*Blätter für die Kunst*' (1892 ff.) conversely appears as a battle waged against formlessness both of mind and art. George once more demanded the binding power of rhyme. Both, however, meet on common ground in their yearning to endow poet and poetry with the element of the sublime.

In the tenth book of '*Poetry and Truth*' Goethe describes Klopstock's genius in the happy hour of its ascendancy: 'Everything converged in Klopstock to create such an epoch.' These words betray Goethe's unbounded admiration for the older poet, and this in spite of the fact that Klopstock's moral admonitions in a letter written to Goethe in 1776 might justly have aroused his rancour and acrimony. The author of the '*Messias*' and the so-called *enthusiastic odes* was the first to give German poetry, which had already attained a certain freedom from the emotional point of view, true grandeur and power. His poetry was passionately religious. The eruptive force of its emotion was bound to have a violent effect on the reader. Klopstock became the prophet of the divinely fervent heart.

The verse-form he chose was essentially German in its tense vitality which followed the bounding curve of Klopstock's fervour in phrases now long, now short, now wide, now narrow. Even the hexameter takes on a German guise, as Klopstock explains in his fragment, '*Über Sprache und Dichtkunst.*' His hexameter has often something rugged and sharp, the sublime standing in immediate juxtaposition to the sweetly gentle. This type of metre thus appears by no means alien to the German genius. Many a poet had tried his hand at it already at the close of the Middle Ages, particularly, however, in the sixteenth (Fischart) and in the seventeenth centuries. The results had, however, sounded so unnatural that Schottelius and others opposed such experiments. Gottsched once more took up the dactylic six-beat metre. Thus Klopstock cannot be said to have inaugurated the adoption of the antique heroic verse, but he was the first to reconcile it with the spirit of the German language. But for him Goethe's '*Hermann und Dorothea,*' '*Reinecke Fuchs,*' or Schiller's six-foot dactyls, or ultimately Platen's verse, could never have been composed. Prior to Klopstock we find J. I. Pyra, whose premature death fell in the year 1774, and S. G. Lange († 1781). Their poems, '*Thirsis und Damons freundschaftliche Lieder*' (1745), vainly attempt a synthesis of Christianity and classic paganism, but their solemn fervour nevertheless seems to foreshadow something of Klopstock's odes. In the latter, the German renaissance at last finds its consummation after a century-long struggle to reconcile antithetical ideals. Herein lies Klopstock's momentous significance for German literature. Klopstock's German hexameter is not based on quantitative metre, but adapts itself to the nature of German verse, and thus at times completely ignores the difference between dactylic and free rhythm. As the founder of German free verse Klopstock soon won many an imitator, amongst them that sincerely passionate admirer of Frederick the Great, Karl Wilhelm Ramler (1725–1798), author of '*Triumph*,' an ode written in what may almost be called free verse. Frederick is here hailed as *Prinz der Brennen*, in the *bardic* manner of the period. Klopstock himself was acclaimed the passionate bard of this movement.

In his attempts at free verse Klopstock is directly dependent on Pyra and Lange, though he travels far beyond their range. Pyra's fight against rhyme was not founded on principle but directed against the stylistic flatness of Gottsched's school, which he sought to replace by noble pathos and variety of form. In this manner Pyra and Lange of Halle freed the German iambic metre from the trammels of the caesura and enjambement. Gleim, on the other hand, adopted rhymeless style for no other reason than that of its greater ease. Pyra's and Lange's versification can hardly be called free rhythm in the full sense of the word, but Lange's translation of the Psalms (1746) adopts a mixed rhythm which certainly appears as a first step towards a truly emancipated style.

Klopstock follows in Pyra's wake. As we have seen, he was not exactly the originator of German free verse, but he was the first true genius to adopt the form. In contrast to Lange, Klopstock favours the falling rhythm; he uses enjambement, and thus is not so much influenced by classic literature but gathers inspiration rather from the Psalms. His ambition was to become not a German Horace, but a German David. Herein he far excels Pyra, though he did not, like Herder, possess a historic attitude towards literature. He thus failed to realize immediately the fruitlessness of such imitations, which could have no other advantage than that of providing a means of developing originality of style. The perfection of the natural German idiom was not achieved till Goethe, and his immediate source was not Klopstock but Herder, who recommended him Klopstock's free verse as a model. Of course Goethe was concerned only with the earlier forms of Klopstock's verse. For after 1764 the poet of the '*Messias*' arranged his free rhythms in apparent patterns of four lines each, just as Goethe himself was wont to do, though the latter was herein guided more by an instinctive feeling for harmony, whereas Klopstock tended to apply a formula.

We should already at this juncture point to an essential difference between Goethe and Klopstock, namely the former's emotional language and the latter's imagination. Klopstock's frequent conditional phrases and phantastic imagery afford a pronounced antithesis to the work of Goethe whose '*Künstlers Morgenlied*' must rank as an exception amongst his works. Whereas Goethe strives towards greater reality Klopstock forsakes the earth for the realm of the abstract. His is the language of profound religious emotion uttered in praise of God. Even in moments of bounding earthly vitality, as in his poem on skating ('*Eislauf*') he touches the sublime. He cares little for colour and palpable illusion and seeks to render the ecstasy of the soul. His passion for the mysteries of the spirit also provides the keynote of the '*Messias*,' lending it as we must admit something of monotony.

It is customary but hardly accurate to think that the '*Messias*' had an *immediate* effect on German literature. Only Klopstock's nearest friends and above all the poets of the *Bremer Beiträge*, in which the first three cantos appeared in 1748, realized that the sublime spirit of this poetry heralded a new springtide for German literature. The self-assured and determined character with which Klopstock's father had endowed his family of eight boys and nine girls in Quedlinburg was combined, in the case of his eldest son, with a poetic gift that gave him courage to assert himself amongst the laureates of his age. It was not very long before the '*Messias*' drew to itself the attention of the literary world. Klopstock's visit to the Zürich critic Bodmer in 1750 led to a breach in the friendship of the two poets, who had little in common either as regards age or character. He thereupon accepted an invitation to the court of the Germanophil Danish king Frederick V in Copenhagen, where, with certain interruptions, he passed twenty years of his life. From here he journeyed to Hamburg, the harbour of his spirit whence he had fetched his wife Meta (Margarete Möller). Royal honours were showered upon him when, in 1803, his body was borne in state to Ottensen near Hamburg. It was the year in which Schiller's '*Braut von Messina*' and Goethe's '*Natürliche Tochter*' were produced on the Weimar stage. Yet at the time of his death Klopstock's fame was already a thing of the past. The year 1773, in which the '*Messias*' was at last completed, witnessed the publication of the *Blätter* '*Von deutscher Art und Kunst*,' Bürger's '*Lenore*' and Goethe's '*Götz von Berlichingen*.' When, in the following year, Goethe's '*Werther*,' Lenz's '*Hofmeister*' and J. Möser's '*Patriotische Phantasien*' appeared in print, Klopstock published his last great work, the '*Deutsche Gelehrtenrepublik*,' eagerly awaited whilst still in the press, and scoffed at on its appearance. This vast plan for the foundation of an intellectual society was finally doomed to failure by Joseph II's hesitation and ultimate death.

Thus Klopstock suffered the tragedy of surviving his own downfall. He had remained to the last the "immortal German youth." Even his work underwent no momentous change in the course of his life. The frequent obscurity of his idiom was certainly a stumbling-block to popularity, for few could follow him in his ecstatic flights. It was his yearning, as we read in the '*Zürchersee*' ode, to conceive the Creation anew. The world was to him the revelation of the Almighty in its heroic as in its pettiest aspects. Even the glow-worm (cf. the '*Frühlingsfeier*') is no less than the planets, the work of God. He sees everything through the light of salvation, and the vagueness of his images is not born of poetic inability but of his own irrational nature; and he does not, in the manner of Brockes, allow theological proofs of divinity to intrude into his descriptions of nature. In spite of this characteristic trait, many a critic (even to some extent Paustian) numbers Klopstock among the enlightened poets. Even Korff ranks him near Lessing because Klopstock lays more stress on the virtue than the individuality of his characters. Above all in the '*Gelehrtenrepublik*' we may admit the influence of enlightenment which had reached Germany from England by way of France through Voltaire (François Marie Arouet, 1694–1778) and Lord Bolingbroke. It is true that Klopstock does not, like Voltaire, make a ruthless differentiation between *honnêtes gens* and *canailles*. The Frenchman held only the former worthy of the blessings of enlightenment in spite of the fact that he simultaneously hurled the insult of his motto *écrasez l'infâme* against the ecclesiastic hierarchy.

To us Klopstock, for all his emotional poetic constructions, is first and foremost the prophet of the irrational and the emotional language of the heart. Thus he has the elemental force of the *Stürmer und Dränger*, particularly in his odes. The lack of any really worthy selection of the odes and hymns may in some measure be responsible for the fact that Klopstock's mighty rhythms seem to attract so few readers today.

Heavenly and profane elements intermingle in his works. The boldness of his images, his words and syntax in which terseness alternates with lengthy cadences reveal his irrational concepts. God, freedom, the fatherland, friendship, his love for his cousin Fanny and for Meta (=Cidli), of whom death robbed him so soon, prove the varying burden of his lofty song. Klopstock frequently indulges in eulogies on his friends in his poems. Many of them, for instance Cramer and Ebert, died before him. He even sings the praise of his favourite sport, skating. Klopstock betrays a decided partiality for noble thoughts which find utterance already in his early ode '*Die Stunden der Weihe*,' a characteristic example of Klopstock's love of conciseness and pathos—an antithesis resulting here in a lack of formal unity. The opening lines of the ode are charged with a dynamic rhythm, but its keynote of holy solemnity appears sadly incompatible with the almost frivolous end, which is suggested by an accidental personal experience and is not worked out to form an organic part of the poem.

Nature became a ruling passion in Klopstock's life. He transfuses it with his burning zest for love, fame, friendship, though its outlines remain vague. External action only appears in transient, intangible images, as though magically suspended between the landscape and the poet's emotion. In his best passages the poet avoids mere description no less than abstract analysis of emotion —e.g., in his great ode '*Der Zürchersee*' (1750) with its asclepiadean verse-construction, a form already favoured by Horace:

*Schön ist, Mutter Natur, deiner Erfindung Pracht,*
*Auf die Fluren verstreut, schöner ein froh Gesicht,*
*Das den grossen Gedanken*
*Deiner Schöpfung noch einmal denkt. . . .*

Goethe's '*An den Mond*' seems to contain a faint echo of the last verse of Klopstock's ode. The *suchende Seele* recalls '*Iphigenie.*' The compound word *Schattenwald* (in place of the adjective plus the noun) appears again in the language of young Goethe and belongs to the *Sturm und Drang*.

Klopstock's dithyramb on the '*Frühlingsfeier*' (1759), which represents in German literature the first great poetic rendering of a tempest, and at the same time foreshadows Goethe's *Prologue*, was originally conceived in free verse (see Lessing's literary epistles, No. 51), but was afterwards, much to its detriment, recast in quatrains. Rhythm and language (cf. the Bible with verses 2, 15, 18, 27) imbue this hymn on the drama of nature's elemental conflict with a terrible and mysterious power that caught Goethe in its spell during his Werther years:

*Nicht in den Ozean der Welten alle*
*Will ich mich stürzen, schweben nicht,*
*Wo die ersten Erschaffnen, die Jubelchöre der Söhne des Lichts,*
*Anbeten, tief anbeten und in Entzückung vergehn.*

*Nur um den Tropfen am Eimer,*
*Um die Erde nur will ich schweben und anbeten.*
*Halleluja! Halleluja! Der Tropfen am Eimer*
*Rann aus der Hand des Allmächtigen auch. . . .*

The fatherland and heroism also play an important part in Klopstock's odes. Nevertheless, for all his praise of the great Prussian king, he could not forgive the latter's scorn of the German muse. The dream of liberty kindled a transient enthusiasm for France in Klopstock's heart until the horrors of the revolution brought bitter disillusionment. He dedicated his song to the fatherland, the great age of the Staufen, the fiery spirit of Arminius and the naïve German maiden; cf. '*Ich bin ein deutsches Mädchen . . .*' This '*Vaterlandslied*,' (1770) was soon to receive a counterpart in Claudius's '*Ich bin ein deutscher Jüngling . . .*'

Thanks to the *Bardendichtung* of the sixties Klopstock's patriotic lyrics unfortunately became involved in academic mannerisms which vainly strove to put the classic gods to flight. A general confusion between Celts and Teutons, playful nicknames such as *leader of the Brennen hosts* (the ancient tribes inhabiting

Brandenburg) for Gleim, *Frederick's bard* for Ramler, *Werdomar* for Klopstock, *Thorlaug* for Gerstenberg, etc., likewise Kretschmann's bardic howlings, could not render these songs on Germania's halls, heroes, oaks and harps immortal. This pedagogic masquerade soon degenerated, in spite of the earnest endeavour to resurrect German and Teutonic mythology. Gerstenberg's poetry ('*Gedicht eines Skalden*,' 1766), which exerted much influence on the German bardic manner, and particularly on Klopstock, is probably artistically the most significant product of this renaissance of ancient traditions. After a thousand years the Northern hero Thorlaug rises from his grave to invoke the glory of the old Northern gods and heroes in the face of the Christian world. Prior to Gerstenberg Klopstock's own handling of the Edda and Nordic history may have aroused interest in literary circles. Other far-reaching influences on bardic poetry in Germany were the poems of J. Macpherson's '*Ossian*' which appeared in a German translation already in 1764 (and in 1768 in the Jesuit M. Denis's version), Percy's '*Reliques*' (1765), the sentimental affectations of the period, Rousseau, and the military exploits of Frederick the Great.

A comparison between Klopstock's ode '*Ihr Tod*' and that of Wieland '*Auf den Tod der Kayserin-Königin*' provides another conclusive instance of those characteristic traits in Klopstock's art which belong essentially to the high-flown tone of the ode and not to the simple song. Klopstock's poem has seven quatrains with lines of unequal length and is unrhymed. The ego plays the chief part whilst death is mentioned but once, though receiving emphasis in the central line and in the title '*Ihr Tod*.' The stammering, emotional accent of the poem is effective in its veiled obscurity: *Doch ein Laut . . . Ein Flammenwort. . . .* It adopts the rhetorical monologue. The allegory *Räucheraltar* almost recalls the baroque manner of making each detail absolute. The language is equally lacking in sensuousness elsewhere: *Die Laute stand.*

Wieland's poem on the other hand is not so concise, and is relatively formal in its construction. The poet does not assert his own feelings so strongly but the composition of the poem is far inferior to that of Klopstock.

Just as Opitz's star had once shed its light over the whole German realm, so Klopstock's earlier works exerted direct and indirect influence on his contemporaries, and if only for a short period, at any rate decisively. We need not emphasize here that not only the correct Ramler but even Herder, Goethe and others were acutely aware of the baroque flavour of Klopstock's free rhythms. As we shall see later on, Klopstock also influenced the church hymnal; though the latter could never have become his true province, for his vital genius urged him to a personal emotional form of expression which was to find its consummation in Goethe. Moreover, Klopstock may in a certain sense, namely in regard to his metric idiom and his innovations in prosody, be called a forerunner of naturalism. In opposition to Opitz he championed the cause of natural German verse, and in his fragment '*Über Sprache und Dichtkunst*' laid the foundations of modern prosody, thereby actually striving towards the goal which the naturalistic movement before the Great War radically demanded both in poetry and theory, upholding that content and formal expression should be inseparable and that the verbal medium should reduce the boundary between object and word to a minimum. Klopstock did not yet draw such extreme conclusions from similar ideas, but in the last pages of the abovementioned treatise he clearly states that vital expression must on the whole fit the content. Herder discusses the same topic in his '*Fragmente zur deutschen Literatur*' (third collection) though in a more poetic manner. To him thought, emotion, and expression must transfuse each other. He accepts the Platonic idea of body and soul. Thus Herder maintains that the true poet must needs write in his mother tongue.

The seed of the 'storm and stress' movement which Klopstock had helped to sow had in the meantime broken into a riot of growth above the stubble of outworn traditions. Rousseau's exhortation to return to nature and his hatred of civilization roused Europe from its sleep, inciting it to a regeneration of man and the state. The poetry of Haller and Ewald von Kleist's '*Frühling*' had already awakened in German literature a passionate yearning for nature and the desire to flee 'from the choking miasms rising from the cities' gilded prison.' Similar ideas, clad in less flattering speech, now issued from Rousseau's treatise on science and the arts. Society was in his eyes the ruin of humanity, progress an illusion of the devil, possessions the cause of class differences: *l'origine de l'inégalité*. Education, as prescribed in '*Émile*,' should enable man to regain his innocence. In the '*Contrat social*' Rousseau attempts to restore those innate rights of humanity which man has lost. He had previously given vent to his yearning for the regeneration of mankind in '*La Nouvelle Héloise*' (1761), of which an anonymous German translation already appeared in the same year in the Weidmann Verlag, Leipzig. With Rousseau, Europe plunged into a pessimism dictated rather by the social conditions than by subjectivity, (as in Strindberg). The latter believed that pessimism resulted from inhibitions produced by the conscious on the unconscious mind ('*The Development of a Soul*'). Nor is Rousseau's pessimism similar to Wedekind's, whose desire to rediscover the elementary nature of man turns to eroticism. Rousseau waged war first and foremost against a world of petrified formal conventions and bourgeois morality.

The German *Sturm und Drang* spurred these processes of thought to a madness of activity which soon developed from sentimental effusions to revolutionary deeds.

The *Superman* becomes the ideal of the day. Anacreontic verse and bourgeois resignation suffer an inglorious end. The youthful champion of the 'storm and stress' campaign wallows in grim horrors. He clenches the storm in his fist, plays with the sun like a juggler with his ball, and stuffs his brain with bizarre monstrosities. He rages against traditions, or like Lavater's friend, Christoph Kaufmann, plays the part of a wandering prophet and feels himself *ein ganzer Kerl*, a Titan inflamed with the elemental passionate fire of love and courage. Edward Young's '*Conjectures on original composition in a letter to the author of Sir Charles Grandison*' (1759) found actual embodiment in these self-termed 'geniuses' who also worshipped at the shrine of Shakespeare and Pindar. Like Young in his '*Night Thoughts*,' they abandoned rhyme. In vain did Lichtenberg († 1799) cast derision on these unfettered originals. In his '*Parakletor, or Consolations for those unhappy souls who possess no original genius*,' he ridiculed the necessity of a lack of symmetry as a means of originality and advised that children should be given a slight blow on the head with a clenched fist so that their brain should lose its symmetry.

The young generation could not slake its thirst for thrills and horrors which it employs in drama and ballad.

G. A. Bürger (1747–1794), who, as we now know, did not become acquainted with Percy's '*Reliques*' until 1777, inclined to maintain the ballad form on which he had modelled his '*Lenore*' (1773). The tonal colour, the palpable lurid drama and popular phrasing of the poem—its formulas, diminutives, repetitions and refrain became very popular amongst young writers. Bürger himself, who in '*Lenore*' had outgrown the melodrama of the pseudo-Shakespearean romances (e.g. Hölty's '*Töffel und Käthe*,' 1772), once more forsook the tragic for the comic vein or the tone of the balladmonger, adopting the ironic note in such ballads as '*Die Weiber von Weinsberg*.'

In spite of its macabre burden—graveyard, charnel-house, coffin, gibbet, Death with his hour-glass and scythe—*Lenore** remains immortal. Two dialogues, the first between Lenore and her mother, the second between Lenore and Wilhelm, give the ballad a fine equilibrium. Whereas in the former case the maiden's despair bursts out in uncontrolled spasms, the emotional element in the second dialogue is restrained in order to break forth with double violence in the breathless crescendo of the ghostly ride with its three lurid glimpses of the landscape illumined by the lightning's flash. But when, at the climax, pigtail and tuft fall from the skull and the body shrinks to a skeleton, the teeth of the modern reader will scarcely chatter like those of Bürger's contemporaries. '*Hasi, Hasi*' is probably only possible as a substitute for '*Ha! Sieh*' when the ballad is recited. To modern taste, the moral conclusion must needs detract from the effect.

How strong an influence Bürger's ballad exerted on Goethe, not only in regard to content, but also to rhythm, is seen in Goethe's

* cf. *Sammlung deutscher Balladen von Bürger bis Münchhausen* (Verlag—M. Niemeyer), Halle, 1934.

This most valuable selection of German ballads with critical notes was produced by the Berliner Germanisches Seminar. Stress is laid upon the highlights in the development of ballad poetry from *Lenore* onwards. Special reference has been paid to Goethe's *numinose Ballade* of his earlier period, to Uhland and to Droste, Miegel, etc. It is pointed out somewhat uncompromisingly that in some periods in romanticism, naturalism, and expressionism the genre cannot thrive in its purest form. A definition of the ballad is conscientiously avoided. The selection bears a preface by Münchhausen who had already gained renown as ballad writer and critic. In his *Meisterballaden*, which gives a subtle analysis of various ballads, he suggests that most ballads reveal a double action. The *Sammlung* renders this point of view convincingly. The book is most welcome in an age which, owing to the wireless, seems to bear signs of a revival of ballad poetry.

'*Der untreue Knabe.*' The latter is an open burlesque of the spectral romance, though not of Bürger's, whose poetic gift Goethe in his youth deeply revered. The most overwhelming influence on Goethe's literary development had in the meantime come from J. G. Herder (1744–1803), whose name is indivisible from that of Hamann (1730–1788).

In Hamann's '*Sokratische Denkwürdigkeiten*' (1759) faith is enthroned above the powers of reason. This work was published in the same year as Young's '*Conjectures*,' with which Hamann was probably acquainted, as we surmise from his opinion on genius. In his '*Kreuzzüge eines Philologen*' (1762) he draws an obscure image of poetry as the mother-tongue of the human race: Just as horticulture is older than agriculture, painting older than writing, song older than declamation, thus, too, the natural language of passion and the senses existed before rationalism. The Northern sage's burning desire for a magic in which elemental nature should be transfused with revelation, description with symbolic meaning, exercised a far-reaching influence on Herder. Hamann's reference to Shakespeare's irrational realm of imagination belongs to another chapter.

In his dependence on the Bible, Hamann's attitude diverges from that of Rousseau, who in other respects fascinated the German philosopher. But the latter's yearning for elemental nature on the other hand affords a barrier between him and the poets of the romantic movement that followed, for these allowed their fancy to play with emotion.

Thus we touch both on fundamental affinities and differences between 'storm and stress' and romanticism which will only become quite evident in the course of our argument. But we may here point to one or two characteristics. The romantic poets favour sound values more than rhythm. They dedicate their lives solely to their art, and indeed verge on the threshold of *l'art pour l'art* or lose themselves in nebulous theories, whereas the *Faust* of the 'storm and stress' period defies erudition. *Faust* ultimately became a mirror of the world, as *Wilhelm Meister* reflected the life of its period. Romanticism, however, denies such objective realism for the sake of its subjective virtuosity. More than two decades earlier Herder had originated a new conception of the folk-song which was to exert its influence far beyond the pale of romanticism.

Herder's legacy to the German language as an imaginative and emotional medium has not been fully exhausted yet. He was one of the pioneers of modern literature and kindled the spirit of its greatest representative, Goethe. It was Herder's tragedy to have to suffer eclipse through his own pupil. He introduced Goethe to Ossian and Hebrew poetry. He repudiated a one-sided over-estimation of Greek classicism and maintained that there was no absolute criterion of beauty. In that Herder combined a national and individualistic with a universal outlook he was especially appreciated by the romantics.

To Herder poetry, and in particular the lyric, represented the central core of all art, as he asserts in *Terpsichore* (1795–1796). As a moralist he regards poetry as the servant of humanity, but he possesses a very generous conception of the term. He was not only acutely sensitive to the past and the world of dream, but to the present, and thus transfuses classic and oriental philosophy with a new emotional significance. Words are symbols to him, a revelation of the divine essence in man. He encouraged a wider study of Indian literature, thus foreshadowing Friedrich Schlegel, Rückert, and others. Moreover, he provided German literature with new material through the romance cycle of the *Cid*, translations of Italian sonnets, and the discovery of a famous neo-Latin German poet of the seventeenth century, the Jesuit Jacob Balde († 1668). Herder translated many of the latter's odes (*Lyricorum libri* and *Silvae*). Being in the Latin tongue Balde's nature idylls and the *pathos* of his descriptions of mountain scenery (a novel feature in his own period) had unfortunately remained a closed book to the majority of the German people. Nevertheless Balde betrays the taste of his epoch and was probably influenced by the Pegnitz pastorals, for instance in his use of that favourite motif of cutting poems in the bark of a tree (*Silvae*, IX. 8, 15): '*Ergo in Apollineis incidam carmina ramis, quae crescent crescentibus ipsis*,' a theme reminiscent of Shakespeare's *As You Like It*.

It was not by mere chance that Herder's interest was aroused by Balde. In his youth he had himself employed the baroque habit of emphasis which had been furthered by Klopstock. It is true that Herder translated Balde's poems at a time when he had outgrown the mannerisms of his juvenilia, but in doing so he reinvoked the spirit of his youth.

A comparison between Gryphius's and Herder's translations of Balde immediately proves (cf. Bielmann *DuV* 1936, H.4) the immense gulf between Herder and the passionate rhetoric of the high baroque, for Herder has a far more sympathetic ear for Balde's lines:

*Ut se feroces denique littori*
*Stravere fluctus!*

cf. Herder's translation:

*Wie sich des Meeres wildste Flut zuletzt*
*Am Ufer leget!*

with Gryphius's rhymed alexandrines:

*Wie schläft der tolle Sturm der ungeheuren Wellen*
*so sanft an diesem Strand. . . .*

Herder's influence did not only affect literature, in the narrow sense of the word, but the whole outlook of his age. As an upholder of 'genetic' philosophy he attacked Lessing and Kant, but he did not realize that Kant in his '*Kritik der reinen Vernunft*' (1781), which appeared in the year of Lessing's death, actually denounces both materialism and dogmatism in science. Herder beheld in Kant's theory rather an enlightened rationalization of the irrational, for it appeared to him that Kant laid too much stress on the intellect as though the latter were the supreme creator of life.

What strikes us most in Herder is his championship of originality, racial unity, primitive culture and the folk-element in poetry. Both as theorist and poet he emphasized the close relationship between the language, poetry, and individual character of his nation. His interest in the folk-song exerted an immediate influence on Bürger and Goethe. Thus there developed a new attitude towards nature and life until with Goethe it blossomed to a vital imagery in which content and form were perfectly fused. Herder's '*Fragmente über die neuere deutsche Literatur*' (1767) and in a yet deeper sense the collection of essays '*Von deutscher Art und Kunst*' (1773), which he published anonymously at the age of twenty-eight, were not only manifestoes heralding in the 'storm and stress,' but reflected spiritual concepts from which German style and thought could benefit right through the period of romanticism.

Herder favours an intuitive and direct emotional idiom which expresses spiritual ideas in sensuous imagery. How much Herder depends on the senses is shown by his treatise '*Über den Ursprung der Sprache*,' in which he attempts to prove that language developed from the five senses.

Thus Herder found the new generation ready to fight for a type of lyric poetry that is really rooted in the people. He certainly rediscovered the folk-song and gave it its name, even though his theories about originality and his vague ideas about the community are today either exploded or forced to undergo strict revision. Rousseau's concept of an ideal people, living in a state of natural innocence, still plays some part with Herder, whereas later in the romantic period the brothers Grimm, Savigny, and others lay more stress on the organic principle than the 'storm and stress' had done. Only Goethe possessed the genius which could reconcile the antithesis through the miracle of his personality, in which human being and poet were welded to so rare a unity. Goethe's classic humanism will receive special attention in a later chapter in contrast to the 'third humanism' of Stefan George. The following words should, therefore, be read in conjunction with the chapter on George, as we can only arrive at a true understanding of Goethe's genius by investigating his significance for our present age. In this way Schopenhauer's idea of Goethe and Nietzsche's picture of 'the sage of Weimar' will shift into their proper perspective.

## *GOETHE'S LYRIC POETRY*

To the present age Goethe provides a subject of sharp controversy. The youth of today has yet to discover its own valuation of the poet and sage.

'More Goethe.' With these words Heinz Kindermann, oppressed by the flood of researches that threatened literary history in 1932, opened his acutely discriminating survey of literature on Goethe. In spite of the fact that classicism was pronounced dead, the years preceding the centenary had seen a ceaseless output of literature on Goethe as an artist, as a conversationalist or a member of convivial society, on Goethe's relations to the intellectual activities of his time, to philosophy (Plotinus, Leibniz, Spinoza), religion, history, politics, nature, music, æsthetics, psychology, language, etc. Stone by stone indefatigable source-hunters piled material into a veritable mountain. Many of these recent publications on Goethe bear the mark of their age.

A growing interest in the more individual aspect of the divine poet's personality betrays the modern critic's yearning to free himself from the mass-consciousness of the present age. But whereas Gundolf's scholarly yet æsthetic vision almost exalted Goethe to a legendary myth, facile journalists dished up a palatable bourgeois version of the poet's life and work for the man in the street. Irreconcilable demands confront each other; mass vies with personality; cf. H. Kindermann: *Das Goethebild des 20. Jhs.*, 1952.

Goethe's genius rose star-like in the dawn of the German lyric's glory. In Goethe intellect and sensuousness were transfused to a harmony as though by the secret processes of nature, whereas Schiller was only able to become what he did through ceaseless bitter struggle. The mystery of life unfolded before Goethe's sensuous vision, whilst Schiller built a gigantic world of heroic dream tearing us from the earth on the winged flight of his passionate spirit. This antithesis between an intellectual (sentimental) and natural (naïve) type of creative power continues to the present day. Only strong minds of Hebbel's calibre were able to overcome the dualism through a valiant affirmation of individual will against inexorable nature. Lesser spirits were shipwrecked in their quest of a harmony which in Goethe had developed as an innate part of his being.

Goethe's lyric poetry of the Leipzig period (1765–1768) is still rooted in the *tradition galante*. The view that the six Leipzig songs are born of true experience cannot altogether hold good.

'*Die schöne Nacht,*' however (sent to Behrisch in 1768, published in 1770), only appears rococo at first sight, for the emotional element breaks the rigid convention. Luna rises *durch Busch und Eichen* on a summer night that is no longer described in the traditional manner. The bold idiom *wandle mit verhülltem Schritt* foreshadows the poetic power of his future verse. The poem ends with an antithesis: *Tausend solcher Nächte* and *eine*.

The passionate strains of '*An Luna*' reveal the poet's intense love of nature: *Nebel schwimmt mit Silberschauer, nächt'ge Vögel, tagverschloss'ne Höhlen.*

An unusual tone runs through the poem: '*Glück der Entfernung*':

> *Ew'ge Kräfte, Zeit und Ferne,*
> *Heimlich wie die Kraft der Sterne,*
> *Wiegen dieses Blut zur Ruh.*

Amor's teasing in the '*Brautnacht*' is intermingled with the flickerings of a mystic flame. As in the other poems the mood is yet veiled by anacreontic conceits.

The same applies to '*Schadenfreude.*' Wearing the shape of a butterfly the poet spies on two tender lovers, fluttering away mischievously when the maiden tries to catch him.

The close of the poem '*Wechsel*' is also based on antithesis, though here, too, we are keenly aware of the poet's love of nature and his sensibility to the precious hours of fleeting life. Lying in the stream he stretches out his yearning arms to the wanton waves.

During his sojourn in Frankfurt a. M. (1768–1770), Goethe's spirit was mellowed through the influence of Fräulein von Klettenberg. Pietist doctrines found a ready echo in his heartsick mood. It was not until his sojourn in Strassburg and Sesenheim (1770–1771), and later in Wetzlar (May–September 1772), and Frankfurt, that Goethe's poetic genius developed its individual character. Certain experiences impressed themselves on his sensitive mind with the power of revelation. Strassburg Cathedral, Hamann's philosophy, Herder's gospel of poetry as the mother-tongue of humanity, the rediscovery of the folk-song, the glory of genius as revealed by Homer, the Old Testament, Ossian, Shakespeare, and above all nature, threw the poet into a state of ecstasy doubly inflamed by his love for Friederike. Goethe's creative impulse was now liberated, though we might hardly think so from the first Friederike songs which are still trammelled by traditional mannerisms, e.g. those poems whose authenticity has been questioned: '*Balde seh ich Riekchen wieder,*' '*Erwache, Friederike.*' In the latter poem Goethe scarcely probes beneath the surface. It is true that he gives them movement and development, not mere playful formalisms of the type of Opitz's '*Ach, Liebste lass uns eilen.*' But

Goethe's emotional language is still limited to clichés (Philomela), *pointe*, and schematic forms. Even '*Mit einem gemalten Bande*' is not altogether free from such conceits. Nevertheless there is a peculiarly vital charm about such poems as '*Willkommen und Abschied.*' Its first version betrays Goethe's guilty conscience:

*Du gingst, ich stund und sah zur Erden. . . .*

The '*Heidenröslein*' was destined to become one of the rarest treasures of popular song. It is based on a folk-song which may be found in an elaborated version in Paul van der Aelst's collection (1602). The '*Mailied*' is transfused by pantheistic feeling. The poet in the ecstasy of inspiration has grown one with his material, so that instead of reading a description we seem to feel the very rhythm of spring and budding youth itself.

The more tumultuous side of Goethe's nature is revealed in Götz, Werther, and Faust. Thanks to Herder, Goethe's lyric verse has much of the soaring flight of Pindar's odes. From the latter Goethe culled his image of the charioteer who seizes the tempestuous moment with the morning's strength. Later, in the '*Seefahrt*' (1776), Goethe once again uses a similar symbol of the leader, this time that of the virile self-control of the steersman who faces wind and weather undaunted on the ocean of life:

*Doch er stehet männlich an dem Steuer;*
*Mit dem Schiffe spielen Wind und Wellen,*
*Wind und Wellen nicht mit seinem Herzen;*
*Herrschend blickt er auf die grimme Tiefe*
*Und vertrauet scheiternd oder landend,*
*Seinen Göttern.*

A characteristic feature of Goethe as a lyric poet at this period is his convincing manner of mingling sensuous and intellectual elements, and also his use of adjectives suggesting movement. Thus he employs not the past participle which through its sense of finality would destroy the dynamic effect, but the present participle: *reifende Frucht*, *türmende Ferne*, *schwebende Sterne* ('*Auf dem See*'), *fruchtende Fülle* ('*Herbstgefühl*'); *sturmatmend* ('*Wandrers Sturmlied*'), *allliebender*, *umfangend* ('*Ganymed*').

Goethe also betrays a partiality for dynamic tension, not, however, of a baroque type but of a symbolic character. We thus find intransitive verbs used as transitives: *euch umsäuselt*, *euch betauen* (*'Herbstgefühl'*); prepositions or adverbs combined with verbs or adjectives: *grüne herauf* (*'Herbstgefühl'*); *wolkig himmelan* (*'Auf dem See'*); *anglühen* (*'Ganymed'*); *erzechen* (*'Seefahrt'*); *eratmen* (*'Schwager Kronos'*); *entgegen singen* (*'Wandrers Sturmlied'*); *entgegen heben* (*'Adler und Taube'*); intellectual verbs and sensual active energies: *zum Teiche hemmen* (*'Mahomets Gesang'*); adjectives used in combination: *freudehell*, *jünglingfrisch* (*'Mahomets Gesang'*); *ahndevoll* (*'Schwager Kronos'*); compound nouns: *Sternenblick*, *Führertritt*, *Flammengipfel* (*'Mahomets Gesang'*); *Scheideblick*, *Rebengeländer* (*'Herbstgefühl'*); *Gebetshauch*, *Rettungsdank* (*'Prometheus'*); frequent use of the prefix *all*: *allliebender* (*'Ganymed'*); *allgegenwärtig*, *allheilend* (*'Adler und Taube'*) etc. . . . reflect the poet's pantheism, whilst richer forms help to create a solemn, hymnal tone: *verlässest* (*'Wandrers Sturmlied'*), *quellet* (*'Herbstgefühl'*). Burdach (*Vorspiel*) has proved how much the language of the young Goethe owes to Klopstock, e.g. (*a*) the combination of the intransitive verb with *auf*, *er*, *an*; e.g. *töne . . . herauf*; (*b*) accusative of the intrinsic object: *Wonne schauern*; (*c*) particle joined to noun: *himmelan*; (*d*) simplex in place of compound: *hellen* (*erhellen*); (*e*) a partiality for words such as *dunkel*, *still*, *golden* . . .

It was, however, Herder who, kindled by the baroque fire of Shakespeare's and Klopstock's passion, and invoking emotion, not reason as his muse, did most to inspire the vehement tide of Goethe's storm and stress lyric. Thus Herder coins dynamic combinations of verbs and prefixes: *erjauchzen*, *hinächzen*, and employs intransitive verbs as transitives: *erschweigen*, *wegbeben*. . . . Using examples of this kind as his model, and steeping himself in nature and eros, the young Goethe was enriched not only by compounds but (as with Herder and Klopstock) by simplex in place of compound; cf. Goethe's *'Wandrers Sturmlied'* (*decken* instead of *bedecken*), or *'Herbstgefühl'* (*brütet* instead of *ausbrütet*).

It was not only Herder the translator and imitator (as Fittbogen wrongly assumed) but Herder the creative poet who was of momentous importance to Goethe's development. It is true that he directed Goethe's interest towards Ossian, Pindar, and the Psalms; but Pindar's influence, which we have already had cause to mention, must not be overestimated, for Goethe would have arrived at free rhythmic verse without him. Literary criticism has long since realized how little of the Pindaric vein is to be found in such poems as the '*Wandrers Sturmlied*' (April 1772). Equally remote from the classic ideal are the remaining hymns of the young *Stürmer und Dränger*. Parallelism, inspired particularly by the Psalms, and alliteration strengthen the structure of Goethe's verse, but with a natural sensuous ease of rhythm and diction that caused Herder's heart to swell with admiration for his pupil. That Goethe does not lapse into formlessness even in these hymns, but creates distinct rhythmic units, thus producing verses of almost regular metre though filled with passionate content, is proved by such poems as '*Mahomets Gesang*.'

In the years of 'storm and stress,' the young titan glories in an almost god-like sense of victory. The poet of the '*Wandrers Sturmlied*' feels his genius lift him like the skylark warbling to the rainy clouds. On wings of fire he hovers high above the muddy road. He is filled with the divine assurance of the elect. '*Mahomets Gesang*' (1772–1773) mirrors the poet's own development in the symbol of the water that, gushing from the spring in the rock and swelling to a stream, then to a river, flows through the plain and the desert and through prosperous cities to empty itself into the eternal sea. In the lyric '*An Schwager Kronos*' (October 10, 1774, written in a postchaise), the god is the postilion who drives the postchaise of the world. '*Prometheus*' (1774) is an embodiment of self-confident genius who ignores the divine powers. Spiritualized passion and a burning desire to fathom the mysteries of the universe kindle the verses of '*Ganymed*' (1774):

*Wie im Morgenglanze*
*Du rings mich anglühst,*
*Frühling, Geliebter!*
*Mit tausendfacher Liebeswonne*

*Sich an mein Herz drängt*
*Deiner ewigen Wärme*
*Heilig Gefühl,*
*Unendliche Schöne!*

*Dass ich dich fassen möcht'*
*In diesen Arm!*

*Ach, an deinem Busen*
*Lieg' ich, schmachte,*
*Und deine Blumen, dein Gras*
*Drängen sich an mein Herz.*
*Du kühlst den brennenden*
*Durst meines Busens,*
*Lieblicher Morgenwind!*
*Ruft drein die Nachtigall*
*Liebend nach mir aus dem Nebeltal.*

*Ich komm', ich komme!*
*Wohin? Ach, wohin?*

*Hinauf! hinauf strebt's.*
*Es schweben die Wolken*
*Abwärts, die Wolken*
*Neigen sich der sehnenden Liebe.*
*Mir! Mir!*
*In eurem Schosse*
*Aufwärts!*
*Umfangend umfangen!*
*Aufwärts an deinen Busen,*
*Allliebender Vater!*

As a '*Wanderer*' (1772) through classic lands he feels the power of generation which creates man that he may reap all he can from life.

How deeply Goethe already suffered under the doom of solitude is betrayed in his poem '*Adler und Taube*' (written probably before 1773), and yet more strongly in the '*Harzreise*' (December 1777). His spirit could never be appeased by the dove's self-sufficiency but must soar triumphant from darkness to light.

From Lili Schönemann the poet received '*Neue Liebe, neues Leben*' (1774–1775) bringing him who had just outgrown the melancholy of '*Werther*' new sorrows and new joys. Only flight saved him from the fetters of premature matrimonial ties. '*Auf dem See*' (June 15, 1775) remains the precious poetic fruit of this attachment. The poem expresses not only a lament on his lost love, but his ultimate victory over pain. The outward journey is full of merriment, but the rhythm of the poem changes as soon as memories of Lili rise before his eyes, and yet again when, on recovering from the blow, peace once more inhabits the soul of the poet. Goethe was about to reach maturity when circumstances brought him to Weimar, where he went through an aftermath of 'storm and stress.' Goethe's youthful period can be said to reach its real close about the time of the appearance of Schiller's '*Robbers*.' Nevertheless his vision begins to mature from the moment he came to Weimar.

It was not in sceptic denial of the unseen powers but in his continual striving towards a nobler concept of humanity that the creator of '*Iphigenie*' and '*Tasso*' tempered his ego by renunciation and control. And still during the journey to the Harz in the winter of 1777 he feels uplifted in the proud realization of being the chosen one. But Goethe already knew the secret of self-surrender; Goethe who, in '*Prometheus*,' had sung of the unflinching self-conviction of genius, or in '*Ganymed*' of the spirit cleaving infinity like flame. Beneath Frau von Stein's sheltering wing, Goethe's soul ripened to harmonious equilibrium. The landscapes of the '*Harzreise*' may be said to mirror this process of the poet's awakening from the mists of emotion into the light of self-criticism. In the '*Lied an den Mond*' (1777) the rhythmic flow of the verses is magically inwoven with the spells of evening. This poem is quite wrongly still connected with the suicide of Fräulein Christiane von Lassberg, who in January 1778 drowned herself in the Ilm. A copy of '*Werthers Leiden*' was found on her person. But Goethe's poem on the moon dates back to the summer of the year 1777.

A comparison between the three different versions and the original poem shows how, under the influence of Frau von Stein, its passionate idiom was gradually tempered (*Liebster* becomes *Freund*) and how much the final form has gained dramatically and æsthetically, but lost from the emotional point of view. In the '*Gesang der Geister über den Wassern*' quiet melancholy broods over the poet's reflection on the transitoriness of life, and in '*Ein Gleiches*' (1780) his yearning for peace is clothed in utter simplicity. Zelter's musical accompaniment rightly interprets the mood of the poem as a yearning for sleep, and thus causes the last line to fade into nothingness. The poem is rich in symbolic melodious assonance and sound values: *allen / allen; Gipfeln / Wipfeln; kaum / Hauch / auch; Walde / warte / balde; schweigen / Vögelein.* And yet the acoustic element is not overstressed. Optic values such as mountain, forest, man, and beast are borne on the gentle ebb and swell of a yearning rhythm. Through its poignant simplicity poetic emotion is here widened from personal to universal significance. The erstwhile titan now recognizes man's limitations. He is reconciled to fate and feels the pantheistic harmony between nature and man. Even before his journey to Italy he confesses in '*Ilmenau*':

> *Allein wer andre wohl zu leiten strebt,*
> *muss fähig sein, viel zu entbehren.*

The '*Zueignung*' also, already restrained as far as its form is concerned, demands renunciation: 'Know thyself, live at peace with the world.' Thus Goethe turns gradually to the world of reality by a remorseless purging of all visionary abandonment. To this period of victorious humanity belongs also the fragment called '*The Secrets*,' with its burden of Christian wisdom:

> *Von der Gewalt, die alle Wesen bindet,*
> *Befreit der Mensch sich, der sich überwindet.*

In place of the grail, the cross, wreathed in roses, shall be erected. Not until he reached the South did Goethe's creative spirit, which threatened to pale beneath the paralysing influence of such abstract moral concepts, awaken to new life. There he was reborn as *Griechenmensch*. Thus Goethe, rejecting the dæmonic principles of life, strove towards the ideal of *kalokagathos*. Plato already wrote of the true dæmon which every man must discover in his own way through self-discipline, and which Goethe himself strove to find. In Christianity the laws of being were rendered yet more profound through belief in a personal Divine Spirit. But all too soon St. Paul's austere conception of man's responsibility was hurled from its lofty pinnacle. Gradually temporal power asserted itself against the *Civitas Dei*. The Machiavellian spirit turned that sense of responsibility to ever more worldly use, until it deteriorated to an arbitrary cult of personality. The ego no longer stood at the judgment-seat before God, but only answered to the voice of its own conscience.

Goethe was one of the first to feel again the thrill of the irrational that descends on the human spirit through the grace of

God. In his '*Urworte. Orphisch,*' he speaks of the *Dæmon* of his life, and of *Tyche* (accident), *Eros*, *Anagke* (necessity) and *Elpis* (hope)—the impersonal powers that govern his existence and actions.

Awe of the mystery of ἐπικρατεῖν (gain mastery) endured. Maturity had not brought disillusionment in its wake. As classic poet Goethe now sought above all else the abiding laws manifest both in the rational and the irrational, though he never robbed life of its profundity. But he curbed all transcendental flight that the soul might be ennobled through reality itself. Not from its fevered dreams, as it had done in his youth, should the spirit fashion his reality, he writes to Frau von Stein.

In Italy Goethe's restrained sensuousness awoke to new life beneath the Southern sun; here the poet matured to classic harmony. His '*Römische Elegien*' (first published in Schiller's '*Horen*' in 1795) are the work of a thankful joyous spirit. The picture he paints of his wife Christine Vulpius bears traits of Faustina Antonini, a young Roman widow. The form of the poems was inspired by Catullus, Propertius and Tibullus. Goethe had now come to experience things above all through an eye that dwelt in contemplation on plastic beauty: *sehe mit fühlendem Aug'*, *fühle mit sehender Hand.*

The '*Venezianische Epigramme*' (1790) breathe a very different atmosphere. Goethe had in the meantime come to know the joys of domestic bliss, and it was only reluctantly that he once again set forth to meet the Duchess Amalie in Venice. When the rosy spectacles were suddenly discarded, and he stood face to face with the naked truth of Italian politics, bitter words fell from his lips. He feels himself a German, and the father of a family. His poem '*Gefunden*' (1813) was written as a reminiscence of his first meeting with Christiane. Like the '*Epigramme,*' the '*Xenien*' suggest the influence of Martial. The '*Elegien*' (*Disticha*) represent a decided development in formal ideals, in that hexameters are no longer abruptly contrasted with pentameters, but follow rhythmically one on another.

Through his friendship with Schiller, Goethe now enters a new span of literary activity. The so-called *Balladenjahr* (1797) not only bears witness to mutual inspiration between the two poets but also to fundamental differences, visible not only in such poems as '*Heidenröslein*' (1771), '*Der König in Thule*' (1774), '*Der Fischer*' (1777), or the '*Erlkönig*' (1782), but also in his later ballads, '*Der Zauberlehrling*' (1797), '*Der Schatzgräber*' (1797), '*Der Gott und die Bajadere*' (1797), '*Der getreue Eckart*' (1813), '*Ballade*' (1813), '*Der Totentanz*' (1813), and others.

Goethe's conception of the ballad form is illustrated by his review of *Des Knaben Wunderhorn* (1806, *Jena Allgm. Lit. Ztg.*) and his essay on the *Ballade* (Weimar edition, 41, 1), in which he describes it as something that contains the element of mystery: The mysterious quality of the ballad depends on its recitative nature. The singer . . . thus uses each of 'the three fundamental types of poetry' in turn, his primary object being to express that which will kindle the imagination and keep the intellect employed; he can begin in a lyric, epic, dramatic tone and as he continues, vary it at will. Indeed, prosody in general could be elucidated by a selection from these poems, for here (in the ballad) the individual elements are not yet found divided but together as in a 'primal form of egg' (*Urei*).

The three fundamental types of poetry cited by Goethe are clearly displayed in his '*Ballade*,' the lyric refrain, the epic narrative (verses 2–6), the dramatic meeting between the father of the two boys and the singer followed by the final unveiling and solution of the mystery (verses 7–11). Actually Börries, Freiherr von Münchhausen, interprets the ballad in a very similar way when in his book on the *Meister-Balladen* he differentiates between a 'lower' or sensually real and a 'higher' or spiritual process.

According to Goethe, the Scottish ballad '*Edward*' was the prototype of its genre, indeed, he used it as a model for the '*Erlkönig*.' Here the narrative is dramatic rather than descriptive e.g. the fragmentary nature of the account, the intense crescendo of the three verses dealing with the *Erlkönig* himself (vv. 3, 5, 7), the feverish dreams of the child, and the reassuring words of the father. The reader himself is drawn into the drama: *Wer reitet?* The ride through the night, the hallucinations of the dying child, landscape and fantastic vision dissolve in one. The mist, the wind and the willows breed terror in the heart of the boy, whose fears are rendered doubly convincing through his sick state. At the same time sound and rhythm help to create an atmosphere of twilight and horror—like the Danish ballad of the *Ellerkonge*, Goethe's ends on the fatal word 'dead.'

Goethe had no craving for ghoulish tales of horror, but found inspiration in folk-legends and fairy tales. Like Schiller he is sensitive to the irrational forces of existence. But whereas the former sings of the integrity of the hero who rides through danger unscathed ('*Die Bürgschaft*') or of the mystery of Divine Providence ('*Die Kraniche des Ibykus*'), Goethe keeps nearer the earth, seeking to enthral the dæmonic powers of nature in symbols. But Goethe's ballads embrace a wide range of subjects including topical events ('*Johanna Sebus*'), the vampire legend ('*Die Braut von Korinth*') that was later to become so popular in France and in which Goethe so poetically contrasts pagan sensuousness with the transcendental Christian faith; or he chooses an Indian subject ('*Paria,*' 1823) in order to expound the dualism in man's nature. For forty years Goethe turned ever and again to this theme which indeed provides the keynote of '*Gott und die Bajadere*' (1797). This ballad appears more conscious in its construction than the '*Erlkönig*' or '*Der König in Thule*', e.g. its strict trochaics rhymed *a b a b c d c d* followed by the dactylic conclusion *e e d*, whilst the final line reverts to the type of the preceding part. Eight solemn lines form a striking contrast to the lively tone of the three last. But in the seventh verse, evidently for the content's sake, the rhythm suddenly appears to change to its reverse, with the result that the poem suffers an effective rupture at this point. The trochaic metre is filled with violent momentum and the *Abgesang* adopts a tone of solemn ritual: *Es singen die Priester* . . . Thus the dancing rhythm of the lines: *Sie rührt sich die Zymbeln* . . . balances the metre of the concluding moral:

*Es freut sich die Gottheit der reuigen Sünder;*
*Unsterbliche heben verlorene Kinder*
*Mit feurigen Armen zum Himmel empor.*

## *THE 'GÖTTINGER HAIN' AND MATTHIAS CLAUDIUS*

Goethe had soared far beyond the limits of his generation. The forerunners of the 'storm and stress' to whom the *Göttinger Bund* also belonged could never reach those heights. The Göttingen circle was founded in 1772, but was dismembered as early as 1774. Klopstock had been their guiding spirit. The word *Hain* itself suggests the bardic cult. Of this small company of poets Hölty was doubtless the most gifted, but the most active member was J. H. Voss, who exerted much influence over his contemporaries through his almanacs and translations. Fr. Leopold Graf zu Stolberg (1750–1819) inspired the circle with a glowing enthusiasm for liberty, simultaneously lending it the glamour of his presence. His ballads '*Die Büssende*,' etc., have won him the name of creator of the German *Ritterballade*.

Horrors are blended with moralizing admonitions:

*Und schon hält er in der Linken*
*Einen Schädel, spült ihn rein,*
*Giesset Wasser dann hinein,*
*Hält's ihr schweigend dar zu trinken. . . .*

*Unsre Frauen zu belehren*
*Hab ich solches kund gemacht. . . .*
*Auch die Herrchen zu bekehren. . . .*

When a youth he had become a friend of Goethe who, one year his senior, had made a profound impression on him through the fiery tone of his verse. Later on Stolberg became a convert to Roman Catholicism, a fact which Voss never forgave him. Stolberg's brother Christian completed the pamphlet which Stolberg, shortly before his death, had drawn up to rebut the bitter accusations which his former friend Voss was levelling against him. Poetry and life, Stolberg believed, must be born of noble emotions and passionate feeling, not a mere ebb that knows no flood. In his youthfully lyrical prose essay *Über die Fülle des Herzens* (1777) he gives vent to those fervent ideals which almost seem to foreshadow Goethe's mighty hymn on nature:

'. . . all noble emotions spring from one source, love, courage, compassion, piety, awe of good, and horror of evil, joy that fills the heart in the presence of nature; behold, seven rays of a seven-coloured bow, seven rays streaming from an overflowing heart which like the sun pours forth life and warmth. . . . Sad it is, when a heart opens too wide and must half-close itself again. This cannot happen without pain and yet, I believe, it must be harder still to know that of all one feels, so little can ever be expressed. . . . From the ever-spending bourn of your plenitude let me now drink. O you whom I revere as my mother and love as my bride. Nature! Nature! at whose breast I can alone find the peace of rapture! As a small child you rocked me in your arms till I found blissful ease in the shade of your forests and by the murmuring stream. . . .'

Such ebullitions of the heart perforce remained alien to the matter-of-fact Mecklenburger, Johann Heinrich Voss (1751–1826). But what he did possess was a peculiar power to blend classic ideas with a popular folk-element. Through Heinrich Christian Boie, whose sister he married, Voss found a means of livelihood. His German rendering of the *Odyssey* (1781) represents the high-water mark in Homeric translations up to that date and it has remained famous to the present day. His very accurate *Iliad* lacks the *Odyssey's* freshness. Voss won equal recognition through his idylls, the poetic genre in which he felt most at home. He does not deck his characters in pastoral array as Gessner had done, but sees them in their natural peasant settings, or in the midst of German domesticity, as in the *Siebzigster Geburtstag* or *Luise* where, with Homeric leisure, he enters into the hymeneal joys of Luise and her pastor. Though many a passage may appear fatuous to us today: *die trippelnde Mama, die verständige Hausfrau; der küssende Papa; der edle, bescheidene Walter*, etc., the description of the preparations for the wedding are rendered with a charming grace and restraint.

The most promising member of the *Hainbund* was Ludwig Christoph Hölty (1748–1776) of Hanover who died at such a premature age. He had steeped himself in Klopstock's verse with adoration. The keynote of his poetry is elegiac, but it abounds in a variety of nuances; at one time he affects the anacreontic vein, at another he invents ludicrous tales of horror ('*Töffel und Käthe*'). Drinking-songs alternate with romantic contemplation of the moon and the grave. His ballads inspired Bürger, but the importance of the '*Nonne*' has perhaps been overrated by W. Kayser. Now and again Hölty adopts a hearty moralizing tone as in those rather unequal verses in '*Der alte Landmann an seinen Sohn,*' or touches on the popular folk element, e.g. in '*Rosen auf den Weg gestreut.*'

Other subjects which inspired Hölty in the short span of his life were patriotic enthusiasm (reminiscent of Klopstock), social defiance in which virtue puts class prejudice to shame ('*An einen Freund, der sich in ein schönes Dienstmädchen verliebte*'), Catholicism, and even the crusades, e.g. in the '*Siegeslied*' which to our mind suffers from too short a metre. The content and melodious style of his poetry provided a stepping-stone to romanticism, as we can well understand if we turn to the lines of his harvest song '*Das Erndtelied*': *Sicheln schallen / Ähren fallen / Unter Sichelschall.*

Hölty but seldom let the beauty of his verse flag. He was an adept at composition both in the German and classic (sapphic-alcaic) style. His elegy *Maynacht* in the asclepiadean manner is characteristic of that unity of tone which Hölty knew how to maintain so well:

*Wenn der silberne Mond durch die Gesträuche blickt*
*Und sein schlummerndes Licht über den Rasen geusst,*
*Und die Nachtigall flötet,*
*Wandl' ich traurig von Busch zu Busch. . . .*

Even Goethe's Sesenheim song: '*Mit einem gemalten Bande*,' which could be compared with Hölty's may-song: '*Alles liebet, Liebe gleitet durch die blühende Natur, . . .*' lacks the Hanoverian poet's finality of form, although Goethe had a profounder sense of reality and pierced the mask of playful virtuosity.

Hölty's elegiac mood found a kindred spirit in Friedrich von Matthisson (1761–1831), cf. *Vaucluse* and *Adelaide*, though on the whole the latter is more closely related to Schiller than to the Göttingen tradition. A melancholy that faintly recalls Schiller and Hölderlin, though never reaching their far horizon of dreams, may be found in the work of J. G. von Salis-Seewis (1762–1834). Neither of the two poets last-mentioned have much left in common with the ideals of the *Hain*.

Matthias Claudius (1740–1815) from Schleswig-Holstein, though not immediately connected with the Göttingen circle, yet appears vaguely related by kinship of spirit. He was nicknamed after one of his publications, the *Wandsbecker Bote*. Politically his home was Denmark and he certainly regarded himself as the German Dane amongst his lyric contemporaries. Political stagecraft had at that time secured cultural relations between the two countries. Frederick V summoned German scholars, poets (Klopstock and J. A. Cramer, the editor of the *Nordischer Aufseher*), and the German statesman Bernstorff to his court. Thus when, shortly before Claudius's death, Denmark's alliance with Germany's enemy resulted in the disruption of the German colony, the poet felt the blow all the more sharply.

His songs are full of humour and downright peasant simplicity. There is a delightful frankness even about the announcement of his *Bote*, with its title '*Asmus, omnia sua secum portans*,' and its copper engraving of Death, the patron saint *Freund Hain*. The opening words read:

> 'I want also to collect my works and publish them. It is true that contrary to custom no one has asked me to do so, and I know better than any kindly reader how little would be lost if my works remained as obscure as my own person, but it is so nice to get subscriptions and be an editor. . . . The price is two marks good money and three marks for the critics and journalists.'

From the heart of this whimsical poet of the people who took a simple carpenter's daughter as wife, flowed the tenderest songs. It was P. Gerhardt's '*Nun ruhen alle Wälder*' which inspired Claudius's '*Abendlied*':

> *Der Mond ist aufgegangen,*
> *die goldnen Sternlein prangen*
> *am Himmel hell und klar;*
> *der Wald steht schwarz und schweiget,*
> *und aus den Wiesen steiget*
> *der weisse Nebel wunderbar. . . .*

In spite of its disturbing didactic element it belongs to the golden treasury of German eventide poems, and actually possesses more of the true folk element than Matthisson's moonlight songs.

The nature poems of Claudius and others also provide striking proof of the change the German poets' attitude towards nature was undergoing in the eighteenth century. It is significant not only that nature now begins to play a greater part in lyric poetry, but that it is now regarded in an entirely different light. Whereas at the time of Luther, Dürer, Altdorfer and the folk-song of the fifteenth and sixteenth centuries, the poet and artist cared above all for the detail of nature, the baroque lyric poet (see Gryphius, Gerhardt, and others) modelled nature to his arbitrary will, treating it as the plaything of his mood and whim. In art as in poetry, originality, preciosity and masquerade counted above everything (cf. the seventeenth-century lyric). In the eighteenth century, however, the poet ceases to regard nature from the vantage point of his intellectual or æsthetic conceits, but turns to her in awe or as though towards a refuge. Often, it is true, he seeks in vain to lose himself in nature, but she remains to Claudius the universal mother, his solace and his friend.

Claudius's proverbs are popular for the apt manner in which they hit the nail on the head as for instance in the '*Golden A.B.C.*':

*Zerbrich den Kopf dir nicht zu sehr,*
*Zerbrich den Willen, das ist mehr.*

or the '*Silver A.B.C.*':

*Im Anfang war die Erde leer,*
*Am Ende sind's die Köpfe mehr.*

Joy and sorrow blend with the tranquillity of Claudius's lyric verse. How sweet a solace breathe the last verses of his poem '*Täglich zu singen*'.

Claudius often likes to begin his poems with a description in the present tense, e.g. in '*Die Sterne*': *Ich sehe oft um Mitternacht*. The poem might well have ended with the third verse. However, there follow two more in which the poet directs his gaze towards the future. The poem should bear its original title *Sternseherin Lise*, for then the lambs and pearls would have introduced additional significance and a delightful touch of irony. Likewise the expression *satt sehen* could more happily apply to Lise than to the poet himself. Few singers today know that that famous patriotic song, '*Stimmt an mit hellem, hohem Klang*,' was based on Claudius's '*Neujahrslied*.'

K. G. Lappe (1773–1843), now almost completely forgotten, is the author of the once famous song: *So oder so*. Some of his simpler songs much remind one of M. Claudius's poetry.

## *SCHUBART, SCHILLER AND THE WAY TO ROMANTICISM*

The province of Swabia can boast many a name of renown, amongst others Weckherlin, Schubart, Schiller, Kerner, Schwab, Hölderlin, Schelling, Uhland, and Mörike.

The musician and poet Christian Friedrich Daniel Schubart (1739–1791), doomed to ten years' penal servitude on the Hohenasperg (1777–1787), became an almost legendary figure as martyr in the cause of freedom during an epoch of political and individual persecution. All the contradictions of the 'storm and stress' are united in this violent patriot who so ardently admired Frederick II and sang the king's praise in his works. Klopstock was Schubart's model, though enlightenment and the French revolution found enthusiastic reception in his journal '*Deutsche Chronik*,' which was later to break his life. His greatest passion, however, was dedicated to the fatherland under whose wings he found so poor a refuge as he himself complains in his autobiography which he dictated during his sojourn in prison. Even in the year of his liberation Schubart was forced to experience how the Duke of Württemberg sold his subjects to the Dutch East Indian Company at the Cape of Good Hope for a pocketful of gold. In his '*Kaplied*' he bids them a poignant farewell:

*Auf, auf, ihr Brüder, und seid stark,*
*Der Abschiedstag ist da!*

Schubart's denunciation of tyranny in the '*Fürstengruft*' (1779), written during the first years of his imprisonment, flowed from the depths of his heart, and is akin to the revolutionary spirit of the author of the '*Robbers*' who was twenty years his junior. Schubart, however, was not only related to the 'storm and stress.' His '*Ideen zur Ästhetik der Tonkunst*' have many points in common with romanticism, in particular that of synaesthesia. Schubart thus ranks as a pioneer of the doctrine of tonal colour, tones *and* thoughts appearing to him to possess their own colour values.

Swabia it was that gave birth to Germany's great dramatist and philosophical lyric poet, Friedrich Schiller (1759–1805). Already at the military academy the young cadet was able to practise his gift of rhetoric by holding orations on virtue and felicity. Though Schiller may not have been inspired to 'storm and stress' through the immediate influence of Rousseau, the spiritual atmosphere of the day was pent with ideas which now exploded with all the volcanic force of youth in the '*Robbers*,' the drama in which Schiller much resembles Shakespeare. Particularly Karl Moor's plea for absolute justice, and the way in which the web of calculated intrigue is torn asunder, herald a departure from the ideas of enlightenment. The *Robbers* appeared in the very year (1781) in which Justus Möser of Osnabrück had published his courageous defence '*Über die deutsche Sprache und Literatur*,' directed against Frederick II's '*De la littérature allemande, des défauts qu'on peut lui reprocher*.' Möser maintains that noble emotions are often kindled by great events, and he makes his excuses for German poetry on the grounds of such a lack. But this argument no longer held good, seeing that he himself might well have beheld a great future for German poetry through Klopstock, Goethe and Bürger.

Schiller's first *Anthology* (for the year 1782) was printed privately. It shows a great variety as regards both form and subject-matter but clearly reveals the characteristic style of the poet with its overladen metaphor, intellectual speculation and a lack of simplicity. '*Die Schlacht*' (1781) is not based on an actual happening like Körner's '*Freiheitslieder*,' yet it is full of sincerity and the best poem in the collection. The odes on Laura are lyric effusions of abandoned sensuality that are sublimated to the sphere of metaphysics. Although they sprang from a definite situation, poems such as '*Laura am Klavier*' seem peculiarly unreal: *Wenn dein Finger durch die Saiten meistert*, whilst images and rhymes are crude and far-fetched:

*Wo verlornes Heulen schweift,*
*Thränenquellen der Cocytus schleift. . . .*

Schiller's *Anthology*, which included contributions by other poets, provides the best document of young Schiller's literary development and touches on the three concepts—God, love, and death. Fundamentally Schiller's attitude towards life was optimistic and idealistic, even though he was given to gloomy pessimism and vacillated between idealism and materialism. The anthology is filled with a yearning for infinity. Brockes, Haller, and Klopstock in particular appear the literary ancestors of the poet. The pietist atmosphere of his Württemberg home and the devout tenets implanted in the boy's soul by his parents had made him profoundly religious. This faith in divine justice and providence coupled with a conviction of the nullity of existence was turned in a new direction during his sojourn at the military academy or *Hohe Karlsschule* as it was later called.

In the academy he made a study of the philosophy of Leibniz, with whose works he had already become acquainted through the poetry of Uz and Haller. Philosophy played a great part in the educational system favoured by Karl Eugen and his noble friend Franziska von Hohenheim. Schiller's favourite teacher J. Fr. Abel encouraged the poet's natural gift of speculation. He also read passages from Shakespeare aloud to the boy and fired his creative imagination. Through direct or indirect contact with the philosophy of Sulzer, Mendelssohn, Grave, Shaftesbury and his disciple Ferguson, Schiller was brought face to face with at any rate a good number of the æsthetic, ethic and religious problems of the day.

Naturally we must not look for a complete philosophy in the anthology. In spite of his especial partiality for Leibniz's concept of universal harmony, Schiller not only knew, but personally felt, the pessimism that in England and France had been interpreted as a philosophic system. Experience and milieu represented important forces to young Schiller. Restrictions and constraint at the academy, intrigues at the petty Versailles of Württemberg, and the exploitation of its subjects nourished the 'Rousseau mood' in the author of the '*Robbers*'; whilst his craving for the horrible, the passionate and the tragically heroic were fostered by Gerstenberg's '*Ugolino*,' Leisewitz's '*Julius von Tarent*,' and in particular by Goethe's '*Götz*,' Schubart's '*Fürstengruft*' and many another 'genius's' hatred of tyranny. This wallowing in horror is found to a certain extent in the anthology, for instance in '*Eine Leichenphantasie*' or '*Die Kindesmörderin*.' Untrammelled emotion is lauded, the hypocrisy of virtuous society puppets reviled. Rousseau's influence must not be overestimated here. Schiller was certainly acquainted with his works, though probably only indirectly through an article by J. G. Jacobi in Wieland's *Deutscher*

*Merkur* of 1778. To this must be added the influence of Klopstock and the sentimental literature of England. Schiller's spirit tossed on the restless tide that surged within and around him. When his teacher Abel introduced him to Leibniz's philosophy he discovered therein the philosophic counterpart of his infinite yearning for harmony.

Schiller's '*Geheimnis der Reminiszenz*' expounds the idea of preexistence which already appeared in Plato's *Symposium*. Once upon a time Laura and the poet had been one: *Du und ich des Gottes schöne Trümmer*. . . . Love moves the spheres, we learn in '*Phantasie an Laura*,' '*Die Freundschaft*,' '*Der Triumph der Liebe*.' . . . The world is as regulated as a timepiece ('*Melancholie an Laura*'). Without love it would be dead. The passionate hymn '*Der Triumph der Liebe*' ends with the verse:

*Selig durch die Liebe*
*Götter—durch die Liebe*
*Menschen Göttern gleich!* . . .

To such love as this, friendship is closely related. Schiller distinguishes so vaguely between friend and beloved that many people today still believe that Laura is a fiction of the brain, a theory, which however is a mistake. Schiller believes in a divine sympathy between world and soul. This blissful concept is not, however, born of material success or the whim of fortune or culled from some philosophic system. It ultimately flows from his inmost being which valiantly battled with the evil forces around him. Thus even an uninhibited cynical outburst had no power to mar his idealism.

After Schiller had fled with Streicher to Mannheim, his energies were directed towards the drama. Indeed Schiller is fundamentally a dramatist and not a lyrical dramatist of the type of Grillparzer, whose characters (Jason, Jaromir, Medea) are but marks of the poet's subjective emotions. If one justly dismisses that rather shallow song '*An den Frühling*' as being uncharacteristic of the poet, one can say that Schiller lacks the truly lyric temperament. His stay with Christian Gottfried Körner in the years following 1785 enabled him to reconcile the conflicting forces that harrowed his soul and prepared the way for new developments in his lyric poetry. The ode '*An die Freude*' (1785), on which Beethoven based the final chorus of his Ninth Symphony, rings out triumphant with faith in the brotherhood of man and that power which sweeps through the universe and joins the humblest of earth's creatures to the stars. The ode is composed as a two-part song for solo and chorus, a form which Schiller was later to use on a far larger scale in the '*Lied von der Glocke*,' in which the contrast between the verses of the bellfounder and those belonging to the poet's reflection mirror the relationship between reality and the supernatural, the image of the bellfounding being but a mask. The reflections themselves fall into two groups, one embracing personal human values (birth, marriage, death, childhood, manhood), the other, problems pertaining to the life of the community and the state. The poem does not illustrate the life of an individual but of humanity in general. Thus the thread is broken in the spinning. It was just this impersonal quality, this sense of being removed from time and place that, combined with strict almost architectonic construction, gave Schiller's words a pregnant power that defeats even the travesty to which they have so often been subjected. In a magnificent tribute to the classical master of rhetoric and 'pathos' Thomas Mann, the ironical master of nuance, just before his death in 1955, recognized the most prominent feature in Schiller's poetic work and human suffering—greatness. Greatness was also the basic theme in H. v. Hofmannsthal's praise of Schiller.

After completing '*Don Carlos*' in 1787 Schiller became a devotee of Greece, and tempered his 'Titan' spirit to more controlled utterance. In the '*Götter Griechenlands*,' which appeared in 1788 in Wieland's '*Merkur*,' he contrasts Hellas's golden past with the godless abstract life of the modern age. The synthesis of nature and ethos appeared to him the ideal which reality will not suffer us to achieve:

*Was unsterblich im Gesang soll leben,*
*Muss im Leben untergehen.*

It was this poem which Fr. L. von Stolberg attacked so violently because in it Schiller spoke of God as the 'divine barbarian,' and betrayed polytheist tendencies in his adoration of the Greek gods. Schiller mitigated some of these heresies in a revised edition!

The crown of Schiller's intellectual lyric verse is '*Die Künstler*'

(1788–1789), after which his poetic output suffers an interruption. In contrast to the pessimistic conclusions of the '*Götter Griechenlands*,' '*Die Künstler*' appears optimistic. To the poet, who is now a professor of history, the present represents a renaissance of classicism. Art alone, he believes, can once more unite those divided forces, sense and spirit. Man can only be truly single-minded (in the sense of Hamann and Herder) in æsthetic creation. Through art he can once more attain nobility of character, knowledge, and truth. It was the lack of this concept of art which Schiller deplored in his scathing criticism of Bürger's poetry (*Allgm. Lit. Ztg.*, 1791). The above philosophic poem with its burden of thought and brilliance of word falls into three parts. The first seeks the origin of all cultural values in art:

*Nur durch das Morgenrot des Schönen*
*Drangst du in der Erkenntnis Land. . . .*

The middle part provides a historical survey of the development of man's delight in beauty, of the influence and application of its canons in Europe. The third part elucidates the general theme by an allegory: Now that man has reached perfection Venus Urania (wisdom) discards her girdle of beauty (Cypria). Thus the promise of regeneration through art is fulfilled:

*Was wir als Schönheit hier empfunden,*
*wird einst als Wahrheit uns entgegen gehn.*

It is the duty of the artist to preserve and enhance human dignity. But he remains at the same time the 'freest mother's free son.' His only law is beauty, whose sisters are morality and science.

For some years afterwards the historian, æsthete and philosopher in Schiller exercised a monopoly over his creative powers. In 1795, shortly after he joined forces with Goethe, his poetic genius was kindled to new flame by his treatise on '*Naive und sentimentalische Dichtung*.' Schiller had reached his classic period. The intellectual clarity he had gained in the foregoing epoch enabled him to render his poetry all the more harmonious and lucid. '*Der Tanz*' (1795) is the symbol of passion tamed by beauty. The dancer is subject to the law of rhythm but is otherwise free to follow his own path. '*Die Würde der Frauen*' (1795), which would more happily bear the title '*Anmut*' or '*Wert der Frauen*,' starts with the subject of social life to turn to theories about the difference between man and woman, a theme to which the earlier romantics were later to revert when investigating the problem of genius; cf. Schiller's conception of intuitive genius in his poem '*Der Genius*' and '*Das weibliche Ideal*,' which praises the surety of woman's soul. It is remarkable to note that in the above poems Schiller, though once a medical student, does not enter into the question of sex at all.

The elegy '*Der Spaziergang*' describes a landscape and an actual situation in a style which suggests Lessing's term *Nacheinander* (sequence). The various stations on the promenade give rise to meditations on man's cultural life in village, town and country. The sequence is actually a juxtaposition and does not always tally with the intellectual idea, e.g. the boat which has lost its mast. Likewise the poet was not always able to force visible images (village and town), which rest simultaneously in space, into an empiric concept moving in time. The finale closes with a eulogy on eternal nature, here beheld in a somewhat Ossianic light:

*Und die Sonne Homers, siehe! sie lächelt auch uns.*

Certain verses contain fascinating pictures, such as in the following lines:

*Leicht wie der Iris Sprung durch die Luft, wie der Pfeil von der Sehne,*
*Hüpfet der Brücke Joch über den brausenden Strom. . . .*

But this poem in particular must not be judged by details, but by the wonderful panorama of human culture it presents.

'*Das verschleierte Bild zu Sais*' with its didactic moral affords an interesting contrast to Novalis's novel '*Die Lehrlinge zu Sais*,' which was inspired by Schelling's idea that nature is spirit made manifest, spirit: manifest nature. On one occasion Novalis solved the *Sais* problem in the sense of Fichte by saying: 'What did he see? Oh! miracle of miracles—himself.'

Schiller's *Gedankenlyrik* is however diametrically opposed to romantic ideals. He does not 'think in sweet tones' (Tieck) but concentrates on philosophy, which often touches on the concrete and is poeticized, the content being spiritualized or sensualized through wilfully powerful and emotional language. Herein Schiller excelled all his predecessors—Brockes, Haller and E. v.

Kleist, e.g. in his great poem: '*Das Ideal und das Leben*' (1795); cf. also '*Aufriss*' II. p. 209, W. Stammler ed.

A comparison with Goethe suggests itself immediately. Both poets seek truth as far as epigrammatic acumen and rhetoric is concerned. Here Schiller, as the *Xenien* prove, is Goethe's peer. The latter on the other hand paints sensuous tangible images, whereas with Schiller the personal element dissolves in imaginary situations or in intellectual reflections on reality and the ideal. We find this particularly in those old favourites of the recital platform, the '*Bürgschaft*' and the '*Kraniche des Ibykus*,' '*Der Ring des Polykrates*' and other poems, though the '*Kraniche*' as symbol of retribution are all the more convincing on account of the unobtrusive manner in which they are introduced.

A surfeit of detail however expands Schiller's ballads all too much. Goethe experienced an innate necessity to see the world and every event in its organic relation to nature; Schiller however does not rest in himself like Goethe. To the former an image crystallizes to an idea, to the latter an idea becomes a natural image. Schiller was urged by an impulse to affect others and he gives vent to his rhetoric in solo and chorus. In his relation to Goethe he certainly not only received but gave, for instance in the case of '*Faust*.' On the other hand Schiller gained much from Goethe's experience of the world and æsthetic vision, a fact to which the correspondence between the two poets relating to the '*Kraniche des Ibykus*' bears striking testimony. Goethe shows Schiller a way in which he can make the miraculous vengeance of Ibykus's murder convincing. At the dread moment not merely two, but a whole flock of cranes fly past. Schiller followed Goethe's hint but luckily drew the line at the idea that the murderer's shouts should only be heard gradually.

The basic idea of the '*Kraniche*' is also contained in the title of Chamisso's poem, '*Die Sonne bringt es an den Tag*,' in which poem the murderer Master Nicholas hides the secret of his guilt for twenty years until one day, by mere chance, memory loosens his tongue and he tells his garrulous wife of his victim, who with the death-rattle in his throat had warned him of the vengeance that must come: 'The sun will bring your guilt to light.'

The *Balladenjahr* of 1797 (the title is Schiller's own) affords an illustration of mutual and reciprocal influences. Goethe too for a short time at any rate inclines to subordinate action to an idea, with the result that the magic of the true ballad was forced to yield to the daylight of common sense and morals, e.g. the '*Schatzgräber*' (1797), which was inspired by a picture.

With Schiller description is often merely the illustration to an abstract idea. *ὕβρις* holds sway over the '*Taucher*,' *νέμεσις* over the '*Kraniche*' (1797), the jealousy of the gods overshadows the '*Ring des Polykrates*.' Self-conquest is the burden of the '*Kampf mit dem Drachen*,' triumph of good over evil is praised in the '*Gang nach dem Eisenhammer*,' power of friendship in the '*Bürgschaft*' (1798), invincibility of love in '*Hero und Leander*,' and divine influence in the '*Graf von Habsburg*' (1803). The joy of seeing poetry soar phoenix-like from the ruins of political disaster inspired Schiller's proud words about 'the German muse':

*Von dem grössten deutschen Sohne,*
*Von des grossen Friedrichs Throne*
*Ging sie schutzlos, ungeehrt.*
*Rühmend darf's der Deutsche sagen,*
*Höher darf das Herz ihm schlagen:*
*Selbst erschuf er sich den Wert. . . .*

As we shall see later, notwithstanding æsthetic and human affinities, a gulf separates Schiller from the coming generation, that of the romantic poets. Personal misunderstandings soon widened the gap between him and the brothers Schlegel, who had once been his disciples. New intellectual and political ideas ruled the day. At the beginning of the nineteenth century Europe was in a state of transition. Political boundaries had been undermined. The Holy Roman Empire was shattered. The *Rheinbund* joined Napoleon. Prussia suffered losses both in the East and West, Austria in the West. Dynasties trembled. A year after Schiller's death this state of uncertainty was driven to a climax by the battle of Jena in 1806. It was the signal for rousing the German nation from the lethargy of dreams, which had sought a substitute for the universality of medieval Christianity in a cosmopolitan state, and thus paved the way for Bonaparte. This led to a nationalist rising, incited by Fichte's speeches addressed to the German nation. But monarchism turned the victory over Napoleon to its own ends, as seen in the hapless *Wiener-Kongress*. In literature these events are largely mirrored in German romanticism, which was originally *not* a revolt against Schiller and classicism but rather an enlargement and continuance of those ideals. At the beginning of their career the brothers Schlegel condemned any association between literature and politics, in accordance with the resigned attitude Schiller adopted in his *Horen*. Had he not said in his poem '*Der Antritt des neuen Jahrhunderts*' (1801): 'Freedom can only exist in the realm of dreams'? But as far back as 1796 Novalis had already an admiring eye for King Friedrich Wilhelm III of Prussia.

The poets of the 'storm and stress' had hailed a modern Machiavelli in their dreams. Classicism had sought ideal humanity as embodied either in Goethe's '*Iphigenie*' or Schiller's epistles on the æsthetic education of the human race. As the classic writers were unable to find their ideal of the 'tamed dæmon' in reality, they fled to the realm of poetry and dream. They sought typical and universal values based on ethic concepts. They aimed at stylistic unity whilst the romantics desired a stylistic variety that should adapt itself to the theme in question. Here they not only found points of contact with Herder and Goethe but even in spite of fundamental differences with Schiller.

The latter's '*Naive und sentimentalische Dichtung*' reveals the cleft between the old world and the new. It was from this work that the opponents of classicism culled many an idea for their programme. In their desire to combine the past and the present they were able to turn to Schiller. His '*Braut von Messina*' is classic in form, but its theme belonged to contemporary life. The '*Jungfrau von Orleans*' (1801) is perhaps the most expressive of Schiller's dramas that can be said to possess romantic traits, e.g. faith in miracles, divine grace, biographic description of the hero, the figure of the black knight, the pastoral idyll and the patriotic note. In '*Maria Stuart*' Catholicism, in the shape of the Holy Communion, is rendered convincing to the audience as an æsthetic spectacle, and in '*Wallenstein*' the hero alone believes in the influence of the stars. But in the '*Jungfrau von Orleans*,' which in its lyric moments also betrays romantic formal ideals, the spectator's faith in the divine is taken for granted. The tragic irony of victory in Mary Stuart's death and various other motifs might be regarded as a bridge between Schiller and the earlier romantics, who derived material from '*Wilhelm Meisters Lehrjahre*' and, like Goethe in his '*Divan*,' dreamed of uniting East and West. This yearning for universality which allies them to Herder is indeed one of the chief characteristics of the early romantic poets. Their influence radiated in every direction and had, for one thing, a most beneficial effect on German philosophy. They steeped their minds in metaphysical speculation and, to begin with, followed Schiller in steering clear of politics, though they regarded the latter as more worthy of poetic treatment than he did. They too harboured dreams of reforming life through art (Novalis's '*Ofterdingen*'), but they had more contact with their own period than had Schiller. Moreover they felt burdened by his ethics which were to their mind all too redolent of Kant. The romantic poets' amoral tendencies alienated them from Schiller but brought them into touch with Heinse, the author of the important *Kunstroman Ardinghello* (1787); also the group of the *Jungdeutsche* were later to recognize Heinse as their forerunner.

It is this dual development of romanticism from and against classicism which makes it so difficult to obtain a clear view of the new movement, for, in contrast with the dawn of the 'storm and stress,' romanticism did not proclaim an absolute revolt against tradition. Schiller's æsthetic ideals maintained their influence but his ethics found opposition. Goethe's liberal attitude on the other hand, including the erotic element, was appreciated. The objective realism of '*Wilhelm Meister*' was welcomed as an antidote to Schiller's idealism, though it is true that here, too, form holds an undebated prerogative over content.

# VII

# HÖLDERLIN

(1770–1843)

FRIEDRICH HÖLDERLIN's poetry lacks Goethe's breadth of vision, yet it soars to heights of dream which perhaps only Schiller and Shelley reached. Did not Hölderlin, Hyperion-like, himself become a myth—the light-bringer to whom Hellas was not a bleak idol of intellectual morality or cultural snobbery, but religion itself? In Diotima he beheld, as, later, Stefan George in Maximin, the embodiment of the divine. As we shall note when referring to George, Hölderlin's attitude to Greece has little in common with that of the modern poet. They are fundamentally different even in their first approach to Hellas. Hölderlin was drawn thither through Pindar, George through Greek sculpture. Above all the crystallized angularity of George's verse is utterly remote from the mighty rhythmic flux of Hölderlin's hymns. Nothing in literary history is perhaps so poignantly tragic as the suddenness with which Hölderlin's genius sank into spiritual night.

Of all the seventy-three years of his earthly existence he was destined only for seven to know the poet's joy of creation. Whilst still at school at Tübingen young 'Holder' was said to walk through the classroom like an Apollo. It was here that as a youth of twenty he, in company with Hegel and Schelling, studied the philosophy of Kant and Plato as well as Friedrich Jacobi's letters to Mendelssohn on the subject of Spinoza. Later on his friendship with Schiller at Jena led to that disastrous meeting with Goethe in Schiller's house of which we learn in a letter to Neuffer (1794). There is no doubt that Schiller was the chief formative influence in Hölderlin's development, involuntarily fostering in him an inclination for those very abstractions which, according to Goethe's advice, he tried to make him avoid. The correspondence between Schiller and Hölderlin during the Diotima period in Frankfurt (1795–1798) provides a key to the riddle of his life. We must on principle beware of drawing too many parallels between personal experience and poetry. Nevertheless there is scarcely another German poet who has poured so much of his soul into his work as the author of '*Hyperion*.' In 1802 he writes: 'As it is said of heroes, I might well say of myself that Apollo has vanquished me.'

The realization of the god's vengeance on the visionary poet struck like a sword's point at his soul. Hurled suddenly from the Olympian heaven of his brief Icarian flight he fell into the abysmal shame of madness.

For all its sensuousness, Hölderlin's language is the soul's purest utterance. He confronted life with the almost religious fervour of heroic youth. Even after his fall he stretched the broken wings of his eagle-spirit until utter helplessness dragged him down to the level of the ridiculous. A carpenter in Tübingen provided board and lodging for the broken poet, who liked to call himself Scaliger Rosa of S(c)ardanelli. Fits of convulsion, during which he reviled himself, were often followed by extreme exhaustion. Scandalmongers regarded his malady as the result of his attachment to Diotima. Nowadays some writers attribute the occasional baroque form of his verse to madness, an accusation which could only hold good in the case of the late formalistic rhymes written after the outbreak of his illness. We cannot fathom the ultimate secrets of destiny. H. v. Kleist committed suicide, Shelley was torn from life in youth, Novalis died inwoven in his death-yearning. More ruthless yet was the fate which the gods meted out to Hölderlin. He was forced to silence and yet had to live.

He threw himself into his work as though he almost foresaw his future. In a letter to Neuffer (1793) he writes that he rises punctually every morning at four o'clock, makes his coffee, and stays in his 'cell' until evening, 'often in the company of my divine muse, often with my Greeks, at the present moment once more in the school of Kant.' The conviction of his mission as a poet filled him with proud strength. He discovered the secret holiness of language through his own creative efforts. In his first songs and letters it is easy to trace his literary models—Rousseau, Ossian, Young,

Schubart, Klopstock, and in particular, Schiller. Hölderlin sings of friendship, immortality, heroism, love, the fatherland, liberty, human nobility and Schiller's ideal of the *kalokagathos*. He sets out in quest of purity, goodness and truth, combining a belief in progress with God and immortality. His yearning for Greece must not be taken in a literal sense but as the wish-phantasy of his German soul in its search for a regeneration of Germany to which Christianity and Hellas should lead the way.

To what rhythmic glory his song could rise already in his Jena period we see in his hymn '*An die Unerkannte*':

*Kennst du sie, die selig, wie die Sterne,*
*Von des Lebens dunkler Woge ferne,*
*Wandellos in stiller Schöne lebt,*
*Die des Herzens löwenkühne Siege*
*Des Gedankens fesselfreie Flüge,*
*Wie der Tag den Adler überschwebt. . . .*

But Diotima was the first to free his profoundest poetic thought. He saw her moving in changeless beauty, as transient nature amidst the realm of the gods, as a divine image amidst the darkness of despair. Their love of beauty, Greece and immortality kindled an overwhelming passion that could never have found consummation on this earth, and whose destruction cast the poet an exile upon the world.

One of the most beautiful of Hölderlin's poems of this period is his hymn (in hexameters) '*An den Äther*,' in praise of the divine spirit inhabiting finite form. It appeared in a revised version in Schiller's *Musenalmanach* of 1798. Apart from Schiller, Pindar, probably also Goethe's '*Ganymed*' and Heinse's '*Ardinghello*,' all contributed to Hölderlin's concept of the divine spirit which sweeps through the whole universe. Schelling's '*Weltseele*,' which appeared in the same year, bears affinity to this idea:

*An den Äther*

*Treu und freundlich, wie du, erzog der Götter und Menschen*
*Keiner, o Vater Äther! mich auf; noch ehe die Mutter*
*In die Arme mich nahm und ihre Brüste mich tränkten,*
*Fasstest du zärtlich mich an, und gossest himmlischen Trank mir,*
*Mir den heiligen Odem zuerst in den keimenden Busen.*

*Nicht von irdischer Kost gedeihen einzig die Wesen,*
*Aber du nährest sie all mit deinem Nektar, o Vater!*
*Und es drängt sich und rinnt aus deiner ewigen Fülle*
*Die beseelende Lust durch alle Röhren des Lebens.*
*Darum lieben die Wesen dich auch und ringen und streben*
*Unaufhörlich hinauf nach dir in freudigem Wachstum. . . .*

Whereas Schiller in his *Das Ideal und das Leben* complains of the unbridgeable gulf between the joys of the flesh and the soul's beatitude, Hölderlin does not separate spirit and flesh. Rather he venerates in Nature what he considers to be her great principles—the Earth, the Aether, and the Light—the trinity with which man has been acquainted since the Eros-myth of Plato's *Symposium.* The conception of Aether was probably also inspired by Pindar, Goethe's *Ganymed* and Heinse's *Ardinghello.* Schelling's *Weltseele* is also usually regarded as an influence, but here Hölderlin was giver rather than receiver, as Schelling introduced the Aether concept into his philosophy at a later date. The above trinity of forces is expressed in Hölderlin's poetry by his beloved tripartite structure: cf. *Germanien, Wanderung, Mutter Erde, Patmos, Brod und Wein,* etc.

It is often difficult to draw a distinct boundary line between Hölderlin's hymns and odes. Viëtor in his history of the ode points to the poet's lyrics as tending since the Diotima period first to the ode, and thence back again to the prophetic hymn. He groups the poet's works into various headings, e.g. the short 'dialectic ode' (e.g. '*Sokrates und Alkibiades*'), the odes to the '*Zeitgeist*' or the '*Tod fürs Vaterland*;' further, those tragic odes in which the poet's soul holds communion with the cosmos, and yet again mythical odes such as '*Der gefesselte Strom,*' '*Der blinde Sänger*' (1801), etc. There follow further hymns full of communal feeling and religious fervour.

Critics are inclined to ignore the fact that Hölderlin's language is often most simple, and gains its effects through some peculiarity in the order of its words. This is sometimes accompanied by a surging rhythm characteristic of the struggle between the poet's realization of the external world and his own heart.

Even Hölderlin's philosophical novel '*Hyperion*' is inspired by lyric genius. It is the *credo* of his passionate faith in Greece, which is not merely an æsthetic dream or intellectual concept as in the case of the brothers Schlegel. Neither is it escape from life, a balm for social misery nor neo-Hellenistic philosophy which sets up an idol of humanity (Plato's ἀρετή, σωφροσύνη) amidst an age of mechanism and mass psychology. It is religion. '*Hyperion*' and the tragedy '*Empedokles*' represent a synthesis of all that his inmost being felt to be his mission as poet. The former work streams from the yearning of his soul's solitude, the latter stresses the necessity of sacrifice.

'We are nothing, what we seek is everything,' says Hölderlin in the fragment of '*Hyperion*' that appeared in the *Thalia*, in which he invokes the spirit of ancient Greece. The southern climate and the example of heroic deeds gave birth to divine beauty. 'Man, however, is a god as soon as he is man. And if he is a god, he is beautiful,' is the burden of Hölderlin's song of Hellas. Herder's, Schiller's and Goethe's concept of humanity and the perfection of man was not very different. Again, Hölderlin writes of *art* that it is the 'first-born child of human, divine beauty.' 'Beauty's second daughter is religion—religion is love of beauty.' Once more we are reminded of Herder's and Schiller's correspondence on æsthetics. The Greek ideal of the golden mean avoids all extremes, whether represented by the restless wilfulness of the Gothic or by the Egyptian's mania for the colossal.

It is hardly possible to analyse the philosophic and religious elements of this work without doing violence to the lyric mood of the poetry. We can only marvel at this extraordinary fusion of simplicity and profound culture. We are led back to the days of the antique, of childlike innocence where spring, peace, and freedom reign supreme. Gods and children are spared by the avenging Nemesis which smites Empedokles for his presumptuousness. In such a divine concept of life man is the centre of nature. Love alone is able to find that unity which Herakleitos called a Singleness embracing all aspects of the same thing: ἓν διάφερον ἑαυτῷ. The unity of the sensual and intellectual marks the zenith of existence, but can only be attained through sacrifice by a heroic nature. Empedokles journeys this path of pain in order to atone for his lust for power. Through his self-sacrifice which reminds one of the death of Christ, life is renewed:

*Am Tode entzündet mir das Leben sich zuletzt. . . .*

Hölderlin was far more definitely than any before him a poet of prophecy. The magnificent formal patterns into which he ultimately cast his ideas were achieved only shortly before his spiritual eclipse, as though his prophetic lips had been closed before his lyric tongue outstripped the limit of human utterance.

Poets are the holy vessels in which the 'souls of the heroes are preserved' (*Buonaparte*). They believe in the gods because they are themselves divine. Whereas we are burdened (cf. '*Reif sind*') with the fate of the ripe earth (*Uns wiegen lassen, wie auf schwankem Kahne der See*), the poet faces the lightning-flash of the tempest that he may grasp the divine fire for mankind through his verse:

*Doch uns gebührt es, unter Gottes Gewittern,*
*Ihr Dichter! mit entblösstem Haupte zu stehen,*
*Des Vaters Strahl, ihn selbst, mit eigner Hand*
*Zu fassen und dem Volke ins Lied*
*Gehüllt die himmlische Gabe zu reichen . . .*

(*Wie wenn am Feiertage.*)

His equally famous *Schicksalslied* vividly recalls Pindar's eighth ode and Goethe's *Parzenlied*. The ruthless antithesis of our human lot and the gods' beatitude is echoed in the rhythm itself.

We have already seen how Hölderlin's love of Greece led him to believe in a heroic Germany, not by way of romantic enthusiasm for the fatherland but through the renaissance of the religious classic spirit. His hatred of the present was born of yearning for a noble future. Hellas became his world and his legacy to German thought. Through his vision of Greece he beheld the German past and the dream of a new German future:

*Gesang des Deutschen*

*O heilig Herz der Völker, o Vaterland!*
*Allduldend gleich der schweigenden Mutter Erd'*
*Und allverkannt, wenn schon aus deiner*
*Tiefe die Fremden ihr Bestes haben.*

The heroes of the classic age were joined by Christ, before whose radiance their own light paled; but still the poet's passion for Hellas burns unquenchable. Hölderlin's dream-clouded verse in distichs, *Brod und Wein* (1801), represents the reconciliation of Christ and the Olympian gods.*

* I have modernized Hölderlin's spelling throughout this chapter; *Brod* of course should be *Brot*.

*Ringsum ruhet die Stadt, still wird die erleuchtete Gasse,*
*Und, mit Fackeln geschmückt, rauschen die Wagen hinweg.*
*Satt gehn heim, von Freuden des Tags zu ruhen, die Menschen,*
*Und Gewinn und Verlust wäget ein sinniges Haupt*
*Wohl zufrieden zu Haus; leer steht von Trauben und Blumen*
*Und von Werken der Hand ruht der geschäftige Markt.*
*Aber das Saitenspiel tönt fern aus Gärten; vielleicht, dass*
*Dort ein Liebendes spielt, oder ein einsamer Mann*
*Ferner Freunde gedenkt und der Jugendzeit, und die Brunnen,*
*Immerquellend und frisch, rauschen an duftendem Beet.*
*Still in dämmriger Luft ertönen geläutete Glocken,*
*Und, der Stunden gedenk, rufet ein Wächter die Zahl.*
*Jetzt auch kommet ein Wehn und regt die Gipfel des Hains auf,*
*Sieh! und das Ebenbild unserer Erde, der Mond,*
*Kommet geheim nun auch; die schwärmerische, die Nacht kommt;*
*Voll mit Sternen und wonl wenig bekümmert um uns,*
*Glänzt die erstaunende dort, die Fremdlingin unter den Menschen,*
*Über Gebirgeshöhn traurig und prächtig herauf.*

This first part of '*Brod und Wein*' provides an important key to the style of Hölderlin's philosophic lyric verse. It consists of eighteen lines in which a striking alternation between hexameter and pentameter renders the content highly stylized, so that it appears freed of the material. The passage quoted divides itself into three parts: lines 1–6 introduce reality and the world's activity, lines 7–12 start off with the antithesis *aber* (man's yearning and solitude), lines 13–18 change the theme. The trilogy is moreover based on optic and acoustic phantasy. The poem might indeed end with the twelfth verse. It is particularly in the second part that we feel the melodious element become so audible: *Liebendes spielt*; *einsamer*, *Freunde*, *Jugendzeit*, etc., and still the music of his *Brunnensehnsucht* lingers on in the lyric verse of Eichendorff, Nietzsche, and Däubler. The third part begins with a description of nature: *Jetzt auch kommet ein Wehn* . . . Through the triple repetition of the word *kommet* the atmosphere becomes ever more tense until with the fall of night the poem concludes on an elegiac note.

In the '*Hälfte des Lebens*,' with its poignant contrast between a wistful late-summer dream and icebound wintry wind, the subjective note has been utterly transfused with the image:

*Mit gelben Birnen hänget*
*und voll mit wilden Rosen*
*das Land in den See,*
*ihr holden Schwäne,*
*und trunken von Küssen*
*tunkt ihr das Haupt*
*ins heilignüchterne Wasser.*

*Weh mir, wo nehm ich, wenn*
*es Winter ist, die Blumen, und wo*
*den Sonnenschein*
*und Schatten der Erde?*
*Die Mauern stehn*
*sprachlos und kalt im Winde*
*klirren die Fahnen.*

Hölderlin wrote this poem thinking he stood in the noonday of his life, but before long he lay enfolded in his spirit's darkness.

In an article on: '*Hölderlin und das Wesen der Dichtung*' Martin Heidegger rightly interprets the essence of poetry not through Goethe but through Hölderlin, for is he not indeed the poet's poet? We shall conclude this section by citing what Heidegger maintains to be the five main ideas in Hölderlin's poetry. (*a*) Poetry is the most innocent of all occupations; it appears in the guise of a plaything. (*b*) But language is at the same time the most dangerous of all possessions. It can range from sublime purity to utter baseness. (*c*) Language unifies humanity. It is only through its agency that we men can find community. (*d*) The poet creates immortality through words. (*e*) Poetry is not an ornament of life but life itself. The poet invokes God in words, he is only subject to the will of the Almighty.

To no other poet was it given that the divine fire should thus descend on him.

## *GOETHE'S LYRIC VERSE AFTER SCHILLER'S DEATH*

In 1788, the year in which Goethe returned from Italy to Weimar, Hamann, the prophet of the 'storm and stress,' died at the residence of Princess Gallitzin.

New paths now opened up before the author of '*Iphigenie*' and

V HÖLDERLIN (Pastel by F. C. Hiemer)
(*From 'Hölderlin', Historischkritische Ausgabe; Propyläen Verlag, Berlin*)

VI WUNDERHORN (2ND VOLUME)
HEIDELBERG, 1808

'*Egmont*.' New problems, new friends were sought and found. At first, alienated by the '*Robbers*' he was but little attracted to Schiller although he supported the latter's successful application for the post of professor of history in Jena. On the outbreak of the French revolution in 1789 will-power and a philosophic turn of mind helped him to maintain an objective attitude. He was no longer the impulsive youth who at the age of twenty-six had been summoned to the court of Weimar. At that time the Duke and his family had themselves stood in the heyday of their youth. The Dowager Duchess Anna Amalia (a niece of Frederick II) was Goethe's senior only by ten years. Her son Karl August, who had just succeeded to the throne, was but eighteen, his wife Luise of the same age. One year later (1776) Goethe was appointed councillor to the embassy and in the following year privy councillor. Major von Knebel, who enjoys a certain renown as the translator of *Propertius*, was five years older than Goethe. Only Wieland (born in 1733) had reached an advanced age and even he was carried away by enthusiasm for the personality of the young poet. Weimar itself basked in the glory of its noble patron Karl August. Between him and Goethe there developed an intimate friendship which happily survived official dissensions in later years. The small town which then boasted but six thousand inhabitants and was moreover cut off from the great arteries of public life would nowadays be stamped as provincial. But under the influence of Goethe and the Duke it became a place of pilgrimage for poets, artists, scholars and politicians from every land. Weimar soon came to be regarded as the symbol of German thought and poetry, a name which it has preserved to the present day.

After Schiller's death Goethe was more solitary than ever. It was the result not of crankish peculiarity but of the unique quality of his personality which could never hope to find another equal. Goethe's dæmon, which was passing through classicism to a yet maturer stage of development, now strove to achieve an ultimate reconciliation of nature and art by endowing the typical with the significance of the symbolic. A striking example of this abandonment of one-sided classicism for more romantic ideals is afforded by Goethe's sonnets (1807–1808). Yet force and restraint retain the harmonious balance so characteristic of the poet's nature.

The '*Urworte. Orphisch*' (completed in 1817, a year after Christiane's death) present a succinct document of Goethe's attitude towards life in his old age. As we have seen before, the poet herein describes the primal forces which ruled his life: the *Dæmon* or inexorable law governing our being, *Tyche* or accident, *Eros*, *Anagke* to which even the Gods are subject (cf. '*Prometheus*': *meine Herren und deine*) and *Elpis* which conquers the inscrutable *Anagke* and, by fostering the hope of freewill in the individual, mitigates the cruelty of fate. He who in Leipzig had torn himself away from Käthchen and simultaneously freed himself from the convention of a literary fashion, he who, in spite of his anguished yearning for Friederike and Lili, had resisted the temptation of a bourgeois home, nevertheless discovered in *Eros* the secret of reconciling freedom and control:

> *Gar manches Herz verschwebt im Allgemeinen,*
> *Doch widmet sich das edelste dem Einen.*

To Goethe the value of history appeared at the most to lie in its power to arouse enthusiasm. Its burden of memories was as unsympathetic to him as later to Nietzsche. He sought to discover true humanity through a life of action which, in his case, was concentrated in the spirit. Goethe's ideas on the position of the individual in the state will be discussed later when we are dealing with George's concept of the poet. Behind the chaos of appearances Goethe divines the existence of a common primal form manifesting itself in life, in history and in poetry as the sublimation of the ego.

In 1819 Frommann of Jena printed Goethe's '*West-östlicher Divan*' for the publishing firm of Cotta. To the poet its creation had meant rejuvenation, and at the same time a recognition of catholicism in the widest sense of the word. He surrendered plastic form in favour of the alluring beauty of the transient impression which, as a Western poet, he, however, welds to stricter form ('*Lied und Gebilde*'). The grotesque and overladen nature of Indian idols was anathema to him as he says in the '*Zahme Zenien.*'

Orient and Occident, Timur and Napoleon, Persia and Heidelberg are united. Goethe has become a wanderer pressing forward from the individual to the universal, from impulse to idea, not through a desire to escape but rather to sublimate life, in order to discover the eternal in existence itself.

*Buch des Sängers (Moganni Nameh)*

*Hegire.*

*Nord und West und Süd zersplittern,*
*Throne bersten, Reiche zittern,*
*Flüchte du, im reinen Osten*
*Patriarchenluft zu kosten,*
*Unter Lieben, Trinken, Singen*
*Soll dich Chisers Quell verjüngen.*

*Dort im Reinen und im Rechten*
*Will ich menschlichen Geschlechten*
*In des Ursprungs Tiefe dringen,*
*Wo sie noch von Gott empfingen*
*Himmelslehr' in Erdesprachen,*
*Und sich nicht den Kopf zerbrachen. . . .*

The truth of the ever-recurring cycle of things leaves a profound impression on his spirit causing him for instance to write the parable of the leaf ('*Gingo biloba*'). No spiritual paralysis threatens his mind. Though he stands in the midst of European upheaval he knows that whatever may come, life is good ('*Es ist gut*'). The work of the aged Goethe holds the secret of rejuvenation through the springtide of love. His philosophy of 'Die and be reborn' attains its zenith in such poems as '*Selige Sehnsucht*' (1814):

*Und solang du das nicht hast,*
*Dieses: Stirb und werde!*

cf. E. H. Zeydel's fine translation
in '*Goethe, the Lyrist*,' 1955.)

and in the cosmogenetic eroticism of the poem '*Wiederfinden*' (1815). Similar ideas are expressed in the '*Weltseele*' (1802) which was influenced by Schelling.

Goethe's formal ideal also suffered a change, but it did not give way to confused imagery. The voyage appears as a symbol of the spirit's progress. A Western heart beats behind the Oriental mask, for Goethe only uses content to which he is drawn by natural affinity; e.g. cypresses for the beloved, Saki-Schenk, Suleika, Hatem, etc. Thus, poems such as the *Schenkbuch*, in which he describes a studious boy's passionate adoration of his master's learning, are thoroughly Western in form; or we read of the doge's marriage to the sea. Goethe's spirit carried him to the ends of the earth. His historic genetic '*Noten und Abhandlungen*' cover a period reaching from primitive times to the modern age.

Inspiration for these poems had been culled from the most various sources. Already in his youth the author of the '*Divan*' had been captivated by the Bible, in particular by Moses, the Song of Songs and the Book of Ruth. The translation of the fourteenth-century Persian poet Hafiz's work by Hammer-Purgstall, the editor of '*Fundgruben des Orients*,' proved a mighty spur to Goethe's imagination. In Goethe's '*Gott und die Bajadere*' and the prologue of '*Faust*' we may trace the influence of Kalidasa's Indian drama *Sakuntalâ*, written about A.D. 500 and translated into German from the English version of Sir William Jones. Further inspiration was provided by the following factors: Goethe's friendship with Professor Eichhorn and the brothers Humboldt, the presence of the Mongols in Weimar in 1814 who mumbled the prayers of the Koran, Diez's translation of the *Book of Kabus*, and a version of the fifteenth-century Persian poet Jāmī's *Medschnūn and Leila*, a study of the Koran, of the *Arabian Nights*, *Mo' allaqât* (dating from the pre-Islamitic Beduin period), the *Persisches Rosental* (Gulistān) by Sa'dî, and above all the epoch-making foundation of Indian studies in Germany through Friedrich Schlegel's treatise, '*Über die Sprache und Weisheit der Indier*' (1808). As we have seen, Goethe's state of mind provided fertile soil for the germination of such seed. In the days when European states were crumbling to dust the poems of Hafiz awakened in Goethe not a longing to escape from life, but a new joy in creative existence. In 1814 Goethe became acquainted with Marianne von Willemer, from whom he was to part forever on his second journey to the Rhine in 1815, fortified in renunciation by his tranquil optimistic heart. She had been his Suleika before whom as Hafiz he could pour out his soul. Herself a poet, she more than any other woman was able to comprehend Goethe's spirit.

The '*Divan*' contains twelve books to which the '*Noten und Abhandlungen*' are added. The work ends with an incitement to action—action as the path to life's fulfilment:

*Denn ich bin ein Mensch gewesen*
*Und das heisst ein Kämpfer sein.*

Similar thoughts are expressed in Goethe's '*Vermächtnis altpersischen Glaubens*':

> *Schwerer Dienste tägliche Bewahrung,*
> *Sonst bedarf es keiner Offenbarung.*

Thus Goethe's conscience paid a debt for his own passive attitude towards the Wars of Liberation. He sought infinity to return again to the finite. The secret of *diastole and systole* symbolizes the reconciliation of the polarity: analysis and synthesis, inspiration and expiration, darkness and light.

Goethe's concept of the organic unity of man and the universe was fostered by Plotinus's *Enneads*, but it had obsessed him since his youth as something of which he ever again found proof in word and thought (Plotinus, Shaftesbury) and in nature. Novalis and Schelling had expressed similar ideas on the subject of polarity. Even from a stylistic point of view, and quite apart from the catholicity of its subject-matter, the '*Divan*' bears an affinity to romanticism. The free rhythms, however, point back to the period of 'storm and stress' and many of the rhymed proverbs which hover so strongly between restraint and passion are rooted in the favourite and ancient German tradition of didactic learning. It was here that Nietzsche found a starting-point for his devastating satire.

Apart from the '*Paria*,' an Indian theme expressing the dualism in our nature which Goethe strove for years to weld to its ultimate form, the '*Trilogie der Leidenschaft*' (1823–1824) represents Goethe's last great lyric work. The aged poet's passionate wooing of Ulrike von Levetzow ended in painful renunciation but without bitterness. His last strength, which had been sorely shattered by the death of Frau von Stein (1827) and Karl August (1828), was concentrated on the completion of '*Faust*.'

*Transition*

Goethe's '*Divan*' is deeply rooted in the romantic movement of the period which, as has been explained, derived from the 'storm and stress' as well as from classic hellenism and idealism; for the new generation's attitude towards Greece changed very slowly. Kant had paved the way for the so-called German idealism which now received its philosophic form through Fichte, Schelling, Hegel and others. But the actual literary spur to idealism was not Kant but the 'storm and stress' with its yearning for uncontrolled self-expression and its passion for monumentality, force, nature, freedom, the irrational and the infinite. It was these ideals to which both classicism and romanticism returned, raising them to a higher plane. Herder appeared to us as a mediator in this respect. His moral point of view, however, separated him from the older romantic poets, just as it did from Kant, whose conception of beauty as disinterested æsthetic pleasure was irreconcilable with Herder's ethics. We have already touched on Schiller's attitude to the budding generation and to Hellas. It is true that he possessed no very perfect knowledge of classic life but he made up for it by his passionate enthusiasm. To him as to Herder life meant combat. Freedom within rule represented the ideal to the author of the '*Tanz.*' It was absolute beauty that he sought. Beauty was to him a necessity of life, the only means of achieving harmony, and only *die schöne Seele* could hope to find the guerdon of that quest. For Goethe this struggle against materialism appears fraught with less toil. Compared with Schiller's his poetry seems to have enjoyed an easier birth. From the naturalism of the 'storm and stress' he develops to the idealism of '*Iphigenie*,' and from here to that ultimate æsthetic realism which provided a direct bridge to romanticism.

# VIII

# GERMAN ROMANTICISM PROPER AND FURTHER DEVELOPMENTS

*The Brothers Schlegel, Novalis, Tieck*

We have already pointed out that German romanticism did not originally develop as an absolute antithesis to classicism. Modern research in the field of biography, history, ethnology (Nadler), philosophy (Ziegler, Spranger, Unger, F. Koch), æsthetics (Wölfflin, Worringer) has done much to further our understanding of the irrational sublimation and dissolution of classic harmony. Rationalism thus appears, one might say, as the thesis, irrational 'storm and stress' as the antithesis, classicism as the synthesis. As romanticism is their sublimation, it must by no means be regarded as a symptom of decadence. Today we recognize in romanticism features which are common to all European literature of the period. The old-fashioned conception of 'romantic schools' developing from one centre (Jena) and subsequently dividing into older and younger schools can no longer be taken seriously. Romanticism appeared simultaneously at the most various places and one cannot possibly speak of a later movement developing from an earlier one, since F. Baader, for instance, is more nearly related to the 'storm and stress' than to early romanticism. Moreover, romanticism is rooted in spiritual and psychological inclinations which vary according to the individual and the race. In our present study, however, we are concerned with the particular qualities of German romanticism as a phenomenon that appeared at a given moment in history, namely at the beginning of the nineteenth century.

A comparison between romanticism and other literary movements helps us to understand its peculiarities. We have already pointed to its love of phantasy in contrast to the emotional vehemence characteristic of the 'storm and stress,' yet both movements betray a tendency towards the irrational which indeed inhabits classicism itself, for in the latter finite harmony contains the mystery of infinity. Thus we cannot set up distinct boundaries between the various movements. It is, moreover, particularly difficult to reduce romanticism to a formula since, in addition to the problems appertaining to generation, style, racial history, the powers of dream and consciousness, its genius is subject to eternal flux. The 'fragments' in the '*Athenäum*' (1798–1800), founded by Friedrich and Wilhelm Schlegel, stress this idea of the progressive nature of universal poetry:

*Die romantische Poesie ist eine progressive Universalpoesie. . . . Sie will und soll auch Poesie und Prosa, Genialität und Kritik, Kunstpoesie und Naturpoesie bald mischen, bald verschmelzen. . . .*

These fragments are, moreover, of great importance in other respects, and represent a characteristic document of their period. They still derive from the past, particularly from Schiller's æsthetic cultural ideals and his isolation from politics. Thus continuing the *Horen* programme, they form a contact with Herder's conception of genius as the natural state of humanity. Goethe's *Wilhelm Meister*, the French revolution, and Fichte's intellectual doctrines appeared to them as the leading forces of the age. Strange as the trilogy Dante, Goethe, Shakespeare may sound to us, Friedrich Schlegel manages to render such and other analogies extraordinarily convincing.

In place of the drama the novel now attains sovereignty over literature. The most heterogeneous elements were combined to form some sort of unity; every possible type of poetry was attempted, and the latter became a pattern-book of linguistic forms. Poetry and prose, poetry and philosophy, native and foreign elements intermingle as a result of this universal breadth of vision. Classic equilibrium yields to a composite mixture of art, nature and wit. And yet in the '*Athenäum*' the intuitive quality of poetry plays an outstanding part. The romantic poets seek in beauty a symbolic representation of infinity, or in Schelling's words, infinity within the finite. Such a doctrine would have been useless to rationalism, but it could find some affinity with Schiller who saw in beauty freedom made visible. The romantic poet believed that this yearning for beauty is manifest in earthly and divine love. Here the '*Athenäum*' is more catholic than Schiller and Hölderlin, who aspired only towards the spiritual. *Wanderlust*, *Waldeinsamkeit*, and *Waldweben* arouse yearnings that can never be stilled.

As yet the romantics made only tentative references to the fatherland. Patriotic enthusiasm was scarcely kindled until the Wars of Liberation. At present æsthetic problems stand in the foreground. One of the chief characteristics of the romantic style is its synaesthesia. Tieck in particular taught the art of 'thinking in dulcet tones' and the transfusion of acoustic and optic elements. Romantic irony is a characteristic feature in the '*Athenäum*' fragments. Its philosophical justification may be found in Fichte's intellectual idea that the human spirit can create the objective world from out its own being, and further in our realization of the existence of a transcendental life beyond this world. We cannot express the latter in words; hence the greatest freedom may reign in poetry. To these romantics and to Schleiermacher, religion is largely a matter of private conscience, whilst for Novalis it was certainly not bound to the church.

In contrast with the 'storm and stress' movement, to which as to *Faust* 'name' is merely *Schall und Rauch*, romanticism analyses emotion. It demands emotion and the understanding thereof. Above all, it investigates the dark side of nature (*Nachtseite der Natur*), active and passive consciousness, the characteristics of animal magnetism, and the secrets of the world of dream and somnambulism. To write poetry is to bind the mysterious spirit of the world in words. All science should become art and all art science. Progressive universal poetry should, according to the '*Athenäum*,' comprise present, past, and future. The very irony of romanticism is always based on idealism. The poet must be able to enjoy the freedom of creation. Other categories already discussed, such as totality and organism, are represented as fundamental values in the '*Athenäum*,' in which many romantic ideas of import are foreshadowed, and which, by the way, clearly betray a legacy from classicism.

Strich's differentiation of two distinct types of poetry (*Deutsche Klassik und Romantik*), based on the dualism: finality and infinity, runs the risk of reducing values actually dependent on historic circumstances to all too simple generalizations. Thus it would almost appear that classicism is in every way superior to the 'expressive' style, whereas Shakespeare, Rembrandt, Bach, Beethoven, the young Goethe, Schiller, Novalis, and Kleist are surely sufficient evidence to support a strong defence of 'expressive' art. Moreover, since Nietzsche, we have come to realize that Greek classicism, which knew nothing of Schiller's moral ideal of duty or humanitarian ethics in the modern sense, bore little relation to the classicism of Weimar. Already during the renaissance we are aware of a preponderance of spiritual values asserting themselves as the result of Christianity in the face of all attempted paganism. The lack of real portraiture in the classic art of Hellas is a further proof of the difference underlying the Greek and modern attitude. Lastly as we have already inferred, the greatest poets and artists, indeed the truly classic spirit itself, seem to reconcile the antithesis to a harmonious synthesis of classicism and romanticism—'a harmony of finite form in which yet lingers the music of infinity' (H. Priebsch Closs's *Art and Life*, 1936, Oxford).

The romantics in the narrower sense, however, must be said to reject the sensuous aspect of the world of appearances in favour of the hidden mysteries of the soul. Gazing on the rising moon or the glittering stars they are inspired to melodious phantasies. The individual and the universe no longer maintain the perfect equilibrium which they enjoyed in the writings of Goethe and recovered in different measure with E. Mörike, G. Keller and, to a certain extent, Droste-Hülshoff, T. Storm, and others. Later on the impressionists once more turned to the visible world, but we must realize that the German romantics also discovered a path to the latter through their love of nature and the folk-song.

Friedrich Schlegel (1772–1829) began as a classic poet. As to Schiller in his '*Ästhetische Erziehung des Menschen*,' the ancient Greek appeared to him as ideal man, κατ' ἐξοχήν. He stresses the quality of ethical and æsthetic values. F. Schlegel's ideas on the piquant element in modern art are deeply rooted in Schiller's theory of the naïve and *sentimentalisch*. It soon, however, came to a break between Friedrich Schlegel and the editor of the '*Horen*' who, according to the opinion of the former, suffered from sublime excessiveness. Wilhelm's wife, Caroline, whom Schiller called *Frau Lucifer*, supported Schiller's antagonists, whilst Goethe retained an open mind and kept up his connection both with

Schlegel and Schiller. Friedrich Schlegel's chief fault was that he recognized and combated a rationalist in Schiller. After writing '*Lucinde*' (1798-1799), which affords a practical example of the romantic style and an antithesis to Schiller's ethics, Friedrich Schlegel's rejection of classicism becomes more complete. Shakespeare, Goethe, Dante, Ariosto, Cervantes, Petrarch, Tasso, are numbered among his favourites. At the beginning of the nineteenth century, particularly after his journey to France, his patriotic conscience awakened. The influence of Fichte's '*Reden an die deutsche Nation*' (1808) and similar writings encouraged this tendency. When Friedrich and Dorothea became converts to Catholicism in 1808 the expression of his religious convictions provided the chief material of his literary output. As a lyric poet he would scarcely have attained immortality. His '*Romanze vom Lichte*' (later entitled '*Rückkehr zum Licht*') deserves special attention on account of its mythology and the influence of Jacob Böhme's and Schelling's philosophy. The earth loves the atmosphere (the light) under whose influence the life of the earth flourishes and develops. Love kindles man's imagination. From such poetic phantasies light at length finds its way home.

Friedrich's elder brother August Wilhelm Schlegel (1767–1845) won renown through his translations and study of Shakespeare. He also was a disciple of Schiller and was wildly enthusiastic for '*Die Götter Griechenlands*.' Wilhelm's own poetry is not romantic. He cared above all for form both intellectually and in social life, and unlike his brother did not adopt the Roman Catholic faith. He did not profess *one* style, for he adopted both classic and romantic forms at will (cf. '*Das Sonett*'). He expresses passion through rhythm. His poetry is conscious. He seldom reaches such poetic heights as displayed in the last lines of his poem '*Romeo and Julia*':

> *Die wie durch Zauber fest geschlungen waren,*
> *Löst Glück und Ruh und Zeit mit leiser Hand;*
> *Und jedem fremden Widerstand entronnen,*
> *Ertränkt sich Lieb' im Becher eigner Wonnen.*

It was Novalis (Friedrich von Hardenberg, 1772–1801), born of Herrenhuter stock, who first gave the romantic poets of the Jena circle poetic symbols for the infinite in the finite. The early death of his beloved Sophie von Kühn († 1797), the philosophy of

Plotinus, Hemsterhuis, Fichte, Schelling, Schleiermacher, Franz Baader, and Johann W. Ritter, were decisive influences in Novalis's poetry. His yearning for death was not pathological but was born of his deep faith in immortality. To him death appeared not as the destroyer, the end of all, as it had done to Catullus: '*Vivamus, mea Lesbia, atque amemus*. . ., *cum* semel *occidit brevis lux, nox est* perpetua *una dormienda*. . . .' Though death had robbed him of his bride, Novalis's belief in a future life remained unshaken. Just as Fichte found a path to science through the imagination, Novalis's dream of immortality leads him to true life, though he was spared the bitterness of Schiller's struggles and was not doomed to shipwreck like Werther. The world of appearances was to him but a symbol of the inner life. Thus the poetic world of his romances becomes reality to him. In the *blaue Blume* he beholds a visible image of the secret world whose existence he divines and in which science and poetry are indivisible. Here even the state—not a republic but a monarchy—should become poetic.

In the fragmentary novel '*Die Lehrlinge zu Sais*' Novalis clothed his and Schelling's concept of 'nature as visible spirit and spirit as invisible nature' in the guise of a romantic fairy tale *Hyazinth und Rosenblüth*. Characteristic is Novalis's belief in the unity of reason and nature which every human being should reach of his own accord in dream. The '*Hymnen an die Nacht*' (1797–1799) present similar phantasies and are the most perfect of Novalis's lyrics. Their most important parts also appeared in prose form (*Athenäum*):

> *Welcher Lebendige, Sinnbegabte, liebt nicht vor allen Wundererscheinungen des verbreiteten Raums um ihn, das allerfreuliche Licht—mit seinen Farben, seinen Strahlen und Wogen; seiner milden Allgegenwart, als weckender Tag.*

The praise of light modulates to a hymn to night and sleep whose closing lines we quote from the poetic version:

> *Zugemessen ward*
> *dem Lichte seine Zeit*
> *und dem Wachen—*
> *aber zeitlos ist der Nacht Herrschaft,*
> *ewig ist die Dauer des Schlafs.*
> *Heiliger Schlaf!*

*Beglücke zu selten nicht*
*der Nacht Geweihte—*
*in diesem irdischen Tagwerk.*
*Nur die Toren verkennen dich*
*und wissen von keinem Schlaf*
*als dem Schatten,*
*den du mitleidig auf uns wirfst*
*in jener Dämmrung*
*der wahrhaften Nacht.*
*Sie fühlen dich nicht*
*in der goldnen Flut der Trauben,*
*in des Mandelbaums*
*Wunderöl*
*und im braunen Safte des Mohns.*
*Sie wissen nicht,*
*dass du es bist,*
*der des zarten Mädchens*
*Busen umschwebt*
*und zum Himmel den Schoss macht—*
*ahnen nicht,*
*dass aus alten Geschichten*
*du himmelöffnend entgegen trittst*
*und den Schlüssel trägst*
*zu den Wohnungen der Seligen,*
*unendlicher Geheimnisse*
*schweigender Bote.*

To Novalis *night* is a potent force, the symbol of death which bears life anew. Hence it achieves religious significance. The path to the inner life is free. Ethereal images and adjectives are heaped into short sentences, their effect as a whole being melodic rather than rhythmic. Striking parallels to Richard Wagner's '*Tristan*' suggest themselves in spite of the negative results of R. Park's enquiries concerning proofs of Novalis's influence on the composer. According to Adam Müller the fifth hymn contains the germ of a great religious tragedy. Without doubt the hymns may largely be interpreted as expressions of the poet's personal experiences in his relation to Sophie, but also as variations on the theme: night and death are one. The hymns are an initiation into the supernatural world which leads us to God. Regarded from this point of view they appear as hymns of humanity and its yearning to escape from the prison of earthly existence into eternity.

Novalis's '*Geistliche Lieder*' are associated with certain church festivals such as Christmas and Good Friday, Easter Sunday, etc. He praises Mary as the symbol of the infinite in the finite.

Novalis sets out in quest of a religion of profound faith. In his prose fragment, '*Die Christenheit oder Europa*,' he glorifies the harmony of the Middle Ages which the reformation destroyed. Emotion, he says, must once more be our guide. Ancient papacy has long lain buried. Now Christianity must be awakened again and with it the all-embracing spirit of God. The latter ideas betray the marked influence of Schleiermacher, who himself attempted to arouse religious feeling. Indeed, this disciple of Spinoza possesses much in common with Novalis. To both 'reflection' is the conscience of mankind, for we must become what we are; death is a gateway to eternity, religion is a matter of personal feeling, and not reason but the heart must reign supreme.

In Novalis's lyric novel, '*Heinrich von Ofterdingen*,' the world is dissolved to mysterious poetic images of pure emotion. The novel is a panegyric on poetry and is divided into two parts. The first describes how Heinrich becomes a poet, the second brings the consummation: *Die Welt wird Traum, der Traum wird Welt*. Dream and reality become one. In contrast with Goethe's '*Wilhelm Meister*,' the world, nature, war, and history are transfused to poetry. Everything becomes a symbol. The legend of Eros (the son of reason and the heart) and Freia (daughter of Sophie and Arktur, i.e. Friedrich Wilhelm III) forms the basis of the novel. The fairy tale is indeed the primal form of all creation, for art and philosophy are dependent on phantasy. It is very probable that Jacob Böhme's mystic cosmogony exerted a direct or indirect influence on certain ideas expressed in the fragment. According to the Silesian philosopher there are four stages in the egocentric world: the first three being fire, water, and light, which is born of the first two. In the fourth sphere the worlds of light, of stone, and of evil oppose one another. Our natural instinct bids us seek the eternal realm we have lost. Light helps us to liberate our soul.

Ludwig Tieck (1773–1853), the son of a Berlin ropemaker, was born in the year which witnessed the publication of Goethe's '*Götz*.' The precocious boy soon betrayed a partiality for lurid fancy and the horrible. Tieck's versatile nature and his peculiar assimilative power caused him to pass through many vicissitudes —a youth full of boundless enthusiasms and a period of literary hackwork under Nicolai in the service of superficial enlightenment. Then in 1797 he announced the appearance of *Peter Lebrechts Volksmärchen*, in which he maintained a free attitude towards his sources. Tieck's version of the '*Wundersame Liebesgeschichte der schönen Magelone und des Grafen Peter aus der Provence*' provides the starting-point for his characteristic intermingling of colour and tone. Here for the first time we meet with the *Stimmungsbild* of the fountain and the whispering trees so loved by the romantic poets. Here, too, are the germs of the characteristic synaesthesia of romanticism, e.g., the green rushing Rhine, strains of the violin like the tints of the rainbow, the green sound of the huntsman's horn, the sky-blue flute, the silvery tones of the lute (which we already find in Klopstock). In Tieck's poem '*Liebe denkt in süssen Tönen*' the boundaries of the senses dissolve in verses of unforgettable beauty. Brentano most nearly approaches such 'romantic fusions.' A. W. Schlegel avoids them completely, Friedrich Schlegel makes scant use of them, Novalis applies them only in relation to colour. Arnim avoids them for the sake of lucidity, but Eichendorff loves the dark-green atmosphere of the forest and is influenced by Tieck's dawn and twilight *Stimmung*.

In Tieck's '*Der blonde Eckbert*,' an original tale of incest, a unified fairy-tale atmosphere is exquisitely maintained throughout the narrative and song. The chiaroscuro of the landscape dims the contours of the chief characters. The transfusion of fairy-tale and realistic element is far more successfully achieved than in some modern stories such as Stehr's '*Geigenmacher*.' Above all, Tieck's poetic prose sustains the magic keynote of his tale. Note the melodious play on the alternative vowel sounds *ei—eu—eu—ei* in *Waldeinsamkeit*:

*Waldeinsamkeit,*
*Die mich erfreut,*
*So morgen wie heut,*
*In ewger Zeit,*
*O wie mich freut*
*Waldeinsamkeit.*

If Tieck had at first displayed a craving for the lurid and terrible, and then turned to the folk-story and legend and exaggerated satire ('*Der gestiefelte Kater*'), his taste, as we gather from his fragmentary novel '*Sternbalds Wanderungen*,' was ennobled through the influence of Wackenroder, Novalis, and Goethe. In his fairy drama, '*Leben und Tod der heiligen Genoveva*,' he attempted to combine the epic, lyric, and dramatic styles. His other fairy drama, '*Kaiser Octavianus*' (1803–1804), might be called a handbook of romanticism. It is at once allegorical, lyrical, and dramatic, and aims at a rejuvenation of mythology. In the '*Aufzug der Romanze*' the figure of Romantic Poetry appears in person. The genealogy of the romance contains many symbols such as Venus and Eremit, Love and Faith, Romance, Jest is Love's servant and Courage the handmaid of Faith. Pagan and Christian ideas intermingle in this phantasy, which bears Love and Faith as its theme. '*Faust*' and Shakespeare's '*Tempest*' (Caliban) must have played some part in the poet's inspiration. The song about the moon's magic:

> *Mondbeglänzte Zaubernacht,*
> *die den Sinn gefangen hält,*
> *Wundervolle Märchenwelt,*
> *steig' auf in der alten Pracht*

became a model of romantic poetry. To the latter we may add the synaesthesia already mentioned, *Waldeinsamkeit*, Christian imagery and a partiality for the cycle, e.g. the collection of stories entitled *Phantasus*, which caused Tieck to be regarded as the chief inaugurator and representative of romanticism. Tieck understood how to act a part, an important asset to the romantic poet. He immersed himself in a study of Nicolai and also Wackenroder, who idealized the Middle Ages, and like young Goethe sang the praise of the old German style.

In his lyrics Tieck seldom gives expression to some actual occurrence, but lets his fancy roam at will—hence his kaleidoscopic imagery. *Traumhaft* (dreamy) is one of his favourite adjectives. Music, he believes, has power to bind all. Thus in his poem '*Zeichen in Walde*' the vowel (*u*) is repeated for the sake of atmosphere almost to the point of absurdity. As far as the linguistic aspect of *Stimmung* is concerned Tieck's contemporaries learned more from him than from Goethe. The '*Mondscheinlied*':

*Träuft vom Himmel der kühle Tau,*
*tun die Blumen die Kelche zu . . .*

shows how Tieck sacrificed the visual image to musical atmosphere. Already the first verse betrays in its details little power of exact observation, e.g. *tun zu*, also a partiality for personification, *Spätrot*, *Ruh*; likewise the second verse, *bleiben auf*, and the third, *Dunkelheit*, *Finster*. In the seventh verse we meet with that unfortunate image: *hüpft wie der Quell*. Taken as a whole, however, the poem shows a surprisingly well calculated sense of structure. Verses 1 to 3 describe the encroaching night, verses 4 to 6 the rising moon and vivacious fancy; 7 to 8 are steeped in yearning. We are thus made aware of a sense of strict composition on the part of the poet. Double lifts (*Spätrot*, *Berggipfel*) disturb its rhythmic flow, which ultimately fades to a mere play of fancy bereft of any goal. The optic illusion is quickened to movement till it creates a scenic effect. A flimmer and quiver of light and shade creates the atmosphere of a moonlit night.

*Heidelberg*

The brothers Schlegel and Tieck were restless spirits. The fate of many a German poet of the romantic movement was symbolic of the character of German romanticism. The brothers Schlegel started at Göttingen; in Jena early romanticism throve for a time under their guidance. Soon, however, the centre of its activities was shifted to Berlin, Vienna and Dresden, and it was in the last town that Tieck made his home. In the Dresden gallery A. W. Schlegel and his wife Caroline discussed their views on art and published them under the title of '*Die Gemälde*' in the *Athenäum*. The home of the musician Reichardt in Giebichenstein also attracted many a poet. In Cologne dwelt the brothers Boisserée, the Rhine and Cologne Cathedral luring many of their old friends to sojourn there. But above all, Heidelberg under the influence of Brentano, Arnim, Creuzer, Görres, Eichendorff, and for a short time J. H. Voss became the centre of the romantic school. Rome, whither the Nazarenes had fled from the tyranny of the Viennese Academy and where they now intended to devote their art to a religious cause, held an irresistible temptation for Tieck and many another. Not only art but that innate yearning of all

Northerners for the South led them thither. The greatest romantic painters, however, are K. D. Friedrich from Greifswald, who stressed the emotional and reflective element in art, and the poet-painter, Philipp Otto Runge from Wolgast on the Baltic, whose most famous work, '*Die vier Tageszeiten*,' illustrates this painter's curious concept of symbolism of colour:

*Der Morgen ist die grenzenlose Erleuchtung des Universums.*
*Der Tag ist die grenzenlose Gestaltung der Kreatur, die das Universum erfüllt.*
*Der Abend ist die grenzenlose Vernichtung der Existenz in dem Ursprung des Universums.*
*Die Nacht ist die grenzenlose Tiefe der Erkenntnis von der unvertilgten Existenz in Gott.*

The arabesques that surround the pictures accentuate their musical quality. Mathematics, colour, and music appear here fused to the unity which Tieck had so much desired. The whole series of paintings is likewise tinged with deep religious feeling.

The so-called *Heidelberg romanticism*, which we mostly connect with the names of Arnim and Brentano, despite their fundamental differences as lyric poets, bears a character all its own. Through them a German university was enabled for the last time to exert a deep influence on literary movements. Clemens Maria Brentano (1778–1842) was the grandson of Sophie de la Roche and the son of an Italian who had settled in Frankfurt. After years of restless wandering he went to Heidelberg whither Arnim came in 1805. In the same year there appeared as fruit of their united labour the first volume of '*Des Knaben Wunderhorn*,' with two hundred and ten songs dedicated to Goethe. The second and third volumes appeared in 1808. These folk-songs aroused the enthusiasm not only of Goethe but of Uhland, Görres, the brothers Grimm and others. The value of the folk-song had already been recognized by Herder. It was his spiritual legacy that now burst into full blossom. Certainly people's conception of *Volk* still remained, but vague and misted by Rousseau-like ideals. Herder laid too much stress on the primitive's originality, as though no *Kunstdichter* could possibly create a 'popular' song (see Uhland's '*Kamerad*'), whilst W. Grimm exaggerated the unconscious element. According to Goethe, the *Volkslied* passed from mouth to mouth. Today we know that there is no organic difference between the *Kunstlied* and the *Volkslied*, even if H. Naumann's theory of the so-called debased *Kulturlied* and primitive communal song is not accurate. (See our chapter on the folk-song.)

Whereas Goethe's theory about the folk-song did not, as we have seen, add any really new ideas to the subject, his famous review of *Des Knaben Wunderhorn* still lives today in the memory of the German people on account of many a pertinent remark (cf. *Weimarer Ausgabe*, 40, 337 ff.). Karl Bode has investigated the relation of original and adaptation in the *Wunderhorn*. From him we learn how systematically Arnim and Brentano studied the folk-song collections of the sixteenth, seventeenth, and eighteenth centuries: Forster, Regnart, Schein, Nicolai, Elwert, Gräter, and others, further the Limburg and other chronicles. In the Eschenburg collection they found the later '*Hildebrandslied*.'

The editors of the *Wunderhorn* did not attempt to give precise references concerning their sources. In their treatment Brentano betrays conservative, Arnim modern taste. The former has a partiality for archaic forms; the latter makes efforts to adapt the songs to modern taste, in the course of which he does not avoid changes, contractions and additions, the metre becoming all too smooth. Through Arnim's independent procedure the defiant deserter and Landsknecht becomes a sentimental Swiss youth who '*Zu Strassburg auf der Schanz*' dreams of his lost Alps, and neglects his duty as a soldier in listening to the music of an alpine horn. From a purely scholarly point of view such licence may deserve a reprimand, but Arnim's intention was to give the old traditions of his country new vitality. It is characteristic that the poet and collector Arnim never managed to write a true folk-song, whilst Brentano's own songs (included in the *Wunderhorn*) sometimes achieved a real folk-song air, e.g. his '*Wieviel Sand in dem Meer . .*,' '*Spinn, Mägdlein, spinn*,' or '*Der Reiter zu Pferd*,' probably an old dance-song. Brentano's playful manner and his partiality for tonal colour is noticeable in his poem, '*Wacht auf, ihr kleinen Schülerlein*,' which Bode calls the counterpart to one of Spee's. The charm of this collection of songs lies in particular in its manifold motifs and forms, which a more unified collection would probably lack. In his essay '*Von Volksliedern*,' at the end of the first volume of the *Wunderhorn*, Arnim rightly complains of the levelling influence his bourgeois era exerted over literature. His complaint might appear even more justifiable if applied to present-day conditions. Yet we may find consolation in the thought that the old songs still survive and remain a constant source of poetic rejuvenation.

No other poet steeped himself so deeply as Brentano in the world of huntsmen, soldiers, tramps, and outcasts, or infused old melodies with such new life. His chameleon-like character was very different from the versatile but steadfast personality of Goethe. In his fairy-tale, '*Gockel, Hinkel und Gackeleia*,' Brentano was able to give free play to those untamable fancies which also fill his '*Weltliche Gedichte*.'

The poem entitled '*Sprich aus der Ferne*' will serve as a typical model of Brentano's work:

*Sprich aus der Ferne,*
*heimliche Welt,*
*die sich so gerne*
*zu mir gesellt.*

*Wenn das Abendrot niedergesunken,*
*keine freudige Farbe mehr spricht,*
*und die Kränze still leuchtender Funken*
*die Nacht um die schattige Stirne flicht:*
*Wehet der Sterne*
*heiliger Sinn*
*leis durch die Ferne*
*bis zu mir hin.*

*Wenn des Mondes still lindernde Tränen*
*lösen der Nächte verborgenes Weh,*
*dann wehet Friede. In goldenen Kähnen*
*schiffen die Geister im himmlischen See.*
*Glänzender Lieder*
*klingender Lauf*
*ringelt sich nieder,*
*wallet hinauf.*

*Wenn der Mitternacht heiliges Grauen*
*bang durch die dunklen Wälder hinschleicht,*
*und die Büsche gar wundersam schauen,*
*alles sich finster, tiefsinnig bezeugt,*
*wandelt im Dunkeln*
*freundliches Spiel,*
*still Lichter funkeln,*
*schimmerndes Ziel.*

*Alles ist freundlich wohlwollend verbunden,*
*bietet sich tröstend und trauernd die Hand,*
*sind durch die Nächte die Lichter gewunden,*
*alles ist ewig im Innern verwandt.*
*Sprich aus der Ferne,*
*heimliche Welt,*
*die sich so gerne*
*zu mir gesellt.*

Its musicality is its chief point. The rhythm is closely attuned to both the sense and structure of the lines. The verses have eight lines, of which four contain four lifts, the others (the coda), however, only two. The long lines describe nature, the short ones express the life of the soul, though the boundaries between the two worlds dissolve. The poem opens on a rhetorical key. A hypothetical *wenn* at the beginning of the second, third, and fourth verses introduces his nature-pictures which lead up to a climax: sunset, the rising moon, midnight. Few of these images appeal to the eye (see *des Mondes Tränen, in golden Kähnen*). On the other hand we find an abundance of emotional adjectives: *heimlich, freudig, still, verborgen.* The poet's soul feels deep affinity with the night, but the lack of clear imagery is accentuated by an excess of clumsy rhyme: *spricht/flicht, verbunden/gewunden.* Nevertheless the poem possesses undeniable charm on account of its melodious nature and unified atmosphere.

Brentano's '*Romanzen vom Rosenkranz. Die Erfindung des Rosenkranzes,*' begun in 1803, but not published until 1852, form a highly romantic work based on a predominant ideal. To understand its purport more completely it is well to turn to Brentano's correspondence with Philipp Otto Runge. Man's primal sin is erased by the Virgin Mary, who tramples on the serpent's head. The conflict between Good and Evil appears in the form of various symbols in the course of the poetic cycle, whilst Mary remains the central theme.

In the meantime, after the death of his first wife Sophie Mereau († 1806), who was herself a poet of some talent, feverish unrest once again assailed Brentano's spirit, until in 1816 he became acquainted with the pious authoress Luise Hensel, whom he wooed in vain. When in Dülmen, during the years 1818–1824, he recorded the ecstatic visions of the stigmatized nun Anna Katharina Emmerich, he appeared to have reached the close of his poetic career. Nevertheless, his spirit remained productive even after 1818, as his plan for a great mystic epic bears witness.

Compared to Brentano's iridescent, bendable nature, that of Achim von Arnim (1781–1831) appears strong as an oak's. His chief merit lies in his resuscitation of long-forgotten treasures of German literature, for as an original lyric poet he has left us little of value. It is not surprising that the friendship existing between the two poets earned the name of a marriage of the soul. But their differences in character were too large to allow the bond to be maintained for ever. Arnim was of aristocratic lineage from the Eastern marches, by confession a Lutheran, whilst Brentano, the restless, wandering spirit, was devoted to the Catholic faith, especially under the influence of Luise Hensel and afterwards. As early as 1809 Arnim came to Berlin and within a short space of time married Brentano's sister Bettina. At that time Arnim as a fiery prophet of patriotic regeneration could only find signs of the national unity for which he craved, in the '*Wunderhorn*.' Herder's collection of songs had still been international, whilst Brentano's and Arnim's was German and rooted not only in the individual but in the whole people.

*Patriotic enthusiasm*

Poetry, like the political fate of Germany, reflected the spirit of revolt against Napoleon and the tyranny of petty states. Even learning did not remain untouched. In 1807, J. J. Görres (1776–1848) published '*Die teutschen Volksbücher*,' and in 1817 '*Altdeutsche Volks- und Meisterlieder*.' Two years later appeared the first volume of Jacob Grimm's '*Deutsche Grammatik*.' Wilhelm Grimm's '*Die deutsche Heldensage*' was published in 1829, long after the chief representatives of the Heidelberg school of romantics had parted company (1808) and Baron de la Motte Fouqué (1777–1843) from Brandenburg had at A. W. Schlegel's suggestion undertaken a rendering of the Sigurdsaga in dramatic form. Fouqué still enjoys fame as the author of '*Undine*' and the song '*Frisch auf zum fröhlichen Jagen*.' The '*Wunderhorn*' also aimed at kindling the spirit of romantic Germany through the memory of its past. It appeared a few years before military victories heralded by many a fiery bard liberated Europe from the tyranny of Napoleon. Philosophers and statesmen such as Fichte, A. Müller, F. v. Hardenberg, Stein, Scharnhorst, and others built a new heroic ideal from the ruins of their country. Others fought through poetry and incited vengeance against Napoleon; thus H. von Kleist (1777–1811) in his drama '*Hermannsschlacht*:' or his poem '*Germania an ihre Kinder*,' with his challenge 'the Germans shall live free on their own soil and destroy their arch-enemies':

*Alle Triften, alle Stätten*
*färbt mit ihren Knochen weiss. . . .*

But before his nation was freed from the yoke of oppression that 'forced its neck under the prerogatives of a son of hell,' Kleist's own spirit was broken. He committed suicide by the Wannsee near Berlin on the twenty-first of November, 1811, after he had fulfilled the last wish of his friend Frau Henriette Vogel by shooting a bullet through her heart.

German patriotic poetry had already played a part in the Seven Years' War, cf. the *Bardendichtung*, to which we have already referred. When, however, Germany was forced to suffer the ignominy of defeat through Napoleon this intellectual poetry straightway disappeared.

Through his own death Karl Theodor Körner (1791–1813) gave significance to his passionately patriotic songs, '*Leyer und Schwerdt*.' Even today the challenge of 1813 (*Aufruf*.):

*Frisch auf, mein Volk! Die Flammenzeichen rauchen,*
*Hell aus dem Norden bricht der Freiheit Licht . . .*

his posthumous song:

*Das Volk steht auf, der Sturm bricht los,*

or the sword-song, '*Du Schwerdt an meiner Linken*,' which Körner composed but a few hours before his death, can appeal to the public. Certainly many others of his poems are immature and all too reminiscent of Schiller. In his father's house at Dresden, Körner was already able to enjoy a wide education. His love of music and poetry was strengthened by his facile productivity. Thanks to his attractive nature and his personal circumstances he soon enjoyed the coveted position of court-poet in Vienna. Whether he would have gradually sunk to the mediocrity of a Kotzebue it is not for us to say. His death has cast glamour over both his personality and poetry.

A greater and more virile poet was Ernst Moritz Arndt (1769-1860) from Rügen on the Baltic, whose song '*Der Gott, der Eisen wachsen liess, der wollte keine Knechte*,' has become the battle-cry of his nation's fight for freedom. In Arndt, Arnim found a spiritual brother who inflamed the hearts of the young fighters with his passionate love and hate. Schill's death in 1809 brought the conflagration to a climax. The dream of a mighty Germany rose before the eyes of the poet. The saying: '*Der Rhein, Deutschlands Strom, nicht Deutschlands Grenze*,' so often quoted today, also comes from the pen of Arndt.

Max von Schenkendorf (1783-1817) also wrote a poem in honour of Schill, though of less pointed nature than Arndt's. It is milder in tone, less definitely political than the latter's. The same may be said for instance of his song: '*Freiheit, die ich meine* (*minne!*), *die mein Herz erfüllt*.' Austrian poets also joined in the fight for freedom, amongst them Heinrich J. von Collin, an imitator of Schiller and Kotzebue, whose '*Wehrmanns-lieder*' defend the emperor Franz and the Habsburg throne.

On the other hand we find Napoleon's admirers, a great many of whose songs are represented in the '*Napoleon Album*' (1842), edited by E. Brinckmeier, and illustrated by H. Vernet, V. Adam and A. Meyer. Amongst the poets appears in addition to Heine and others Freiherr Franz von Gaudy, the author of the '*Kaiser-Lieder auf Napoleon*.'

*Eichendorff, Chamisso*

The influence of the Heidelberg school of romantics is clearly visible in the work of the Catholic poet Josef Freiherr von Eichendorff (1788-1857), a native of Upper Silesia. He, too, composed many a passionate song in praise of his fatherland, and when in the year 1813 king Friedrich Wilhelm III's proclamation was read before the people, the poet exchanged his pen for the sword and joined the ranks of the Lützowian army in which Theodor Körner served. Fundamentally, however, Eichendorff was not of a militant nature, and also had little sense for political verse. As a true poet he could not feel neutral; nevertheless, he avoided overburdening his verse with literary content. In his treatise on romanticism: '*Über die ethische und religiöse Bedeutung der neuen romantischen Poesie in Deutschland*' (1847), a work that exerted but small influence on modern literary criticism, he speaks of the use of poetry and its significance in the life of the nation: 'The cries of passion and despair do not yet in themselves produce poetry. True poetry is religious and makes poetry of religion.' He thus demands high moral values of æsthetics. His songs about wanderlust, love and spring are, for all their robust worldliness, transfused like his romances with something of the transcendental. He possesses the power of rendering the mysterious music of nature, of the forest, the sea, the wind, the sky, and the flowers in verse:

*Schläft ein Lied in allen Dingen,*
*die da träumen fort und fort,*
*und die Welt hebt an zu singen,*
*triffst du nur das Zauberwort.*

Eichendorff casts the true romantic spell over our hearts—moonlight, the murmurings of the forest, loveliness, wanderlust, the postillion's horn, slumbering fountains, a world clouded in dreams; cf. '*Mondnacht*':

*Es war, als hätt' der Himmel*
*Die Erde still geküsst.*
*Dass sie im Blütenschimmer*
*Von ihm nun träumen müsst.*

*Die Luft ging durch die Felder,*
*Die Ähren wogten sacht,*
*Es rauschten leis die Wälder,*
*So sternklar war die Nacht.*

*Und meine Seele spannte*
*Weit ihre Flügel aus,*
*Flog durch die stillen Lande,*
*Als flöge sie nach Haus.*

His poem '*Sehnsucht*,' one of the '*Wanderlieder*,' is also typical of his style:

*Es schienen so golden die Sterne,*
*Am Fenster ich einsam stand*
*Und hörte aus weiter Ferne*
*Ein Posthorn im stillen Land. . . .*

The subject-matter is wanderlust. The arrangement of the lines, like that of his images, is characteristically lax. Their order might indeed often be changed and they do not end on a finite note. One would perhaps expect a logical conclusion, namely that the poet would take to the road and set out like the two young fellows whom he heard singing.

Eichendorff seems to have found no difficulty in adopting the student and folk-song tone as in his popular '*Prager Studenten*,' or '*In einem kühlen Grunde, da geht ein Mühlenrad*.'

Of the latter poem Kerner tells an amusing anecdote. In 1812 Eichendorff sent it to him inscribed with the signature *Florens*. A puff of wind blew the page which had just arrived high above the roofs and tree-tops of Welzheim in Württemberg. Kerner had little hope of recovering it. On the following day, however, a Tirolese pedlar arrived with mouth-organs, bracelets and rings, one of which was wrapped in a piece of paper which he had found an hour's walk distant amidst a flowering meadow of flax. It was the page containing Eichendorff's poem, which soon after sped as a *fliegendes Blatt* all over Germany.

The author of the '*Taugenichts*' was by no means only a dreamer. He was a magnificent swimmer, an adept dancer and rider, and often a mischievous comrade who delighted in frightening his companions by harmless practical jokes. There is a tale that walking along the banks of the Oder one day with his parents he suddenly caught up his five-year-old sister and plunging into the water swam with her across the river. It was in Halle, where Schleiermacher, Steffens and F. A. Wolf held many a student under their spell, that Eichendorff first became acquainted with the romantic poets. In Lauchstädt he saw the *Weimar Theater*, and even beheld the Olympian poet at work. But it was above all the literary circles of Heidelberg and Vienna which attracted him, and where he enjoyed the hospitality of Friedrich Schlegel, A. Müller, Wilhelm von Humboldt, Friedrich von Gentz and others. In Berlin he conversed with Savigny in the house of the banker J. Mendelssohn, the son of the philosopher. Later sojourns in Breslau, Danzig, Königsberg, Dresden and Vienna brought him into contact with the leading spirits of his age. Through him romanticism found consummation. But as far as influences were concerned it was a matter of give and take. Thus for instance Eichendorff's conception of the state may be termed romantic. Like A. Müller (1779–1829) he wished it to represent a vital unit. The former, who became a friend of Eichendorff's in Berlin and Vienna, had been connected with Kleist as fellow contributor to the journal *Phöbus* (1808). A. Müller was born in Berlin. In Vienna he became a convert to Catholicism, enjoying the patronage of Metternich and Friedrich von Gentz, and the friendship of Friedrich Schlegel, and others. His philosophy and æsthetic ideals stood in strong opposition to the French revolution and the doctrine of natural rights. He defended positive historic right against absolute ideals, rejecting æsthetic systems in favour of the doctrine of organic law as upheld by Herder, Burke and Novalis. In his eyes the family represents a vital cell in the structure of the state in which the aristocracy and the bourgeoisie must form a necessary bond. In art also antitheses must be reconciled. Reason and phantasy should join one another in beauty. An important feature of Müller's philosophy is his belief in the myth of an original dual sex, of the Androgyne of Plato's *Symposium*. The necessary contrast between male and female, and their final synthesis on which A. Müller lays so much stress, is in part a continuation of Schiller's and W. von Humboldt's concepts.

Herder's idea of the organic unity and natural evolution of society also bore fruit in the works of F. K. von Savigny (1779–1861). The latter ranks as the founder of the historically-minded school of law which can be understood as the natural offshoot of a romantic concept of the state.

Karl Ludwig von Haller's '*Restauration der Staatswissenschaft*' (1816) on the other hand represents the unromantic attitude, a return to reactionary ideals that would reassert the absolute sovereignty of the ruler. The subsequent disillusionment which political conditions bore in their wake increased a yearning for a new springtime of the nations, whose advent and dénouement Eichendorff, Adam Müller's friend, was still fated to witness.

Adalbert von Chamisso (1781–1838) came into contact with romantic circles in Berlin. French ancestry and Gallic temperament mingle with his German sentiment to create a unique personality. When he was twenty years old he abandoned the French language for German. Through Napoleon, the emigrants who had fled in 1790 from Boncourt were enabled to return to their native land, but Chamisso's ancestral home had been laid waste, and the young lieutenant had already begun to look on Berlin as his home. Varnhagen's salon, Fichte and A. W. Schlegel attracted him. The defeat at Jena threw him into deep dejection, for he himself stood halfway between the two countries. Affinity of taste brought him for a time into the company of

Madame de Staël. In 1813 Chamisso was carried away by the tide of German patriotism, and felt himself a true German. He devoted his time to the study of medicine, botany, geology and anthropology as his favourite subjects. His scientific interests led him to the South Sea Islands to study their flora. By this time he had found recognition and esteem as a scholar. His fame as the mysterious 'shadowless man,' and as a globe-trotter, resounded all over the land of his adoption. The home of his mother found a literary memorial in his verses on '*Schloss Boncourt*.' But the fate that hurled him from the privileged state of a born aristocrat into the life of a burgher is symbolized in the famous story of '*Peter Schlemihl*.' In the active pursuit of his scientific studies and in the limitations of bourgeois existence the erstwhile enthusiast at length found peace of mind. It is characteristic of his nature that his best poems were written after his marriage in 1819, amongst them '*Schloss Boncourt*.' One of the reasons for his comparatively late development as a writer may have been the fact that he was bilingual. His German models were Schiller, the '*Wunderhorn*,' Fouqué and Uhland, the last exerting particular influence on his romances. But the story of such poems as the '*Tragische Geschichte*' of a pigtail, the '*Riesenspielzeug*' or '*Der rechte Barbier*,' etc., etc., is drawn from the treasure-house of his own phantasy, or represents his very individual rendering of German legend and anecdote. His song-cycle *Frauen-Liebe und Leben* became famous through Schumann's composition. Occasionally Chamisso betrays a streak of cruelty as in his poem *Das Kruzifix*.

*Swabia and Alemannia.*

*Uhland, Schwab, Kerner and others*

Under Ludwig Uhland (1787–1862), German romantic lyric poetry, in particular the ballad, definitely approaches a more classic idea. Uhland robs his knights and ladies of every individual trait and presents them as types invested with all the noble virtues that ever inhabited a knightly heart—freedom, manly prowess, honour, faithfulness, the integrity of action, the sweetness of love. A mature reflective quality transfuses Uhland's works which those of Eichendorff alone could rival in popularity. Here we find nothing of the abstruse phantasy of Tieck playing havoc with traditional lore. No Brentanesque whimsies make a mock of Uhland's noble morality. Ecstatic ebullitions have given place to a lucid tempered idiom that expressed his wholehearted love for the fatherland. Uhland's verse is not only patriotic; it has the genuine ring of folk-poetry ('*Der Wirtin Töchterlein*,' '*Der gute Kamerad*') interspersed with romantic illusion and disillusion ('*Der Traum*'). When his lyric gift began to fail him, though he grew silent as a poet, he continued to fight as an undaunted orator for the rights of his people and particularly of his own Swabia.

Uhland's compatriots were justly proud of their history and above all their poets. His generation brought with it hopes of a new literary triumph. Nevertheless, one cannot speak of a Swabian school, but only of affinities through common ancestry, friendship and patriotic enthusiasm. In his '*Schwabenspiegel*' (1838), Heine amused himself at the expense of Swabia where everybody is *hübsch patriotisch*, *gemüthlich*, *hübsch ordentlich*, and treats his Swabian contemporaries with derision. Heine regards Gustav Schwab as the herring amongst saltless anchovies, Karl Mayer is a 'tired fly,' Gustav Pfizer a 'reflective bat,' Justinus Kerner a 'great fool.' Nevertheless, genuine admiration causes him to refrain from mocking at Uhland. Already in his volume on the '*Romantische Schule*' Heine refers with undisguised wistfulness to the tournaments, the knights and noble ladies, the monks and nuns, the minnesingers and Nordic heroes of Uhland's poems, amongst which he most loved the verses:

*Der schöne Schäfer zog so nah*
*Vorüber an dem Königsschloss;*
*Die Jungfrau von der Zinne sah.*
*Da war ihr Sehnen gross. . . .*

Heine's yearning for the past is simultaneously mingled with his love-hatred of Germany, with the result that he accuses Uhland of a lack of originality and calls his heroes respectable imitations of Arminius and Thusnelda. This narrow judgment may, perhaps, contain a germ of truth, for we must admit that Uhland's heroes are idealized to a great extent, and the past appears in too rosy a light. But Heine's scornful references to 'sickly sentimental melancholy' do not fit Uhland, whose weakness is only a frequent tendency to oversimplify his characters, as for instance in the case of the king and his liegemen in some of his ballads. We can obtain a clear insight into the manner in which Uhland draws his types in order to achieve the popular tone by a study of the ballad '*Bertran de Born*,' which was inspired by Diez's '*Leben und Werke der Troubadours*.' Many further examples, e.g. '*Es zogen drei Bursche*,' might be cited. The latter possesses an Indian parallel. Heine's '*Bertran de Born*' appeared after Uhland's poem, and by its side seems but a skeleton, or rather a playful conceit of decadent romanticism.

Uhland was particularly adept in matching popular content and form, as we see by his *Nibelungenstrophe* in the '*Sängers Fluch*.' No other poet was so suited to the task of writing a '*Geschichte der Dichtung und Sage*,' or on '*Alte hoch- und niederdeutsche Volkslieder*.' Though his partiality for epic breadth caused him to enjoy only a passing fame as a dramatist ('*Ernst, Herzog von Schwaben*,' '*Ludwig der Bayer*') he will remain immortal as a popular lyric poet as long as the German race has pride in its poets. Uhland's '*Der gute Kamerad*' (1809), remodelled from a *Landsknechtslied* in the *Wunderhorn*, unites and will ever unite his compatriots in times of suffering or of joy.

We are only gradually beginning to realize how much Uhland, after one hundred and fifty years, means to Germany. As a politician, a scholar and a poet he had wanted to appeal to the German people. Uhland's faults cannot be disguised. He started from a romantic conception of the folk-song; he read a feeling for Nature into the minnesong, which rightly belongs only to the *niedere Minne*; he was too often influenced by book-reading instead of mingling with the peasants. But he was a 'conservative democrat,' full of passionate faith in a pan-German community. He rejected all individual subjective art and tried to root himself in the life of the people. Uhland's language at its best, e.g. in his most beautiful poems, '*Die linden Lüfte sind erwacht*,' '*Droben stehet die Kapelle*,' etc., is of a lucid simplicity that makes him a true poet of the people. It is not surprising that the Swabian poet Hans Heinrich Ehrler, born in 1872, was able to use Uhland as the starting-point of his own verse. Ehrler's '*Heimatlied*':

*O Heimat, wir sind alle dein,*
*Wie weit und fremd wir gehen . . .*

which sounds like a solace after the misery of the war, may rightly be regarded not only as the expression of nostalgia for Swabia, but as the spiritual legacy of Uhland.

Of far less significance are the remaining Swabian writers, with the exception of Mörike, the greatest of the nineteenth-century poets since Goethe and Hölderlin. Wilhelm Hauff still enjoys popularity as a writer of lyrics through his two songs, '*Reiters Morgensang*' (*Morgenrot! Leuchtest mir den frühen Tod*) and '*Soldatenliebe*' (*Steh ich in finstrer Mitternacht*). Like Hauff, Justinus Kerner from Ludwigsburg cared more for the world of the occult than for the German muse. Already as a youth he was sensitive to the mysterious ways and warnings of fate. For this reason he seems more closely allied to the romantic school than other Swabian poets. When as a youth he came to Tübingen to study science he fell asleep exhausted upon a bench in front of the hospital. Just as he awoke a medical prescription fluttered down from one of the windows. The accident decided the course of his studies. As a doctor he achieved world-wide fame by his observations of the case of a somnambulant woman, known as 'the visionary of Prevorst,' in Württemberg. Kerner diagnosed in her certain manifestations of the magnetism of the animal or human world. The little blue flame which the visionary beheld in the right eye of animals was explained by him as the soul. He moreover noticed that minerals had a strange effect on the somnambulist, producing sleep and magnetic attraction. These experiences seemed to Kerner to confirm ideas which he had long harboured, namely that supernatural forms are as real as the sensual. In his frequently morbid inclination towards the demonic, the 'night-side of nature' he differs greatly from Uhland. Many of Kerner's songs are melancholy, for example, his '*Wandrer in der Sägemühle*':

*Dort unten in der Mühle*
*sass ich in süsser Ruh*
*und sah dem Räderspiele*
*und sah den Wassern zu. . . .*

From his pen came also that well-known wanderer's song: '*Wohlauf! Noch getrunken den funkelnden Wein.*'

More productive as a lyric poet was Gustav Schwab (1792–1850), who must also rank amongst the later romantics. What a gulf lies between him and Goethe is revealed by the dogmatic abstract tone of his '*Erste Liebe*.' How ponderous and ornate is the language in which he addresses his '*Pauline*': *liebes frommes Mühmchen* . . .

Side by side with weak rhyming and long-winded description we nevertheless find some powerful ballads, such as '*Der Reiter und der Bodensee*,' and above all the '*Gewitter*,' which justly ranks as the finest example of his art as a ballad-writer.

An Alemannic poet, more than thirty years his senior, Johann Peter Hebel (1760–1826), composed a poem bearing the same title, which is, however, of a very different type. Whereas in the case of Schwab's ballad the lightning destroys four lives, Hebel's tempest subsides and gives place to an atmosphere of humorous tranquillity. The child continues to slumber undisturbed in its cradle:

*So helfis Gott, und b'hüetis Gott!*
*Wie zuckts dur's G'wülch so füürigroth*
*und's chracht und toost, es isch e Grus,*
*ass d'Fenster zitteren und's Hus.*
*Lueg's Büebli in der Waglen a!*
*Es schloft, und nimmt si nüt drum a.*

On the whole Hebel appears more akin to Claudius than to his immediate South German compatriots. His poetry inclines towards the idyllic. His pious temperament was content with a humble field of activity, and it was not until Goethe praised his work in the *Jenaische Literaturzeitung* that the world took much notice of him. Even success did nothing to alter his innate modesty. In his homely Alemannic dialect he describes the '*Habermuss*,' the man in the moon ('*Lueg Müetterli, was isch im Mô?*'), the evening star, Frau Holle, and the little witch, or he tells us that even the smallest creatures of nature, insects, the little spiders and flowers have souls. Translation into High German robs such poems of all their magic.

# IX

# AUSTRIA, BIEDERMEIER, GRILLPARZER

WHEN German literature is spoken of, few are aware of the prominent part Austria played in its formation, not only in modern times but more especially during the Middle Ages. The traditional picture of the *gemütlicher*—happy-go-lucky Austrian—has given rise to the proverb: 'In Austria beats the German heart, in Berlin the German brain.' But Austrian history and literature tell another story, for they were not created by dreams and tender melancholy alone, but by manly deed. Placed between East and West, Austria, and especially Vienna, has been the stage of many a mighty conflict.

Two thousand years ago Vindobona was a Roman fortress. It was here that the royal philosopher Marcus Aurelius wrote his essay *Ad se ipsum.* Following the disintegration of the Roman empire the ravaging tide of the fierce Huns swept over the land, and after the death of their leader Attila, the Eastgoths, Langobardian tribes, and later the Avari settled temporarily on the fertile soil of the Danubian valley. It was, however, Charlemagne who in his struggles with the Avari first founded the so-called Ostmark (East border country) which constitutes the germ of the later Austrian empire, and from the end of the tenth century onwards the famous dynasty of the Babenberger, under whom the minnesong lyric flourished, made of Austria a fortified gateway to the East. In 1273 the Habsburgs came into power and held it for nearly seven hundred years until 1918, which saw the breakdown of Austria after the Great War.

Vienna became a world-centre of culture. Here in the fourteenth century the second German university was opened, and soon afterwards it became the residence of the German emperors. With the Great War the political power of Austria was shattered. Only the core of a vast country remained, but music, poetry, and art yet retain their magic power. Here the South German genius, in which the Bavarian, the Franconian, and the specific Austrian characteristics are blended, found its most perfect expression in the so-called Austrian baroque. Illusion and reality are interwoven in poetry. The Austrian theatre revels in baroque splendour and 'panache,' and society is bred in an æsthetic atmosphere.

On the threshold of the German renaissance stands Kaiser Maximilian I († 1519), called the last of the knights, who held his court at Innsbruck and founded in Vienna (1502) the *Collegium Poetarum et Mathematicorum.* He was not only a patron of this humanistic movement or renaissance of the scholarly world, but himself a poet. His epic *Teuerdank* describes the chivalrous adventures of his life; it is of distinctly allegorical character, and the last product of the courtly epic. His prose work *Weisskunig* is a chronicle of battles and personal experiences. The marriage of his grandson Ferdinand von Österreich into the house of Ladislaus secured the inheritance of Bohemia and Hungary for Austria. 'Austria, happy by marriage,' was well on the way to the consummation of its power. During the following years, however, Vienna had to stand its trial in the wars against the Turks. But even beneath the travail of the Thirty Years' War Austria's power remained unshaken, nor did the ravaging plague of 1679 and the second siege of Vienna by the Turks in 1683 blight its poetic vitality. Austrian baroque flourished especially during the reign of the Emperor Leopold I.

In contrast to the art of the renaissance, baroque architecture has the reputation of being formless and overloaded. Its effect is often that of unrestrained magnificence. This style must ever seem incomprehensible to classicists. But Austrian baroque is not mere bombast. Leibniz has given it philosophical justification. The subordination of the atom to the whole and the simultaneous recognition of the atom constitute the formative principle of baroque. We find in German and Austrian baroque poetry a peculiar intermingling of intellectual and sensual thought somewhat similar to that met with in the poems of Donne and Crashaw. And we may note that Austrian baroque architecture in the hands of Fischer von Erlach, Lucas von Hildebrandt and Prandauer, has a lightness, a musical flow, that removes it far from the overloaded Italian manner. Indeed it takes on a romantic allure which enables it to blend with nature, as in the monastery of Melk and in the little church of Dürnstein on the Danube.

As the genius of Goethe and Schiller rose, Austrian baroque fell into decay.

After the golden age of Maria Theresa, Joseph II, her successor, set out to realize the great reforms dreamed of by his mother. Education was furthered; state and church were reorganized on a more tolerant basis. Mozart's dream of an enlightened mankind, as expressed in the '*Magic Flute*,' may indeed have been inspired by the spirit of Joseph II, and Sarastro, High Priest of the Temple of Wisdom, bears a resemblance to this tolerant benefactor of his people. It was Joseph II who opened the Austrian national theatre to which every lover of drama would fain make a pilgrimage. The names of Schreyvogel, Laube, Bauernfeld, Kainz, and Anton Wildgans († 1932) have since added fame to the Burgtheater, where frequent performances of Shakespeare provide an everlasting bond between Austria and England. Stage art and music celebrated many a triumph here, but in the meantime *Weimar* had become the great cultural centre of literature and thought, and the spirit of Goethe, that universal genius of the modern age, shed its light on Austrian culture. At the same time Goethe himself gathered from the latter more than one inspiration, as for instance from the Orientalist Hammer-Purgstall, and from the scholarly and literary circles in Bohemia, at Karlsbad, Teplitz and Franzensbad. Moreover the theatre in Weimar, directed by Goethe, developed under the influence of Vienna.

The fall of Napoleon and the rise of Metternich brought about a reaction in Austria. We generally term this period the *Biedermeierzeit* (about 1820–1850). Freedom of thought and public opinion were suppressed, and when at the Wartburg-Fest in 1817 rebellious liberal students made a bonfire of pigtails, stays, and canes (the symbols of reaction), matters were only made worse. Two years later the student Sand murdered the diplomat-author Kotzebue, which led to liberalism being completely crushed. Metternich has been held responsible for this reactionary campaign, but it was rather the work of the system than of the man himself, who indeed could appreciate liberal thought and even enjoy a poem of Heine's. Under this difficult state of things the Austrian bourgeoisie sought refuge and sweet oblivion in the music and poetry of home and salon. The tumultuous wave of rebellion, echoed in Beethoven's dæmonic symphonies, had ebbed. Schubert's gentler melodies soothed the troubled soul.

It is, however, a misconception to consider this period, the so-called *Biedermeierzeit*, one of bourgeois spiritual tranquillity. We speak of it as the good old times, but in reality it was inflamed with revolutionary ideals. A new social class was fast rising, parliamentary reforms developing, and the press gaining universal power.

The term '*Biedermeier*' still provides a point of dissension in contemporary criticism. Grolman considers its use in regard to a definite literary epoch unjustified. Nevertheless the latter interpretation has been proved correct by Pongs, Kluckhohn, Weydt, Bietak, and others. Pongs calls the entire bourgeois culture of the nineteenth century *Biedermeier* and allows its limits a large scope. His conception appeals to us personally far more than one which would press such poets or scholars as J. Grimm, Ranke, G. Keller, Grillparzer, Droste, Raabe, Stifter into a narrow definition. G. Keller, for instance, and many another writer bears affinity to the *Biedermeier* spirit only in certain ways. Moreover, one cannot possibly say that Schubert's '*Antikenlieder*' belong to this category.

But even the *Biedermeier* epoch is not lacking in the dæmonic element. What heroism can be hidden behind bourgeois existence, what cruel forces imperil it one may apprehend through the stories of Gotthelf, O. Ludwig or Droste. The powers of light and darkness in and around us ever threaten each other. Bourgeois values such as home, respect of history, tradition and custom, a flair for collecting, a love of the folk-element, all appear as a natural defence against excess. The bourgeois spirit certainly expresses itself somewhat differently in the Austrian and Prussian poet; nevertheless an affinity of mood is unmistakable. It would not be right to call the latter mere resignation, although the French revolution and the fall of Napoleon had shattered the era. We should rather discern in the *Biedermeier* an ethic attitude which of its own free will applies the leash to its passion, and in place of personal freedom seeks to secure the liberty of the family, the bourgeois community, and the nation. For this reason we often find the destructive element sacrificed to the family unit and clan spirit. The abysm of the dæmon world yawns behind this world of bourgeois morality.

Only in comparison with our own times does this period seem one of ease and security. The loyal Austrian loved his opera and sang his national anthem to Haydn's melody, which had been inspired by *God save the King*, and in the Schubert circle forgathered the so-called *Schubertiaden*—circles of leading poets, actors and musicians of Austria.

Here Grillparzer (1791–1872), Austria's greatest poet since the Middle Ages, was a welcome guest. With him German literature experienced the Indian summer of its classicism. His genius incorporated many characteristic Austrian traits. He was like Walther von der Vogelweide, sociable yet solitary at heart, dreamy of mind, sensitive, but slightly ironical, and withal a conscientious official. Melancholy, disciplined subordination, frankness and irony—these specifically Austrian characteristics are expressed in his story of '*The Poor Fiddler*.' He who understands the fiddler's character will also comprehend Grillparzer's temperament, which falls precipitately from rapture into disillusionment, freezes in the sun, and would fain flee far from the madding crowd.

Grillparzer kept aloof from literary fashions and moreover stood in opposition to the German nationalist movement. He towers above such second-rate Austrian authors as Johann Gabriel Seidl (author of the popular poem '*Die Uhr*'), Johann Nepomuk Vogl ('*Heinrich der Vogelsteller*'), Ernst von Feuchtersleben ('*Es ist bestimmt in Gottes Rat*'), Karl Egon von Ebert ('*Frau Hitt*') and Freiherr Joseph Christian von Zedlitz ('*Die nächtliche Heerschau*').

Imagination and reason were but rarely reconciled in Grillparzer's genius. This discord affected not only his poetry but his personal life. His temperament made the thought of marriage with Katharina Fröhlich, his lifelong betrothed, impossible, and she herself possessed a charming but obstinate little head. He paints her picture in '*Allgegenwart*':

*Abends, wenn's dämmert noch,*
*Steig' ich vier Treppen hoch,*
*Poch' ans Tor,*
*Streckt sich ein Hälslein vor;*

*Wangen rund,*
*Purpurmund,*
*Nächtig Haar,*
*Stirne klar,*
*Drunter mein Augenpaar.*

In the poem '*Jugenderinnerungen im Grünen,*' he confesses why his spirit that was continually drawn anew to hers could never find true union with her being. 'Our hearts burnt but never melted,' Grillparzer says of his love, and in his drama, '*König Ottakars Glück und Ende,*' which unmistakably alludes to the fall of Napoleon, the poet commemorates his beloved Käthe.

Though Grillparzer's nature was fundamentally passive and often succumbed to fits of profound melancholy, it is wrong to identify this passivity with the Austrian mentality, a mistake made by critics (such as O. Zausmer) even today. His attitude towards the state was as problematic as that towards love. He was faithful to the Austrian dynasty, though not blind to all its faults. The fact that he is sometimes branded a reactionary conservative is an injustice, due perhaps to his personal abhorrence of the upheaval brought about by the French revolution and the German national movement of 1848. Above all, it was the patriotic German students who turned against him when in 1848 he burst into eulogies on '*Feldmarschall Radetzky*' and his army. At the bottom of his heart, however, Grillparzer was an adherent of liberal monarchism (particularly of his ideal, Joseph II), and an open enemy both of democratic standardization and Metternich's bureaucracy. The humanitarian ideal of Weimar appeared more noble in his eyes than the nationalist cause, and a greater Austria meant more to him, the admirer of Napoleon, than a unified German realm. Thus it is of his beloved land of the Danube that he sings such heartfelt praise in '*König Ottokars Glück und Ende*' (Act III):

*Es ist ein gutes Land,*
*Wohl wert, dass sich ein Fürst sein unterwinde! . . .*

It was long before his works were acknowledged by the public either in Austria or abroad. Some wrongly saw in him a clever imitator of Schiller, and censorship put obstacles in his path. This was one of the causes of his choosing ancient Greece as background for the action of his characters.

Bourgeois liberal ideas and Schopenhauer's pessimism are voiced in his dramas. The freedom of one is the ruin of the other, and man cannot strive against his predestined fate—writes the poet in his trilogy, '*The Golden Fleece.*'

One might apply the words spoken by Grillparzer at the grave of Beethoven to the work of the poet himself:

> 'Since the beginning of time poets, heroes, singers, and men beloved by the gods, have lived that the crushed soul of man may be fortified to remember its origin and goal.'

But it was only through suffering that Grillparzer was able to attain such glory. His poem: '*Abschied von Gastein*' (1818):

> . . . *Denn wie der Baum, auf den der Blitz gefallen,*
> *Mit einem Male strahlend sich verklärt. . . .*
>
> *Indes in dieser Flammen glühndem Wallen*
> *Des Stammes Mark und Leben sich verzehrt;*
> *Der, wie die Lohe steigt vom glühnden Herde,*
> *Um desto tiefer niedersinkt zur Erde . . .*

provides a key to the understanding of his work. As artist he did not flee from life in the manner of many a modern symbolist, but his spirit was so broken by antagonistic forces in and around him that he could never attain that note of sublime prophecy which was Hölderlin's.

The weighty content of Grillparzer's poems often finds little support in his careless metre, and herein too we may be tempted to see a symbol of his dualistic nature, which also colours his attitude towards religion. In '*Die Ruinen des Campo Vaccino*' he exalts classic paganism to the detriment of Christianity. Nevertheless, it is only from the point of view of æsthetics, and not for want of faith, that he here laments the decline of classicism. In vain did Grillparzer try to defend himself against the attacks of the church. He only won the reproaches of the emperor, who never forgave him.

The year of revolution (1848) saw the fall of Metternich, but none the less brought with it disillusionment. In the political entanglements that followed Austria and Prussia confronted each other as enemies, and in 1866 Austria met with defeat. This heralded a new era in Austrian literature, of which we shall hear in a later chapter.

# X

# THE POLITICAL LYRIC ROUND ABOUT THE YEARS 1830 AND 1840–1848

We have already met with the political lyric in connection with the Wars of Liberation. Though we regarded it largely from the point of view of content we are conscious that it is also dependent on a certain formal sense and attitude towards life. Even the greatest poetry has not only an æsthetic purpose but betrays some particular conviction of the poet's mind. In its narrower aspects, to which we shall confine ourselves in this chapter, these convictions take on the form of political agitation. It is, therefore, unjust to apply a purely æsthetic criterion to such verse, for its intentions are quite different; it aims at rhetorical effect, seeks to rouse violent emotion, and convince the reader. It champions a social class, or 'the nation' in the party-sense. It employs ideologies and describes actual events ('*Rheinlieder*' and others). At the same time political poetry can use æsthetic means (by way of palpable description) in order to render its argument the more effective. The boundary between form and content is thus indistinct, nevertheless the chief point is political agitation.

Christian Petzet has given us an informative study on the nature of political verse. A history of the ideas and thematic development characteristic of this genre of poetry is, however, found only in Benno von Wiese's exhaustive work, which we may regard as a starting-point for our present survey. He shows in what manner the non-political attitude prevalent in Germany at this period reacted to the French revolution. On the whole the latter interested the Germans from the point of view of ideology. The fact that after the execution of Louis XVI enthusiasm rapidly cooled down only proves that in Germany the French revolution had been regarded as an idea, and not as an immediate political necessity for France. In the *Horen* Schiller definitely repudiated politics in favour of the realm of humanity and the perfect æsthetic state. Classicism threatened to lose itself in timeless ideals. Nevertheless, Goethe was able to find contact with his contemporaries and reality, whilst Schiller discovered a balance to his æsthetic cosmopolitan attitude in his passionate love of the fatherland. Even the preceding period of 'storm and stress' showed itself unwilling or unable to make its verse the mouthpiece of contemporary politics. It raged against tyrants, but usually only in a vague abstract manner, and in similar terms gushed about liberty and humanitarianism. Nevertheless, the noble robber Karl Moor finally gives himself up to the law. The results of the French revolution cast the fiery enthusiasts into an abyss of disillusionment. They began to harbour grave doubts as to the omnipotence of 'enlightenment,' or even rejected it openly. The restoration took advantage of the situation and by winning the support of the Catholic church, and poets and scholars such as Friedrich Schlegel and A. Müller, set out to build a bulwark against the revolution. Church and state were now united, and their efforts to re-establish the old order of things were furthered by the fact that romanticism with its æsthetic patriotism was now giving way to classic ideals, and dreamed of a united Christian Europe.

On Napoleon's ascendancy not only the face but the soul of Europe underwent a change. The Germans were forced to leave their æsthetic dreams for the material world of deeds and politics. Classicism and romanticism had both, in the political sense, represented escape from life. Culture had appeared more significant than the affairs of the day and political conviction. Now, however, Arndt, Fichte, Görres and others began to hurl anathema on the enemy. And still they tried to protect the German *spirit* from Napoleonic contamination. They fought in the name of moral freedom, honour and God. They incited their country to a holy war against the arch-enemy. Herein lies the chief distinction between these religious patriotic *Freiheitsdichter* and the romantics, who lacked any real interest in political activity. Later, when the restoration began, and Metternich's absolutism nipped all dreams of freedom in the bud, the persecuted *Burschenschaften* still guarded their honour and their faith in old ideals, which many of them were able to defend on the field of battle. As yet lyric poetry had not sunk to the level of propaganda. The ideals to which the students aspired in their gymnastics were on the whole still connected with an enthusiasm for liberty that was partly the legacy of enlightenment.

German political poetry during the thirties was up to a point international, for it shared its yearning for freedom with similar movements in Greece and Poland. But in the forties it concerned itself chiefly with its own patriotic cause. Byron's sudden death (1824) in the service of the Greeks, followed three years later by the ultimate Greek victory over the Turks, fanned the flames of the German cause of liberation. The revolt of the Poles against the political tyranny of Russia in 1830 threw a fresh brand on the fire. But soon afterwards the Russians had avenged their defeat.

German lyric poetry of the period mirrors these foreign events. Wilhelm Müller, famed through Schubert's musical rendering of his songs, composed a number of '*Griechenlieder*' which, though exhilarating as political propaganda, lack all originality. Few realize that the quasi-wistful '*Müllerlieder*' (*Das Wandern ist des Müllers Lust, Ich hört ein Bächlein rauschen, Ich schnitt es gern in alle Rinden ein*) were the outcome of certain social games in which the poet and his friends were wont to indulge at the house of Stägemann where Luise Hensel, whom Müller courted in vain, played the part of gardener. Many of Müller's '*Reiselieder*' (*Im Krug zum grünen Kranze, Am Brunnen vor dem Tore*) are still in vogue today.

The fate of Poland inspired Lenau and Platen to write their '*Polenlieder*.' Also Julius Mosen, the author of that song so loved in Austria, '*Zu Mantua in Banden*,' was inspired by Polish patriotism.

At Hoffmann and Campe's in Hamburg, the publishing house which produced the works of the Jungdeutschen, there appeared in 1831 the '*Spaziergänge eines Wiener Poeten*.' The author, Anastasius Grün (pseudonym of the Austrian count Auersperg), wisely published these attacks on Metternich and his arbitrary censors and clerical firebrands anonymously. The songs in '*Schutt*,' '*Nibelungen im Frack*' likewise serve political ends. Grün appears as an imitator of Uhland, Heine and others, but his scathing wit is his own. He wields his weapon with an æsthetic gesture and thus does not yet appear as that truly political type of author who asserted himself in the forties, when the poet (Herwegh, Freiligrath) became the mouthpiece of a political party inciting revolution.

The individual representatives of the political lyric of 1840 and 1848 by no means belong to one and the same party. Each reacted to the trend of the times in his own way, either as a *radical* (Herwegh), a *liberal* (Hoffmann von Fallersleben), an *internationalist* (Heine), or even as a *conservative* (Geibel).

When Friedrich Wilhelm IV succeeded to the throne in 1840 patriotic Germans were full of hopes for the future. Turnvater Jahn was set free. This and other generous gestures on the part of the government kindled the people's love for their country and their king. When the latter, however, began to assert even more strongly the theory of Divine Right promulgated by the restoration party, disillusionment was rife.

In 1840 the patriotic poets were able to find themes of momentous significance, such as the problem of the Rhine, which aroused wild enthusiasm. N. Becker hurled his challenge '*Sie sollen ihn nicht haben, den freien deutschen Rhein*' at the French, who were once again about to claim the Rhine as their own. Those opening lines of the song were soon on every tongue and inspired a whole number of '*Rheinlieder*.' Herwegh, Prutz, Dingelstedt (author of the '*Lieder eines kosmopolitischen Nachtwächters*') joined in praise of the Rhine. Max Schneckenburger's famous '*Wacht am Rhein*' was written shortly before Becker's song, but did not attain popularity till later, since when, however, it has remained a favourite. In his old age, E. M. Arndt (born 1769) wrote a song on the Rhine. His verses (1841): '*Was ist des Deutschen Vaterland?*' incited the Germans to unite. In the same year Hoffmann von Fallersleben composed the national anthem '*Deutschland, Deutschland, über alles*.' These verses, which were set to music by Haydn, have, like his charming children's songs, '*Winter ade! Scheiden tut weh*,' '*Summ summ summ*,' '*Ein scheckiges Pferd*' and others, won him an eternal place in every German heart. He suffered deeply under the consciousness of his country's lack of political unity and was filled with disgust at the sight of many an armchair patriot. His poem '*Rotwälsch*' and the '*Allemanische Lieder*' were furnished with a glossary. Fallersleben may well be called the last of the wandering minstrels.

France accepted Becker's challenge. Musset answered the German poet in tones of boundless scorn. Lamartine on the other hand regarded the Rhine as a symbol of brotherhood between the two countries.

*Jung-Deutschland*, in whose name Wienbarg composed his '*Ästhetische Feldzüge*,' found a glowing orator in Georg Herwegh. To the latter strife was the mother of all progress. His '*Gedichte eines Lebendigen*' (1841) created a sensation. He was honoured by an audience before the king, Friedrich Wilhelm IV, but the poet's shyness in the presence of his sovereign, his subsequent tactless behaviour, and his hopeless failure when, in the revolution of 1848, he had the chance of proving himself courageous in the face of danger, caused him to become a figure of fun. The pun: '*Herwegh =Herr, weg mit dir*' is symptomatic of the scorn with which the once-famous patriot was met even amidst his own circle of friends. Idealism and reality represented in him a crude and tragic antithesis. Nevertheless his fame as the most radical poet of the forties remains unquestioned. Who has ever thrown such defiance into verse as rings through his '*Aufruf*':

> *Reisst die Kreuze aus der Erden!*
> *Alle sollen Schwerter werden?*

Who has ever sung with such determined hate as in the refrain:

> *Wir haben lang genug geliebt,*
> *Wir wollen endlich hassen?*

His poem on '*Die deutsche Flotte*' and the unity of a Germany guarded by an efficient fleet has become famous. Herwegh, whom Heine called the 'lark of iron,' believed himself to be a second Hutten when, in '*Jacta alea est*,' he sang: '*Ich hab's gewagt!*' . . . His rider's song:

> *Die bange Nacht ist nun herum,*
> *Wir reiten still, wir reiten stumm*
> *Und reiten ins Verderben.*
> *Wie weht so scharf der Morgenwind!*
> *Frau Wirtin, noch ein Glas geschwind*
> *Vorm Sterben, vorm Sterben . . .*

is uncannily powerful in its fey vision. As a political poet Herwegh depends on the topics of the day. His rhetoric is rich in antithesis, exaggerated and full of phrases, though not altogether lacking in sincerity. But his heart quailed before deeds and he ended in disgrace.

When Freiligrath wrote that the poet looks on the world from a higher vantage-point than the battlements of party politics:

> *Der Dichter steht auf einer höhern Warte*
> *Als auf der Zinne der Partei . . .*

Herwegh openly acclaimed himself a servant of 'radical liberalism.' Geibel, in his poem '*An Georg Herwegh*,' soon confronted Herwegh with an equally bold and manly song that flowed from his veneration of the enduring conservative forces in life.

Ferdinand Freiligrath from Detmold stood as *Jungdeutscher* on the side of the Swabian poet Herwegh, with whom however he was, as we have seen, destined to clash in many respects. Both as poet and man he shows true character. His political '*Glaubensbekenntnis*' was written with heartfelt conviction. He sacrificed the pension which had been granted to him by the king and in 1844 accepted the fate of the exiled demagogue. In the year 1848 he once more returned to his native country and was persecuted on account of his poem '*Die Toten an die Lebendigen*,' but was finally liberated. Later on he again fled to England. Through his translations of Burns, Victor Hugo, and others he became an interpreter of English and French literature in Germany.

The force of Freiligrath's political songs carries one away, but his character is greater than his art. The integrity of spirit which gave birth to his '*Ça ira*' songs, his revolutionary dreams of justice and personal (also political) independence, for which he was forced to lead the life of an exile, deserve our sympathy and admiration. Of his songs, the German Marseillaise lives only as a name today. Apart from the song '*O lieb, so lang du lieben kannst*,' or '*Prinz Eugen, der edle Ritter*' (*Zelte, Posten*), almost all his poems have sunk into oblivion, yet the memory of the poet's combative spirit still endures. His marked partiality for Oriental splendour often loses itself in sterile fancy.

After 1850 the political lyric suffered a decided check. The working classes were still too weak in numbers and in will to make good their demands. The growth of industrialism and the increasing prosperity of the bourgeoisie stifled the poet. The so-called *Gründerzeit* which followed drained culture and human values of their vitality and paraded them as a hollow mask. A new 'storm and stress' arose to quell the social and cultural life, this time from the ranks of the proletariat and bourgeoisie. Naturalism shattered the illusion and allied itself to social and political ideologies of which we shall hear more later.

# XI

# HEINE, PLATEN; RÜCKERT, LENAU; THE MUNICH CIRCLE

---

HEINRICH HEINE, who was born in Düsseldorf in 1797 and died in Paris in 1856, was a herald of this movement. He belongs simultaneously to the climax of 'Young Germany,' and the dissolution of German romanticism. His genius has been represented in the most varied light both in Germany and abroad. Whereas foreign countries often regard him as the most representative German poet after Goethe, German criticism is probably unanimous in claiming that his reputation has been assessed too high. We ourselves consider Mörike, not Heine, to have been the greatest poet of the nineteenth century after Goethe and Hölderlin. The disrupted state of Heine's character and attitude towards life makes it wellnigh impossible to deliver any objective judgment. He continually changes his tone, which is now full of destructive dialectics, now romantic and dreamy, now heroic (cf. the poem '*Die Grenadiere*'), now *blasé*. As the most brilliant journalist of 'Young Germany,' he can hardly be given sufficient praise. The air of a martyr, which he was so often wont to affect, has a habit of suddenly turning into irony. Many of his readers, and particularly Germans, find it disturbing that, for instance, in the case of the literary scandal concerning Platen and others, Heine throws all personal pride to the winds, annihilating his literary rival by scurrilous revelations of the latter's intimate life.

It is certainly right and necessary to subtract a good percentage of Heine's '*Weltschmerz*' as mere masquerade. This mask does not always reveal profundity in the sense of Nietzsche's. Heine often *wanted* to suffer and appear interesting, and must not always be taken too seriously. Gentle whispers such as '*Leise zieht durch mein*

*Gemüt*' (cf. '*Neue Gedichte*') alternate strangely with the poem '*Frieden*' or the philosophic '*Seegespenst*,' which suffer from an uncertainty of character to which their romantic irony bears witness. A song so often met with in *Stammbücher*, '*Du bist wie eine Blume*' (cf. '*Buch der Lieder*'), seems too full of conscious effect with its calculated triplet: *so hold und schön und rein* inverted in the last line, and thus disillusions the reader. In '*Pornography and Obscenity*' D. H. Lawrence characteristically points to the flaw in the poem when he accuses Heine of insincerity:

'for a few more years, then she'll be an unhappy old maid, and not pure nor beautiful at all, only stale and pathetic. . . .'

Similarly critics were able to detect the all too obvious construction of '*Ich hab im Traum geweinet*.' In the course of its three verses the poet relates his dreams, and each time awakens to describe his sentiments: sadness, pain, and yet greater pain.

But Heine's spirit was purged in the fire of actual and bitter suffering, and everyone must be moved to sympathy in the face of all he was forced to endure, and his almost superhuman efforts to withstand fate during his years of paralysis. In his lines '*Where?*'

(*Aus dem Nachlass*)

*Wo wird einst des Wandermüden*
*Letzte Ruhestätte sein?*
*Unter Palmen in dem Süden?*
*Unter Linden an dem Rhein?* . . .

he has perhaps given us the sincerest poetic record of his feelings on leaving his Rhineland home for alien lands; cf. also the following poem in his '*Neue Gedichte*':

*Ich hatte einst ein schönes Vaterland.*
*Der Eichenbaum*
*Wuchs dort so hoch, die Veilchen nickten sanft.*
*Es war ein Traum.*

*Das küsste mich auf deutsch und sprach auf deutsch*
(*Man glaubt es kaum,*
*Wie gut es klang*) *das Wort:* '*Ich liebe dich!*'
*Es war ein Traum.*

Heine's genius was rooted in German romanticism from which it struggled gradually to free itself. Already early in his career the folk-song had made a profound impression upon him. He gathered strength and inspiration from his German mother-tongue, which he made an instrument for gibes on his fatherland, such as none in his time could rival. The '*Lyrisches Intermezzo*' and the '*Heimkehr*' in his '*Buch der Lieder*' are in themselves sufficient testimony of Heine's power as a lyric poet: cf. '*Im wunderschönen Monat Mai . . .,*' '*Lehn' deine Wang an meine Wang . . .,*' '*Auf Flügeln des Gesanges . . .,*' '*Ich grolle nicht . . .,*' '*Du schönes Fischermädchen . . .,*' '*Herz, mein Herz, sei nicht beklommen . . .,*' '*Der bleiche, herbstliche Halbmond . . .,*' '*Das ist ein schlechtes Wetter . . .,*' '*Die Wallfahrt nach Kevlaar. . . .*'

The religious atmosphere of the last poem, like that of

*Im Rhein, im schönen Strome,*
*da spiegelt sich in den Well'n*
*mit seinem grossen Dome*
*das grosse, heilige Köln . . .*

is, however, purely æsthetic. The sensual element shines through the veil of piety. In '*Die heil'gen drei Kön'ge aus Morgenland,*' which opens like a fairy-tale, a childlike spirit still balances the irony, but religious feeling is no more than a foil.

How lightly Heine could adopt alien material and represent it as a part of his own amorous sufferings is proved by his '*Lorelei*' (1823). She is to him the image of the destructive powers of nature. The legend is centuries old and was already known to Celtes. It may originally have expressed a poetic image of the echo. Brentano, probably in imitation of '*Die Nonne*' in the '*Wunderhorn,*' composed the first German '*Lorelei*' ballad in 1802, altering the name of *Lurelei* (*luren* = to lurk; *lei* = rock) to *Lorelei*. Associations with the name Lore had certainly played some part in the choice. A few years later Niklas Vogt recounted the Rhenish legend about the *Zauberfräulein*, intermingling tradition with Brentano's ideas. Two years before Heine's '*Lorelei*' there appeared also a romance by Count Löben bearing the same name, so that Heine was able to turn to models and deck his Rhenish fay with all the alluring magic of his verbal art. The peculiar fascination of the poem is partly due to the poet's ability to transfuse the subject-matter so utterly with his own emotion.

In the other poems Heine was wont to indulge in extreme

subjectivity, as for instance in '*Erklärung*' in the '*Nordsee*' cycle, in which the poet's boundless passion for Agnes spurs him to hyperbolic phantasy. His heart beats more wildly and 'with a strong hand' he tears out the tallest fir of Norway by its roots. He dips the tree in glowing Etna, and with this 'giant pen steeped in fire' he addresses his words to the dark firmament: *Agnes, ich liebe dich!* All through the night future generations will be able to read these letters of fire.

Nevertheless, it is particularly in the '*Nordsee*' cycle, which is written in free rhythm, that Heine looks on nature with the true eye of the poet. Indeed, not only in jest but in perfect earnestness he called himself 'the poet of the North Sea,' which appears in poetry but seldom between the time when '*Kudrun*' was composed and the age of Heine and Geibel. A comparison between Goethe's and Heine's free verse, however, soon makes one aware of the latter's weaknesses. A cold irony, which in Heine's case springs not so much from a dæmonic urge driving him from mood to mood, but rather from the antithesis between poetic dream and actuality, destroys the emotional unity of the poem. Behind the scorn we may yet discern Heine's bitter cry of despair.

Thus also the literary and political satire '*Atta Troll*' (printed in 1843) is a characteristically bizarre Heinean protest against the pious German lyric, above all against Menzel and the Swabian poets. In his tendency to destroy any kind of political ideal he surrenders his own individual attitude. In spite of his attack on the reactionaries, the biting scorn which he pours on Germania in '*Deutschland. Ein Wintermärchen*' (1844) is aimed also at the liberal enthusiasts. Heine, it is true, composed a *Weberlied* for the working class, and was a devotee of Saint-Simon's gospel, foreseeing the revolution of the proletariat and the fatal suppression of all individuality.

According to Dr. S. S. Prawer's research on Heine, among the poet's three creative periods (marked respectively by the *Buch der Lieder* of 1827, the *Neue Gedichte* of 1844 and the *Romanzero* of 1851) the middle period is the least highly regarded. 'Wrongly so: for this period saw Heine create—almost without models and without a living tradition—a great satirical poetry in the German language. . . . His genuine sympathy with the oppressed could not conceal from him that the victory of the cause he championed would not ameliorate his own lot. The future in which his ideals would have become reality Heine envisaged with secret horror—a horror embodied in the spectral "Doppelgänger" of chapters VI and VII of '*Deutschland. Ein Wintermärchen*'. Here Heine shows himself deeply involved with the very things he had pledged himself to destroy—a very modern dilemma. . . .' Heine's poem his second Ego, a 'key-figure', will live on through Schubert's unforgettable composition, but in his excellent monograph *Heine the Tragic Satirist* (a study of his later poetry, 1827–1856), Cambridge, 1961, Dr. S. S. Prawer makes the startlingly pertinent remark about Heine settings: 'One may perhaps be forgiven for feeling, with Theodor Adorno, that the nearest musical "equivalent" of this poetry is to be found, not in the five thousand or so extant Heine settings, but in the work of a man who never set a single one of his poems: in the folk-song compositions, the scherzos and the funeral marches of Gustav Mahler.'

Heine was soon disillusioned. The victory of the masses did not turn out to be the fulfilment, the third kingdom of which he had dreamed. He turned from Börne, whose narrow democratic conscience regarded Goethe as a panderer, and a manifestation of bleak Hellenic serenity. For Heine, Goethe always remained the greatest German poet. Certainly he himself was far removed from the Olympian's classic ideal, for his heart was ever on his tongue. Goethe's works were to him as statues with which he could not fall in love. His meeting with Goethe in Weimar has been described in a memorable manner by Heine himself:

'I was near addressing him (Goethe) in Greek, but when I saw that he understood German, I told him in German that the plums along the road between Jena and Weimar were very good' (see H. G. Atkins, p. 59, '*Heine.*')

Heine and August Graf von Platen-Hallermünde (1796–1835) were irreconcilable literary and political rivals, yet both belong to an era of *Epigonen*. It is true that Platen attacked Heine first, because the latter had allowed Immermann's verses against Platen to be published. In the fifth act of his '*Romantischer Ödipus*,' Platen mocks at Heine, the 'seed of Abraham,' and his ally Nimmermann (Immermann). Heine avenged himself thoroughly for that insult in the '*Reisebilder*' ('*The Baths of Lucca*'), casting Platen's hapless homosexuality before the public and making cheap jokes about Platen's distorted style. Even today the latter poet is still thoughtlessly misrepresented as emotionally cold and an enemy of life, whilst his language is deemed frigid and stark. When Platen sings:

*Ich möchte gern mich frei bewahren . . .*

*Und nichts geniessen, als die Helle*
*Des Lichts, das ewig lauter bleibt,*
*Und einen Trunk der frischen Welle,*
*Der nie das Blut geschwinder treibt*

it is unfair to ignore the conclusion ('*Antwort*') as Spiero did:

*Denn, ach, die Menschen lieben lernen,*
*Es ist das einz'ge wahre Glück!*

Loneliness caused Platen to suffer almost more keenly than any other poet, for his passionate blood being unnatural, he was forced to conquer it in heroic solitude. In '*Tristan*' he found profound expression for his quest of beauty:

*Wer die Schönheit angeschaut mit Augen,*
*Ist dem Tode schon anheimgegeben. . . .*

Different and far less morbid are the words of Epimetheus in Goethe's '*Pandora*':

*Wer von der Schönen zu scheiden verdammt ist,*
*fliehe mit abegewendetem Blick!*

The strict form of Platen's odes, in particular his famous '*Sonette aus Venedig*,' is born of conscious discipline, the rock at which he clutched in his shipwrecked existence. In preparing a second edition of his poems he was still more rigorous and rejected many from the early volume.

Beneath the mask of a distinguished aloofness was hidden a tormented soul that struggled in vain against its perverted instincts and the consciousness that he was but a follower of classicism. A long sojourn in Italy where, at Naples, he found a friend in August Kopisch, the discoverer of the Blue Grotto at Capri and author of the popular '*Heinzelmännchen*,' failed to bring him the freedom of spirit for which he had yearned, and an abiding melancholy was his lot. He thus fell into *l'art pour l'art*, not for lack of profundity but in order to conquer the tragedy of his physical and spiritual existence. A dark fate ruled over his life, to which an overdose of drugs against cholera in Syracuse put a sudden and untimely end.

A late exponent of romanticism was Friedrich Rückert (1788–1866), who introduced his friend Platen to the elaborate forms of Oriental poetry. To both form was the path and goal of life; on both weighed the burden of an excess of culture and their wide knowledge of European and Oriental languages; both, in their virtuosity of form, lack intuitive power in regard to emotion and vision. Of the vast mass of Rückert's songs only a few have any appeal for us today: '*Du bist die Ruh*,' '*Aus der Jugendzeit*,' '*Du meine Seele, du mein Herz*,' and the ballad '*Der alte Barbarossa*.'

The scholar obscured the poet. Just as Creuzer believed that all religions had a common root, so Rückert believed in a common origin of all languages. After an unsuccessful beginning as *Dozent* in Jena he discovered himself as a poet and a patriot. A journey to Rome strengthened his inclinations in the latter direction, which is not surprising in view of the tone of his previously published '*Geharnischte Sonette*.' In 1826, at the age of thirty-eight, he became professor of Oriental languages at Erlangen. Later on he went to Berlin, and retired in 1848 in order to devote all his time to linguistic studies and to his poetry.

As an erudite poet he became the most important interpreter of Oriental poetry in Germany. He imitated the Persian '*Ghasels*' of the thirteenth-century poet Jalāl-ud-dīn Rūmī, and rendered songs of Hafiz and Firdousī into German. He translated the Arabic '*maqāmas*' of Harīrī (about A.D. 1100) and other works from the Indian (*Mahābhārata*), the Latin and the Greek, etc. He felt especially drawn to the rhymed prose of Harīrī with its amazing virtuosity of tone, rhyme and word: *Widersacher—Widersager*, *Neuntöter—Leuntöter*, *Rauf—Kauf—Schnauf—Laufleute*, and many another play upon words by himself. In the poems entitled '*Östliche Rosen*' Rückert, in contrast to Goethe, appears as a master of accurate costume and adaptability to alien ideals (Hafiz). On the other hand, in the book of proverbs, '*Die Weisheit des Brahmanen*,' which was in part influenced by Scheffler's '*Cherubinischer Wandersmann*,' the mask scarcely conceals the true German content. As in the volume called '*Liebesfrühling*' and other collections, the poems differ considerably in quality and suffer from redundancy. Rückert, who had sung praises of the common fly (see his '*Nachlass*,' II, 76) and composed many a poem on the seasons and family life, also wrote wild battle-songs, which he characteristically cast in sonnet form.

Nikolaus Lenau (Niembsch von Strehlenau, 1802–1850) is a singer of gloom and melancholy. In his poem to Lotte Gmelin, '*Mein Stern*,' we hear the voice of a torn spirit:

> *Um meine wunde Brust geschlagen*
> *Den Mantel der Melancholei,*
> *Flog ich, vom Lebenssturm getragen,*
> *An Dir, Du Herrliche, vorbei. . . .*

In his introduction to Lenau's collected works Anastasius Grün describes the life-story of his hapless friend. He calls Lenau at once fiery and wistful, aristocratically independent, full of soldierly courage and unbridled fancy—a mixture of Hölty and Byron. Solitude weighed heavily on the soul of him who wrote the '*Schilflieder*,' the '*Heidebilder*,' and the '*Drei Zigeuner*.' He boldly attempted a version of *Faust* in order to cast off the curse of feeling himself but a follower. He wandered from place to place, unable to find rest. We have already made his acquaintance as the writer of the '*Polenlieder*.' He shared the *Stürmer und Dränger's* hatred of tyranny and cast *Schädellawinen* at the feet of the victor. Rebelliously he put the poet before the ruler. His reckless, passionate originality, alas, lacked the power to weld itself to form. When Lenau, on his first attack of madness in the autumn of 1844, jumped up from his friend's breakfast table with a cry of despair and defiance, and to his horror beheld his ravaged face in the mirror, his tormented spirit was symbolically bared to the world.

All his life he was a man of moods, driven by his passions and homeless. His ancestors were probably of Slav origin. Though he himself was Hungarian by birth and early education, he was German-Austrian in thought and expression. Even Swabia and particularly Lotte's home, Stuttgart, where he found both a friend and his first great patron in Gustav Schwab, the editor of the *Cottasches Morgenblatt*, could not become a home for him.

In his melancholy '*Schilflieder*' he indulges in sorrowful resignation. He set out for America with buoyant hope, dreaming of prosperity through the purchase of land in Crawford County in Ohio, and the ultimate healing of his soul's sickness. Even this proved a fiasco; America repelled him, appearing in his eyes as some vast insurance establishment inhabited by rogues and avaricious emigrants who were destroying the kindly and human American Indians. Only the primeval forest of Ohio, the Hudson Valley, and the Niagara Falls kindled his poetic soul. It is characteristic that the pearl of the collection '*Reiseblätter*' is the poem '*Der Postillon*':

*Lieblich war die Maiennacht,*
*Silberwölklein flogen,*
*Ob der holden Frühlingspracht*
*Freudig hingezogen. . . .*

It is not a romantic wandering song in the sense of Eichendorff's, but a poem that enables one to feel the deep restlessness of his spirit. The '*Postillon*' was composed in America, but bears distinctly German traits. Whilst Lenau still harboured rosy hopes of America, he composed the defiant '*Abschied*' of an emigrant who with a glad heart exchanges the home of tyranny for the new free world:

*Meer, spüle mir hinweg die Kluft,*
*Die von der Freiheit noch mich trennt!*

After his disillusionment he longed to return to German oaks and the land of his fathers. In '*An mein Vaterland*' he sings:

*Dein liebes Angesicht verschwand*
*Mir, wie mein Jugendglück!*

In the end he believed he could find peace through his love for the clever wife of a Viennese government official, Löwenthal, but even here his dreams were frustrated, for though he remained enamoured of Sophie until soon after writing the epics '*Savonarola*' and the '*Albigenser*,' madness fell on him and broke him utterly. In his spirit's darkness his violin remained his only consolation. The last fire had been spent in the poet who had once wandered and ridden wildly through the Hungarian pusta and composed those magnificent pictures which we meet with in the *Heideschenke*:

*Es schwieg der Sturm, das Wetter schwand;*
*Froh, dass es fortgezogen,*
*Sprang übers ganze Heideland*
*Der junge Regenbogen. . . .*

Lenau is not always so happy with rhyme and form as in the above poem. Thus for instance his poem of two verses, '*Bitte*,' suffers from a lack of balance, as a comparison of the third line in each verse clearly shows:

*Weil' auf mir, du dunkles Auge,*
*Übe deine ganze Macht,*
*Ernste, milde, träumerische,*
*Unergründlich süsse Nacht!*

*Nimm mit deinem Zauberdunkel*
*Diese Welt von hinnen mir,*
*Dass du über meinem Leben*
*Einsam schwebest für und für.*

Moreover, the verb *schwebest* (instead of *ruhest*!) lacks suggestive quality. The *dunkle Auge* (the night) seems in this strangely static poem to be an omen of the insanity into which his spirit was doomed to plunge.

### *The Munich Circle*

In the history of lyric poetry the members of the Krokodil-Bund, Leuthold, Lingg, Bodenstedt, Grosse, Schack, and others, cannot be said to reach very great heights, for in their æsthetic attitude towards life their imagination lacked power to create poetry from reality, and moved in a fictitious world. Nevertheless these confederates of the Munich circle are not mere imitators of Goethe or of *Weimar idealism*, but stand on stable feet in the midst of their contemporaries. Emanuel Geibel (1815–1884) from Lübeck is all too often underrated (see *Ermatinger*) or branded as a poet for 'flappers.' Yet it cannot be denied that he lays most stress on formal values, as we see in his epic poem '*Sanssouci*,' in which he causes Frederick II to speak in an entirely un-Prussian manner. Geibel, however, proved not only a master at formal imitations of Matthias Claudius, Goethe, Uhland, Eichendorff,

Heine and others. His life and his art are by no means shallow. It is true that fortune twice smiled upon him, firstly when after a sojourn in Greece he was summoned to Schloss Escheberg, near Kassel, by the Hessian chamberlain Karl Otto von Malsburg, in order to arrange the library. Geibel's conservative, noble attitude during his conflict with the radicals gave rise to a literary feud that caused him to throw a manly challenge in Herwegh's face:

*An Georg Herwegh.*

*Es scholl dein Lied mir in das Ohr*
*So schwertesscharf, so glockentönig,*
*Als wär' aus seiner Gruft empor*
*Gewallt ein alter Dichterkönig.*

*Und doch! Ich weis' es nicht von mir,*
*Ich muss dich in die Schranken laden. . . .*

When the Prussian king Frederich Wilhelm IV rewarded him with a pension Geibel, in spite of this second stroke of luck, was able to face envious rivals with a clear conscience and the words: 'I never strove for guerdon. I sang but as inspiration moved me.'

Once again Germany was inflamed by his songs when, during the struggle for Schleswig-Holstein, he raised his battle-cry: '*Protestlied für Schleswig-Holstein,*' with its refrain:

*Wir wollen keine Dänen sein,*
*Wir wollen Deutsche bleiben.*

The year 1848 brought Geibel dire distress. Later on a happy marriage and King Maximilian II's invitation to a *Symposium* at Munich, where he stayed from 1852 to 1868, restored his pecuniary and spiritual independence. His pan-Prussian inclinations deprived him of the patronage of Maximilian's successor, Ludwig II, but won him the favour of the Prussian king. A few years later he experienced the consummation of his patriotic dreams through Bismarck.

An æsthetic desire to temper passionate expression, coupled with his sensitive ability to adapt foreign metres, enabled Geibel to translate from the Romance, Greek and Latin lyric poetry, including fifty of Horace's odes.

The winner of the Nobel prize, Paul Heyse (1830–1914), was

likewise an adept at translation, in particular of Leopardi's *Canti*, whose power of suggestion exerted no little influence on his own works. Heyse, however, was more opposed to everyday existence and poetic naturalism than Geibel. To him it seemed that life and art must of necessity represent two alien worlds if creative power was not to be sapped at the roots. He suffered from the irreconcilable antithesis between actuality and ideal, bourgeois existence and art, though unlike the 'Nazarener' he never preached escape from life or joined in the weary dirges of the *fin-de-siècle*.

As a son-in-law of the historian Franz Kugler, author of the students' song the '*Rudelsburg*,' he was already able to gather around him an æsthetic circle in his native town Berlin, whilst through Kugler's influence he was also introduced to the literary society known as the *Tunnel*. But it was only in Munich that he was able to find poets and friends truly matched to his taste. The younger generation during the eighties levelled most of their taunts at him as the representative of harmonious æsthetic classicism. Heyse's strength lies in his talent as a short-story writer.

The rest of the Munich poets moved in the shadow of Geibel, to whom many were much indebted. Friedrich Bodenstedt won a name for himself through the virtuosity of his '*Lieder des Mirza Schaffy*,' a branch from the tree of the '*Westöstlicher Divan*.' Hermann Lingg, the ambitious and sometimes even moving author of the epic '*Die Völkerwanderung*,' and Felix Dahn unite in their mutual enthusiasm for history, which the latter uses for his novels and stories and the former for his poems. The Swiss writer, Heinrich Leuthold, possessed a strange dual character. The bohemian in him drove him to rack and ruin and insanity, but not in the realm of art, where he ends as an 'elegant snob' (cf. Ermatinger).

The Alemannic poet, Josef Viktor von Scheffel (1826–1886), was closely and personally related to the Munich circle. He was born in the same year that the *Monumenta Germaniae historica* saw the light. Today Scheffel is still remembered as the author of such songs as '*Frau Aventiure*,' and in particular '*Gaudeamus*,' his epic '*Der Trompeter von Säkkingen*,' and the historic novel '*Ekkehard*.' Nevertheless, he is but little read. True, his song:

*Alt Heidelberg, du feine,*
*Du Stadt an Ehren reich,*
*Am Neckar und am Rheine*
*Keine andre kommt dir gleich . . .*

still quickens every German heart, but it did not save him from being accused of banality and nineteenth-century sentimentality. How hackneyed appear such verses as:

*Das ist im Leben hässlich eingerichtet,*
*dass bei den Rosen gleich die Dornen stehn*

with their refrain:

*Behüt' dich Gott!*
*Es wär so schön gewesen,*
*behüt' dich Gott!*
*es hatt' nicht sollen sein.*

His *Butzenscheibenlyrik* became a special target for taunts. Nevertheless, it was not Scheffel so much as his followers, Julius Wolff and Rudolf Baumbach, who indulged in intolerable triviality. Scheffel's students' songs, which are in part full of rollicking life, his drinking ditties, '*Wanderlieder*,' and enthusiastic patriotic songs are worthy of a revival, for which the time now seems ripe. The songs, e.g. '*Der Ichthyosaurus*,' which were produced under the immediate influence of cultural and scientific societies, would drop out, as would the satires and various pedantic antiquarian compositions in '*Frau Aventiure*,' and much of the little-known and learned '*Bergpsalmen*.'

The influence of the Munich circle, or a certain affinity to the latter's ideals, may also be traced in the work of such lesser talented poets as Otto Roquette, the author of the song '*Tage der Rosen*' (*Noch ist die blühende goldene Zeit*), Oskar Freiherr von Redwitz, Hugo Salus, the author of the poem '*Kammermusik*,' and others. The Austrian poet Robert Hamerling († 1889) sang the 'swan-song of romanticism.' Martin Greif (Frey) also bears some similarity to the Munich circle. The works of all these poets are scarcely remembered today, any more than is that once hackneyed song '*Allerseelen*' (*Stell' auf den Tisch die duftenden Reseden*) by the Tirolese opponent of the Jesuits, Hermann von

Gilm, who stands quite apart from the Munich circle. Whether Gilm is really, as H. Greinz upheld, the greatest poet of Tirol, is open to question in view of the claims of Adolf Pichler. Both belong to the rank and file of the *Epigonendichter*, and were certainly surpassed by their younger compatriot, F. von Saar.

# XII

# DROSTE-HÜLSHOFF

ANNETTE VON DROSTE-HÜLSHOFF (1797–1848) stands half-way between romanticism and realism. During her life her fame was overshadowed by the noise and clamour of *Jung-Deutschland*. Today she is justly regarded as Germany's greatest poetess. Both her personality and her art defied formulation on the part of her critics. Convention and a sense for the dæmonic attained a peculiar equilibrium in the soul of this aristocratic poetess from Westphalia. Her common sense was strong enough to curb her natural inclination towards the phantastic.

The sensuous element is predominant in her descriptions of nature, the symbolic playing but a secondary part and not, as in the case of Conrad Ferdinand Meyer, acting as the pivot of the poem. On the whole the latter poet attempts to base his poem on a single vision or idea, whereas in Droste's case the central theme is dissipated in the detail of her sensitive descriptions of nature. Her ability to render the visible world profounder through vision, symbol and dream is proved by her poem on sleeplessness: '*Durchwachte Nacht*,' in which impressionist effects are interspersed by a vision. The '*Hünenstein*' inspired the fancy of the poetess in such a way that the superficial impression yields to a deeper and more spiritual apprehension. This manner of passing from the outer to the inner vision is peculiarly characteristic of Droste.

The writer of the '*Heidebilder*' has justly been called a forerunner of impressionism both of the physiological and psychological type. The latter stresses the spiritual element and tends towards the symbolic. The former sacrifices the ego altogether and demonstrates the unity of all detail through the means of atmosphere, which, however, can ultimately also be a spiritual factor. But the chief feature of physiological impressionism is an abandonment to the objective world. Droste's poems, '*Die Lerche*,' '*Hirtenfeuer*,' '*Heidemann*' and '*Der Weiher*' belong to this group:

*Der Weiher.*

*Er liegt so still im Morgenlicht,*
*So friedlich wie ein fromm Gewissen;*
*Wenn Weste seinen Spiegel küssen,*
*Des Ufers Blume fühlt es nicht:*
*Libellen zittern über ihn,*
*Blaugoldne Stäbchen und Karmin,*
*Und auf des Sonnenbildes Glanz*
*Die Wasserspinne führt den Tanz;*
*Schwertlilienkranz am Ufer steht*
*Und horcht des Schilfes Schlummerliede;*
*Ein lindes Säuseln kommt und geht,*
*Als flüstr' es: Friede! Friede! Friede!*

Nevertheless her poetry does not represent a direct path to German impressionism of the end of the nineteenth century, for her aristocratic attitude towards life, her Catholic faith and moral inhibitions regarding nature and human beings are of a very different calibre. She possesses, however, an extraordinarily acute sensibility to the infinitesimal miracles of nature, in which her womanly instinct stood her in good stead. Her clear sharp vision separates her from romanticism just as her ethic convictions stand between her and impressionism. She steeps herself in her subject with an almost motherly love and the zeal of a collector. For this reason critics were inclined to recognize in her works traits of the *Biedermeier*, whose style she in some ways actually suggests. Nevertheless, when applied to Droste's art clichés appear hopelessly fallible. Her spiritual ancestors were amongst others Goethe, Schiller, M. Claudius, Hölty, Matthisson and Tiedge (author of the once popular didactic poem: '*Urania über Gott, Unsterblichkeit und Freiheit*,' 1801). At the same time her soul was steeped in the tradition of her native country and her religion.

It was in the solitude of nature that she found solace when Levin Schücking bade her farewell. Suffering did not bow her head, and with high-hearted courage she wrote letters to her beloved friend giving him sound advice about his marriage.

To be solitary belonged indeed to her inmost being. Her spirit was attuned to the dæmonic in nature, and in the moorland and forest she conjured up the elemental creatures that haunt her works; cf. her '*Bilder aus Westfalen*,' e.g. the fiddler in '*Der Knabe im Moor*.' It is characteristic of Droste's imaginative power that the '*Heidebilder*' were composed not in Westphalia but in Meersburg on the Bodensee. Her ballads also are charged with the lively fancy that rendered her attitude towards nature anything but passive: cf. '*Geierpfiff*,' '*Vergeltung*.'

A cycle of poems entitled '*Das geistliche Jahr*,' published posthumously in 1851, seems to bear little relation to Droste's other lyrics. They are pious Catholic verses for Sundays and for church festivals of the Catholic year. The poetess here turns to God. Faith, hope and charity guide her doubting soul. Fear and a painful consciousness of the sinfulness of life, *Frau Welt*, torment her. The poems do not fit any narrow theological doctrine or system, though they sometimes recall the ideas of Diepenbrock and the Fürstin Gallitzin.

The '*Laienbrevier*' (1834–1835) by Leopold Schefer, born in 1784 at Muskau in the Oberlausitz, bears witness to Droste's poetic power. Schefer's edifying works, which once enjoyed great popularity, have long since fallen into oblivion.

### *The German Religious Song in the Nineteenth Century*

Gellert the moralist, the rhetorical Klopstock, Herder, Wieland, Schiller and Goethe had none of them presented the Protestant faith with any song which could have achieved lasting popularity amongst the devout community. Klopstock's sublime phantasy remains a closed book to the simple layman. Matthias Claudius's verse breathed too sensitive a spirit to find its introduction into the straitlaced punctiliousness of ecclesiastic song, and thus the latter remained devoid of fresh inspiration until the days of romanticism. Novalis's '*Wenn alle untreu werden*' or '*Wenn ich ihn nur habe*,' or E. M. Arndt's '*Geht nun hin und grabt mein Grab*' found much response. The greater bulk of Protestant songs in the nineteenth century were, however, written by Julius Sturm († 1896), whose songs like those of Gellert were also gladly adopted by the Catholics. The reason for this was probably not only the lack of truly great inspiration in the religious song of the time, but also the interconfessional outlook of many tolerant believers who were not perturbed by this mutual use of material, and it is not until 1867, on the foundation of the Catholic *Allgemeiner deutscher Cäcilienverein*, that official hymn-books were introduced, though even these did not achieve orthodox form.

With its renaissance of the past and of traditional poetry, romanticism might have endowed the religious song with a new lease of life, had Brentano, Eichendorff, Görres ('*Marienlieder*'), Luise Hensel ('*Müde bin ich geh zur Ruh*' . . .) or others been less subjective in their emotional poetry. A comparison between their style and that of the old church-song at once reveals the gulf between them. Heinrich Bone's Catholic '*Cantate*' (1847), which were to enjoy many a new edition right up to the twentieth century, afford a landmark in the history of German religious song. For Bone not only created new songs but also brought many a long-lost treasure to light. Even Richard Wagner recognized the worth of the old German religious song and in theory, at any rate, issued a warning against the practice of allowing the voice to be drowned by the instrument. The voice, he said, should be accompanied by the organ alone.

The ritual of the Roman Catholic service, however, stood in the way of the development of the hymn. Valiant efforts to found a German church on the part of B. M. Werkmeister at the end of the eighteenth century, and V. A. Winter at the beginning of the nineteenth, were doomed to failure through the power of Rome. The *Cäcilienverein* was invested with the responsibility of preserving the purity of Catholic liturgy. Nevertheless the German song triumphantly pushed its way into the Catholic service in spite of clerical resistance. Thus Franz Schubert composed his '*Deutsche Singmesse*' (1826) to the text of J. Neumann. The individual songs at the beginning of the mass, '*Wohin soll ich mich wenden*,' the gloria: '*Ehre, Ehre sei Gott in der Höhe*,' the further passages leading to the gospel and the Credo: '*Noch lag die Schöpfung formlos da*,' the offertory: '*Du gabst, o Herr, mir Sein und Leben*,' the Sanctus: '*Heilig, heilig, heilig ist der Herr*,' are still sung in Catholic circles.

## *MÖRIKE*

Like Droste, the Swabian poet Eduard Mörike (1804–1875), Germany's greatest lyric poet of the nineteenth century since Goethe, Hölderlin, and Novalis, also had little sympathy for the literary movement known as *Jung-Deutschland*. He sought to master the disintegrating influences of romanticism, which he regarded as sinister powers, and to curb the irrational yearning for the infinite by forming it to plastic images. Thus he leads unruly romanticism over the threshold of a new classic ideal, though he transfuses the latter with a dæmonic element, which neither Heine nor Platen was able to achieve fully. Mörike's love for his gypsy-like, irresponsible Peregrina (Maria Meyer), his separation from his wife, and other disasters, plunged him into the depths of despair, from which his faith in God and in his art saved him. By a symbolic interpretation of life born of self-sacrifice Mörike was able to conquer the adversities against which he had continually to struggle, first as pastor of Cleversulzbach and then as a teacher of German literature in the *Mädchenstift* at Stuttgart.

In his poem '*An einem Wintermorgen vor Sonnenaufgang*' the poet regards himself as mirroring the polarity of the world. His spirit seems to hover between rest and flux in that state of pure sublimity which before him Goethe alone achieved:

*. . . Zu fluten scheint mein Geist, er scheint zu ruhn. . . .*

When Mörike as here or in the *Peregrina Lieder* endows individual emotion with universal significance he transcends all his contemporaries. But beauty was won by him only through renunciation: *Was aber schön ist, selig scheint es in ihm selbst*, so ends his poem '*Auf eine Lampe*':

*Noch unverrückt, o schöne Lampe, schmückest du,*
*An leichten Ketten zierlich aufgehangen hier,*
*Die Decke des nun fast vergessnen Lustgemachs.*
*Auf deiner weissen Marmorschale, deren Rand*
*Der Efeukranz von goldengrünem Erz umflicht,*
*Schlingt fröhlich eine Kinderschar den Ringelreihn.*
*Wie reizend alles! lachend und ein sanfter Geist*

*Des Ernstes doch ergossen um die ganze Form—*
*Ein Kunstgebild der echten Art. Wer achtet sein!*
*Was aber schön ist, selig scheint es in ihm selbst.*

The construction of this poem is based on a series of lucid proportions in each single part; 3+3+3 lines +1 as finale. Comparison with Rückert's humdrum verses on '*Die Lampe*' (*Nachlass*, II, 30–31) immediately proves how much profounder in form and feeling is Mörike's poem, even if we leave all æsthetic associations with Rembrandt's *Disciples at Emmaus* or Donatello's *Dancing children* out of count. In analysing this poem, Adolf von Grolman emphasizes the words *noch* in the first line and *scheint* in the last. They appear to him to give the poem that characteristically elegiac tone which is born of Mörike's realization that the gods have forsaken the dwelling-places of men, and that the integrity of art, which is here symbolized by the tranquil beauty of the lamp, is now threatened by the day.

Mörike's '*Um Mitternacht*':

*Gelassen stieg die Nacht ans Land,*
*Lehnt träumend an der Berge Wand,*
*Ihr Auge sieht die goldne Wage nun*
*Der Zeit in gleichen Schalen stille ruhn;*
*Und kecker rauschen die Quellen hervor,*
*Sie singen der Mutter, der Nacht, ins Ohr*
*Vom Tage,*
*Vom heute gewesenen Tage.*

*Das uralt alte Schlummerlied,*
*Sie achtet's nicht, sie ist es müd';*
*Ihr klingt des Himmels Bläue süsser noch,*
*Der flücht'gen Stunden gleichgeschwung'nes Joch.*
*Doch immer behalten die Quellen das Wort,*
*Es singen die Wasser im Schlafe noch fort*
*Vom Tage,*
*Vom heute gewesenen Tage*

attained a truly classic level. Rest and movement here attain real harmony. The polarity 'day and night' is happily expressed by the symbol of the weights with the equally laden scales. An effect both of contrast and unity is attained by the division of the poem into two verses, and each verse into two metrically, rhythmically opposed parts (restful iambics and lively anapaests or iambics). An immense gulf yawns between such passionate formal concentration and the romantic disintegration of Brentano's '*Sprich aus der Ferne*.' Mörike fuses images and emotion to a wonderful unity, whilst in Brentano's case the imagery is submerged in a flood of musical expression. Nor does Mörike lose himself in details like Droste. A comparison between Mörike and Keller will be attempted in the following chapter.

The destructive element which we already discovered in the *Peregrina* songs is frequently apt to illumine the closing lines of a poem like a lightning flash rending dark clouds, as for instance in the moving poem at the end of the novel: '*Mozart auf der Reise nach Prag*,' entitled '*Denk es, o Seele*' in the collected lyrics. Two small black horses canter merrily from the meadow back to the town. Soon they will pace slowly bearing a hearse:

*Vielleicht noch eh'*
*an ihren Hufen*
*das Eisen los wird,*
*das ich blitzen sehe!*

In the poem '*An einem Wintermorgen*,' which we have already mentioned, the day bursts forth with a vehemence reminiscent of Wolfram's dawn-song:

*Es träumt der Tag, nun sei die Nacht entflohn;*
*die Purpurlippe, die geschlossen lag,*
*haucht halbgeöffnet süsse Atemzüge;*
*Auf einmal blitzt das Aug' und, wie ein Gott, der Tag*
*beginnt im Sprung die königlichen Flüge!*

The elementary powers and the eeriness of legend take on palpable anthropomorphic form in his ballads: '*Der Feuerreiter*,' '*Die Geister am Mummelsee*,' '*Elfenlied*,' etc. The supernatural element subsides to serene merriment in '*Schön-Rohtraut*' mingled by a faint note of renunciation and rococo frivolity: *Und küsst Schön-Rohtraut auf den Mund*. Recurrent phrases give the ballad an air of tranquillity. Interesting too is the use in this poem of sound-effects: *den ganzen Tag* (*a—a*), *kleine Weile* (*ei—ei*).

Mörike's sense of humour is also evident in the '*Märchen vom sichern Mann*,' a satire on Schelling's natural philosophy, also in part of the novel '*Maler Nolten*' and in the idyll of '*Der alte Turmhahn.*' Yet conscious and unconscious nature and fate only find reconciliation in rare moments of harmony. His stanzas on his '*Besuch in Urach*' complain of man's inability to find the key to the mysteries of Nature: '*Doch sie bleibt mehr als der Mensch verwaist. . . .*'

Mörike's unique genius drew from the unconscious a sure intuitive apprehension of truths which science and psycho-analysis have since attempted to explain. In his poem '*Erstes Liebeslied eines Mädchens,*' a girl's passion and fear are expressed by the symbol of a snake. From such phenomena psycho-analysis has, alas, deduced fixed concepts as though poetry had not the right to create free images of its own.

What Mörike was often too shy to reveal in word, burst forth with elementary passion in the musical rendering of his songs by Hugo Wolf. In this sense one might justly say that H. Wolf perfected Mörike's work. The disciple of R. Wagner liked to maintain a single theme expressing the poetic idea throughout one song (e.g. '*In der Frühe*'). He often caused the voice to break off suddenly at the end of a song in order to let the accompaniment complete the idea. The chief distinction between Schubert's and Wolf's songs is that the latter lays more stress on the significance of the word. Herein we see the legacy of Wagner.

## *THE SWISS LYRIC POETS:*
### *G. Keller, C. F. Meyer, C. Spitteler*

Gottfried Keller (1819–1890) was a true native of Zürich. Today its inhabitants still point with pride to the *Haus zum goldenen Winkel* in which their greatest author was born. Keller is more of an epic writer than a lyric poet, but even so he has given the German nation some precious songs. His style is clearer and robuster than Mörike's, and he more easily reconciles the romantic with the realistic element. Indeed, Keller stood with his feet well planted on the ground and a sense of humour prevents him from falling into the romantic vagueness of such poets as Eichendorff. Nevertheless the major part of Keller's lyrics was written before he came under the influence of Feuerbach and other representatives of the materialistic school of philosophy. Keller's words:

*Die Zeit geht nicht, sie stehet still,*
*Wir ziehen durch sie hin . . .*

are characteristic of his tendency to confine the flux of time within the limits of space whereas in Tieck's case it rushes on, an untamable flood: '*In dir trägst du die wechselnde Zeit.*'

Keller was forced to travel a hard road before he was able to find his true métier as a writer. He began as a lyric poet. Gradually however, by a process of renunciation and self-discipline, he came to adopt the narrative form. His sojourn in Munich, where it was his dream to become a painter, ended in the disaster which he described in '*Der grüne Heinrich.*' The revolution dragged him into the midst of political liberal activity. He became acquainted with Herwegh, Freiligrath, Bakunin, Richard Wagner and other 'knights of the spirit,' who as exiles had formed a home amidst the German colony in Zürich. A. L. Follen was instrumental in forming many a friendship between these men. Keller's straightforward honesty of mind invigorates the reader. His attitude towards politics is both noble and human:

*Trau keinem, der nie Partei genommen*
*Und immer im Trüben ist geschwommen.*
*Doch wird auch dir jener nicht frommen,*
*Der nie darüber hinaus will kommen.*

Love too assailed his heart during these troubled years. His open-hearted, clumsy offer of marriage to Luise Reiter is worthy of being remembered. It reflects the true Keller. The year 1848 witnessed an important change in Keller's spiritual development. Switzerland received its liberal constitution. He himself was given a scholarship at Heidelberg University, where he heard Hettner and Feuerbach, and then at Berlin, where he joined the 'Tunnel' circle and met Varnhagen von Ense, Chr. Fr. Scherenberg, and others.

These years were of considerable influence on his writing and helped him to conquer his subjective outlook on life. This may be gathered from a perusal of the amendments of his own poems, e.g. '*Abendregen,*' '*Trübes Wetter.*' He now became a novelist and bade the lyric farewell, though he took it up again in later years. When Keller returned to his beloved Switzerland, in praise of which he composed that unforgettable hymn '*An das Vaterland*,' he came into contact with F. Vischer, T. Storm, and especially C. F. Meyer. At this time he wrote his '*Züricher Novellen*.'

A serene joy illumines Keller's art. He possessed the broad restful vision and humour untroubled by overwrought fancy and subjective hysteria. Within the solid walls of bourgeois life he could practise renunciation without indulging in agonized writhings of the soul and even without the painful tension of a Mörike. A comparison of the latter's poem '*Um Mitternacht*' with Keller's '*Stille der Nacht*' marks their differences:

*Stille der Nacht.*

*Willkommen, klare Sommernacht,*
*Die auf betauten Fluren liegt!*
*Gegrüsst mir, goldne Sternenpracht,*
*Die spielend sich im Weltraum wiegt!*

*Das Urgebirge um mich her*
*Ist schweigend wie mein Nachtgebet;*
*Weit hinter ihm hör' ich das Meer*
*Im Geist, und wie die Brandung geht.*

*Ich höre einen Flötenton,*
*Den mir die Luft von Westen bringt,*
*Indes herauf im Osten schon*
*Des Tages leise Ahnung dringt.*

*Ich sinne, wo in weiter Welt*
*Jetzt sterben mag ein Menschenkind—*
*Und ob vielleicht den Einzug hält*
*Das vielersehnte Heldenkind.*

*Doch wie im dunklen Erdental*
*Ein unergründlich Schweigen ruht,*
*Ich fühle mich so leicht zumal*
*Und wie die Welt so still und gut.*

*Der letzte leise Schmerz und Spott*
*Verschwindet aus des Herzens Grund:*
*Es ist, als tät' der alte Gott*
*Mir endlich seinen Namen kund.*

In Keller's case the 'polarity' is also maintained throughout each verse, but not in the form of a hopeless conflict or as antithesis, but as a reconciled equilibrium. Even the superficial form of the poem is symmetrical. Its rhythm in contrast to Mörike's does not vary. The first verse stresses the optic element: the harmony between clear night and the glory of the stars; external and internal movement are unified in the cosmic image of the primeval mountains and the foaming swell of the sea. Compare also the polarities in the following lines: West and East, death and resurrection, scorn and reverence of the divine. The visual element triumphs over the musical power of the word. A great simplicity enhances the beauty of the poem. It is no choral chant and has nothing of religious ecstasy or supplication, but is filled with sincere piety. Night is to Keller the symbol of infinity. Under the stars he feels himself one with the universe, as did Novalis and Eichendorff, though Keller's expression and imagery are far more precise. Keller's reverence of nature and the least of its creatures springs from his deep religious fervour. In this sense he even describes the death of a midge in his '*Kleine Passion*' as a fatality not without significance. His great trust in Nature, his understanding of the folk-element, his poetic originality and a divine sense of humour achieve a rare synthesis. He regards the world both in its physical and spiritual aspects with the keen eyes of an artist. Through his poem '*Augen, meine lieben Fensterlein*' he immortalizes the 'dear little windows.' In Keller's works clear vision unites with an intense power of realization. Knowledge and emotion become one, and in poems such as '*Winternacht*' in which he looks on the snowbound landscape as on a corpse, nature is conceived as wearing the significance of a myth.

Conrad Ferdinand Meyer (1825–1898) was also born in Zürich, two years after his compatriot Dranmor (Ludwig Ferdinand Schmid), whose anguished life was a source of inspiration to the former poet. Meyer was never able to achieve direct emotional language such as Goethe's, but he managed to express his own passionate feelings objectively. Michelangelo was his model. Meyer's creative genius awoke comparatively late. In the ivy ('Eppich'), which bears old and new leaves at the same time—winter and spring, he sees a symbol of his own life. Educated bilingually as a child he wavered between French and German as a means of poetic expression until the events of 1870–1871 decided him once and for all in favour of German. The spirit of autumn broods over his songs. His love of fading garlands and the melancholy of evening is neither romantic nor classic, but a symptom of his overwrought hypernervous being. He, however, conquered his æsthetic attitude by descriptions of heroic deeds.

The 'pictures' and happenings in his poetry are impregnated with lyric symbolism. One can easily comprehend the meaning of the two sails in his '*Zwei Segel.*' With true artistic insight he nobly sacrifices the subjective for the sake of the objective. In place of uncontrolled self-confession he expresses his feelings through a distinct picture, a definite event (see '*Ein Pilgrim*'), or a symbolic line such as '*Das grosse stille Leuchten*' . . . from his patriotic poem '*Firnelicht.*'

By subjecting the object or action to this spiritual process he frees it of its crude materialism. This manner of endowing the objective world with symbolic significance was already found in Mörike's poems, e.g. '*Auf eine Lampe*' and later appears above all in the *Dinggedichte* of Rilke ('*Römische Fontäne,*' '*Panther*'). C. F. Meyer's '*Der römische Brunnen*' is not only the best-known but the most perfect *Dinggedicht* amongst his lyrics, though he does not develop this category of poetry as far as did Rilke.

Although little is said of the actual structure of '*Der römische Brunnen,*' it seems nevertheless to be plastically and palpably suggested through the rhyme and metre—for instance in lines 1, 3, 5, which by means of their broken rhythm express the dynamic process of the water filling the three basins. Again lines 2, 4, 6, through their fluent unbroken rhythm, render the broken resistance of the stone and the overflowing of the water. At the end of the poem we get a wonderful sense of the upward and downward movement of the water in the harmonious alternation of flux and tranquillity. A strong contrast is afforded by Rilke's poem, in which the plastic image is sacrificed to the expression of eternal flux.

Through endowing the object with symbolic significance, C. F. Meyer escaped the danger of mingling two forms of art which Lessing pronounced irreconcilable. The means by which this may be achieved are various and include direct address (cf.

Blake's '*Tiger*'), moralizing didactics (cf. Brockes), *Stimmung* in Lenau's poems, and symbolization as in the case of C. F. Meyer. In the latter's poem '*Schwarzschattende Kastanie*' the symbol represents the significance of the tree which the poet regards as a living being. Thus he is not concerned with the impression, but the outward form is seen as the manifestation of its essence.

It is not surprising that C. F. Meyer's poems often present close analogies to the plastic arts. Michelangelo was his ideal. In the latter's statues, particularly the Slaves and Moses, he beheld a symbol of his own being. We indeed find true 'picture-poems' amongst Meyer's works in which he translates works of art into poetic form. The antithesis between sculpture and present-day existence is often a theme of such poems, e.g. '*Die Karyatide*' appears as the symbol of carved peace in the tumult of modern life (cf. also '*Der Triumphbogen*'). Paintings also tempted him to take up his pen and write such poems as: '*Nach einem Niederländer*' or phantasies inspired by Böcklin's '*Flut und Ebbe.*' The poet loved to ponder on the events of history and visualize them with the full strength of his mind's eye, which, as we have stated, was able to win such an objective picture of historic facts. His poem '*Begegnung*' proves how irresistible was his urge to see himself as a third person. In the strange rider he sees *der jungen Augen wilde Kraft, des Mundes Trotz und herbes Schweigen.* This necessity of describing himself through history leads him to seek suitable material, which he uses not as a means of escaping from himself but as a heroic mask.

C. F. Meyer's attitude towards history bears little resemblance to that of the Munich poets. To him circumstances are a symbol both of his own and of universal being. He believes that it is heroic deeds above all which cause man to find his true self, and these he seeks in all their tragic greatness. As Ermatinger has shown with reference to the *Monumenta Germaniae historica* and to Niebuhr, Ranke, Sybel, Mommsen, Burckhardt—the period of scientific historicism doubtless played an important part in influencing C. F. Meyer in this direction. To this may be added the poet's own vacillation between æsthetics and ethics, a problem which he expressed in his novels, epics and romances as the universal struggle between power and justice. The names of Hutten, Jürg

Jenatsch, Thomas à Becket, Angela Borgia, Gustav Adolf, Pietro de Vinea and others, suggest the type of theme. In his ballads: '*Die Füsse im Feuer*,' '*Miltons Rache*,' '*Die Rose von Newport*,' '*Kaiser Friedrich der Zweite*,' and others he gives new life to history, a similar sense of excitement and concentrated pathos of word.

As in the case of Gottfried Keller, C. F. Meyer's improvements and alterations of his own works are of great help in tracing his development. Meyer was not always so happy in his visual effects as has been suggested by the poems already discussed. '*Lenz Wanderer, Mörder, Triumphator*,' for instance, suffers from irregular composition, as does the third part of this poem: '*Frühling, der die Welt umblaut*,' which could well stand by itself in an anthology. The *Siegespforten* here mentioned do not quite fit the mood of humility (*niedrig*) described. We are also disturbed by the final conjunction *dass* in the last line but one. But herein we again have a proof of C. F. Meyer's peculiar trend of thought which caused him on other occasions often to arrive at unrivalled heights.

Like C. F. Meyer the philosophic poet Carl Spitteler (1845–1924) was influenced by Burckhardt's conception of history, but he might be called a more indirect lyric poet. His brilliant virtuosity is too burdened by intellectual problems and scintillating metaphors to allow of his achieving sensuous poetic vision. His partiality for cycles, e.g. '*Schmetterlinge*' (with symbolic motifs inspired by the life of the butterfly), moreover his '*Balladen*' and '*Glockenlieder*,' point to the conscious energy of his creative genius. In spite of Spitteler's heroic struggle to achieve vivid emotional expression, his poetry remains on the whole intellectual. It glitters but has no warmth, though it abounds with profound and brilliant thoughts. He was denied pure lyric feeling such as was given to Theodor Storm, and thus out of a sense of his own weakness he invoked Hellenic sublimity:

*Nicht Gedicht von hitzigen Gebärden*
*Und von vielem Fühlen und Lieben,*
*Eitel selbst sich auseinander dichtend,*
*sondern dichtend leuchtende Gestalten. . . .*

## *NORTH GERMAN LYRIC POETS:*

### *Hebbel; Storm; 'Der Tunnel über der Spree'—Fontane; Strachwitz; 'The Plattdeutsch Lyric'—Groth; Reuter*

Friedrich Hebbel (1813–1863), the greatest poet between 1840 and 1860, was the son of a mason from Wesselburen in Norderdithmarschen (Holstein), which at that time belonged to Denmark. A fateful star reigned over the year of his birth. It was the year of victory in the Wars of Liberation. G. Büchner, O. Ludwig and R. Wagner belong to the same generation. But it was also the year of Wieland's and Körner's death. To Hebbel life and poetry were one endless heroic battle. Man's guilt appeared to him as the inevitable tragedy of man's existence. It was not material want, hunger and misery that roused his passion, but the tragic fact that the individual in order to assert himself must ever stand in opposition to God and the universe. The universe breaks down the barriers of the ego, but the individual seeks his own peculiarity, see Hebbel's letter to Elise Lensing, April 1837:

'It is the realization of the absolute contrariness in things, it is in short that sickness which you will never comprehend, because you were able to ask about it.'

Such an attitude towards life knows no compromise. Life, says Hebbel, forces one to action:

*Man geht nicht in die Schlacht als Held,*
*Man kommt als Held heraus . . .*

or he writes those defiant lines in the cycle entitled: '*Dem Schmerz sein Recht*': *Alles Leben ist Raub . . . ein heiliger Krieg. . . .*

The drama was destined to be Hebbel's true métier, nevertheless he also appears as a lyric poet of the first order.

We may easily discern the influence of Schiller and Uhland in his earliest works. But his later poems such as the serene '*Herbstbild*' are among the rarest treasures of the German lyric. So are his powerful ballads, e.g. the '*Der Haideknabe*,' in which the poet describes how a boy dreams of his murder and then dies a horrible death. In regard to the reflective nature of Hebbel's poetry we would join with Professor Edna Purdie in saying:

'At its best, his lyric poetry is reflective, but indirectly so; reflection is the outcome and not the origin of the poetic conception.'

Emotion and intellectual thought are not always so completely fused as in the '*Herbstbild*,' but the problem of the interdependence of both worlds remains a leading motif in his lyric poetry. It mirrors the rift between the individual and the universe, nature and God. With what dire toil unity of body and soul are achieved, often enough in vain, is shown by the following analysis of '*Weihe der Nacht*' (1840):

*Nächtliche Stille!*
*Heilige Fülle,*
*Wie von göttlichem Segen schwer,*
*Säuselt aus ewiger Ferne daher.*

*Was da lebte,*
*Was aus engem Kreise*
*Auf ins Weit'ste strebte,*
*Sanft und leise*
*Sank es in sich selbst zurück*
*Und quillt auf in unbewusstem Glück.*

*Und von allen Sternen nieder*
*Strömt ein wunderbarer Segen,*
*Dass die müden Kräfte wieder*
*Sich in neuer Frische regen,*
*Und aus seinen Finsternissen*
*Tritt der Herr, so weit er kann,*
*Und die Fäden, die zerrissen,*
*Knüpft er alle wieder an.*

Already in the first part of the poem the sensual is transformed to the spiritual through the words *heilig*, *göttlich*, *Segen*, *ewig*. The second verse opens suddenly (apparently for rhythmic reasons) with the preterite form of the verb *lebte*, where we should actually have expected the present tense, whilst it ends with the present *quillt*, thus effecting a connection with the first part. The latter added to the third would form a complete unity.

The *Finsternisse* represent the night in which God now appears.

The phrase *So weit er kann* is mere padding and can hardly be regarded as fortunate. Moreover, we had previously heard nothing about the *Fäden, die zerrissen*, and *zerrissen* was probably introduced here only to help the rhyme. We are aware of a determined effort to accentuate the conclusion. The abstract nouns *Stille* and *Fülle*, further *säuselt, was*, and *es*, manifest the reflective nature of the poem, which lacks lucidity and emotional unity. Translated into prose the contents imply that man looks upon the night as a refuge and bringer of peace. The stars pour down blessings and energy, giving us power to attempt new deeds.

One should not forget that the title of the poem was originally '*An meine Seele*,' which indeed suits its monologue-like character. The word '*eingefroren*' (first edition) can scarcely be termed happy.

We treated this example of Hebbel's poetry in detail, not in order to belittle his power of blending form and subject-matter, but to illustrate the peculiarity of his reflective verse. What we may call the '*intimate* lyric' with its indifference to monumental content was alien to his being. It is that form of poetry in which another North Saxon poet Theodor Storm, Hebbel's antithesis, excelled. From out the stormridden night of Hebbel's introspection we enter the intimate circle of Storm's bourgeois world.

Theodor Storm (1817–1888) was born in Husum. Bourgeois life, home, family, memories that live in old furniture, or in a gesture, are given a new significance through his poetic sensibility. They provide the keynote of his poetry, but are not yet considered in the light which Thomas Mann was later to cast on them. That Storm, like Gottfried Keller, did not fight shy of a humdrum profession as a balance to his imaginative life suggests at once the difference between him and the author of '*Tonio Kröger*.' It is obvious that Storm both in his poems and short stories avoids abstract and didactic speculation. He fills his verses with simple images drawn from his home circle: cf. '*Gode Nacht*':

*Över de stillen Straten*
*Geit klar de Klokkenslag;*
*God Nacht! Din Hart will slapen*
*Und morgen is ok en Dag . . .*

or '*Die Nachtigall*':

*Das macht, es hat die Nachtigall*
*Die ganze Nacht gesungen;*
*Da sind von ihrem süssen Schall,*
*Da sind in Hall und Widerhall*
*Die Rosen aufgesprungen.*

*Sie war doch sonst ein wildes Kind,*
*Nun geht sie tief in Sinnen,*
*Trägt in der Hand den Sommerhut*
*Und duldet still der Sonne Glut*
*Und weiss nicht, was beginnen. . .*

Thus of necessity he limits his horizon to a miniature world of house and garden into which momentous, historic events and philosophic problems scarcely intrude. The state and church usually appear in his lyric verse only in so far as they are connected with family life. But Storm does not succumb to naturalism. On the contrary his use of colourful description is most reticent, and he employs symbolic images rather than surface texture. Sometimes his poems appear little more than a skeleton, so that they produce almost the effect of an epigram: e.g. '*Trost.*' Through this limitation of material and style Storm was forced to renounce much. But the simple bourgeois life which he depicts mirrors human fate in all its poignancy. Certainly the dæmonic element, which was a feature of Mörike's poetry, is here far milder. Nevertheless, in a few terse lines Storm succeeds in investing sensual imagery with profound spiritual significance. Such simplicity is not really unconscious and naïve. In the introduction to the '*Hausbuch aus deutschen Dichtern*' Storm defines the limits of what he considers the pure lyric, to which he refuses to admit the political and true reflective lyric. He considers that poetry should appeal to us not through thoughts but through images and not through an *a priori* determined metric pattern but through a form that is a vital expression of human life. That Storm did not remain absolutely true to his theory goes without saying. Storm's theory of the absolute lyric only represents the final scientific conclusion of his ideas. The trilogy—intellect, fancy, emotion or thought, image, feeling—should, according to Storm, be considered as a unit and expressed as such. The idea is not ruled out but must be experienced as part of the poet's fancy and emotion.

Storm's flexible metre and rhythm possess a peculiar magic that is accentuated through tonal effects, as for instance in the poem: '*Schliesse mir die Augen beide*,' and especially in '*Meeresstrand*':

*Ans Haff nun fliegt die Möwe,*
*Und Dämmrung bricht herein;* . . .

Storm achieves this effect not through regular metre but through the power of words. The emotional element is only suggested, cf. the lines *Wie Träume liegen die Inseln. . . . So war es immer schon.*

In spite of the almost arithmetically calculated construction of the verses, the very obvious cæsura and the equal division between *optic* (verses 1–2) and *acoustic* (verses 3–4) effects, the poem does not seem mechanical, for its strictly proportioned structure is enveiled in a mist of ever-changing hues and movement. In the creation of *Stimmung* that hovers so strangely between the mathematical components of his verse lies Storm's unique quality as a lyric poet. See also p. 367.

We have already referred to Storm's love of outline. Not that he always achieves it. Even where he apparently reduces a poem to a skeleton as in the two verses of '*Schliesse mir die Augen beide*,' one might still argue that one verse would suffice, for the second introduces no fresh motif but is little more than a musical variant of the first. At the same time the words *Welle*, *Schlag*, and the personified *Schmerz* are all too metaphorical for such a gem. Also the verb *füllest* is too ponderous for this little poem that should end on a liquid melodious note, lulling the mind to sleep.

Under the pseudonym of 'Tannhäuser' Storm joined the poetic society known as *Der Tunnel über der Spree* from which the Munich circle of the *Krokodile*, under the leadership of Geibel, had culled many an idea in regard to organization and ceremonial ritual. The Berlin *Tunnel* had actually been founded by the Viennese critic M. G. Saphir, but in its further development this circle became the centre of realism in Berlin. In the autobiography of his youth '*Von Zwanzig bis Dreissig*' Theodor Fontane (1819–1898) describes the life of this society in which Strachwitz, Geibel, Heyse, Franz Kugler, Hesekiel, Heinrich Seidel (the author of '*Leberecht Hühnchen*') were wont to move, as well as Christian

Friedrich Scherenberg (who must not be confused with his relative Ernst Scherenberg) who is the author of that impressive poem '*Der verlorne Sohn*,' and one or two battle-epics, such as '*Waterloo*.'

From the point of view of literary history Fontane is of utmost importance on account of his relation to naturalism. In spite of his age he preserved a buoyant heart which beat in sympathy with the youth of the eighties, and was indeed able to lead them. Certainly he was not blindly addicted to the *milieu* craze, nor did he make the worker the hero of his ballads. Nevertheless, he joined the young rebels who worshipped the seventy-year-old poet in their open war against false pathos and falsehood in poetry and life. Fontane's warm-hearted exuberance enchanted all who came into contact with him. An admixture of French blood may have played some part here, but in his novels, his '*Preussiche Soldatenballaden*' and his politics he is thoroughly German and true to the Prussian ideal. More than one protracted stay in England widened his horizon. He composed ballads on English themes, e.g. '*Die Brücke am Tay*,' '*John Maynard*,' and above all '*Archibald Douglas*' (1854), a panegyric of man's love for his fatherland:

*Der ist in tiefster Seele treu,*
*Wer die Heimat liebt wie du . . .*

Whereas in the two ballads first mentioned the dramatic structure of the *Naturstimmung* tends to dissolve in impressionistic lyric effects, the Douglas ballad is perhaps the masterpiece of the *Tunnel* poetry. Karl Löwe set it to congenial music. This ballad is remarkable for the lucid division of its predominating points. The alternation of quadruple and triple lifts lends vitality to the rhythm. The word *war* in the first verse which Münchhausen criticized is surely in its right place, for the sense of the phrase is: *Da war sie für mich öd' und leer*.

Moritz Graf von Strachwitz (1822–1847), a Silesian whom brain-fever doomed to a premature death, likewise wrote a Douglas ballad: '*Das Herz von Douglas*.' Both poets achieve a most dramatic effect and it is difficult to say which of the two poets deserves the laurels. Strachwitz's ballad lacks Fontane's fine psychological study of the king's character, which changes from glowering passion to joyful enthusiasm, and his material is indeed different. But it, nevertheless, does not fall short of Fontane's poem in power. It is nobly proportioned, the various parts presenting formal analogies, the numeric relationship being 2, 1, 8 and 2, 1, 4+4 and 2+2, 4. Repetition is used with striking effect as for instance in verses 16 and 17, in order to produce on the one hand a *ritardando*, on the other a *prestissimo*. Palpable images, short sentences (the first verse contains four imperatives) and the way in which the hero's words are held back until verse 21, are signs of a true and not too conscious poetic art. The break between verses 11 and 12 appears to us insignificant.

Thus Strachwitz's imagery (*es sei im Banner das Kreuz entrollt*), his dramatic power and versification are by no means inferior to Fontane's, though the latter won the applause of the future through the stress he lays on the psychological element.

New influences flowed in on the lyric from the direction of dialect verse.

Klaus Groth (1819–1899) from Schleswig-Holstein freed the way for dialect poetry when in 1852 he published his *Quickborn*. Thus the ice was broken for Reuter and other Low German lyric poets. Until then dialect had been regarded as an impassable barrier which had been set up by the second sound-shift. It was easier for Upper German poets to find a place in German literature. Amongst these may be mentioned the Tirolese poet K. Schönherr, Franz Stelzhamer from Upper, J. F. Castelli from Lower Austria, the Bavarians Karl Stieler and Franz von Kobell, the Alemannic J. P. Hebel, the Alsatians August and Adolf Stöber, and the Styrian Peter Rosegger who has long enjoyed fame in European literature.

Low German poetry, however, which had once flourished under the Hansa and only fell into oblivion when its last star was eclipsed with Jürgen Wullenwever, had first to overcome the prejudice of doubt as to its literary possibilities. The political struggle for Schleswig-Holstein furthered an interest in Low German literature.

Klaus Groth, who had himself adapted many High German traits, both in regard to form and emotion, now burst forth in praise of his '*Modersprak*.' His '*Plattdeutsch*' (*platt* originally meant clear, comprehensible and not flat!) was now to be considered worthy of literature. Certainly he laid himself open to the accusation of having made a compromise between High and

Low German, but only recently he found more than one defender who restored him to his rightful place in German literature and gave him precedence over other Low German poets, in particular Brinckmann. Groth was never put in the shade by his numerous compatriots right up to Hermann Claudius, the great-grandson of the famous Matthias Claudius. Enthusiasm for *Platt* grew so quickly that a certain August Dühr († 1907) actually undertook the task of translating the *Iliad* and the *Odyssey* into Low German —alas, with but partial success.

Only one author surpassed Groth to any great degree—Fritz Reuter (1810–1874) from Stavenhagen in Mecklenburg. He wrote with a true Low German heart and in the true Low German tongue. He would tolerate no compromise. A seven-year imprisonment of terrible duress (1834–1840), to which he had been sentenced as a corporation student, avowedly on account of his rebel spirit, seems to have broken his spirit. He began to drink and fall into fits of melancholy. At the age of forty he married, and sunshine fell once more on his path. When Groth's '*Quickborn*' appeared soon after, he too ventured publication, and in 1853 (i.e. a year after the appearance of Groth's work) appeared his own '*Läuschen un Rimels*' (*Läuschen*=*Leise*, *Schwänke*) which brought him immediate fame. Through his later novels, in particular '*Ut mine Stromtid*,' he won himself a name in European literature. Today his notorious *Inspector Bräsig* is as well known a figure as any of the North German characters of the artist W. Busch's, from whose pessimism Reuter however remains free.

In the course of these last chapters we have often crossed the threshold of tradition and entered the realm of modern literature. Seen from the present-day angle, the new 'storm and stress' at the turn of the century appears as the manifold expression of a general spiritual unrest, the cause and effect of which we shall attempt to sum up in the following chapter.

# XIII
# CHANGING VIEWS

## *NIETZSCHE*

*Naturalism, Impressionism—Neo-Romanticism, Expressionism*

During the French revolution of July 1830, when Hegel and Goethe, the immortal exponents of the idealistic school of thought, were reaping the harvest of their creative life, newly awakened forces bearing the banner of progress and democracy broke forth.

True classicism had not rejected life for the sake of art, for Goethe (like Plato) recognized the world of appearances, although he saw therein the reflection of a purer world, purging reality of the dross of materialism through his sense of organic form.

Romanticism, which is *not* a symptom of decadence, mingled reality and dream with almost religious fervour to create from them a synthesis which itself could be termed a higher reality. But as soon as belief in God as an 'infinite individuality' had been shattered, Schleiermacher's creed of 'individuality mirrored in the object' could no longer find realization. Artificially stimulated self-confidence hardly sufficed to hide disruption and eclecticism. 'We suffer from a surfeit of ideas' is the plaint of the day, as we already see from '*The correspondence of two Germans*' (P. A. Pfizer, 1831) which simultaneously throws classic culture to the winds.

Only Hebbel's rugged force was able to close the wound of divided existence by heroic affirmation of the individual amidst the inimical universe, whilst in the Indian summer of Gottfried Keller's genius soul and body found ultimate reconciliation. 'Through his verses flashes and thunders Goethe's gold,' writes Arno Holz. Lesser poets were wrecked, and their fate appears as a fulfilment of Keller's own words, 'The spirit hovers not over a glass of water but over the waters!' Heine plunged back into life in despair, only to fall exhausted. He had deemed himself the God-chosen herald of a heaven on earth. Influenced by Count Saint-Simon and his followers, Bazard and Enfantin, he sought in the new religion of sensual pantheism a realization of romantic dreams and yearning. Socialism, originally borne on the wings of ethical ideals, and freedom allied themselves with economic principles which attempted to set the structure of society on a purely scientific basis. Rodbertus, the founder of scientific socialism in Germany derived benefit on the one hand from the free trade and valuation theories of Ricardo (the disciple of Adam Smith), on the other from Saint-Simon who defended the worker's claim of full profit. The conflict between relentless egoism (M. Stirner) and communal idealism heightened the antagonism of the parties. Culture was supplanted by civilization, or in the words of Spengler, creativeness by construction, tragic *Herrenmoral* by the 'frog perspective of the plebeian mind' which regards everything from the standpoint of material security. To Karl Marx, who, in company with Friedrich Engels, set up the famous 'communistic manifesto' of 1848, economic co-operation appeared in place of abstract idealism as the sole means of unifying mankind. Fifteen years afterwards Lassalle in his '*Public Retort*' presented the later social democratic party with its programme. Lassalle's incipient *rapprochement* with Bismarck was, however, nipped in the bud the following year by his fatal duel with Prince Janko von Racowitza. On the threshold of this century, on the occasion of the party meeting at Dresden in 1903, Bebel declared war against bourgeois society. The seed had germinated and mass-consciousness was fully aroused. The revolution was apprehended not only in the political field but in the world of art.

In company with the psychology of the individual appeared the group and racial psychology of the age of commerce. Yet long before the triumphant ascension of socialism and the days of Max Kretzer, Bettina von Arnim wrote her social-political work on the misery of Berlin, '*Dies Buch gehört dem König*' (1843), whilst Robert Prutz in his novel, '*Das Engelchen*' (1851), arraigned the sufferings to which the lower classes were subjected. Adam Müller's romantic conception of the state as a community, 'a totality of human circumstances' was eclipsed by the new principles of freedom and equality. The *Volksgeist* (cf. G. Freytag, W. H. Riehl) as it revealed itself in language, custom, law and history appeared as the antithesis of the 'spirit of the age,' which was dominated by the economic determinism of nineteenth-century thought. The conflict of these two concepts is mirrored in the work of Immermann. But his bourgeois world now yielded to the proletariat. The modernists, likewise, were able to find a forerunner in Spielhagen; less, it is true, where formal matters were concerned, but certainly in his ideas of progress. Nature now appeared no longer as the symbol of the *Weltgeist*, but was considered subordinate to the physical law of cause and effect. The tension between conservative and revolutionary forces had now reached its climax. The foundation of the empire was the fulfilment of a people's *Barbarossa-Sehnsucht*. The craving for monumentality so characteristic of the epoch is reflected in the grandiose rhetoric of Treitschke's history. From out an unfathomable flood of reality and dream, of superhuman heroism and modern psycho-analysis, arose the gigantic musical myths of Richard Wagner.

Friedrich Nietzsche (1844–1900) followed in these sublime paths until an apprehension of ultra-sensitive decadence in his idol caused his passion to turn to irreconcilable revulsion. Life was to him the will to power. Against Schopenhauer's passive confession of suffering he pitched the ruling force (*Herrenmoral*) of his superman. The decadence of the waning nineteenth century appeared to him as the curse of mass-morality and self-sufficient virtuousness. Darwin's theory of evolution provided Nietzsche with the basic idea of man's triumph over suffering. The naturalistic movement which developed in the eighties was definitely nurtured on Nietzsche's revolutionary ethics, whilst so-called 'neo-romanticism' in its symbolistic aspects culled inspiration rather from his attitude to life, or in its impressionist tendencies from his concept of form. Naturalism was concerned chiefly with social problems. Salvation from the boredom of existence, writes the Danish philosopher Kierkegaard in his '*Either . . . or*,' can only be achieved by an intenser life of the spirit. Nietzsche, who was not acquainted with the latter work, conquered nihilism, like Kierkegaard, through a belief in the ever recurring appearance of similar forms. The antithesis between the highly moral admonishment to live in such a manner that one desires to live again and the fatalistic conception of the eternal cycle of existence remains unreconciled in Nietzsche's works.

Friedrich Nietzsche exercised the greatest influence on German expressionism. He who preached the gospel of heroism became the idol of the exponents of this expressionist movement. He triumphed over Schopenhauer's pessimism, and yet few of his enthusiastic followers realized that his affirmation of life in reality springs from an essentially tragic conception of human existence. Through suffering he came to know joy. Of the Greeks he said in the last chapter of '*Die Geburt der Tragödie aus dem Geiste der Musik*' (1871–1872): 'How must this people have suffered in order to attain to such a realization of beauty.' Thus Greek art is born of the conflict between the Apolline (serene sublimity) and Dionysian (tragic passion), a dualism coined by Nietzsche. Neo-classicism knew only 'negation,' and froze movement to stark rigid geometry. It borrowed the outward gesture and fitted emotion into a scheme. Our tragic instincts 'weakened by Socratic and Christian morality' are revived again by music. In Bach and Richard Wagner, Nietzsche recognizes its outstanding representatives.

In his '*Unzeitgemässe Betrachtungen*' (1873–1875) he claims Schopenhauer and Wagner as the leaders of humanity, and like many thinkers today he disdains the catchword 'progress.' History only 'weakens' personality and produces self-complacent and impotent tolerance. Soon afterwards Nietzsche's life and philosophy underwent a profound crisis. Like Schopenhauer he violently attacked the hypocritical mass-instinct, nevertheless unlike the latter he found release not in the buddhistic Nirvana but in his affirmation of life. The breach with Richard Wagner acted as a great blow to his spirit. He now saw in Wagner only love of effect and morbid negation of life. Nietzsche's new outlook is reflected in '*Menschliches, Allzu Menschliches*' (1878–1879). He lost all faith in heroes, saints and art. Good and evil became only relative terms to him. It was but a passing mood born of the bitterness of disillusionment. With prophetic frenzy he now fights against the 'moral prejudices' ('*Moralische Vorurteile*,' 1881) of modern civilization. 'Good' is that which rouses our emotion, 'evil' is the synonym of a feeble spirit. He lives well who shapes his life in such a way that he would long to live it again.

At the height of his poetic inspiration in the inebriation of creative joy he wrote '*Also sprach Zarathustra*' (1883–1885), the apotheosis of the superman which was put to music by Delius. The German expressionists drew much inspiration from its poetry. The keynote of his philosophy is to be found in the poem '*Das trunkne Lied*':

*O Mensch! Gib acht!*
*Was spricht die tiefe Mitternacht?* . . .

'*Zarathustra*,' like Nietzsche's allusion to the 'blond beast,' gave rise to much misunderstanding. It was not untamed lust but the joy of the free spirit whose praise he sang. He calls sensuality the holiest of wine. His superman is impelled by a noble will to power ('*Wille zur Macht*').

Nietzsche's contemporaries revered not only his works but also his life. Already at the age of twenty-five he became professor of classical philology—an abnormal occurrence in German scholarship. He fell victim to a mental disease in the prime of life. For eleven years his mind was deranged until death released him. The insatiable flame of his life had consumed itself. Yet his philosophy lived on to guide the young generation who had to go through the upheaval of the Great War and the fevered time that preceded it. A heroic regeneration of mankind meant to Nietzsche a philosophic affirmation of life. The private, egoistic individual must be sacrificed for the sake of a nobler objective existence which future generations shall attain. Nietzsche's '*Dionysos-Dithyramben*' give passionate expression to this fundamental antithesis between spirit and life. He who loved Dürer's engraving of the Knight, Death and the Devil as an image of man's solitary quest, dauntless in the face of danger and death, was nevertheless an admirer of Claude Lorrain, who had likewise so strongly appealed to Goethe. But it was music which exerted the strongest influence on Nietzsche. Abstract thought, he maintained, must become vital. Music and Hellas were his spirit's realm. It was not a tendency towards the *vita contemplativa* which led him thither. To him Caesar-Napoleon was the manifest superman, warfare our fate. 'The silver bow wakens terror' in the ears of the faint-hearted burgher.

This passionate will for a nobler life is similarly expressed in Nietzsche's '*Sprüche*':

*Ecce Homo.*

*Ja! Ich weiss, woher ich stamme!*
*Ungesättigt gleich der Flamme*
*Glühe und verzehr' ich mich.*
*Licht wird alles, was ich fasse,*
*Kohle alles, was ich lasse:*
*Flamme bin ich sicherlich!*

They contain some of the finest gems of German gnomic poetry which could boast a live tradition through Hans Sachs, Goethe ('*Divan*'), and others. In Nietzsche we already find something of the disintegrating sarcasm of the era of decadence.

If any poet experienced the mysterious impulse of inspiration to the full it was the poet of the famous '*Dionysos-Dithyramben.*' Already here life and spirit appear as the great antithesis. In the years that followed, the years of '*Zarathustra,*' he was swept forward on its flood until in 1889 his spirit was engulfed in darkness. In the nineties appeared his '*Trunkne Lied*' ('*Zarathustra*'), as well as the nine '*Dionysos-Dithyramben*' (1884–1888). They open with the question as to what are truth and morals. Intellect and instinct, abstract thought and eternal life, egotistic isolation of the individual and a nobler community represent the antithesis on which this series of hymns is based and which closes with the problem of truth.

Nietzsche holds that profound understanding conquers egoism and that the individual must submerge himself for the sake of mankind. Thus the will to power is stripped of its arbitrariness and becomes the will to self-sacrifice. The gentle joyousness, of which Nietzsche so often speaks, is an expression of this heroic 'and yet' attitude towards life. The will to become superman must steel itself in solitude. In his demand of self-sacrifice Nietzsche approaches the spirit of Hölderlin and Rilke. His rejection of the rational for the sake of the irrational is somewhat reminiscent of Herder.

The language of the '*Dithyramben*' is quite peculiar. Its musical element persists through each single word, it is rich in assonance, repetition, and inner rhymes. A playful untroubled freedom ripples through rhythm and tone. All this is, however, not virtuosity. It is formal necessity which almost demands that the dithyrambs should be read not by the eye but apprehended musically by the ear; cf. '*Die Sonne sinkt*':

*. . . Rings nur Welle und Spiel.*
*Was je schwer war,*
*sank in blaue Vergessenheit,—*
*müssig steht nun mein Kahn.*
*Sturm und Fahrt—wie verlernt' er das!*
*Wunsch und Hoffen ertrank,*
*glatt liegt Seele und Meer. . . .*

The context of these songs can naturally not be regarded as rigidly systematic, and some of the ideas may appear contradictory; for they are poetry, not philosophy.

The scope of this book forbids further discussion of the spiritual factors which gave birth to that originally passionately patriotic *Sturm und Drang* of which Arno Holz was the most consistent and epoch-making leader. The general trend of this movement was absolutely opposed to the attitude of the classic Schiller or more especially the pseudo-idealism of his followers. Truth not beauty was the watchword—that is, truth in the sense of realism which is not afraid of the bare facts of existence or of poverty, and finds significance in the most trivial detail, even a shoe-heel. Thus naturalism provided at once its own Alpha and Omega. In vain was Nietzsche's warning in the '*Birth of Tragedy*.' The mirror which once reflected keen and mighty features now showed only that petty verisimilitude which the imperfect lineaments of nature itself display.

The term 'naturalism' must be used with great care. It signifies definite renunciation of the world of beautiful illusions (*Die Welt des schönen Scheins*). Hideousness, brutality, and crime, as phenomena of natural truth, add to the poet's material. The fashion of the day demands of literature, as of the law, the expiation of the accused whose crime is but the outcome of milieu and heredity. Moral expositions give way to analysis, fanatic description of detail and impressions of microscopic exactitude that revel in dialectic speech. Ambition and hunger and sex appear as the ultimate forces of human instinct. The individual is represented as the slave of natural processes. Mass triumphs over authority.

Unlike Schiller or, later, Holz's adversary Paul Ernst, the naturalist did not regard existence as a stage for the activities of heroic personalities but weltered in the chaos of those dark and passionate forces whose presence he felt within himself and which he sought to emulate. The *milieu* dramas of the eighties and nineties laid bare the utter barrenness of such an attitude to life which was based on Feuerbach's doctrine of omnipotent materialism: sexual crime, hereditary drunkenness, poverty and slums, capitalist extortion, matrimonial problems in bourgeois and bohemian life, free love, bastardy, prostitution, and pathological perversity clothed in brutality or a decadent *raffinement*. All these invoked a *Götterdämmerung* atmosphere which in gentler natures, such as G. Hauptmann, caused *Weltschmerz* to weave a dream of heaven.

We saw that naturalism stresses the accidents of life and tends towards analytic confession rather than to the development or conflict of individual character, welded to shapes of universal significance. In so far as the empiric world of appearances remained but a transcript of reality it failed to become poetry. Yet even naturalism contained something of an idealistic attitude towards life, namely, in its belief in man's ultimate liberation from the drudgery of everyday existence. The decay of speculative thought betrays itself in philosophy. The doctrine of positivism as preached by Comte, John Stuart Mill, Dühring, H. Spencer and Mach, who dissects the ego as a practical unity of peripheral nervous stimulation, became limited to a purely empiric plane. Materialism as represented by Vogt, Moleschott, and on a more popular level by Büchner and Häckel, based itself one-sidedly on science. Nature was conceived as a reality apprehended by the senses, and man as her dependent offspring. Such were the sources from which naturalistic literature drew its inspiration. Its most important models, apart from Nietzsche, were Ludwig Feuerbach and Max Stirner (Kaspar Schmidt) who tore the mask from the face of sham virtue, and as a radical egoist recognized his bitterest enemies in the family and the state. Thought was based solely on scientific discovery. This new philosophical conviction appeared of momentous importance to the young poets, for it justified rigorous realistic description. Questions concerning the mystery of life, of fate, original sin and accident were attacked anew. Thus the naturalistic poets of Germany could boast a so-called 'realistic ideal' in which they saw the flower of all earthly existence. This ideal was nourished by a belief in progress and the rebirth of harmony. But as is shown by Bölsche's works this aim was limited by earthly values, health, normal existence, and permanent prosperity. Nevertheless reality and the abstract remained irreconcilable, and the world is unillumined by any divine radiance.

Modern research also regards naturalism from the point of view of *Weltanschauung*. According to Dilthey's three types naturalism should be ranked amongst those concepts which exclude ideas of value and reason and recognize as infallible only the theory of cause and effect. With consummate finesse O. Walzel was able to point to hidden laws of construction underlying even the supremely impressionistic *Treffkunst* of F. Poppenberg's '*Bibelots*' and A. Kerr's review of d'Annunzio's '*Gioconda*.' Impressionism which, unlike realism, allows its ephemeral touch to rest only on the surface of things must not be confused with naturalism. In contrast to the latter, impressionism if consistent would reject, though in vain, all spiritual valuations or imaginative concepts (even memory-pictures), and instead passively reproduce the subtle nuances afforded by the broken surface texture of things as they appear under the influence of colour and light.

All subject values are relegated to the province of refined technique, where they linger as a nervous tremolo in the quivering mist of atmosphere and light. The problem of form is exhausted in the rendering of technique. A particularly lucid interpretation of such *Treffkunst* is afforded by Luise Thon's '*Sprache des deutschen Impressionismus*.' Nevertheless naturalism, impressionism and neo-romanticism still require stricter delineation as distinct categories. Hermann Pongs has already pointed to the exaggerated decadent element in neo-romanticism. The latter's relation to expressionism is certainly closer than was hitherto supposed. When the colour flecks appear charged with inner agitation we may recognize therein a first symptom of expressionism.

It is more difficult to trace this development in poetry than in painting. Van Gogh derived from the impressionist school, but his passion for expression would not let him rest content with the passive appearance of things, and his mountains and trees are filled with fierce momentum as though the force of primal creation and the rhythm of the generation yet stirred within him. The rhapsodies offered in praise of the dark powers of instinct and fecundity which represent one side of expressionism (for instance the works of Wedekind) appear more nearly related to naturalism than to the crystalline laws of *cubism*. But the beautiful untamed animal is no longer a transcript of reality but is intensified to such an extent that it seems to move in the sphere of the dæmonic and absolute.

A veritable medley of styles appear to converge or follow on each other's heels during the reign of Wilhelm II. Fontane in his old age borrows the technique of novel-writing from a younger generation though rejecting their mass of detail. The generation coinciding with Wilhelm II's birth (1859) became the champion of naturalism. Not all its exponents, as for instance Richard Dehmel or Paul Ernst, remained true to the community. Almost at the same time or a little later Stefan George and Barlach arose as opponents.

The naturalistic movement centred in Munich and Berlin, whilst Michael Georg Conrad and his circle published their own journal '*Die Gesellschaft*' in Munich. The literary clique founded by the brothers Hart in Berlin favoured more radical views. One and all were, however, outdone by the 'consequent naturalism' of Holz and Schlaf. At the instigation of O. Brahm, P. Schlenther and Max Harden, the *Freie Bühne* came into being, and by presenting first Ibsen's *Ghosts* and then Hauptmann's '*Vor Sonnenaufgang*' irrevocably set the fashion for the new 'storm and stress.'

## *ARNO HOLZ*

### *New Forms in the German Lyric*

On October 26, 1929, occurred the death of one of the most original characters in German literature—Arno Holz. Together with Johannes Schlaf he appears as radical inaugurator of the naturalist school in Germany and creator of a new lyric style. Holz was born in 1863, the son of a chemist in Rastenburg, East

Prussia. An unfavourable criticism was destined to change the whole of Holz's work. In 1885 he published his '*Buch der Zeit.*' This was not well received by the critics. It is a collection of enthusiastic and masterly poems, and a powerful expression of the social atmosphere of our times. Romantic songs are included among those which betray a strong social tendency, so that the work suffers from a lack of harmony. This volume also includes a cycle of thirteen poems, called '*Phantasus*,' the rhythm of which is similar to that of Herwegh's '*Mein ganzer Reichtum ist mein Leben.*' As we shall see, Holz later gave the name of '*Phantasus*' to the whole of his new lyrical work.

The failure of the above book caused him to ponder over his technique. He had enriched poetry with modern problems but not yet revolutionized its form. He next embarked upon the study of critical theories of Zola, whose work he had read in Paris. In addition to the latter writer, Flaubert and the Goncourts were his new favourites. It is characteristic of Holz that with his usual radicalism he outrivalled Zola's theory and became the creator of what in his versatile and dialectic study: '*Die Kunst, ihr Wesen und ihre Gesetze*' (1890–1892), he calls *konsequenter Naturalismus.*

Zola's definition, '*Une œuvre d'art est un coin de la nature vu à travers un tempérament*,' was not radical enough for Holz, who set up the doctrine that art only differed from nature in its medium of representation. His theory finally culminates in the formula, *Die Kunst hat die Tendenz, wieder die Natur zu sein. Sie wird sie nach Massgabe ihrer Mittel und deren Handhabung*; i.e. art tends to be nature which it becomes according to the medium used and the treatment thereof. Art develops; it is not absolute but relative, and there are as many conceptions of art as of nature. Thus distinction between music, poetry, sculpture and painting is unsatisfactory, for art is not limited to separate forms of expression. There are as many forms of art as there are artistic mediums. These may change, exhaust themselves or be replaced by other means, e.g. our conventional dancing is nothing but motion. According to Holz it has ceased to be a medium of expression. He foresees a modern art which only consists of sound and light, and for him no medium is more comprehensive than the word.

To Holz it is of prime necessity to adhere as closely as possible to nature. This concept of naturalism, which we must distinguish from a *purely imitative* and hence unaesthetic impulse, affords an antithesis to an *absolute will to art* which Holz denies at any rate in theory. As a result he came to draw that cheap simile between art and the scribblings on a slate. The question is here not whether the geometric style was the primary stage in artistic evolution, or whether a child's scribblings are actually worthy of aesthetic criticism, but whether we recognize in art a will to abstract form or not. Theoretically Holz endows with sovereign power that base reality which Rilke calls

'an incomplete reality that lies in the streets and in the houses, only that more of it is gathered there than else intrudes into one evening' (Malte Laurids Brigge).

It was characteristic of Holz that about the same time he sought and found a literary companion in Johannes Schlaf. In spite of great hardships, hunger and cold, they finished '*Papa Hamlet*' (1889) under the Norwegian pseudonym: Bjarne P. Holmsen. This cycle of three tales already betrays the naturalistic style whose cause Holz championed also in theory. In 1890 they published the drama, '*Die Familie Selicke*,' which was staged on the *Freie Bühne*. Holz made use of his naturalist method of minute description and phonographic exactness. Soon afterwards both friends published their works together in the volume '*Neue Gleise*,' but from that time on they went separate ways.

Of greater interest are Holz's other works, above all his theories on the lyric which he propounds in the '*Revolution der Lyrik*' (1899). According to Holz novel and drama have found their way back to nature, but not so the lyric. He complains that the form has become detached from the spirit, maintaining that verbal music, rhyme and verse are sufficient in themselves, whilst he believes that even when a poet like Walt Whitman tried to destroy conventional law by free verse, it turned out to be 'pulpit-style' and not artistic form. The '*Moderne Dichter-Charaktere*' (an anthology of lyrics, edited by Conradi, Arent, Henckell and Hart in 1884, to which he had himself contributed a few poems) had also not revolutionized poetry. Holz maintains that it is 'the blood of the language' that must be renewed. The modern poet seeks the inner rhythm which is born directly of the subject and which avoids all amateurish lyrical patterns not truly expressive of the matter. Holz is the enemy of the clanging, jingling rhyme that tires the hearer by the repetition of hackneyed words. To him the verse also seems to have lost its pregnant significance. He hears in every stanza, as soon as it is repeated, a hidden 'hurdy-gurdy.' Even free verse is not always devoid of a 'false pathos' which spoils the essence of the inner form. In returning the words to their original value and their simple meaning Holz sees the salvation of modern lyric form. Yet he does not abolish significant rhythm expressed in utmost simplicity. Consequently, departing from literary convention, Holz also invented a new arrangement in the printing of his poems. The author calls these new verses *Mittelachsenverse* (central-axis verses), that is to say, the lines are built round an 'axis' in order to give beauty and clarity of design. This may be illustrated by the following example from '*Phantasus*' (1898):

*Draussen die Düne.*

*Einsam das Haus,*
*eintönig,*
*ans Fenster*
*der Regen.*

*Hinter mir,*
*tictac*
*eine Uhr,*
*meine Stirn*
*gegen die Scheibe.*

*Nichts.*

*Alles vorbei.*

*Grau der Himmel*
*grau die See*
*und grau*
*das Herz.*

Holz was violently attacked by his literary opponents. He defended the originality of his technique and cleared up a few misapprehensions; he did not mean to abolish subjective art—the poet had to express as directly as possible *what* and *how* he felt.

Here Zola's *tempérament*, once so radically rejected, is re-established! Holz emphasizes the fact that art never becomes nature, but in his fight against æsthetic affectation he had to create a revolutionary formula.

Further explanations were summed up in the book: '*Die befreite deutsche Wortkunst*' (1921), in which he calls the new mode of printing an 'acoustic picture'; it takes the place of the old form of versification. For instance, the writing of two equally long lines, one below the other, must be conditioned by inner form, otherwise his parallelism is 'false pathos.' Compare the above poem: (*grau der Himmel, grau die See*). The repetition of the word *grau* is to emphasize the monotony of the scene.

Holz then refers to the use of 'numerical architecture,' a scheme according to which a certain number of verbs, nouns or adjectives appear 'spontaneously' in his songs. In contrast with the radical rejection of rhyme in the '*Revolution der Lyrik*,' he here returns to the use of the latter, but no more as a hackneyed form, but as a medium of artistic gradation. Impure rhyme becomes for him a useful means of transition from verse to verse. But there is no *a priori* form, no essential difference between drama and lyric; they are one unity, the former indirect, the latter direct, expression.

These were the main points of Holz's theories which inaugurated new lyric forms and which he put into practice in '*Phantasus.*'

But it is truly a touch of irony that it was just his other poems, written in the old style, which attracted the attention especially of the German public, as for instance the '*Blechschmiede*' (1902), a modern Walpurgisnight in its diabolical abandonment and literary satire. In this 'lyric, dramatic, drastic, musical, picturesque and plastic mystery of words,' '*Phantasus*' also appears under various masks. In '*Dafnis*' (1903) Holz proves himself a master of rhyme. It is a 'lyric portrait' in which the poet imitates and tries to excel the style of the seventeenth century often with brilliant skill. Both '*Dafnis*' and the '*Blechschmiede*' are unique in their linguistic mastership and unquestionably influenced the second edition of '*Phantasus*' by their burlesque, Aristophanic style.

Having created a special technique for the representation of every subject and emotion and every conceivable type of character, Holz produced the colossal cycle of '*Phantasus*' (1916) in seven parts. It is a large folio edition of three hundred and thirty-six pages, a giant compared with the edition of 1898–1899. A unique example of expansion is represented by the poem '*Gottseidank*' (Ph. V), which covers ninety-two folio pages. It contains a vast sentence (page 112), the labyrinthian structure of which spreads over fifteen pages, formed of repetitions and variations round an 'axis' which is one single finite verb of one syllable, arithmetically increasing. In the course of nearly three pages, about four hundred nouns are registered. Thus Holz even surpasses Walt Whitman's power of cataloguing. There is a long sentence of one hundred and forty-four lines. Such vast structures are intended by Holz to characterize the content: thus the tiresome climbing of a mountain is symbolized by a sentence of twenty-seven lines.

If we admit a fundamental difference in the conception, '*Phantasus*' presents a counterpart to the works of Rabelais. One is struck by some similarities in style. Both draw material for their work from their wide scientific reading and betray an affinity of style in regard to onomatopoeia, alliteration, assonance, plays upon words, and fantastic combinations, etc. Thus we are led to think of Rabelais's enumerations in his '*Gargantua and Pantagruel*' (cf. Diogenes's *Jolly Tub*). Above all, Walt Whitman's '*Leaves of Grass*' bears some resemblance to Holz's style. The latter, however, rejected the idea of any dependence on the American poet who departed from the conventional metrical scheme and rhyme. His poetry, however, also abounds with figures of speech, antitheses, catalogues and metaphors.

Unquestionably Holz was the first to use the new form systematically, theoretically and practically.

### *Phantasus-Rhythm and Free Verse*

In the foregoing chapter we already referred to the *Phantasus-Zeile*. The latter signifies that ultimate formal unity which Holz indefatigably strove to attain up to the time of his death. Again and again his ear detected elements that disturb the auditory image which to him should constitute the line's unity and render it distinct from its accompanying phrases. As we see by his incessant typographical alterations he was wont to discover ever new tonal valuations. But as the printed word was thus always in flux, even his last amendment could hardly be said to crystallize the rhythmic image to the ultimate form which he avowed it must inevitably wear. In order moreover to counteract mistakes due to the reader's individual interpretation of such symbols as punctuation and other values of expression, elocutionists would have to be especially trained by the poet himself, and kept acquainted with his latest revisions. He was, however, fully aware of the difficulties involved. Only iron discipline and restraint could have withheld such an artist in words as Holz from the pitfall of microscopic accumulative analysis of the sensuous impression, particularly when the subject in hand is the *Leierkasten.* Often indeed we are reminded of '*Dafnis*,' of gargantuan and pantagruelian hyperbole, and the poet cannot escape his craving to register every detail, and eventually falls into mere verbal frippery.

A comparison of the different versions of '*Phantasus*' sheds an interesting light on Holz's method of work. CD* as opposed to AB* clearly show a desire to break rhythmic monotony. Individual images are often intensified. The *blaue Riesenblüte* ('*Sieben Billionen Jahre*') is, in CD, hurled from its state of dream-clad slumber into a whirling chaos of new worlds and scattered like spray on the winds. In place of the single verb *schwamm* in B, we find five in C, seven in the version of 1922, and nine in D.

Certain of the *Phantasus* poems enjoy a terser quality of expression, e.g. '*Draussen die Düne.*' In contrast to A, BCD give the concrete article (*das* Haus, etc.). Apart from this the text remains almost unchanged. The suppression of *I* results in the diminution of the subjective element which is now expressed alone by the possessive pronoun *meine*. The verb is absolutely omitted.

The personal emotional element is just intimated at the end, thus intensifying the annihilating greyness that encompasses us and clutches at the heart. And yet the complete suppression (not surrender) of the ego by the object causes these verses to remain somehow superficial and decorative. Symmetry of rhythm, of which Herder speaks in his edition of the old poem on the rain-nymph with the water-jug, is not found in Holz's verse, for he mingles both metre and rhythm. Just here the regular rhythmic reiteration which Holz tabooed might have rendered the atmosphere of his poem more palpable, in that its very monotony

* A = *Musenalmanach*; B = *Phantasus*, 1898–1899; C = *Ph.* 1916; D = *Ph.* 1925.

would have symbolized the unending patter of rain. How differently Gottfried Keller conceived his '*Trübes Wetter*'! Hope and despair inhabit his mind equally. The complex tension between the powers of external life and the poet's inner vision is reconciled.

In Longfellow's '*Rainy Day*' the monotony of rain expressed first by the 'sensitive,' then by the 'affective' style, yields ultimately to a state of calm reflection:

*The day is cold, and dark, and dreary,*
*It rains, and the wind is never weary.*

The parallelism in the last lines of '*Draussen die Düne*' is peculiarly reminiscent of a poem which Fiona Macleod (W. Sharp) heard an old Gaelic woman sing and of which he gives a rendering in his '*Poems and Dramas*' (1925): '*It is the grey rock I am. . . .*' Likewise we may call to mind the close of the first verse in Macleod's song, '*Leaves, shadows and dreams*' (1900). We have no reason to suspect any conscious relationship between the German and the British poet, but it is interesting to note that Macleod who was acquainted with the works of Turgenev, Baudelaire and Walt Whitman, himself tried his hand at rhythmic prose, for instance in his '*Silence of Amor.*'

As in the first and last lines of '*Draussen die Düne,*' the following lines also betray some formality in their metre:

*Über die Welt hin ziehen die Wolken.*
*Grün durch die Wälder.*
*fliesst ihr Licht.*

*Herz, vergiss!*

*In stiller Sonne*
*webt linderndster Zauber,*
*unter wehenden Blumen blüht tausend Trost.*

*Vergiss! Vergiss!*

*Aus fernem Grund pfeift, horch, ein Vogel . .*
*er singt sein Lied.*

*Das Lied vom Glück!*

With the exception of their arrangement, the lines in C and

D are identical. We would suggest an interpretation of rhythm different to Benoist-Hanappier's reading of the same, and even to Ermatinger's who was led astray by his misunderstanding of the *Mittelachse*. The three verbs: *ziehen*, *webt*, *pfeift*, should surely only be counted as lifts. The *Mittelachse* is solely the external spine, a mere decorative arrangement of the print, not the backbone of symmetrical construction. In spite of this typographic succession of lines, a regular beat of two lifts may be detected. The inversions so loved by Holz here distinctly create first descending, then ascending rhythm. The poem also excels in sensitive contrasts such as movement and rest. As in Goethe's '*Über allen Gipfeln*' we may trace a gradual declining movement from height to depth. But Holz's poem, with its crowd of personifications such as 'magic' and 'solace,' and its alliterative virtuosity, knows nothing of simple statement. The emotional element bursts forth in rhetoric: *Vergiss! Vergiss!* The poet himself defended these lines by maintaining that they alone rendered the pain suggested by the other words of the poem fully significant, and only thus could theme and form be utterly transfused.

Whereas in '*Über die Welt hin*' all action lies in the past, the poem '*Rote Rosen*' calls forth a succession of word-pictures which, as though caught in the spell of a static present, bear no organic relationship to each other. Unfortunately in the version D the poem disintegrates in manneristic expansion. C is a phantasy, a picture in words. The hero suggests the plastic figure of Colleoni, but in its decorative treatment it reminds one of the art of the *Sezession*, in particular the paintings of Gustav Klimt which, notwithstanding the dreamy allure of their symbolism and their sensuous tremulous colour, appear caged in the sterile bleakness of calculated decadent æstheticism:

*Rote Rosen*
*winden sich um meine düstre Lanze.*

*Durch weisse Lilienwälder*
*schnaubt mein Hengst.*
*Aus grünen Seeen,*
*Schilf im Haar,*
*tauchen schlanke, schleierlose Jungfraun.*
*Ich reite wie aus Erz.*

*Immer,*
*dicht vor mir,*
*fliegt der Vogel Phönix*
*und singt!*

These are but momentary impressions ranged side by side, where painting and poetry are crudely intermingled, a misunderstanding of *ut pictura poesis* against which Lessing railed in his *Laokoon.* In spite of the last line *und singt* the atmosphere remains unquickened. Heroic will dies on the stagnant air. Holz was probably aware of it himself for in the version D he re-echoes the final verb thrice. What element of true poetry the verses contain springs less from any lyrical quality than from the tonal colour of contrasts (rigidity and movement), set in an ideal landscape like Böcklin's. All gradations are avoided. The individual images are isolated, not arbitrarily but in opposition to one another. Their relation to the subject 'I' gives this word-painting its lyric note.

What descriptive prose can achieve with the help of the '*Phantasus*' technique can be proved by comparing the *Stimmungsbild* '*Rote Dächer*' with Holz's dreamy memories of youth—the little provincial town with its steep red roofs and long streets, the sleepy fowls and the rose-trees in their green window-boxes. Both passages are prose. Nothing would be lost by rendering the first into acknowledged prose, whereas we destroy the very heart of true poetry by divesting it of its form. How much would be sacrificed by a mere change of words in transcribing Mörike's '*Um Mitternacht*' or Eichendorff's '*Es schienen so golden die Sterne*' into prose! What significance lies in the refrain *Und dann und wann ein weisser Elefant* in Rilke's '*Karussell*' or the hurdy-gurdy rhythm (so despised by Holz) in a lullaby! What depth of passion sounds from Morungen's '*Dô tagite iz,*' or lies in the simple symmetry of those inverted couplets in Gottfried's '*Tristan*':

*ein man ein wîp, ein wîp ein man,*
*Tristan Isôt, Isôt Tristan.*

And though the impressionist poets taught us to experience the most subtle and exquisite charms of some fragment of nature, the older poets were able with a few imaginative lines to suggest emotional experience beyond the range of Holz's elaborately impressionistic analysis of the material world.

Holz lost himself in a chaos of words. Had he been completely consistent in realizing his theories he would have turned to primitive people whose language, both in regard to sound and rhythm, is still closely related to the object or action. The expressions they use are concrete and suggestive. Like the Shilluk the story-teller today still interprets action by naturalistic means when he describes the act of wandering by: he walked and walked and walked. . . . Thus Holz instead of writing: *immer vor mir fliegt* . . . would have had to use a repeated verb: *er fliegt, fliegt, fliegt*. . . . Similarly in his verses on the rain, '*Draussen die Düne*,' the phrase *eintönig der Regen* would have had to be replaced by: *Regen, Regen, Regen* . . . which emphasizes the monotony.

But a return to primitive forms of expression could not of itself regenerate language. We should first have to become primitive ourselves. Only when primeval passion bursts into stammering utterance '*Du, Du* . . .' does such reiteration of word appear born of an inner necessity. Today primitive repetitive forms of speech, when occasioned not by emotional excitement but merely for the sake of emphasis, strike us as verbosity and tautology. Holz does not lead us into this cul-de-sac, but his constructions of syntax, his manner of multiplying nouns around the verb are often (if they do not take the form of dream-phantasies) mere virtuosity or attempted verisimilitude, founded on the misconception that art should rival nature as if it were the highest aim to stuff the carcasses of the dead!

This error produces particularly fatal results where *tempo* is concerned. In describing a journey even a close imitation of the rocking, knocking rhythms of the train does not yet weld the phrases to the shape of a poem. Art has its own laws; it is not an imitation of rhythm apprehended in actuality. Through art two separate worlds, reality and imagination, are fused to a unity. A work of art is a picture not a mirror. Konrad Fiedler, foreshadowing modern ideals, differentiates between the forms of art and those of nature. For the sake of imaginative form defiant anaturalism is almost transmuted to religious significance in the art of Emil Nolde, or in Franz Marc's abstract paintings of animals. Such concepts are, however, not new. How often had the old masters (e.g. Grünewald in his '*Crucifixion*') distorted natural appearances and violated proportion in order to render emotion more intense and enhance the formal quality of their work!

It should be mentioned here that the peculiar arrangement of the printed line in '*Phantasus*,' has since been used in England by the composer Cyril Scott.

## *IMPRESSIONISM AND NEO-ROMANTICISM*

*D. v. Liliencron, H. v. Hofmannsthal, Dehmel, Morgenstern, and others.*

Holz's adamantine strength survived the literary battles of the naturalistic era. Other lyric poets who had also stood in the front rank of the fighting-line were drained of all vitality in their struggles against an outworn tradition and the 'betrayal of nature.' Such was the fate of that passionate spirit Hermann Conradi and the neurasthenic Wilhelm Arent, the brilliant critic Heinrich Hart and the socialist agitator Karl Henckell, who, however, was later to write poetry of a true lyrical vein. Representative of the period are the '*Lieder eines Menschen*' by the atheist and anarchist Ludwig Scharf and the poems of John Henry Mackay, who, though of Scottish ancestry, was educated in Germany. The work of the Baltic poet Maurice Reinhold von Stern, who strove in vain to reconcile his individuality with social idealism, never gained the recognition it merited. Ferdinand Avenarius, founder and editor of the journal *Kunstwart*, and arbiter of æsthetic taste for the young generation, certainly kept aloof from all radical political activities; nevertheless, his infallible instinct had led him to recognize the value not only of naturalism as represented by Holz, G. Hauptmann or Schlaf, but also of the impressionistic experiments of these authors and other movements.

We saw that the era of the new German 'storm and stress' movement, which began about 1880, accompanied by the economic revolution with Marx as its chief exponent, and the scientific revolution initiated by Darwin, was profoundly influenced by Zola. He laid emphasis upon the pathological and social aspect of life, and upon scientific representation of milieu and heredity. The Russians, Tolstoy and Turgenev—Tolstoy as the type of noble demagogue and 'godseeker,' and Dostoevsky as European criminologist and apostle of a stricken proletariat—were the accepted models of

German writers. The strongest influence upon the drama was exercised by the Norwegian Ibsen, whose radical subversion of ethical and social values was combined with an impressionistic treatment of detail. The Swedes, especially Lagerlöf and Strindberg, who later veered round to expressionism, became leaders of the movement. Munich and Berlin became the centre and pivot of the new fashion in Germany.

When naturalism became the triumphant fashion of the day in Berlin and Munich, Austria did not take the lead in this literary movement. New ideas were maturing, as we see by the publication of Hermann Bahr's collection of essays, '*Die Überwindung des Naturalismus*' (1891), in which this sensitive critic and journalist from Linz betrays his keen sensibility to every novel movement. But even whilst Ernst von Wildenbruch was casting acrimony at the '*Augen ohne Geist*,' new paths were being opened up by D. v. Liliencron, who belonged to no clique.

Detlev von Liliencron (1844–1909), born in Kiel, may be said to be the full-blooded pioneer of the decadent impressionist school which followed. The latter might have learned much from his keen sense of reality, and certainly his courageous spirit inspired the young men of the eighties. The discipline and nicety he frequently shows in the choice of his expressions suggest the true artist. Moreover Liliencron breathed the same atmosphere as the young generation, even if he in no way disguised his antipathy towards the levelling effect of democracy. Æsthetic sensibility caused him rather to favour a vulture-like anarchism. Nevertheless, he possessed a passionate love for his country.

D. v. Liliencron's biography unfolds itself like some ever-changing panorama. He was descended from an impoverished aristocratic family, and as a Prussian officer he witnessed his country's triumph and political ascendancy in 1866 and 1870–1871. Debts forced him to give up his military career. He became a teacher of languages in America, and earned a pittance as pianist and painter; but when his first volume of poems '*Adjutantenritte*' (1883) met with success he was able forthwith to dedicate his life to his writings.

It is his fate to enjoy the transient joys of a March day:

*Kurzes Glück schwamm mit den Wolkenmassen;*
*Wollt es halten, musst es schwimmen lassen. . . .*

He clutches at the transient moment, drinks deeply of joy's draught, and shares his high spirits with his companions. He longs to see and hear the wonders of nature, adding impression to impression with lightning speed and without proper continuity or delicate nuances; cf. '*Die Musik kommt*':

*Klingling, bumbum und tschingdada,*
*Zieht im Triumph der Perserschah?*
*Und um die Ecke brausend brichts*
*Wie Tubaton des Weltgerichts.*
*Voran der Schellenträger.*

*Bumbum, das grosse Bombardon,*
*Der Beckenschlag, das Helikon,*
*Die Piccolo, der Zinkenist,*
*Die Türkentrommel, der Flötist,*
*Und dann der Herre Hauptmann.*

*Der Hauptmann naht mit stolzem Sinn,*
*Die Schuppenketten unterm Kinn;*
*Die Schärpe schnürt den schlanken Leib,*
*Beim Zeus, das ist kein Zeitvertreib.*
*Und dann die Herren Leutnants.*

*Zwei Leutnants, rosenrot und braun,*
*Die Fahne schützen sie als Zaun.*
*Die Fahne kommt, den Hut nimm ab;*
*Der bleiben treu wir bis ans Grab.*
*Und dann die Grenadiere.*

*Der Grenadier in strammem Tritt,*
*Im Schritt und Tritt und Tritt und Schritt,*
*Das stampft und dröhnt und klappt und flirrt,*
*Laternenglas und Fenster klirrt.*
*Und dann die kleinen Mädchen.*

*Die Mädchen alle Kopf an Kopf;*
*Das Auge blau und blond der Zopf.*
*Aus Tür und Tor und Hof und Haus*
*Schaut Mine, Trine, Stine aus.—*
*Vorbei ist die Musike.*

*Klingling, tschingtsching und Paukenkrach.*
*Noch aus der Ferne tönt es schwach—*
*Ganz leise bum bum bum bum tsching.*
*Zog da ein bunter Schmetterling,*
*Tschingtsching, bum, um die Ecke?*

Herein D. v. Liliencron shows himself to be the representative of the so-called physiological *Nervenkunst*.

His nature pictures breathe an atmosphere in which the individual element yields to the general *Stimmung*. The profounder realm of the spirit is often lacking here, so that the poet's ego remains obscured by the external illusion of appearances. His only world is that of light, colour and tone. Images inspired by memories, e.g. '*Unter den Linden*,' and usually not developed directly from nature remain inorganic.

D. v. Liliencron gives us rhythm rather than melody. A good example of the latter is his poem '*Schöne Junitage*.' The four verses are each in turn dedicated to a distinct period of the day: midnight, morning, day, evening. The verses begin without an anacrusis, but in *flussüberwärts* the chief accent falls on *ü*. The very lack of verbs in line two of the first, second and third verses causes the poem to sound rhythmic rather than melodic. The season (June) remains vague. The four verses seem indeed to suggest symbols rather than description, a point which is, however, characteristic only of a part of Liliencron's work. Of quite a different calibre, drastic and direct in its verisimilitude is his song: '*Das schönste Mädchen von der Welt*.' Here Liliencron does not hesitate to use either careless jargon or photographically realistic description. For this reason, however, the last line of the third verse with its rococo simile appears all the more disturbing. As a master of *Treffkunst*, D. v. Liliencron represented the art of German impressionism without falling into extremes or making sound an aim in itself at the expense of all logic.

Amongst the most characteristic features of German impressionism are exact registration of acoustic and optic impressions, together with a partiality for dialect, alien words, adjectives producing the desired *Stimmung*, present participles of a passive nature, suppression of the verb and every other possible means of producing delicate nuances. The vague tremulous atmosphere is rendered yet more diffused by the use of *synaesthesia*, compound adjectives and the frequent use of *und*, *man*, *es*, etc. The infinitive in noun form replaces the verb; instead of *es tönt* we find *ein Tönen*.

Whereas the radical naturalist regards the human being as absolutely dependent on social existence, and employing Marxist dialectic exaggerates reality for the purpose of propaganda, the impressionist is essentially non-political. He dissolves the world to a play of colour and mood, not as a harmless dreamer, but often as one who sets up icy barriers to protect himself from the trivialities of bourgeois existence. This attitude towards life is certainly quite alien to that of D. v. Liliencron, who does not set himself up as the pivot of a narrow circle in order to build a new world from within, but abandons his sensual, full-blooded nature to the allurement and devastation of life. Thus he never succumbed to the weary, anaemic decadence into which impressionism often degenerated. His language expresses a keen visual sense and a robust power of observation.

D. v. Liliencron's poetry is, moreover, not lacking in a profounder meaning, a realization of fate. In his '*Leben und Lüge*,' written on the eve of his death, he lays bare the bestiality of the human race, its envy and pride, in the crudest colours—cf. also his poem '*Feudal*,' where the retainer is killed in order that a noble lady may 'warm her feet in his guts.' These grim and rather tasteless horrors are balanced by his ballad on the defiant champion of freedom, '*Pidder Lüng*.'

During the many vicissitudes of his life, D. v. Liliencron's family, his friends, nature, the thought of great men's deeds, and above all his art, were his constant solace. Thus his intrepid spirit fortified him whilst other impressionists were lured into the nirvana of neo-romanticism.

To this neo-romantic group belong, amongst others the talented G. Falke, Max Dauthendey, K. Busse, Schönaich-Carolath, the young H. Carossa, and the once so popular O. J. Bierbaum. The latter was editor of an art journal called *Pan*, at one time managed also by Cäsar Flaischlen, who now and again made use of Holz's *Mittelachse*, and thus superficially appears to owe more to the latter than he actually did.

It is no mere accident that on the threshold of the twentieth century impressionism found a milieu in which it could readily flourish in Vienna. In the movement known as symbolism and neo-romanticism Austria once more took a prominent part. About the year 1892, the date of Gerhart Hauptmann's '*Weber*,' a reactionary tendency had become apparent, and in opposition to the school of scientific realism and socialistic agitation arose a poetry of distinctly individualistic character.

Rilke, Schnitzler, and H. v. Hofmannsthal, who are the chief participants in this movement, endeavour with subtle artistry and sensitiveness to atmosphere to reveal the hidden regions of the subconscious and the irrational in human nature.

In the Viennese poet H. v. Hofmannsthal, who died in 1929, the world lost one of the most refined writers of neo-romanticism. Not all who listen to Richard Strauss's '*Rosenkavalier*,' '*Ariadne*,' or '*Electra*,' are aware that H. v. Hofmannsthal was the author of the libretti. Those who have enjoyed the yearly festival of music and drama at Salzburg will have heard his version of the medieval English morality play '*Everyman*.' In H. v. Hofmannsthal's play the rich man, forsaken by fortune, has to account for his sins before God. In the lyrical drama '*Das Salzburger grosse Welttheater*,' which is inspired by Calderon, H. v. Hofmannsthal makes use of his favourite theme: the purification of mankind through death, and, with some resemblance to Shakespeare's plays and Goethe's '*Faust*,' the stage represents the world, where king, queen, beggar, peasant and workman play their transitory parts.

In the poem entitled '*Ballade des äusseren Lebens*,' the poet sings of our daily lot:

*Children grow up with hollow eyes,*
*And knowing naught, they grow and die,*
*And all men go their way. . . .*

Melancholy and unsatiated desire of life fill his poems. His development was precocious, and at the age of seventeen he was already writing verses reminiscent of Goethe's.

H. v. Hofmannsthal's lyric drama '*Death and the Fool*' (1893) may be considered a characteristic example of the romantic mood of this period. The hero Claudio is swayed between the world of deed and dream. Life and love are mere phantoms, and only when death comes to him and plays a strain that calls up the shades of his mother, his beloved and his friend, does he recognize the worth of reality that he had let slip through his hands:

*In eine Stunde kannst du Leben pressen,*
*Mehr als das ganze Leben konnte halten,*
*Das schattenhafte will ich ganz vergessen*
*Und weih' mich deinen Wundern und Gewalten.*

. . . *Erst, da ich sterbe, spür'ich, dass ich bin.*
(*Der Tor und der Tod*—Insel Verlag.)

The passionate enquiring spirit of Richard Dehmel (1863–1920) had little affinity with that of his friend Liliencron. Yet the two share in common an unshakeable faith in life. Both scorned the *l'art pour l'art* attitude as decadent. In poetry and theory Dehmel regarded art as an expression of man's whole being, as a creative energy forming images and models. Hence he was able to call himself both realist and idealist. Art was in his eyes affirmation of life, and only through its agency did he feel sovereign over chaos. Through a metaphysical understanding of love the individual may gain contact with the community. The senses desire to be reconciled with the spirit. Thus the barriers between art and the layman, between individual and race are demolished. He who sacrifices life attains it. Body and soul, heart and God join in a new community. It is true that our yearning never reaches its goal, but our senses themselves find consummation.

The essence of life is to Dehmel its joy and zest, though its laughter is fraught with tears. Life is abandonment (see '*Venus Regina*'). The intoxication of the '*Trinklied*' is full of riotous affirmation of life in the spirit of Nietzsche's '*Zarathustra.*' Dehmel was evidently profoundly influenced by the latter, even if he rejects the pessimism of that decadent era. At other times also Dehmel betrays himself as the child of his age, when, for instance, he broods over Max Klinger's '*Phantasien,*' or writes '*An mein Volk,*' and dreams that the nations may unite to one great fatherland. In the '*Bergpsalm*' a million tongues clamour for joy and peace. Full of faith in the future he sees the '*Arbeitsmann*' free, beautiful and bold as the birds, but dark clouds also bring presage of the approaching storm, the revolution of the '*Zukunft,*' when grimy fingers will clutch at the white throat of the rich man's pregnant wife. Characteristic of the period is also Dehmel's song '*Manche Nacht*':

*Wenn die Felder sich verdunkeln,*
*Fühl' ich, wird mein Auge heller;*
*Schon versucht ein Stern zu funkeln*
*Und die Grillen wispern schneller.*

*Jeder Laut wird bilderreicher,*
*Das Gewohnte sonderbarer,*
*Hinterm Wald der Himmel bleicher,*
*Jeder Wipfel hebt sich klarer.*

*Und du merkst es nicht im Schreiten,*
*Wie das Licht verhundertfältigt*
*Sich entringt den Dunkelheiten.*
*Plötzlich stehst du überwältigt.*

(S. Fischer Verlag.)

Already the word *manche* robs the night of its universal character. *Versucht ein Stern zu funkeln* points to a peculiar exactness of observation. The second verse and the second line of the third shows a close interest in nature. The conclusion is, as often in Dehmel's verse, epigrammatical and overpowering in tonal power —a feature in striking contrast to the 'open' ending of romantic night-songs.

The ever-recurring dualism—man and woman—appears in the shape of *Herr* and *Herrin*. Dehmel's novel in poetic form, '*Zwei Menschen*,' is fraught with the struggle and fate of two human hearts whose happiness merges in that of the world, and thus exalts the individual to the realm of the infinite. Eros provides the keynote of most of his poems. They are the overflowing of a sensual spirit, inebriated with life. Their breadth of vision saves them from any hint of cynicism. Side by side with them stand delightfully amusing children-songs such as '*Fitzebutze*,' or '*Die Reise*.'

Like Dehmel, Christian Morgenstern (1871–1914) also seeks to find a spiritual meaning in earthly life. His poetry and *pensées*, however, especially towards the end of his short life, turn more towards mysticism. By the irony of fate, the really excellent qualities and truly German spirit of the *Charon* poets: Otto zur Linde, R. Pannwitz, K. Röttger, R. Paulsen have been too much neglected. A great deal of Christian Morgenstern's work has likewise been ignored, yet who is not acquainted with the bizarre shapes mirrored by the prism of his wit in the famous '*Galgenlieder*' and '*Palmström*' poems? It is a world full of superreal senselessness in which the moon adapts itself to the shape of the German alphabet, waning in the form of *A* and waxing as *Z*, or we find some gem like the brilliant dialogue between earth and a cube:

*Ein Würfel sprach zu sich: 'Ich bin*
*mir selbst nicht völlig zum Gewinn:*
*Denn meines Wesens sechste Seite,*
*und sei es auch Ein Auge bloss,*
*sieht immerdar, statt in die Weite,*
*der Erde ewig dunklen Schoss.'*

*Als dies die Erde, drauf er ruhte,*
*vernommen, ward ihr schlimm zumute,*
*'Du Esel,' sprach sie, 'ich bin dunkel,*
*weil dein Gesäss mich just bedeckt!*
*Ich bin so licht wie ein Karfunkel,*
*sobald du dich hinweggefleckt.'*

*Der Würfel, innerlichst beleidigt,*
*hat sich nicht weiter drauf verteidigt.'*

The '*Lattenzaun mit Zwischenraum*,' the lonely '*Knie*,' '*Das ästhetische Wiesel*,' which stands on a *Kiesel* for the sake of the rhyme, the '*Perlhuhn*,' which counts the number of its pearls, or the '*Fisches Nachtgesang*' (without words) have become common property. But this word-comedy expresses in reality a profound earnestness and moral significance which was all too often lost on a hyper-intellectual generation. The consumptive author of '*Melancholie*' was an admirer of Walther von der Vogelweide, Goethe, Paul de Lagarde and Nietzsche. Like the last he struggles to discover the secret of life until, a few years before his death, Angelus Silesius's mystic utterance, '*Mensch, werde wesentlich*,' struck him as a revelation. (Dehmel appears to express very similar thoughts: cf. '*Werde du*.') His heart yearns for the world beyond without, however, rejecting the earthly plane. His epigrams and proverbs bear witness to his unquenchable desire to escape from the *Alltag* into the *All-Tag*.

A few months after Morgenstern's death the young Austrian dreamer Georg Trakl (1887–1914) died in the military hospital at Krakau. His wistful images in '*Abendlied*,' '*Verfall*,' '*Landschaft*,' that seem indeed born of a spirit already fey, express a world of dreams.

*Landschaft.*

*Septemberabend; traurig tönen die dunklen Rufe der Hirten*
*durch das dämmernde Dorf; Feuer sprüht in der Schmiede.*
*Gewaltig bäumt sich ein schwarzes Pferd; die hyazinthenen Locken der Magd*
*haschen nach der Inbrunst seiner purpurnen Nüstern.*
*Leise erstarrt am Saum des Waldes der Schrei der Hirschkuh*
*und die gelben Blumen des Herbstes*
*neigen sich sprachlos über das blaue Antlitz des Teiches.*
*In roter Flamme verbrannte ein Baum; aufflattern mit dunklen Gesichtern die Fledermäuse.*

Hölty and Hölderlin are his ancestors, but in his disintegration of the corporeal image for the sake of spiritual processes Trakl appears as a forerunner of the expressionist movement, to which we shall now turn. As to new English translations of poems by G. Trakl, Morgenstern, George, etc., see Angel Flores's '*Anthology of German Poetry from Hölderlin to Rilke*' (New York, 1960).

## *EXPRESSIONISM*

The aim of expressionism, as its name implies, is to give not the outer appearance but the inner being of a phenomenon. We find similar tendencies in painting. The impressionistic painting of a Manet, Monet, or Renoir yields to the expressionistic art of Munch, Kokoschka, Hodler, Kandinsky, Nolde, Marc, and Van Gogh which reveals the internal processes of nature, with the sun as a symbol and the earth's surface in a state of universal chaos. For this a new sense of form is requisite, a new language and a new philosophy. In the place of Taine, another French philosopher, Bergson, with his doctrine of 'productive development' supplies the intellectual basis of these new aspirations. He seeks emancipation from the intellectual limitations of materialism by means of 'intuition.' Sigmund Freud's psycho-analysis and Rudolf

Steiner's anthroposophical ideas also exercise an influence upon the literature of this period. 'Old' models are rediscovered, whilst Wilhelm von Scholz now veers round from the neo-classic drama to the cult of the mystic and unintelligible. Dostoevsky, the European criminologist and apostle of a stricken proletariat, finds fresh supporters in the new movement.

Language renounces logic entirely and expresses the secret anguish and exultation of the spirit in a new ecstatic idiom of a decidedly Nietzschean character. Another feature of expressionism is the revolutionary tone which, during the Great War, became a clamorous indictment of the past. This was doubtless in many cases no more than a superficial vogue which soon degenerated into the grotesque extravagance of the *Wortchaotiker*, the so-called 'Dadaists.' In the hands, however, of a really great poet it is the outcome of a profound conviction, the expression of a deeply religious longing for the third kingdom, namely of the new man. This idea of the third kingdom was not new. It is found already in Lessing's '*Nathan*,' or with Heine and Nietzsche, in Walt Whitman's '*Leaves of Grass*,' Ibsen's '*Emperor and Galilean*,' or J. Schlaf's '*Das dritte Reich*,' also Gerhart Hauptmann and others. Man, instead of being senselessly borne along on the vortex of everyday life, is now to be transferred to a higher spiritual world, in which there will be an intensified ethical existence without loss of contact with reality. It is from *volkhafte* communion that the longing for the new human being develops in such writers as H. Stehr, H. F. Blunck, and E. G. Kolbenheyer, whilst in the case of the expressionists (K. Edschmid, G. Kaiser, E. Toller, and F. von Unruh) it bears a more social and political aspect. The passionate heroes of A. Mombert recede into mythical regions.

Writers such as Alfred Döblin and others paint utopias of the future with much technical detail. The contrast between nature and the metropolis, spiritual man and the machine, individual and crowd once more become, as in naturalism, the chief problem in German art. The ultimate aim of life as conceived in expressionism may be designated as the realization of the complete human being, and service to the community. Laments on the mad whirl of an age of soul-killing mechanization, a desire to penetrate the secrets of the human soul, and an ecstatic *Rauschkunst*—such are the characteristic features of Toller's, Werfel's and Kaiser's calculated plays.

Franz Werfel (born 1890 in Prague, † 1945 in California) was the acknowledged leader of the young expressionists with a radical tendency. Throughout his collection of poems, which are frequently of a dramatic nature—'*Der Weltfreund*' (1911), '*Wir sind*' (1913), '*Einander*,' '*Gesänge aus den drei Reichen*,' '*Gerichtstag*' (1919)—the prevailing theme is the redemption of the old selfish type of mankind by brotherly, all-embracing love, demand of communal effort, and transformation of the philosophy of 'I am' into that of 'We are.'

Expressionism seeks the essence of things. Its poetry has neither the languor of decadence nor romantic yearning, but is whipped up by the feverish unrest of modern man. Allegory plays a great part. War is described (by G. Heym) as a monster with skulls round his neck. The metropolis is depicted as a brutal prison. Ecstatic visions, strange moods and the horrors of the war years find expression here.

There are also fervent songs of liberty, of the birth and resurrection of a new mankind. Dionysian affirmation of suffering transfigures all our deeds.

Titles of poems such as '*Der Aufbruch*' (E. Stadler), '*Die Dämonen der Städte*' (G. Heym), '*Stimme über Barbaropa*' (A. Ehrenstein), '*Der Panamakanal*' and '*Wassersturz*' (I. Goll), and others symptomize the revolutionary attitude of the period. The German anthology of 1919, '*Menschheits-Dämmerung—Symphonie jüngster Dichtung*' (The dawn of mankind), edited by Kurt Pinthus (Berlin—E. Rowohlt, Verlag) bears witness to this fact. An art of ideas (*Ideenkunst*) take the place of verisimilitude. Satire, baroque eroticism, metaphysics and intellectualism intermingle. Language and metaphors are ecstatic. Carl Sternheim's fever-born novel '*Europa*' or Kasimir Edschmid's collection of short stories '*Timur*' provide many characteristic examples.

The expressionist lyric poets of Germany between about the years 1910 and 1920 are for the greater part, like Werfel, prophets of chaos and the rebirth of the eternal ego. According to their personal attitude, now national, now international, socialist, or religious, the thunder-charged atmosphere of the years preceding the Great War, the upheaval, the dénouement and the ensuing revolt are mirrored in their verse. Karl Bröger, Heinrich Lersch, Gerrit Engelke, Alfonz Petzold, Max Barthel and others take up another line as champions of the working class, though they clearly betray the influence of the expressionists. Poets like Th. Däubler, G. Heym, W. Flex, J. Winckler, Else Lasker-Schüler, E. Lissauer, P. Zech, and E. Stadler went their own way, or appear as forerunners. Others formed literary groups such as the *Aktion*; amongst these we may place J. R. Becher, W. Klemm, L. Meidner, A. Wolfenstein, G. Benn, L. Rubiner, the editor of the anthology '*Kameraden der Menschheit*.'

That the expressionist's attitude towards life was regarded as far more than a mere fashion is proved by the ecstatic theories and the lyrics of the poets of the *Sturm* circle, amongst whom were numbered in particular Lothar Schreyer, August Stramm, Kurt Schwitters, Herwarth Walden, and with certain reservations Kurt Heynicke. H. Walden founded the '*Wochenschrift für Kultur und Künste*' (or *Der Sturm*) four years *before* the war. The artists Marc, Nolde, Klee, Kandinsky, Pechstein, Hodler, Chagall, Kubin, Archipenko, Kokoschka, and others became contributors. The journal flourished for twenty years (1910–1930) and gradually adopted a communistic tone. But it must be definitely asserted that the *Sturm*, at any rate during the first years of its existence, was not a one-sided political or marxist organ. Its tendency was, generally speaking, international. Lothar Schreyer, however, later sought a path of salvation in the racial strength of a people and in religious faith.

On the whole, subject-matter was but of secondary interest to the *Sturm* poets, who considered that art should appeal not to the intellect but to the senses. They were unaware that their theory only led them down a cul-de-sac and that they themselves suffered from hyper-intellectualism. The latter is evident in their dramas, for instance in A. Stramm's '*Sancta Susanna*,' which appeared on the Berlin stage in 1918, three years after Stramm's (1874–1915) death, and set to music by Hindemith. An extreme example is moreover provided by A. Stramm's abstract lyrics.

*Kreise im Kreise*
*Kreis im Kreise*
*Voran Voran*
*In den Anfang*

*Kreis im Kreise*
*In das Werden*
*In*
*Das*

| | |
|---|---|
| *Voran Voran* | *Werden Werden Werden* |
| *In das Ende* | *In* |
| *Voran Voran* | *Kreisen Kreisen Kreisen* |
| *In den Abgrund* | *In* |
| *Voran Voran* | *Die* |
| *In die Höhe* | *Tränen Tränen Tränen* |
| *Voran Voran* | *In die* |
| *In das Sterben* | *Tränen* |
| *Voran Voran* | *In den Raum* |
| *In das Werden* | *In den Raum* |
| *Kreise im Kreise* | *In den Raum!* |
| *In das Werden* | *Tränen kreist der Raum!* |

This is not the result of an absurd pastime, even though serious purport often suffered betrayal at the hand of some plagiarist. The terrible chaos beneath the surface was apprehended too intensely to be termed a whim. The destruction of the phrase was *necessary* to express the horror of realization in those who beheld the skeleton beneath the illusion of appearances. An ascetic restraint in the use of colour and playful arabesques heightens the macabre effect. The individual lines of the poems appear as rings of steel welded to a strict rhythm.

From the example given above we can gain much insight into the expressionist attitude of mind. It rejects any exact transcription of nature. Just as the painter or sculptor uses the image of an elephant's feet to express not elephantiasis but the act of standing, so the writer of the above poem seeks some verbal symbol of the sense of becoming, of eternal flux and whirling rotation in space.

The *words* not the phrase are his instrument. The clash of the single word-blocks produces rhythm, image and tone. Thus one can here speak of an absolute work of art of optic, acoustic, dynamic effect, for the associative quality of the single 'alogical' words counts for nothing, even though the logical explanation could not altogether be effaced—e.g. in the word *und* in the poem below. In addition to such extreme experiments in the expressionist style we find poems that retain an impressionistic flavour, whilst some present examples of so-called *Merzwortwerk*.

Kurt Schwitters, who coined the term, explains this style in the following manner. It seeks to find a short-cut from intuition to the work of art; e.g. instead of *white* pigment the painter attaches a bit of cotton-wool to his canvas; *round and hard* are represented by a porcelain button. Recent rather belated experiments on the part of the surrealists appear to adopt the *Merzwortwerk* or colletage technique, which had degenerated into placard and journalistic advertisement and the grotesques of 'Dadaism.' J. Ringelnatz (Hans Bötticher), who stood somewhat apart from the movement, was able to impregnate it with the matter-of-fact robustness of his biting satire.

It is characteristic that the *Sturm* refers to verbal, not poetic art. The *word* remains the primal root of creation. Instead of an unending list of names we now again quote from a poem of Stramm's, in which, for instance, the word *und* is intended to give the effect of a sudden blow: cf. the poem '*Untreu*':

> *. . . Im Atem wittert Laubwelk!*
> *Dein Blick versargt*
> *Und*
> *Hastet polternd Worte drauf. . . .*

What emotions the poet experienced in writing it we can learn from a letter from Stramm's own hand (published in the *Sturm*) and addressed to H. Walden. Thus the prefix *ver* is supposed to express the sense of passing away, the sequence of the consonants *t—l* should suggest a 'gliding past' (*wittert Laubwelk*) and blowing away. *Laubwelk* seems to Stramm more intense than the softer and more melodious *welkes Laub*.

In Italy and France futurism and cubism might be regarded as parallels to the German expressionist movement. As we saw, the expressionist destroys grammar, as does the futurist Marinetti, who, however, does not pursue the process of disintegration in quite the same way.

We must doubtless regard expressionism as a modern literary 'storm and stress' in revolt against impressionism and neo-romanticism, though the latter two cannot be said to be altogether synonymous. But the spiritualizing element in impressionism had already built a bridge to the new movement. Moreover, in addition to the poets already mentioned, many others had paved the way, such, for instance, as Alfred Mombert with the ecstatic visions of his trilogy '*Aeon*.'

Possibly future years, taking a bird's-eye view of the past, and regarding the whole course of development in broader outlines, will look on the movements from naturalism to the close of expressionism as a unified whole. The war cast its lurid shadows both over the years which preceded its horrors, and over those which followed, which must therefore be included in the reckoning. Between Goethe and the present a new world had sprung into being whose burden of material weighed heavily on many a poet's spirit. What a gulf yawns between Goethe's divine self-assurance in the '*Harzreise*': *Dem Geier gleich . . . schwebe mein Lied*, and such poems as A. Wolfenstein's depressing '*Im Bestienhaus*'!

On the other hand, we may still find in some a burning optimistic affirmation of life. Theodor Däubler (1876–1934) championed the new spirit both as theoretician and poet. His giant work in epic-lyric form '*Nordlicht*' (1910) underwent revision, and *Selbstdeutung* (1921). Since he himself felt the necessity of elucidating its cosmic mythology, Däubler seeks the origin of all life in the male sun (*sol*). Existence means to him a return to the sun for which plants, beasts and men alike ever yearn. The Northern light is the symbol and certainty of the earth's salvation and transformation into a guiding star. The path leads through ice towards light, to God. The first part of this loosely constructed work is autobiographical and sings of Venice, Rome, Florence, and other towns; the second part is a confession of the super-individual, 'lyric' ego, the Adam within us. Perseus, St. George, Roland, Parzival are regarded as the various stages in the hero's quest of perfection of earth. They are guided by their faith in God and the stars. Christ's life as a man is the most sacred proof that salvation awaits us.

# XIV

# RAINER MARIA RILKE

---

RAINER MARIA RILKE (1875–1926) was born in Prague, travelled to the South and to Russia, lived for a time in Worpswede with a little community of artists whom he brought to public notice, and later enjoyed close intimacy with Rodin. His musical power over words, his rare subtlety of expression and his mysticism make it difficult for many to find access to his genius. His verses echo the whispering of the trees, the raging of the storm, the awakening of spring and the murmuring of water. A certain mystic yearning is the keynote of Rilke's poetry:

*This is yearning: to be borne on the wave*
*And to have no home in the span of time.*
*And these are desires: gentle dialogues*
*Between the faint hours and eternity. . . .*

In his description of man and beast he endeavours, as in '*Der Panther*,' to penetrate to the essence of all being. This poem is a masterpiece of empathy into nature: cf. Blake's '*Tiger*' with Rilke's verses:

*Sein Blick ist vom Vorübergehn der Stäbe*
*so müd geworden, dass er nichts mehr hält.*
*Ihm ist, als ob es tausend Stäbe gäbe*
*und hinter tausend Stäben keine Welt.*

*Der weiche Gang geschmeidig starker Schritte,*
*der sich im allerkleinsten Kreise dreht,*
*ist wie ein Tanz von Kraft um eine Mitte,*
*in der betäubt ein grosser Wille steht.*

*Nur manchmal schiebt der Vorhang der Pupille*
*sich lautlos auf—dann geht ein Bild hinein,*
*geht durch der Glieder angespannte Stille—*
*und hört im Herzen auf zu sein.*

(Rilke's *Neue Gedichte*—Insel Verlag.)

Rilke calls his poems experiences, cf. '*Die Aufzeichnungen des Malte Laurids Brigge*' (1910). In order to be able to write poetry, he says, one must visit cities, must get to know men and things, must observe gestures, follow the flight of birds and know how the flowers grow. A poet must command his imagination. His emotion must be welded to form by his creative impulse. It must be born of an inner necessity. In the poem '*Pietà*,' which forms part of the cycle '*Das Marien-Leben*' '*The Life of the Virgin Mary*' 1913, the poet seems to recall a spirit lost since the days when medieval masons had charged the starkness of stone with an emotion almost unendurable.

The collection of poems '*Das Stunden-Buch*' is a modern book of devotion. Amid the vast loneliness of the Russian steppes Rilke meditates on human destiny. He loves not the harsh light of day but the twilight of solitude and death. For him the modern city breeds falsehood, its children are but shadows, and the multitude becomes a herd, but the poet bursts these barriers in his striving towards God. In these and other poems: '*Das Buch der Bilder*,' '*Neue Gedichte*,' '*Duineser Elegien*,' '*Sonette an Orpheus*,' '*Späte Gedichte*,' etc., Rilke has perhaps achieved the highest technical perfection in German poetry since Goethe. His translations of André Gide, Paul Valéry, Maurice de Guérin, Elizabeth Barrett Browning ('*Sonnets from the Portuguese*'), and others betray his sensitiveness to foreign poetry.

In his '*Briefe an einen jungen Dichter*,' Rilke expresses his inmost thoughts. Conceited criticism and irony, he says, are strangers to the true poet. Slowly the poet must mature like a tree, withstanding the storms of spring without fear that the summer may not follow. Rilke's letters to Ellen Key, Lou-Andreas-Salomé, Elsa Bruckmann, the Fürstin Marie von Thurn und Taxis-Hohenlohe, to his wife, to Rodin, H. v. Hofmannsthal, and others likewise provide a key to many problems suggested by his works. He went his own way, ignoring and not even reading criticisms or advertisements. In spite of the manifold experiences engraved so deeply on his spirit during his frequent travels, in spite of changes and development, his poetry ever retains its singular haunting power, the expression of a defined inviolable personality. Rilke's early verse still betrays the elegiac tenderness of a hypersensitive boy who grew up in Prague between two peoples, though he was educated as a German. Only too soon he felt an urge to turn from the sensuous world to a realm of dreams. The local colour which had been a distinct element in his poetry paled; Rilke's tendency towards introspection and the subjective nuance of his attitude towards nature were reinforced by his discovery of J. P. Jacobsen (1847–1885). Yet Rilke did not possess the masterful will of George, but conquered the object through immersing his own personality therein. We have already referred to the influence Russia and Worpswede exerted on the poet, and to a striking comparison often drawn between C. F. Meyer's '*Der römische Brunnen*' and Rilke's '*Römische Fontäne*':

*Zwei Becken, eins das andre übersteigend*
*aus einem alten, runden Marmorrand*
*und aus dem oberen Wasser leis sich neigend*
*zum Wasser, welches unten wartend stand,*

*dem leise redenden entgegen schweigend*
*und heimlich, gleichsam in der hohlen Hand*
*ihm Himmel hinter Grün und Dunkel zeigend*
*wie einen unbekannten Gegenstand;*

*sich selber ruhig in der schönen Schale*
*verbreitend ohne Heimweh, Kreis aus Kreis,*
*und manchmal träumerisch und tropfenweis*

*sich niederlassend an den Moosbehängen*
*zum letzten Spiegel, der sein Becken leis*
*von unten lächeln macht mit Übergängen.*

(Rilke's *Neue Gedichte*—Insel Verlag.)

In the '*Stunden-Buch*' (1899–1903, publ. 1905) Rilke declares his great love of all things. He knows now that life is ever in the right for behind life stands God. Already in his early story '*Wladimir, der Wolkenmaler,*' or in '*Von einem, der die Steine belauscht*' ('*Geschichten vom lieben Gott*'), God is the centre and goal of all man's aspirations. Through the concluding poem of '*Das Buch der Bilder*' 1902, '*The Book of Images*' echoes the medieval *media in vita*: '*Der Tod ist gross. Wir sind die Seinen lachenden Munds. . . .*' In the '*Stunden-Buch*' the poet yearns with religious fervour for death, a death which belongs to each one of us separately, individually:

*O Herr, gib jedem seinen eignen Tod*

or

*Denn wir sind nur die Schale und das Blatt.*
*Der grosse Tod, den jeder in sich hat,*
*Das ist die Frucht, um die sich alles dreht.*

This realization of death in the midst of life stands in strong contrast to the complacent security of the post-classic nineteenth century. But the '*Stunden-Buch*' cannot be called passive or purely mystic, for it does not only seek the contemplative life. What a note of joy resounds through his introductory verses, that praise of work:

*Da neigt sich die Stunde und rührt mich an*
*Mit klarem, metallenem Schlag:*
*Mir zittern die Sinne. Ich fühle: ich kann-*
*Und ich fasse den plastischen Tag.*

And yet the will has its limits. Resignation overshadows all action, a concept which was later to be closely formulated in Rilke's '*Requiem*' (1909) for Wolf, Graf von Kalckreuth.

Some of Rilke's best images arise out of this patient waiting for the hour of change: '*Wer spricht von Siegen? Überstehn ist alles*': 'Who talks of victory, to *endure* is all' ('*Requiem*'), and thinking of the tragic young poet who, overcome by the brutal ugliness of life, shot himself at the age of twenty, Rilke, in the said '*Requiem*' condemns subjectivity and asks the poets to transform their emotions, not to pour them out defencelessly. Instead of lament he demands with determination its transformation into the poetic word:

*wie sich der Steinmetz einer Kathedrale*
*verbissen umsetzt in des Steines Gleichmut . . .*

'doggedly, as the carver of a cathedral transfers himself to the stone's constancy' (tr. by J. B. Leishman).

Not the active but the poor and especially the children are nearest to God. Solitude is our fate. He who loves her conquers her. Thus Rilke arrives at an affirmation of suffering but with more humility than Nietzsche.

How deeply Rilke felt attached to the tradition of his family is seen in his '*Weise von Liebe und Tod des Cornet Christoph Rilke*' (1906, but composed in 1899) in which he writes: *Aus dunklem Wein und tausend Rosen rinnt die Stunde rauschend in den Traum der Nacht*. From magical tones such as these, Rilke built a memorial to youthful heroism.

With the '*Neue Gedichte*' and '*Der Gedichte Anderer Teil*' (1907–1908) which under Rodin's influence grew to imperishable plastic proportions, the mystic poet found a way back to reality. The subjective note appears to be almost eliminated in many of these poems, yet the images, e.g. '*Der Panther*,' '*Das Einhorn*,' '*L'Ange du Méridien*,' '*Die Fensterrose*,' '*Die Flamingos*,' are pregnant with symbolic significance.

Rilke himself regarded the '*Duineser Elegien*' (1912–1922) as his greatest work. Inseparably related to them are the '*Sonette an Orpheus*,' which was composed simultaneously as a by-product (see Rilke's '*Briefe an eine junge Frau*'). They form a complete cycle, whereas the '*Duineser Elegien*' remained a fragment. In the '*Sonette an Orpheus*,' death casts no gloomy shadows over the poet; Rilke's sings a hymn of praise on life, here and in the beyond. Orpheus belongs to the two worlds. He knows that nature is at once the start and the goal, the urge and its control. In the starry constellation of the '*Rider*' (Sonnet XI), Rilke sees a symbol of the totality of existence. The second part of the sonnets is a eulogy on the unicorn, the lovely anemone of conception, the rose, the maiden and the child as the minions of true life. Sacrifice and surrender to life appear as the highest aim of existence.

It is at this point that we find the immediate bridge to the '*Duineser Elegien*' (Duino Elegies), which Rilke himself interprets in his '*Briefe aus Muzot*.' From out hopeless despair the path leads through ever growing enlightenment to the realization of God. The first two elegies (1912) show that man has not yet crossed the threshold to a higher state of existence. Even the lover is one-sided, for he only thinks egotistically of his own happiness. Death alone is a transition to maturity. The following eight elegies, which belong to a later period, illumine the poet's spiritual development —the change from the external to the internal, from sense to spirit. Suffering is affirmed. Even though the gifts of life are transient the poet gives them eternal significance. Here too, sacrifice remains the ultimate meaning of existence. Out of decay life is born ever anew. Life and death are one! Only the angels know that perfect unity of life and the beyond. In this they are superior to us, but we too find consummation on earth through the single experience of our individual existence:

> *Aber weil Hiersein viel ist, und weil uns scheinbar*
> *alles das Hiesige braucht, dieses Schwindende, das*
> *seltsam uns angeht. Uns die Schwindendsten.* Einmal
> *jedes, nur* einmal. Einmal *und nicht mehr*. . . .

Thus Rilke, whose genius stood aloof from the war, yet affirms life through 'his poetic activity.' His whole life was a sacrifice in the service of his art. He has been justly called an *existenzieller Dichter*. It is true that his attitude was reflective, a sensitive 'listening' and 'seeing,' but not in the sense of decadent over-refinement, for his mind was ever crystallizing emotion to form. He rejects the poet who only pours out his feelings in lamentation without forming them, cf. the above '*Requiem*':

> *O alter Fluch der Dichter,*
> *die sich beklagen, wo sie sagen sollten,*
> *die immer urteil'n über ihr Gefühl,*
> *statt es zu bilden.*

Thus his images do not dissolve into an impressionist haze. Through this power to form Rilke triumphed over suffering, but not as a pure mystic, for the love for form was too strong in him:

> *Für dich nur schliessen sich die Dichter ein*
> *und sammeln Bilder. . . .*
> *Und Maler malen ihre Bilder nur,*
> *damit du unvergänglich die Natur,*
> *die du vergänglich schufst, zurückempfängst.*
> (Stunden-Buch.)

Rilke's language is rich in words and idioms which he often coins anew: *torig, knabig, traumig*, etc. He is aware of the dangers of hurried expression. That Rilke himself is inclined to prove a stumbling-block to the translator (quite apart from mistakes such as *douleur originelle = Urleid*) is not surprising. Abstract idioms like those of the '*Requiem*' often defy interpretation. Strange, too, is his frequent use of enjambement and unusual rhyme-construction with pronouns, conjunctions, and prepositions. These peculiar forms create an effect of gentle uncertainty, whereas in the case of Heine, Morgenstern, or W. Busch, this very enjambement and rhyme-play often appears ironic or burlesque. Rilke retains his sensitiveness to the power of words in his own translations. He, too, sometimes finds himself faced by unscalable barriers, for instance when he renders Michelangelo's *parla basso* by *spricht leise*, which is correct according to the sense but loses the proper sound value.

Thus we see that Rilke's genius does not fit either into the category of impressionism, which mirrors momentary appearances, or into that of expressionism, which seeks the essence behind the lying mask. For Rilke stands between the two, even though one cannot deny that in time and place he may seem to stand nearer the latter movement. He also, once again, believes like Hölderlin in life and in the presence of God. But Rilke lacked the all-conquering force which Hölderlin poured into his hymns. Pain clouds his enthusiasm. It is also characteristic that the poet of the '*Duineser Elegien*' looked on Nature only as a symbol of spiritual reflection. Certain it is that the elegies are not born of the German landscape which inspired Hölderlin to sublime utterance. Yet Rilke possesses an almost uncanny power of apprehending the secret life of all things and investing them with symbolic significance through his profound realization of God.

Rilke certainly does not preach escape from life. Instead of throwing one's life away the poet can, according to Rilke's message, save his self from a disenchanted 'collective' and 'factual' world by accepting and transmuting the latter into a realm of poetic symbols.

The precise, 'factual' world of our intellect is, in Rilke's view, not the true, i.e. total world. How often this has been proved in history. In spite of all faultless planning, some mysterious and incalculable accident occurs and destroys the seemingly unconquerable edifice. Rilke compares our existence to a game of ball—we throw the ball, which, however, keeps falling back into our

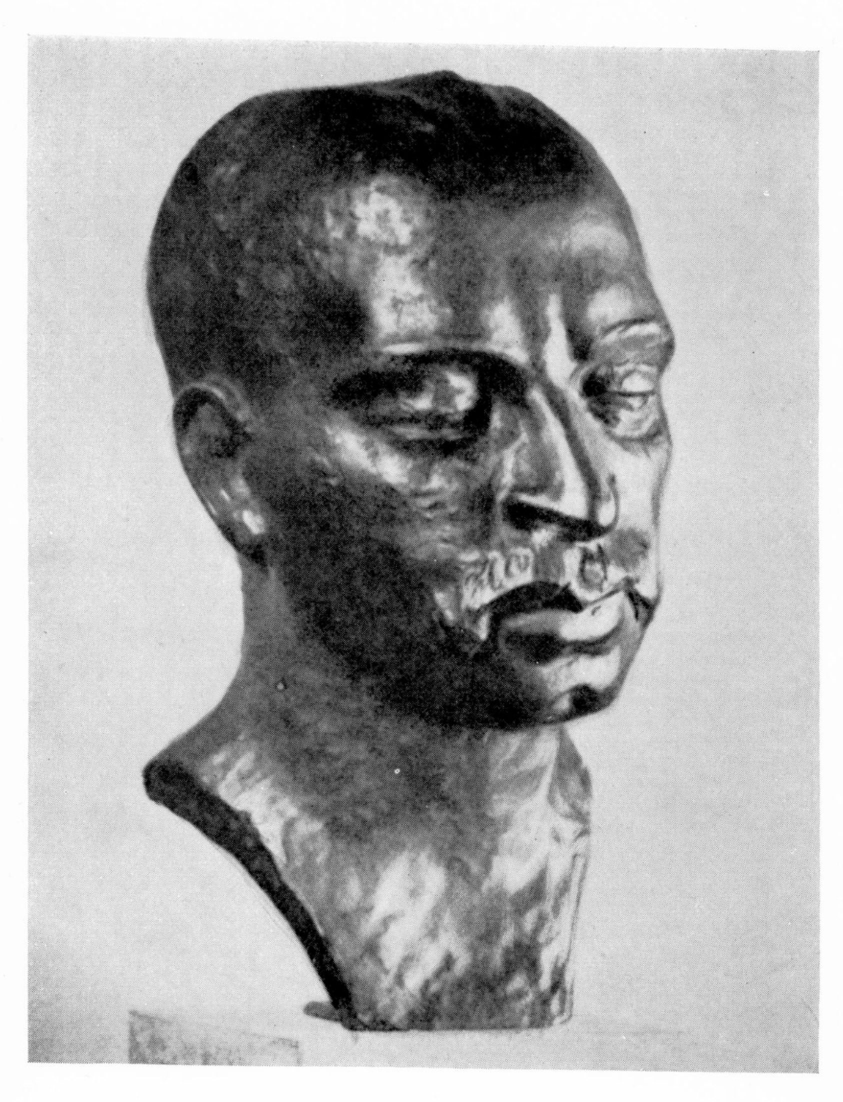

VII RILKE
*Bust by Clara Rilke*

VIII STEFAN GEORGE
(*Kester, Lichtbild-Archiv, München*)

hands. He also favours the motif of the *mirror*, emphasizing thus the difference between the appearance and reality—a conflict which inspires him to praise and lament.

The creative productivity in Rilke's last twenty years was astonishingly rich. Many of the poems not contained in the posthumous volume: '*Späte Gedichte*' ('*Later Poems*') were published by Professor Ernst Zinn in '*Gedichte 1906 bis 1926*' (1953). In his penetrating 'Introduction' to his English translation: '*Poems 1906–1926*' (1957) J. B. Leishman refers to the vast number of Rilke's late poems: 'Many are among the most memorable of German poems. That we should have had to wait for them so long, must surely be a fact without parallel in literary history (the case of G. M. Hopkins is too similar for comparison).' In the first lines of the poem ('*Nicht Geist, nicht Inbrunst wollen wir entbehren*') in the above translation the essence of Rilke's message is revealed:

> 'No intellect, no ardour is redundant':
> *to make one through the other more abundant*
> *is what we're for, and some are singled out*
> *for purest victory in that contention . . .*

## *STEFAN GEORGE AND THE 'THIRD HUMANISM'*

The new attitude which rose to challenge prevailing fashion found its prophet in Stefan George. In George's poem '*Ursprünge*' we hear of the heritage he derived from history, and those living forces of the spirit that enveloped him and his native land. The Rhine, enwoven with myth and legend, graced by its vineyards and merry vintage feasts; the proximity of France; Rhenish soil that the Roman legions had once trodden and where the Catholic church yet preserved the glamour of pagan rites; Büdesheim and Bingen where, in August, 1814, Goethe had participated in the festival of St. Rocchus. These origins did not give George his poetic genius, but they influenced its growth and became his fate.

The age into which George (1868–1933) was born had witnessed the annihilation of the unity of ego, individual, world and God. From its ruins George built the image of a new world—a 'third humanism.' He restored to poetry its formal power, and to words the magic quality of incantation:

*Kein ding sei wo das wort gebricht.*
(*Das neue Reich.*)

Against the theory of material progress he foretold the advent of the *Gesamtmensch* who wrestles with God until he holds Him in his grasp ('*Stern des Bundes*'). 'We were becoming a disfigured and cold-blooded humanity which boasted of its many-sided discoveries and complex emotions whilst great deeds and great love were steadily waning. The masses fabricated law and rule,' writes George in the preface to '*Maximin*' (1906). Solitude is the poet's will:

*Menschlich glück verschwor ich um dein lied*
*Fügte mich der not des wandertums.*
(*Stern des Bundes.*)

These wanderings were in the nature of a definite quest. A strict plan underlay all his actions. In his memoir of the poet (1934) Bondi, George's publisher and host, states that practical matters were not alien to George and that his life, which was by no means bohemian though not bourgeois either, was regulated and planned. A rather too hasty comparison with Goethe is appropriate only as far as superficial matters are concerned.

With this fixed goal in view, George's art and life developed to a unified *Weltanschauung*, based on the consciousness of his election to a mission demanding self-sacrifice. He discovered Eros as a guiding principle of cosmogenetic necessity, and Kairos in readiness to accept the doom of the moment. George is thus seen to revive two ancient Greek precepts. We may trace their development from their tentative beginnings in his own words:

*Wie in die herbe traube*
*Erst mählich duft und farbe dringt,*
*Wie aus dem nächtigen laube*
*Die lerche scheu ins frühlicht schwingt.*
(*Fibel.*)

In his earliest volume of poems, '*Fibel*' (1886–1889), George's language is forced and harshly disciplined. In comparison with naturalistic extravagance or Holz's juvenile ecstasies, it appears frigidly ascetic. Reason lays her cold hands on his burning brow. Every emotion is frozen by an icy breath. George's soul is a lonely house encircled by a sea of mists. Only gradually is his appreciation of nature freed from human torment. A yearning for the South, where the senses know only warmth and beauty and light, awakens in his tortured soul which is 'emptied of passion.' Nevertheless, the '*Legenden*,' a summary of the '*Fibelgedichte*,' seem to foreshadow something of the greatness to come. Eros (whom both Plato and Goethe had deemed indispensable to the attainment of wisdom) and Heros become George's leaders in his quest of knowledge, his search of 'bodies, flowers, clouds, and waves.'

The language of the '*Hymnen, Pilgerfahrten, Algabal*' (1890–1892), is still crude, the heart torn between passion and discipline. The ritualistic atmosphere, the cult-like imagery and artifice that envelops these poems, stand in violent contrast to the era which had substituted quantity for quality, and had sacrificed greatness to mass. George's vision of the priest-emperor Algabal bears affinity to his own personality. At the same time, as symbol of an inexorable will to power in a satiated world, Algabal appears universal. But already the '*Hymnen*' are acquainted with the imperial gesture. Algabal's admonishment to his illustrious grandmother:

*O lass mich ungerühmt und ungehasst*
*und frei in den bedingten bahnen wandeln*

provides an analogy to the incitements of freedom and law during the classic period of German poetry. But Algabal's idea of liberty lacks their organic reconciling harmony, is Roman in its ruthless vigour. The accent falls on the idea that fate is determined by law. Hence his relentless attitude towards the surrounding world.

In the third volume of poems: '*Die Bücher der Hirten und Preisgedichte der Sagen und Sänge und der hängenden Gärten*' (1895) the overpowering historic conscience of our age is crystallized to poetic expression. The spirit of Greece haunts George's arcadian idylls, the cults and mysteries, the election of the leaders, the beauty of the wrestlers, of the singer, their happy relation to the community, fearlessness of death in a world of beauty. George's wish-phantasy of sublime serenity (*hoher und heiterer Wille*) points to classic ideology. The norm, the golden mean, harmony decreed by proportion, principles of selection and the ideal type which Vasari had once called the *buona maniera antica e moderna* are characteristics also of George's classic idea of formal beauty, in the face of which all gothic and baroque, all manneristic and realistic abandonment was made to appear barbaric corruption. Du Fresnoy's *majestas gravis er requies decora* and Winckelmann's noble simplicity and sublime serenity strengthened George's yearning for ideal beauty. George's attitude, however, appears harder, his will more tense.

The peculiar restraint typical of George's portrayal of woman is remarkable in an era of literature saturated in erotic neurosis. Schopenhauer confesses in his '*Welt als Wille und Vorstellung*' (see '*The metaphysics of sexual love*') that the description of sexual love is by far the most frequent theme of both lyric and epic poetry. Whereas in G. Hauptmann's works, e.g. '*Fuhrmann Henschel*' ('*Der Ketzer von Soana*' presents an exception) man appears as the bondman of his sensuality from which there is no release, George's female characters are tamed by masculine will or else sublimated as divine heroines. Like Nietzsche he sees in woman an influence antagonistic, destructive.

George's later volumes contain fewer portraits of women, whilst in the atmosphere of solemn consecration that attends the consummation of the Sublime Law in the '*Stern des Bundes*' and '*Das neue Reich*' they find no place at all. 'The foolish pilgrim' of '*Das neue Reich*' is but sketched in with a light brush. George speaks of love in the abstract rather than giving a picture of the beloved. The very title of one of his works is praise of love, not of the beloved; or he stresses her effect on the spirit rather than her appearance. Similarly in the '*Hirten- und Preisgedichte*' he is interested in the emotions the wrestler and harpist awaken in the people. Again he speaks of the shadows 'swiftly cut as decorations for my hall of memories.'* As in his landscapes George's selective hand places colour by colour as though forming the jewelled pattern of some precious inlay:

*Er nahm das gold von heiligen pokalen.*
*Zu hellem haar das reife weizenstroh.*
*Das rosa kindern die mit schiefer malen.*
*Der wäscherin am bach den indigo . . .*

* All translations of poems, etc., are my own if not otherwise mentioned.

or he gazes on the mirrored image of his fleeting joy:

> *Die hügel vor die breite brüstung schütten*
> *Den glatten guss von himmelgrünem glase. . . .*

Thus on the whole his external images remain vague, obscure. Yet the large simplified lines with which they are frequently drawn exert a peculiarly powerful effect, though in '*Tage und Taten*' the description of Böcklin's '*Pietà*' seems surprisingly sentimental and inapt, for his description of the angel 'stern as God's command' can apply only to a literary rendering of facial expression, not to a sense of form which is pitiably lacking in the picture. How far more fitting might George's designations appear if applied to Rubleuv's '*Old Testament Trinity*,' whose hieratic Byzantinism seems incidentally to bear a closer affinity to the poet's own style.

In '*Sagen und Sänge*' images born of the poet's spiritual experience of the Middle Ages are, like their classic and oriental counterparts in '*Hirten- und Preisgedichte*' and '*Hängende Gärten*,' divested of the impressionistic accidental values of the world of appearances and raised to the dignity of universal symbols. Hence George often discovers 'meanings' which actually lie outside the pale of the medieval conscience.

Having thus treated figures from history, George, in the '*Jahr der Seele*' (1897), approaches the subject of nature. Here too we find that his attitude is for the most part anything but romantic. For we meet with no fervent dream-clouded phantasies, no immediate contact, no abandoned outpouring of emotional reaction, although it cannot be said that the poet's sensibility was not deeply stirred by his theme (cf. '*Dies leid und diese last*,' or his spirit's pain in the poem '*Flammende wälder am bergesgrat*').

But George's landscapes remain fundamentally remote, deprived of organic rhythm, static crystallizations of his emotional state (see H. v. Hofmannsthal's '*Gespräch über Gedichte*,' in which George's magic power of word in painting these landscapes of the spirit is so subtly interpreted). Nature is disintegrated, and the lifeless atoms, like brittle fragments of some mosaic, are set together again to create a perfect pattern. Short sentences interweave like threads in a tapestry to form his pictures. Thus in the poem '*Komm in den totgesagten park*' deep blue, soft grey roses, asters and purple vine, enmeshed with green against the blue of the sky, twine to an autumnal garland.

Man and Nature are to George no unity as they were to Goethe. In poems such as '*Wir schreiten auf und ab im reichen flitter*' we find no invocation of the moon reconciling these two worlds. Objects are not, as in the early days of expressionism, imbued with spiritual activity, but rest satiated within themselves. An interesting contrast is here afforded by Eichendorff's '*Mondnacht*' with its harmonious intercourse between Nature and man, and George's anti-romantic view of Nature in the poem '*Der hügel wo wir wandeln liegt im schatten.*'

Outspoken dualisms—paganism and Christianity, control and abandonment, ecclesiastic pomp and monastic ascetism, South and North, reappear continually in the '*Teppich des Lebens*' (1900). George strives to weld them to a harmonious unity in an ideal realm where Hellas and Golgotha are reconciled.

In the two first 'monuments' of the '*Teppich,*' Greece and the Gothic North stand side by side as allied principles of life. They represent a synthesis of these intellectual 'polarities' which are ever being coined anew by poet and scholar as varying aspects of the one fundamental concept: *rational* and *irrational* = *classic* and *romantic*, *plastic* and *musical* (Schiller, Nietzsche), *South* and *North*, *Naturidealismus* and *Vernunftidealismus* (Korff), *bildend* and *bestimmend* (W. v. Humboldt), *objective* and *interesting* (F. Schlegel), *finality* and *infinity* (Strich), *renaissance* and *baroque* (Wöfflin), *Greek* and *Faustian* (Spengler), *Greek* and *Gothic* (Scheffler), *empathy* and *abstraction* (Worringer), *form* and *creation* (Simmel), etc.

To apply the term 'rational' to classic art in contrast to romantic is just as misleading as the application of the polarity 'realism—idealism,' for the true classic spirit only achieves its consummation through being transfused with irrational values, see here p. 214.

With George this polarity appears in the juxtaposition of the image of the Greek temple with its strong affirmation of life: '*Im maasse mit der landschaft wuchs dein haus . . .*' and the transcendental verticality of the gothic church: '*In wolkige nebel deuten deine türme . . .*' Both these pictures contain those antitheses which by their balance of 'being and becoming,' light and darkness, really produce the classic synthesis:

*Kreuz . . . das licht der erde,—*
*Hellas ewig unsre liebe.*

In the prelude George seeks this classic equilibrium led by an angel, the herald of the life beautiful.

The '*Seventh Ring*' (1907) tells how the poet met Maximin the *Gottmensch. Kairos* and *Hellas* are the forces of fate which guide the poet's footsteps. In the '*Stern des Bundes*' (1914) we leave the rich sensuously coloured world of the '*Seventh Ring*' to enter the realm of immaterial light where the new life in God is prophesied —God is sound and light. The spirit of holy youth is made manifest through Him. '*Das neue Reich*' (1928) proclaims the final fulfilment born of self-control. Now George can say of himself: *Ich bin nur frei weil ein gesetz mich engt*—words that may be interpreted in a sense similar to the Swiss painter Hodler's freedom within rule.

Immoderate yearning can only destroy. That timeless moment *Nu*, already foreshadowed in the '*Stern des Bundes*' and even earlier, is recognized as the ultimate secret of life. A hundred years before, Novalis and Schelling had intimated similar concepts in writing that landscapes dissolve, spirit and dreams wear bodily form. The moment is supreme God, body and soul are only names for the changing aspect of reality. In war and love the world is reborn. George invokes the children of the ocean in his panegyric of the hero whose spirit lives in the murmuring voice of the sea-shell which a boy holds to his ear. Through this image of the shell infinity is made finite.

In our brief sketch of George's development he has appeared before us as a prophet of the spirit of Hellas, a visionary giving eternity to the ephemeral moment, *der den leib vergottet und den gott verleibt*.

This specifically Georgian ideal of the *kalokagathos* is thus seen to have been the basis of George's 'third humanism.' It would be just as wrong to trace this concept purely to Goethe's influence as to trace a straight line of development through the literary movements known as naturalism, impressionism and expressionism. Similarly the biological factors that govern modern European existence are utterly remote from those prevailing in ancient Greece. Moreover, we are well aware that classicism does not represent a cultural unity that can be covered by a single cliché. It embraces historic, aesthetic and psychological values which require lucid and exact interpretation wherever they are newly formulated.

We already noted a fundamental difference between Goethe's and George's attitude towards art and life. It is reflected even in the recitation of their verse. Goethe knew no 'normal *tempo*' whereas George gave his poems an element of incantation, reading them in the monotonous tone of a Gregorian chant.

George's observations about Goethe throw interesting light on their disparities. What Goethe meant to him is evident in two poems: (a) '*Goethe-Tag*' ('*Der Siebente Ring*') and (b) '*Goethes Lezte Nacht in Italien*' ('*Das Neue Reich*'). They not only give us the key to George's understanding of Goethe but also elucidate certain problems presented by the former's verse.

Of particular interest are George's reflections in '*Goethes Lezte Nacht in Italien.*' Like the foregoing poem they at the same time hold up a mirror to George's own being. On the shores of the Mediterranean, where the firs rear their black wings aloft and a single star glimmers silvery in the blue night, Goethe witnesses two youths take a pledge of eternal faith. It is the hour of Goethe's farewell to Italy. On this Southern alien soil he, the truest heir of his race, is overcome by a sense of overwhelming poverty. Only here did he ripen to humanity, and he cries aloud to the German people:

*. . . traget auch fürder in strömen*
*von eurem blute das edelste jenseit der berge. . . .*

For fate had denied the German nation a prophet, a son of Gäa. He, Goethe himself, was only her grandchild. His people 'fumbled in the void,' as he dared not venture 'into the chasms of the grim guardians' to tear from them their magic formula. Yet an apprehension of the divine life burns in Goethe, for he too had felt the divine thrill pass through him—once when as a wild unruly child he had joined the bacchanalian revelry of the Rhineland vintage, and again when he journeyed from the land of dreams and melody and fantastic towers into the realm of the sun. And now he returns thence bearing the vital ray, knowledge of the body's beauty, the divine norm, back to the misty North. In the far future this yearning for the South was to find expression once again in George's '*Maximin*,' 'a boy whom you deified'; cf. 'scion of our own line' ('*Stern des Bundes*').

Such were George's reflections in gazing at those two youthful heroes of the Southern world where frenzy and serenity, roses and marble, sweetness and strength, youth and maturity, meet to form a perfect harmony. If in this poem Goethe is called not the son of Gäa, but her grandchild, who could no more than apprehend the mysteries hidden beneath our earthly plane, George is thinking of Goethe who voluntarily curbed his creative frenzy by iron discipline. It is from the myth of the world-tree Yggdrasil that George borrows the image of the fiends burrowing at the roots of the tree. The poet-visionary must wrest the magic runes from their grasp.

Here as in the '*Jahr der Seele*' we meet with that specifically Georgian apprehension of Nature as an inimical, daemonic force, an attitude absolutely contrary to that of Goethe. It is intimated already in George's *juvenilia*, though there it bears the stamp of neo-romanticism. Alienation from Nature, satiety, hyper-intellectualism, unemployment, disdain of life, narcissism, elaborate refinement of style, aristocratic reserve, a worship of beauty that leads to a yearning for death—all these may well suggest affinity to Hugo von Hofmannsthal. Nevertheless George did not fall into the preciosity, the chill aloofness and resignation of neo-romantic aestheticism. Proof thereof may be found in his attitude towards Nature. It is not his way to hover forlornly in the twilight between life and death. In the '*Urlandschaften*' (primeval landscapes) and the '*Traurige Tänze*' he is seen to possess his peculiarly personal view of nature. It is not merely aesthetic. In silence Nature serves. The druid knows of its secret influence ('*Das neue Reich*,' 'destroying us, you destroy yourselves'). Life is kept awake through magic alone. The necessity of exorcising these powers forbids man's felicitous abandonment to Nature. A phrase such as 'the trace of mighty arms' suggests only conflict and strife.

Remembering George's maxim 'Control next to strength' it might first seem that his ideal of Greece was identical with that of Goethe. But in reality George simplifies it to a gesture of Attic dignity. It is the golden mean which George admires in Böcklin:

*Du gabst dem schmerz sein mass: die brandung musste*
*Vertönen. schrei durch güldne harfe sausen.*

In George's '*Hyperion*' beauty stands hard by action: 'Sparta's steelbound courage wedded to Ionia's grace.' Yet with George tension is stressed more than felicitous balance. And there is yet another point of difference; for whereas Goethe embodies his ideal of humanity in the 'eternal feminine,' George seeks it in the *heroic beauty of a youth.*

George's harsh verbal constructions are born of rigorous self-discipline. Against Goethe's rich idiom they appear bodiless and angular (cf. '*Mühle, lass die arme still*'). The lines seem welded together like blocks of masonry. His enjambements, unlike those of Rilke, seldom dissolve, for each line appears as though cemented within itself by the significance or oral rigidity of the final word.

Rhythm and metre advance with iron tread, usually in heavy trochaics. A frequent use of words of one syllable slows down the pace. George's chantlike diction is echoed in the rigid lines whose sequence can even be interchanged. Phrases are contracted to block-like adjectives: cf. '*das starke bösemferne zeichen.*' These abrupt joints, the compressed participles, the constriction of the sentences remind one of the style of '*Pandora*' concerning which Goethe himself used the term 'as wedged into each other.' Whereas Goethe in his youth seeks to liberate an excess of emotion in Pindaric phrases, the style of '*Pandora*' is consciously contracted by compound adjectives and participles. Through experience Goethe had come to acknowledge the laws of form. Now like Prometheus he could say—'chance ever remains hateful to me.' Epimetheus, his contemplative brother, sees yet deeper. The 'eternal moment' fills Goethe's consciousness in his old age.

George, on the other hand, lacked the abandoned vehemence of youth which in Goethe's case matured to a living classic ideal. A sense of humour saved the creator of Mephisto, of the '*Jahrmarktsfest zu Plundersweilern*,' or the '*Auerbachs Keller*' from stagnation. By the side of Goethe's, George's works appear sapless. We miss the unconscious, joyous harmony of Goethe's Greek ideal. The prophet of '*Das neue Reich*' was reared in a civilization disrupted by social and economic revolution. The comforts of bourgeois ties had been rent asunder, unity of life destroyed. The order of the day was no longer 'live and let live,' but an incitement to an ascetically trained youth to do its duty. The hosts of the 'other realm' break threateningly into the universe that once had been transfused by the Divine essence. We saw how remote is George's attitude towards Nature from that of Goethe or romantic *Stimmungskunst*.

In comparison with Nietzsche's conception of classicism, which in its dynamic tension bears some affinity to George's, Goethe's appears a calm sea after storm. In the fateful year 1918 Paul Ernst published an anecdote: '*Geheimer Ausspruch Bismarcks*,' which alleged that Goethe possessed after all only the soul of a philistine. Such a criticism is just as much a thing of the moment as Nietzsche's aphorism about Goethe, the 'German exception.' Nevertheless, in a way it touches the core of our argument, for we have seen that whereas in Goethe Dionysian and Apollonian principles were merged to an organic harmonious whole, George was only able to attain that unity through a relentless autocratic will. Goethe seeks characteristic individuality and transitory values (in action), George creates an impersonal form. To him Nature and intellect are antithetical. A lack of direct emotional experience is balanced by his extraordinary intellectual and creative capacity to draw inspiration from history and the world of aesthetics. But this very gift doomed him to pursue the path of a solitary, far from the common crowd and far also from all human aspiration. An angel is his guide to the life beautiful. Just as Herder once discovered the origin of culture in the miracle of the divine gift of language, so the visiting angel came to George. But instead of a classic-pantheistic idea of God's omnipresence, the new man now mirrors the divine tension between God and man. The inspiration that Dante once found in Beatrice, Hölderlin in Diotima, comes to George through Maximin, who freed the inmost sources of his being. In Maximin he discovered the consummation of his dream—incarnate God. In order to do justice to George's poetry it is essential to separate it from the excesses of 'Georgeanism.' Apart from E. Bertram, perhaps one of the most distinguished poets of the George-Kreis was K. Wolfskehl who died in exile, New Zealand, in 1948.

## *COUNTER CURRENTS AND NEW PATHS—VOLKHAFTE DICHTUNG. J. WEINHEBER.*

Unquenchable is the German's yearning for the South. George had given it expression through his 'third humanism.' R. G. Binding (1867–1938), and R. A. Schröder, born in Bremen in 1878, rank among the strongest representatives of the classic spirit in German life and poetry. Somewhat younger poets such as F. G. Jünger also tend towards Hellenism. Not until Binding had reached maturity did he realize his poetic métier. It was in gazing on the Hermes in Olympia that he beheld the glory of Hellas, and the mystery of creative death appeared to him as a revelation. In his lecture on 'The German and the humanist concept in the eyes of the future' it is the antique ideal which Binding sees fulfilled in the German, the struggle to attain perfection of body and spirit with a free heart and a free mind. Herder, Winckelmann, Goethe, Schiller, Humboldt, and Hölderlin were his spiritual ancestors. Thus intellectualism was once more trying to discover roots in German soil, as it did also with Rudolf Borchardt (1877–1945), the translator of Dante and author of '*Die Schöpfung aus Liebe*.' Binding, who, though of Swiss birth, chose Hesse as his heart's home, was one of the six who publicly defended the 'New Germany' against the attacks of Romain Rolland. Amongst the others were W. von Scholz and E. G. Kolbenheyer, author of '*Lyrisches Brevier*.'

R. A. Schröder, who was born in the same year as Kolbenheyer, also sings praises of Germany which to him is *Das Land der Mitte*. His art forms a bridge between Germany and Rilke, whose mystic abandonment, however, Schröder does not share, as his religious songs '*Mitte des Lebens*' prove. He has gained fame as a translator from Greek (Homer), Latin (Vergil, Horace) and almost all important modern European languages.

The following summary aims at tracing the radical changes German poetry has undergone since 1933; at the same time it will reveal the traditional forces, which reasserted themselves or found especial official sanction during those years of National-Socialist rule. The ballad once more came into its own. After Strachwitz and Fontane, the three most important exponents of the German ballad became: Münchhausen, Miegel, Lulu von Strauss und Torney.

Goethe had spoken of the ballad as the primal form of poetry, but without using the term in its historic sense. *Urform* does not necessarily imply *uralt*. Today we know that the ballad and dance were not, at any rate in Germany, an essential unity, and that the ballad did not originally spring from a collective art but is individual *Kunstdichtung*. Since Hölty and Bürger created the modern serious *Kunstballade*, the latter remained a favourite with the Germans and often became hackneyed and superficial, particularly at the time of the *Reichsgründung* in 1870–1871. D. v. Liliencron gave it new life, but his tendency toward impressionistic effect only too often disrupted the austere restraint of the ballad form and dissolved it in *Stimmungsbilder*. Even '*Pidder Lüng*' is also not quite free from this fault, although its noble ideal of independence and communal feeling makes one forget this weakness. Naturalism and Wedekind's *Brettldichtung* failed where the ballad was concerned, for hysterical subjectivity ruled the day. The apprehensive dreams and visions of symbolism or Spitteler's mythic sceneries lacked the palpable reality which the ballad demands. Where, however, as in the cabaret-song, we are faced with the actuality and sensationalism of the newspaper, an analogy to the *Bänkelgesang* and *Zeitungslied* of the waning Middle Ages immediately suggests itself. The ballad was, as we saw, rejuvenated by D. v. Liliencron and particularly by Strachwitz and Fontane.

Börries Freiherr von Münchhausen (1874–1945) began as their acknowledged pupil. The noble characters of his poetry spring from their affinity with his own nature. Gradually his images become profounder and clouded by fate. A gesture mirrors the secrets of the soul, as in his masterpiece, the '*Ballade vom Brennesselbusch*,' or in the '*Nobiskrug*.' But B. von Münchhausen does not always maintain this high standard. He has given authoritative expression to his intimate knowledge and understanding of the ballad form in the valuable study called '*Meisterballaden*,' in which he differentiates between external and internal action, e.g. in Miegel's '*Ritter Manuel*,' in which dream and reality interweave to one pattern.

Agnes Miegel, born in Königsberg in 1879, also tries to register the great passions of her heroes—proud love, strong rage, defiant faithfulness. She often lacks B. von Münchhausen's interest in action, but has all the more feeling for the magic of Nature and the world of German fairy-tale. She often elaborates the content with impressionistic *Stimmungsbilder*, as for instance in her ballad '*Die Nibelungen*':

> *Schön Kriemhild kauerte nah der Glut,*
> *Von ihren schmalen Händen*
> *Zuckte der Schein wie Gold und Blut*
> *Und sprang hinauf an den Wänden.*

As a woman she shows a partiality for patient heroines and fairy beings: '*Schöne Agnete*,' '*Die Frauen von Nidden*,' '*Die Domina*,' '*Die Braut*,' '*Marie Antoinette*,' '*Agnes Bernauer*,' '*Jane*,' '*Lady Gwen*.' It is no mere accident that English themes appealed to her, for she spent some time in England (Bristol) during her youth.

As a third German ballad-writer of repute we should mention Lulu von Strauss und Torney (born in Bückeburg in 1873). She also employs the heroic tone but prefers to describe the nobility of simple man as in '*Mara*':

> *Dies war das Lied, das Mara sang,*
> *Wenn rot im Herd die Flamme sprang: . . .*
>
> *Da kam ein Mann den Weg entlang,*
> *Verstaubt sein Kleid und schwer sein Gang.*

It is hardly possible to say which of these three ballad-writers deserves the crown, perhaps Agnes Miegel.

Another North German poet, Ina Seidel born (1885) in Halle an der Saale and Miegel's junior by six years, should be mentioned here not as a writer of ballads but as the author of the *kleine Mythen*. Here she depicts the metamorphosis of the soul into mythic figures: riders, birds, fishermen, huntsmen, shepherds, etc. Freedom and womanly, motherly instinct supply problems for many of her poems. In spite of the fact that she is deeply influenced by German tradition and family bonds, she is aware of mighty counter movements, which she, however, manages to control by a harmonious and steadfast rule of life.

Apart from such well known and comprehensive collections of

poems as Albert Sergel's '*Saat und Ernte*' and particularly Albert Soergel's '*Kristall der Zeit*,' the following anthologies may be regarded as displaying the change in poetic taste during the two decades before the last war. They are literary manifestos, even if they do not set out to be so. Such for instance is R. Kayser's '*Verkündigung*' (1921) in the preface of which political *pathos* is denied but which nevertheless still retains a decided expressionistic and revolutionary bias. G. Benn, T. Däubler (who is all too frequently regarded as only an expressionist), H. Johst, W. Klemm, F. Werfel, P. Zech and others are still represented here. In the foreword we read:

'. . . this period—autumn 1920, and the atmosphere is very languid and stale—shows signs of everything but progress or perfection . . . and only the first pale light of dawn.'

In 1927 appeared R. Fehse's and Klaus Mann's '*Anthologie jüngster Lyrik*.' In the introduction Stefan Zweig also speaks of a period of transition. No dominant voice rings out over the choir of poets to which belong W. H. Maass, W. E. Süskind, M. L. Weissmann, H. Wille, and others.

Stefan Zweig characteristically writes:

'Present-day youth suffers from an abbreviated puberty . . . it has become more matter-of-fact, energetic and less dreamy through the pressure of the age.'

O. Heuschele's '*Junge deutsche Lyrik*' (1928, 1930[7]) already betrays quite a different tone. In the preface it declares its prophets to be R. M. Rilke, Hugo von Hofmannsthal, and R. A. Schröder. This collection is both a synthesis and a renaissance. Amongst other poets, some of whom we have already named, are also Paula Grogger, J. Linke, Ruth Schaumann, and G. Schumann; further M. Hausmann too with his touching poem '*Ich möchte eine alte Kirche sein*,' and R. Billinger with his proud, hopeful song:

*Wir Bauern dulden keinen Spott*
*an unserm Herrn und Helfer Gott!*

The titles of the anthologies and poems in and since 1933 are significant. Many of them have rightly sunk into oblivion: cf. the forcible but now pitiably dated utterances in H. Böhme's

'*Rufe in das Reich. Die heldische Dichtung von Langemarck bis zur Gegenwart*' (1934). The 'Third Realm' had come. Such poets as Dietrich Eckart may be called its forerunners. The '*Ausritte*' almanacs published by Langen-Müller (1933 ff.), were documents of the time. The most typical group of contributors includes the editors of the journal '*Das innere Reich*' = P. Alverdes and K. B. von Mechow, further R. Billinger, G. Britting, H. Blunck, H. Claudius, H. H. Ehrler, P. Ernst, J. von Goltz, H. Johst, E. G. Kolbenheyer, H. Leifhelm, E. W. Möller, Dr. Owlglass, author of '*Kleine Nachtmusik*,' M. Reuschle, G. Schumann, E. Strauss, F. Tumler, W. Vesper, J. Wehner, J. Weinheber, E. Wiechert, J. Zerzer, H. Zillich, author of '*Komme was will*,' and others. These are very largely the same names that appear in '*Das kleine Gedichtbuch*' (1933), partly also in the '*Deutsche Wende*,' which, published by Reclam, is introduced by G. Schumann's '*Wer sich dem Reich verschrieb, ist ein Gezeichneter*.' . . . Songs such as H. J. Nierentz's '*Deutschland, grosse Schmiede*,' B. von Schirach's '*Hitler*,' W. Brockmeier's defiant '*Jungbauernlied*,' H. Anacker's '*Lachend will ich mich verschwenden*,' H. Böhme's '*Verbrenne Mensch*,' further J. Linke's '*Yggdrasil*,' L. F. Barthel's '*Dies hier ist Deutschland*' and many others, in particular songs by German poets living abroad, were intended to be 'witnesses' and 'prophets' of the 'Third Realm.' Many at the same time proved that the folk-song and even the religious song were enjoying a revival, for instance in the '*S. A. Sturm- und Marschlieder*,' amongst which is a new version of the Low German prayer of thanksgiving:

> '*Wir treten zum Beten vor Gott, dem Gerechten. Er waltet und schaltet ein strenges Gericht; er lässt von den Schlechten die Guten nicht knechten. Sein Name sei gelobt. Er vergisst unser nicht. . .*'

Further we may cite the collection named after the notorious *Horst Wessel Lied*, '*Die Fahne hoch*,' and the songs of the N. S. Gemeinschaft 'Strength through Joy': '*Werkleute singen*.'

The working-class song has not died out: e.g. G. Engelke († 1918) from Hanover, A. Petzold († 1923) from Vienna, K. Heynicke from Liegnitz, H. Lersch († 1936) from München-Gladbach, author of the famous song *Soldatenabschied*, with the refrain:

*Deutschland muss leben, und wenn wir sterben müssen!*

To these names may also be added those of M. Barthel from Dresden, and K. Bröger from Nürnberg, author of the '*Bekenntnis*':

*Immer schon haben wir eine Liebe zu dir gekannt,*
*Bloss wir haben sie nie mit einem Namen genannt.*
*Als man uns rief, da zogen wir schweigend fort,*
*Auf den Lippen nicht, aber im Herzen das Wort*
*Deutschland. . . .*

The introduction of the Barthel-Bröger-Lersch poems '*Schulter an Schulter*' is characteristic: *Dieses kleine Buch Gedichte nennen wir 'Schulter an Schulter,' weil wir keine Einzelgänger sind, sondern Schulter an Schulter mit unseren Kameraden marschieren.*

H. Claudius and J. Kneip belonged to the workmen in 'Haus Nyland,' a society for creative work in which the extreme North-west regions of the Reich had once stood under the leadership of J. Winckler. Lastly the radical reformation of the *Deutsche Akademie der Dichtung* was the significant symbol of the new political ideal which, carried on the wings of the Third Realm, rejected the 'manless generation.'

Most of the above names have today been swept away. The aesthetic effect of many a poem and *Sprechchor* was spoiled by immature crudity or propaganda. There was, however, at least *one* outstanding poet, the Austrian J. Weinheber, who with the collapse of Germany and Austria took his own life.

Proudly Josef Weinheber (1892–1945) coined the motto of his chief work '*Adel und Untergang*' (1934):

*Nicht Gnade nahm ich, Frost war mein Stärke.*

He set out on a lonely quest, and it was long before fame crossed his path. He had already achieved unity of form and content when he was one day suddenly acclaimed the greatest living German-speaking poet next to Rilke and George.

Through his '*Gedanken zu meiner Disziplin*' we may gain much insight into his manner of working. The integrity with which he guards the word is incorruptible: 'Language is the reality of spirit and through it man becomes a spiritual reality.' Schopenhauer's dictum that a heroic life is the highest purpose of our existence here attains a new significance: *Uns ziemt zu fallen; jedwedem auf seinem Schilde* ('*Adel und Untergang*').

The singer's duty is to incite, to lament and to warn. Instead of altar and sword, the word gives him strength to render service to his people. Like a cyclops of the antique age Weinheber feels himself hurled into chaos. Now in the '*Einsamstes Selbstgespräch*' he realizes that we possess no home but that which rests within us. Blood is 'not yet *your* blood,' earth not yet *your* earth. To him perfection lies in the word of the poet.

We have already referred to Weinheber's reverence for his mother-tongue. To her he dedicates his undying '*Hymnus auf die deutsche Sprache*.' A comparison between this hymn and Rückert's poem '*An die Sprache*' proves Weinheber's power over words.

Classic and other verse-metres provide him with models for practising his formal art. He tempers passionate outburst and the violence of fate to noble restraint. Regarded in this light his '*Ode an die Buchstaben*' appears not as tonal virtuosity, but as an expression of his profound love of the word with which he embraces far horizons. To one possessing such a talent the temptation to write an unending number of variations on one theme is irresistible. Thus Weinheber takes Hölderlin's ode '*An die Parzen*': applying it now to earthly life, now to the world beyond. Again he breaks up single phrases and remodels them in turn to a notturno, a scherzo, a rondo and lastly creates a hymn from the raw material.

In 1935 appeared his volume of poems entitled '*Wien wörtlich*,' in which the poet of the odes and hymns suddenly falls into the coarsest dialect. We hear the voice of the Viennese in all his suffering and his love for his native home Vienna, whose decay he was doomed to witness, and whose great tragedy was that she was not spared the inflation. Vienna from which life had fled wore but the beauty of stone, and the Belvedere and Schönbrunn stand as silent witnesses of a past glory. The changes that have swept the land are poignantly summed up in the '*Synonyma*': *Muatta, Vatta = Papa, Mama, Bundesstaat = Republik!*

No poet has so successfully welded the everyday atmosphere of Vienna to classic measure, image and tone as Weinheber. None has given us such a delightful picture of the Viennese in his *Kaffeehaus* attitude, at his *Jause* or at the *Heuriger*, within his four walls or promenading to the strains of the Radetzky march, at the *Jahrmarkt* or the carnival, or once upon a time in his profession of *kaiserlich-königlicher* official. Or we enter the spirit of the *Pensionist*, the gallant *Präsidialist*, the philosophic *Biertippler*, the dreamy *Biedermeier*, the frequenter of the *Stammtisch* or the *Wurstelprater*. The '*Ballade vom kleinen Mann*' in the office is European rather than typically Viennese. '*Diethelm Trausenit*' and the '*Elegie auf den Tod eines alten Wieners*' would gain in power if they were shortened.

The '*Späte Krone*' (1936) and '*O Mensch, gib acht. Ein erbauliches Kalenderbuch für Stadt- und Landleute*' (1937) are Weinheber's latest works of importance. In the former he addresses himself more resolutely than before to the racial community and the august duties that belong to a noble mind and heart. Restraint and the golden mean are the principles on which his poetic vision would build a new world. The overreaching temerity of the titan must end as it did with Hölderlin in abysmal fall. Lightning and tempest fall as a divine blessing on man as he sets out on the path of liberty, only flame can free us; cf. '*Empor*.' The poet well knows that man must fall on the way, but he sings of the spirit.

# XV

# GOTTFRIED BENN, FORM-EXPERIMENTS IN GERMAN LYRIC POETRY AFTER 1939-1945

## I

### *Gottfried Benn and The Absolute Poem*

THE Berlin doctor, Gottfried Benn (1886–1956), six years older than Weinheber, became the favourite poet of a disillusioned generation. As a brilliant nihilist and politically controversial character he captivated the imagination of many young German and foreign students. He contrasts the power of the intellect with that of 'worthless' joy in existence, e.g. in '*Sils Maria*':

*Doch wer die Stunden denkt:*
*ihre Welle, ihr Spiel, ihr Wesen,*
*der hat die Stunden gelenkt.*

His poem '*Wer allein ist*' is a rejection of Goethe's 'Die and be reborn':

*Nicht mehr Stirb und nicht mehr Werde:*
*Formstill sieht ihn die Vollendung an.*

G. Benn seeks artistic perfection and '*Entwicklungsfremdheit*' in his '*Statische Gedichte*,' i.e. form alone is to him '*Glaube und Tat*,' belief and action; life is a '*niederer Wahn*,' petty illusion: '*Entwicklungsfremdheit ist die Tiefe des Weisen.*' In his celebrated Marburger Rede: '*Probleme der Lyrik*' (1951), G. Benn advocates the so-called 'absolute poem' in place of the poem of lyrical mood. The 'absolute poem' is a product of artistry. Artistry is the supreme endeavour on the part of the intellectual and isolated artist to experience his own Ego as essential content, in a world of perishing values. The 'absolute poem' is that which is left of a poem when through a process of distillation the artist has purified and 'cleared it of all dregs' such as mood, atmosphere, profundity. This is the antithesis to Shelley's views: 'When composition begins, inspiration is already on the decline.'

According to Benn's diagnosis of modern style the following four symptoms betray an outworn mood or mode of poetry and should be banned: *Andichten*, *Wie-Vergleiche*, *Farbenskala*, *seraphischer Ton*:

1. The Romantic address to Nature can be part of perfect poems such as Eichendorff's '*Sehnsucht*' or Goethe's '*An den Mond*,' but their form as expression is rejected by G. Benn as being 'more than a hundred years old.'

2. The excessive use of similes introduced with 'as' and 'like,' according to Benn, weakens (through epic and journalistic elements) the creative tension of a poem. No doubt, readers will easily find exceptions; for instance we could mention Rilke's '*Geburt der Venus*' and its many similes prefaced by *wie*: '*wie ein junges grünes Blatt, wie Monde, wie eine junge Frucht, wie ein Springbrunnen, wie ein Blumenstiel, wie Hälse von Schwänen, wie Morgenwind, wie Segel, von der Ferne voll, wie aus Umarmung*,' and above all the striking simile: '*wie ein Bestand von Birken im April . . . die Scham.*'

3. The vague Romantic application of colour and the traffic in words which once sounded new (e.g. 'steilen'), are rejected as obsolete.

4. The seraphic tone which often already at the start of a poem propels the reader into 'heavenly spheres,' is ridiculed.

The present-day poet must, according to G. Benn, speak and appeal to his own generation. He, like B. Brecht (1898–1956), thus hammers into his verse scientific and social expressions of his time: Ion, Broadway, Gammastrahlen, Neurogen, etc. But unlike B. Brecht he does not direct his verse to humanity, and although he demands actuality, not l'art pour l'art ('*Man muss dicht am Stier kämpfen*'), he yet seeks to master the 'absolute poem,' i.e. a poem without belief, a poem without hope and without a didactic message, a poem which is addressed to nobody but which, strangely enough, claims to be 'metaphysical.' Its relentless law is static expression and clarity of style. It is not a matter of private concern, but of highest intellectual achievement.

G. Benn's artistic views are, in spite of obvious differences and perhaps quite unconsciously, rooted in Nietzsche's aesthetic concept of the artist in his *Birth of Tragedy*, a book which continues to revitalize and fertilize creative writing even after 1939–1945: according to Nietzsche 'the artist has already surrendered his subjectivity in the Dionysian process; the picture which now shows to him his oneness with the heart of the world, is a dream-scene, which embodies the primordial contradiction and primordial pain, together with the primordial joy of appearance. The "I" of the lyrist sounds therefore from the abyss of being: its "subjectivity" in the sense of the modern aesthetes, is a fiction . . . the pictures of the lyrist are nothing but *his very* self and, as it were, only different projections of himself, on account of which he as the moving centre of this world is entitled to say "I": only of course this self is not the same as that of the waking, empirically real man, but the only verily existent and self-resting at the basis of things, by means of the images whereof the lyric genius sees through even to this basis of things. . . . Hence all our knowledge of art is at bottom quite illusory, because, as knowing persons we are not one and identical with the Being who, as the sole author and spectator of this comedy of art, prepares a perpetual entertainment for himself. Only in so far as the genius in the act of artistic production coalesces with this primordial artist of the world, does he get a glimpse of the eternal essence of art, for in this state he is, in a marvellous manner, like the weird picture of the fairy-tale which can at will turn its eyes and behold itself; he is now at once subject and object, at once poet, actor and spectator.' ['*The Birth of Tragedy*' translated by Haussmann, ed. by O. Levy.] Thus, according to Nietzsche as well as to Benn, only as an aesthetic phenomenon is existence justified. The story of the poet's life and trials is, however, not altogether irrelevant, although the work of art must in itself be more important than everything else.

In a similar way also T. S. Eliot's '*The Sacred Wood*' (1920) became a document of the time, and much of the so-called 'New Criticism' stems from it. Like Nietzsche, T. S. Eliot sees the progress of an artist in a continual self-sacrifice and in a continual extinction of personality. He demands tradition and he rejects the search for novelty; instead of new emotions he seeks the ordinary ones; the process of writing is, according to him, conscious and deliberate: 'The bad poet is usually unconscious where he ought to be conscious, and conscious where he ought to be unconscious . . . poetry is not a turning loose of emotion but an escape from emotion; it is not an expression of personality but an escape from personality.' Therefore he does not seek 'sincere' emotion nor merely 'technical' excellence but the expression of 'significant' emotion which is 'impersonal' and 'which has its life in the poem and not in the history of the poet.'

But T. S. Eliot, in contrast to G. Benn, is conscious of standing in his time and tradition when he says that a 'historical sense compels a man to write not merely with his own generation in his bones, but with a feeling that the whole of the literature of Europe from Homer and within it the whole of the literature of his own country has a simultaneous existence, and composes a simultaneous order . . . no poet, no artist of any art has his complete meaning alone.' Moreover, T. S. Eliot sees art and morals in close interrelationship. We are here reminded of Matthew Arnold's view that poetry is 'a criticism of life,' and also of Shelley's statement: 'the basis of morality is laid not by preachers but by poets,' and of Tolstoy who denies the value of all human endeavours with the exception of those which are valuable to all men.

G. Benn's glittering word-artifices are the antithesis to such views and particularly to those of the author of the '*Dreigroschenoper*.' Although between him and B. Brecht exist fundamental differences, both use the so-called artistic estrangement or 'distantiation' (*Verfremdung*, *Entfremdung*). As B. Brecht at a certain stage of his development deliberately does not reveal the realistic character of his plays to his audience in a too familiar manner and does not want the actors to identify themselves too much with the characters, so G. Benn and also Günter Eich (born 1907), Günter Grass (born 1927), etc., endeavour to create word-artifices in which a direct logical connexion of associations is often lacking, and which live on magic sound effects and playful inventions, dazzling surprises and chiffres, cf. Reinhold Grimm's fine study '*Gottfried Benn, Die farbliche Chiffre in der Dichtung*,' Nüremberg '*Erlanger Beiträge*,' I. 1958. In the sense of G. Benn's theory such poems are precious jewels of 'absolute' value, see e.g. his own '*Welle der Nacht*' (1948):

> *Welle der Nacht—, Meerwidder und Delphine*
> *mit Hyakinthos leichtbewegter Last,*
> *die Lorbeerrosen und die Travertine*
> *weh'n um den leeren istrischen Palast.*
>
> *Welle der Nacht—, zwei Muscheln miterkoren,*
> *die Fluten strömen sie, die Felsen her,*
> *dann Diadem und Purpur mitverloren,*
> *die weisse Perle rollt zurück ins Meer.*

This poem tells no story directly; it is also no re-statement of folk-lore and myth. It requires an almost encyclopædic brain and linguistic ingenuity to grasp the 'meaning' of the obscure references: to the boy Hyakinthos, the plural-form of the stone Travertin, the Meerwidder (cf. '*Faust II*'), and finally the Muscheln—Diadem—Purpur—Perle in those two verses which, according to the poet's own interpretation, refer to the castle Miramar on the Adriatic Sea and by suggestion to the tragic fate of Maximilian, emperor of Mexico. This is an art of bold outlines, an art which (only apparently) rests in no definite time, in no definite place or history or tradition or personal emotion, and which is the declared aim of a number of the present avant-garde poets in West Germany, whilst the integration of experiment and tradition is essentially the goal of the three notable contemporary East Germans: Johannes Bobrowski (born 1917), an admirer of Dylan Thomas, Góngora, Lorca, etc., Wolfgang Hädecke (born 1929) who now lives in West Germany, and, above all Peter Huchel (born 1903), perhaps the greatest living East German poet who will be referred to later on.

## II

### *Form-experiments in German Lyric Poetry after 1939–45*

The post-war poems of R. Hagelstange (born 1912), H. E. Holthusen (born 1913), and K. Krolow (born 1915) testify to the fact that an important inner movement was once again struggling for expression in West Germany. The living springs of German lyricism seem to be inexhaustible. The existence and continuance of a lyrical heritage in German poetry are, as we have seen, sufficiently proved by the naïvety of Hermann Claudius, the forceful free-rhythmic verse of Klopstock, Goethe, Hölderlin, Novalis, Heine and Nietzsche, as much by the rare tension and immediacy of the young Goethe, as by the daemonic maturity of the old Goethe and of Mörike. Finally one might mention the magical incantation of Stefan George's '*Sänge*' and the depth of Rilke's '*Dinggedichte*' and '*Duino Elegies*.' It is no mere concidence that the gifted young poet Heinz Piontek (born 1925) who began under Karl Krolow's influence and who has already published some remarkably original poems in: '*Furt*' (1952), '*Rauchfahne*' (1953), '*Wassermarken*' (1957), is on the side of Hugo von Hofmannsthal's so-called 'conservative revolution' in which the forces of tradition and innovation try to hold the balance.

Baroque characteristics and a Classic heritage are again coming to the fore. Once more contemporary German poets discover the nothingness of all existence when confronted with death. The favourite themes are the unity of life and death, a recognition of the pure spirit and faith in the goodness of creation, despair of life, overpowering apocalyptic visions, the 'comforted despair' which recalls the antithesis of Baroque verse; shattering self accusation (though there are exceptions as in R. Hagelstange's sonnets: '*Venezianisches Credo*,' 1946). There is a desire for the formal discipline of the sonnet which acts as the anchor of salvation for poets such as H. E. Holthusen: '*Klage um den Bruder*' (1947), W. von Niebelschütz (born 1913): '*Posaunenkonzert*' (1947) and occasionally even for Wolfgang Weyrauch in '*An die Wand geschrieben*,' 1950, (cf. '*Am Abend*'). In the Preface to Alma Heismann's '*Sonette einer Liebenden*' (1957), W. Lehmann calls the sonnet a rusty watercan with its mouth clogged up, but at the same time he shows that in the hands of a gifted artist such as Alma Heismann (1885–1943) the sonnet is the appropriate pattern to control and give creative expression to the overflow of emotions. With similar skill it is used by another poet of the older generation: Jesse Thoor (Peter Karl Höfler, 1905–1952) in '*Die Sonette und Lieder*,' ed. by Alfred Marnau (1956), Veröffentlichungen der deutschen Akademie für Sprache und Literatur, Darmstadt. This Academy to which the world of letters must be grateful for rescuing neglected or suppressed authors from oblivion, published, apart from the above works by A. Heismann and Jesse Thoor, also poems by Franz Baermann Steiner, Gertrud Kolmar, Alfons Paquet, Hans Schiebelhuth, Arno Nadel, Eduard Saenger, etc. All these poems stand in a tradition which has never been broken. Stefan Andres (born 1906), author of the story about an episode in the Spanish Civil War: '*Wir sind Utopia*' collected his poems (odes, songs and sonnets) in '*Der Granatapfel*,' in which he gives artistic expression to two fundamental forces in contemporary German lyric poetry: he is master of the sonnet form, e.g. in his renowned '*Requiem für ein Kind*' and he can also create his poetic vision in powerful free verse, particularly in his odes: '*An Orpheus*' and '*An Hellas*':

*Götter von Hellas,*
*Ihr am Baum*
*Himmlischer Sehnsucht Europas*
*Einzig Frucht gewordene Blüte.*

In this connexion some publications of German poetry in New York deserve special mention, particularly Hans Wolff's sensitively controlled poems: *In den silbernen Nächten* (1950) and *Auch der Herbst kommt wieder* (1958). Furthermore, Nelly Sachs, born in Berlin and resident in Stockholm, recently received a Festschrift, published by the Suhrkamp-Verlag which also brought out her collected poems in '*Fahrt ins Staublose*.'

Though in modern German poetry there is a prevailing tendency towards 'free-rhythmic' expression we also find a characteristic predilection for Classical forms, together with a return to a new humanitarianism which through sensitive translations from Classical poetry found its most passionate advocate in Thassilo von Scheffer's '*Die homerischen Götterhymnen*,' '*Die Argonauten*,' '*Die Kyprien*,' '*Ovid. Metamorphosen*.'

In this connexion, Hermann Buddensieg's book: '*Hymnen an die Götter Griechenlands*' (1947), is extremely valuable. The author of these hymns, in contrast to G. Benn, demands a Goethean 'change and rebirth.' According to him, a study of ancient values helps us, because if to-day Aeschylus no longer appeals to us, 'it is not worth living in this world.' As in the days of Goethe, Schiller, Hölderlin and Novalis, the poet is praised as the interpreter and mediator of a mythical world, in which only a brotherly intimacy with death gives to life depth and fullness. If, however, the poet can once more conjure up the words: Mother Earth, Air, Sea, Fire, it is no deification of existence in Stefan George's sense. Man must submit himself humbly 'to the will of the gods.' Our time-bound existence will fall away like an empty shell, for it is unconsecrated and worthless.

The truly great lyric poet only appears to be estranged from the world. Aeschylus's '*Persians*' or Sophocles's '*Ajax*' or Euripides' '*Trojan Women*' are, in a sense, closer to our time than almost anything that our present age offers. It is a question of basic humanity, as it is in Goethe's '*Faust*,' for nervously sensitive 'reportage' acts only for the day, and the feeling of emptiness and the arrogance of analytical comprehension often end in anarchy. The work of the really profound poet is of *this* and *all* time; it is individual as well as universal, i.e. applicable to all ages and to all men. He achieves this by combining Apollo and Dionysus, clarity and visionary ecstasy.

Another significant feature of German lyrical poetry immediately after 1945 is its inwardness. In its intense feeling, poetry has emerged as a force opposing false rhetoric and the threatening total uniformity and utilitarianism of life.

Karl Krolow is the author of an important 'Foreword' to F. Rasche's little and now forgotten anthology '*Das Gedicht in unserer Zeit*' (1946). This booklet, published one year after the last war, reflects some predominant features of German writers in 1945–1946, maintaining that amidst the barrenness of a world politically and morally bankrupt the countryside should be won back again for poetry, and that the rivers, trees, fields, flowers, the stars themselves should speak once more through poetry. Thus, according to K. Krolow, the intimate relations between Nature and mankind, between God and man, should again be kindled or awakened. Moreover, the tendency towards 'intellectual' poetry, towards vague mysticism and a guilt-laden consciousness should yield to a new mode of poetic form, which is beyond time but not timeless. The poet's deepest concern should naturally be the creation of lyric poetry expressive of *our* present age and *our* generation. The most modern lyric, K. Krolow likewise asserts, should be deeply religious, without being limited to creed. Some latest lyrical experiments in West German poetry are, as we shall see, a far cry from such and other post-war manifestoes.

Finally the demand is expressed that in all poetic writings a subtle sense of form be revealed: the sonnet has different functions from those of the elegy, the simple song different ones from those of the ode, etc.

K. Krolow decries the 'world of beautiful machine guns.' He does not avoid the question of guilt, he also does not veil or make the word or deed seem more beautiful than it is:

*Ich bin das Land, das im Gerichte steht,*
*Und allen Ländern bin ich das Gericht.*

But the basic motif is solitude amidst terrifying Nature. Silence is to him like a thunderclap. Nature becomes daemonic, the 'spirit of the time' is rejected. His '*Lobgesang*' is a hymn in praise of the imperishable universe.

Karl Krolow is not alone in his endeavour to preserve old values and build up new ones in post-war Germany. We have already referred to H. Piontek's 'conservative revolution.' In a critical essay, well worth re-reading and entitled: '*Wer heute ein Gedicht wagt*' (*Die Zeit*, 1949), '*Who dares compose a poem to-day*,' the poet Wilhelm Lehmann (born 1882) scorns the dilettantism of many recent verses which revolve continuously round the theme of factories and barracks. Moreover, he makes fun of the foolish imitators of Rilke and the enthusiasts of the hackneyed image of the pumpkin, symbol of massive existence, and above all he attacks the empty versifiers of platitudes and of vulgar mixtures of images and abstractions. He seeks a way out of the conflict between the realists' surface-play of manners and the ecstatic flights of the idealists.

Elisabeth Langgässer (1899–1950) is, in many ways, spiritually related to W. Lehmann. Her work '*Der Laubmann und die Rose*,' 1947, mirrors the poet's return to Nature. The blooming of flowers and herbs over a stony waste of bombed houses is a joyous consolation for the homeless and a hope for the rebirth of the year. Thus the primeval love for the cycles of the years, the acceptance of Goethe's belief in change and permanence and especially in all-embracing Nature, explains itself: 'I become both man and woman, all embracing Nature, released from the spell, root and scent.' Perhaps quite unknowingly, Jacob Böhme's theory of our origin here becomes a song: 'My origin is the breath'; the breath enters into all names, but the names wither like the seeds. 'The world streams in, I breathe it back,' as it does in Goethe's 'diastole and systole.' Thus the rose ceaselessly opens, blooms, bears fruit and changes. In the beginning is the end, in the end the beginning, cf. T. S. Eliot's similar theme in '*East Coker*.'

The unity of all life is made manifest in E. Langgässer's poetry as a unity of the present and the past: the Ancient World and the Middle Ages, and man's intimate relationship with the realm of the lower and higher worlds, with Merlin, Ariel, Klingsor, Rapunzel and Frau Holle. It is a poetry in which the animals and plants of children's fairy tales are friendly to the yellow-hammer, the lark, the dove, the swan, the siskin, the hoopoo, and also to the hare, the lizard, the stag, the bee and the snail. The Norn 'Verdandi' under the ash spins the thread of fate and her magic words cast a spell on seeds and fruits:

*Der Mohn fällt ab. Ein Tropfen rinnt*
*Bis in die Krausblattgrube . . .*
*Der Esche, wo Verdandi spinnt,*
*Verwölkte Murmelkrone sinnt*
*Hinab zur Wurzelstube . . .*

('*Regnerischer Sommer*.')

In an essay written in August 1948 about W. Lehmann, Elisabeth Langgässer points to the two essential forms in German lyrical poetry:

*a*) the 'naïve' expression, *b*) the 'artistic' expression.

But Elisabeth Langgässer whom we have singled out here as representative of a particular group of modern nature poets, like Wilhelm Lehmann himself, takes a '*third*' road, which leads directly from the Romanticism of Novalis and P. O. Runge to Brentano and Droste-Hülshoff. She, too, draws upon fairy-tales: mythology, folk-lore, the magic of Nature, and the old German proverb. Her world with its elves, its woods, and its birds nesting among trees is a very intimate world. It is a dream world, which deliberately devotes itself to magic and incantation.

The main nineteenth-century heir of that heathen-Christian

feeling for nature was for Langgässer without doubt mainly Clemens Brentano. It is no pantheistic merging with the Universe, but it is a feeling for Nature, the desire to approach, physically and spiritually, the mysterious powers within us and around us, and this often indeed in a fairy-tale world, which recalls both Shakespeare's elf kingdom in the '*Tempest*' and in '*A Midsummer Night's Dream*,' and Goethe's Nature spirits at the beginning of '*Faust*' (Part II).

Unfortunately, E. Langgässer's poetry is so heavily laden with names and associations from myths, fairy-tales, the Middle Ages, early history, and botany, that the reader can hardly grasp the sense without a dictionary. Her Nature kingdom is like Klingsor's magic garden in which the names of plants have special significance: e.g. mistletoe, foxglove, especially the symbolical 'wonder of the roses.' North and South are one. Modern European imagination joins with that of antiquity: Persephone with Amfortas, Parzival with Avalun, Morgana with Maria, as in the poem '*Schneeschmelze am Dom*'; and we meet Demeter, Frau Holle and the Norns, Arethusa, Joringel and Jorinde, Ossian and Orpheus, and last but not least Nymph Kora, Hermes and even Unke the toad. In thus merging plants and animals into a new mythology Elisabeth Langgässer's poetry is akin to Wilhelm Lehmann's '*Der grüne Gott*' (1942, 1st ed.) and '*Überlebender Tag*,' (1954). This poetry, too, points to the common source and origin, to Clemens Brentano's '*Romanzen vom Rosenkranz*,' but Langgässer is at the same time ultra-modern in her bold acceptance and interpretation of the cosmological knowledge in our atomic age:

'*Nicht "Gedankenlyrik", da sei Gott ferne! doch denkender Lyriker samt sämtlichen Prämissen: samt dem Unsicherheitskoeffizienten von Heisenberg, dem Umriss der Atomlehre, der Leibnizschen Mathesis universalis und der Philosophie von "Sien und Zeit", der dialektischen Denkübung und der Umwelttheorie von Üxkuell, der Sakramentenlehre moderner Pastoraltheologie und der Soziologie von Max Scheler—er ist es, den wir fordern müssen, soll sich nicht der kosmologische Umkreis der Lyrik zu einem Weideplatz frommer Schäfer verengen, zu einer sanften Insel in ultrablauen Meeren und einer Weltraumrakete, die nach dem Leeren zielt.*'

Whilst W. Lehmann and E. Langgässer praise the roots of nature, and turn to modern science as well as to old myths, the joy of summer being brought out through associations from the saga of Helen and Paris, Hans Egon Holthusen's verse voices the religious fervour amongst the Germans in a time of tribulation. The very title of his book of poems: '*Hier in der Zeit*' (1949) indicates their actuality. The poet, like Hölderlin in his song of fate: '*Schicksalslied*' laments the iron necessity of our existence. We are hurtled into time. Our beginning is a blind fate, so is our end: 'Wir alle sind wie Stürzende.' Time is our death. Earth-bound man becomes his own enemy when he divides time into peace and war. Here on earth fulfilment is denied to us, even in love: '*Glück ist ein Strohfeuer. Aber wir wollen es brennen sehn.*' . . . We are imprisoned by the 'barbaric order' of our blood. Beauty is merely a mysterious poison, because the 'music of lust,' 'the sweet concert of our limbs' results only in despair to the lovers. Under the yoke of the ecstatic moment man and woman are hurled into each other. Yet in love there can be no harmony. We blindly lose ourselves into an 'empty paradise.' Sleep alone can extinguish our senses and re-establish the primeval equilibrium. Such is the theme of the poem '*Nocturno*': '*Schlafen. Lösch uns die Sinne. . . . Finde die Welt ihr uraltes Mass. O lasse uns schlafen!*'

When Holthusen speaks of the guilt of the body he seems to hark back to the Manichaean concept of evil. It is our human intellect, the perpetual wound of the Universe, which sharpens the conflict. Nor does he shirk the question of war-guilt. According to him we *all* are guilty: '*Schuldig wir alle*,' but Germany, lying in the heart of Europe, became 'a crater of evil': '*Du übernahmst die Rolle des Frevlers.*' . . .

In spite of this note of despair, Holthusen affirms life, though a curse seems to lie upon it. He realizes how terrible the individual as well as the nations can be. He maintains that man is already vanquished at his birth: '*Jeder Geborne ist ein Besiegter.*' Yet Nature is unconquerable and God's mercy unending: '*Das Bad deiner Liebe. . . . Weltmeer deines Erbarmens.*'

These two consolations are to reconcile man with time and death. The third comfort is the message of compassion, for we are all brothers in God: '*Aus Millionen erschlagener Russen dèn Bruder erwählen.*'

Thus Holthusen's lament becomes an affirmation of life whose joy is deeper than sorrow, as it is also in Nietzsche's '*Zarathustra*' song: 'Lust tiefer noch als Herzeleid.' Man's tortured nights and God's grace balance each other. The poet's God is like Kierkegaard's God 'fearful,' a primordial rock on which our hands are rent and bleed. Here and elsewhere we feel a certain affinity with Rilke's and Hölderlin's thought and imagery.

His '*Eight Variations about Time and Death*,' published in 1949, (later incorporated in Holthusen's poems: '*Labyrinthische Jahre*,' 1952) resume the theme of the futility and monotony of our human existence: Time means Death. Love seeks Death. We try to seal time with kisses, but in vain. Our body and the coarse aggressiveness of sex are destined to disintegrate and decay. Above all we are consumed by history: '*Geschichte verzehrt uns.*' . . . '*Geschichte, furchtbar und ganz wie umsonst!*'

Human laws and treaties are 'withered into sound.' Truth is the water-mark beneath the motley imprint of Time. The reference to the Germany of 1939–1945 is transparent when Holthusen in dactylic metre speaks of Caesar, 'standing erect in the car, an idol of the masses' and when he describes the last days of Berlin's agony and the dictator's end in the Reichskanzlei. Not until our pride is brought low, can we seek God's grace. Not until we rid ourselves of time and of the flesh, can we reach the true realization of our inner selves: '*Nun und nimmermehr hier, in der Zeit und im Fleisch.*'

In the *Ballade vom verschütteten Leben* (1952) by Rudolf Hagelstange (born 1912) the tragic fate of six German soldiers is raised to the symbol of the threatened existence of our time. The theme is set clearly and vividly before us. On the 17th June 1951 it was reported from Warsaw that Polish workmen whilst clearing away an underground shelter, discovered two men, one of whom fell dead after walking a few steps; they were the last two of six German soldiers, who, as far back as the beginning of 1945, had, according to the story, been cut off from the outside world, by an explosion in a gigantic underground store-house of provisions. Report (which later on turned out to be a hoax) revealed that shortly afterwards two of the trapped men committed suicide in the bunker and two of the remaining four fell and died.

The motif: 'All is dust. There are only steps . . . Now, O man, you are dust and you will return to dust . . .'—*Memento, homo, quia pulvis est, et in pulverem reverteris*—is the keynote of this ballad of night and despair. But the new 'saga of the dust' is at the same time the old saga of the eternal light. At the end the promise is revealed to us that they finally witness 'out of a thousand dark silences a single shining child.' This sudden conclusion comes to us as a surprise, for the whole poem is overshadowed by a spirit of despair and frustration.

The above six victims have been effectively selected by R. Hagelstange according to name and character. The number six itself has significance: six war years, six years of captivity in an apparently golden cage, which then covered the six soldiers in night and dust.

Each single fate has symbolic meaning: for instance Benjamin's death is that of an anchorless dreamer; Christopher's death is that of a steadfastly believing Christian, and the death of the sergeant Wenig is that of a repenting sinner:

'. . . Then he went—the others lay down to sleep—, he loaded his service-pistol and paid what was left to him. It was only a little—, yet the whole 'Wenig' (Little). And he had no more than this. . . .'

This '*Schlaraffenfalle*' is by no means an accidental occurrence, a fatal trap in a golden cellar—it is our own relentless destiny. From time to time the author feels urged to emphasize that symbolism: . . . They knew they were shut in and buried ('We do not know it yet . . .'); or the passage about the eyes in the tenth and final section of the poem: . . . We imagine we can empty a sea with two thimbles. 'Yet—we do not see. Light sees out of us . . . The bright stays bright, and the blind one remains blind.'

The poem is written in a mixture of exalted language, reportage of facts and ornate imagery. There is no doubt that beneath the apparently casual surface there lies in this ballad a well-prepared and powerfully expressed artistic vision. It is perhaps one of the most notable poems published by a poet of the younger generation in Germany after 1945.

---

Another striking feature of contemporary German lyrical poetry is its growing tendency towards autonomy of word-structures, its love of a shock-method, of experimental combinations, of word-effects, of the *dernier cri*, and its 'distantiation' and hatred of tradition: e.g. Bert Brecht's '*Vom armen B.B.*' debunks 'poetic' expressions in order to be able to write true poetry again. The birds are called 'vermin'; the pine trees 'piss'; the poet flings away the empty glass and his 'cigar stump' and disturbedly falls asleep:

> . . . *Gegen Morgen in der grauen Frühe pissen die Tannen*
> *Und ihr Ungeziefer, die Vögel, fängt an zu schrein.*
> *Um die Stunde trink ich mein Glas in der Stadt aus und schmeisse*
> *Den Tabakstummel weg und schlafe beunruhigt ein* . . .

But this acrid satire from the pen of such a powerful author cannot be compared with the forced crudeness of '*An die Wand geschrieben*' (1950) by Wolfgang Weyrauch (born 1904) whose 'ABC' might have benefited from contacts with the art of surrealism where the alphabet is put to a much more effective use. He could also have learned from Paul Celan (born 1920) whose '*Todesfuge*' (in '*Mohn und Gedächtnis*' 1952) is a highly artistic presentation of our contemporary historic tragedy:

> *Schwarze Milch der Frühe wir trinken sie abends*
> *wir trinken sie mittags und morgens wir trinken sie nachts*
> *wir trinken und trinken*
> *wir schaufeln ein Grab in den Lüften da liegt man nicht eng*
> *Ein Mann wohnt im Haus der spielt mit den Schlangen*. . . .

But there is also much arbitrariness in some of P. Celan's abstractions which not infrequently make the impression of crossword-puzzles and 'word-montage' with inverted images.

In the light of many intellectual experiments in West Germany it is a welcome surprise to find among the contemporaries an East German writer such as Peter Huchel (born 1903), the chief editor of '*Sinn und Form*,' who without violation of word-material and without taking refuge in mere reportage and montage can shape present-day events to a poetic vision (e.g. '*April* 1945') which as regards intensity and atmosphere resembles that of A. Gryphius and G. Trakl. P. Huchel is, however, an original poet, e.g. in his poem about the '*Retreat*' in which an individual tragedy is given timeless expression in stark outlines:

*Ich sah des Krieges Ruhm.*
*Als wärs des Todes Säbelkorb,*
*Durchklirrt von Schnee, am Strassenrand*
*Lag eines Pferds Gerippe.*
*Nur eine Krähe scharrte dort im Schnee nach Aas,*
*Wo Wind die Knochen nagte, Rost das Eisen frass.*

The two recently published anthologies of East and West German poetry: '*Deutsche Lyrik auf der anderen Seite*' and '*Junge Lyrik*, 1960' (both at C. Hanser Verlag, Munich) emphasize the difference between those two expressions in present-day Germany. We have, in the chapter about G. Benn's '*Welle der Nacht*,' already referred to the above two kinds of lyrical verse, quite apart from the political consideration. The West, in contrast to the East, is a testing ground for word-artistry. Above all, the West, though teeming with individual theories and contributions about a poet's task, rightly offers no 'official' directives as to a writer's duty to the social order and the state, whereas the DDR (with Johannes R. Becher, † 1958, as its Minister of Culture) demanded and still demands a politically committed expression in art, not an 'ivory tower' poetry.

---

The year 1956 seems to be of particular significance, mainly in the history of experiments in West German lyrical poetry. In that year there appeared '*Das Gedicht*' ('*Jahrbuch zeitgenössischer Lyrik*,' ed. by Rudolf Ibel) which is a challenge to the poetry of Rilke and George as well as Benn and the poets of '*Menschheits-Dämmerung*.' Stress now lies mainly on poetic technique. But in contrast to Benn's call for 'pure' poetry it does not ignore the problem of suffering. Instead of harmony it advocates disharmony; instead of Goethe's totality of human and poetic experience it is satisfied with a fragment of a rapidly shrinking world.

In 1956 there also appeared '*Dichtung unserer Zeit*' (Limes Verlag) which reflects the present-day preoccupation with literary conceits and convulsive mannerisms. Examples are easily found in verses by R. P. Becker, H. Mader, P. Rühmkorf (Pseudonym: Leslie Meier) and W. Riegel. This author tries to build up wild landscapes of syntactical adventures. In his '*Bemerkungen zu Jakob van Hoddis*' Werner Riegel confesses that the mad things form themselves into poetry: '*sammeln sich die verrückten Dinge zum Vers.*' Several other writers of the above '*Kleinbuchreihe*' ('*Dichtung unserer Zeit*') are obsessed with sexual exhibitionism. It is a favourite theme, particularly since Paul Valéry's poetic vision '*La Pythie,*' to depict the poet's creative struggle as a sexual conflict between nature and intellect: '*mes deux natures vent s'unir*'; e.g. Reinhard Paul Becker (born 1928): '*Die Arche unter dem Pilz*' ('*Komm*'), in which he speaks of the womb of language, cf. the expressions: '*Mutterleib meiner Sprache . . . gesegneten Schosses. . . . am Morgentau deiner Nabelschnur . . . Umarmung meiner mütterlichsten Vaterkeit . . . kam die männliche Nacht in mein Bett,*' or Helmut Mader in '*Lippenstift für die Seele*' calls his muse a whore in God's temple: 'Meine Muse war eine Tempelprostituierte.' . . . ('*Notre Dame*').

Last but not least in 1956 appeared '*Transit*' ('*Das Lyrikbuch der Jahrhundertmitte*'), edited by Walter Höllerer. Also here the emphatic utterances of the so-called '*Bekenntnislyrik*' are rejected. There is a clear preference for structural artifices of verse-forms. But in contrast to the tone of utter despair and humiliation, as expressed in Peter Rühmkorf's '*Song deiner Niederlagen*': 'Ich bin Europas verlorener Sohn. Siehe die trübe Gestalt' . . . W. Höllerer strikes a note of hope which rings into the second half of our century: 'Taut the sails as on the first day'—'*Prall wie am ersten Tag die Segel.*'

But this new poetic language has to fulfil a specific task: it does not want to entertain or to please or to sing the praise of the universe; it aims at unsentimental close-ups and at the same time it unfolds vast distances; it aims at dissonances rather than harmony, at fragmentation rather than totality, and at utmost intensity and density of expression. Therefore the predilection for an enigmatic brevity of style which, as also with E. Langgässer and W. Lehmann, etc., does not easily avoid the danger of falling into manneristic expressions reminiscent of old riddles.

## III

### *Epilogue—Some Latest Laboratory Experiments: Technical Oddities. Montage. Sophistication and Satire*

It is perhaps in the outer or inner landscape-descriptions that the trend of the latest experiments in German lyrical poetry reveals itself most clearly. A glance at the different interpretations of Nature by various writers of the outgoing nineteenth and the twentieth centuries will illustrate and strengthen the preceding observations.

Theodor Storm (1817–1888) in '*Meeresstrand*' expresses a natural phenomenon with concrete outlines which form a clear picture in our imagination: the dike—the mud flats—twilight—sea-gulls—voices:

*Ans Haff nun fliegt die Möwe*
*Und Dämmrung bricht herein;*
*Über die feuchten Watten*
*Spiegelt der Abendschein.*

*Graues Geflügel huschet*
*Neben dem Wasser her;*
*Wie Träume liegen die Inseln*
*Im Nebel auf dem Meer.*

*Ich höre des gärenden Schlammes*
*Geheimnisvollen Ton,*
*Einsames Vogelrufen—*
*So war es immer schon.*

*Noch einmal schauert leise*
*Und schweiget dann der Wind;*
*Vernehmlich werden die Stimmen,*
*Die über der Tiefe sind.*

The poem expresses a lyrical mood: evening dusk—the quiet wind—the awakening of the subterranean forces; it is at the same time symbolic of the incomprehensible depth of our existence. Thus the concrete lines mingle with the awareness of the mysterious unity of the universe. Both, outer and inner world, are classically balanced, cf. '*Medusa's Mirror*,' pp. 37 ff.

Georg Heym (1887–1912) in his '*Tod des Pierrots*' which has obviously been inspired by Rimbaud's '*Le dormeur du val*,' approaches Nature in a different, i.e. 'Neo-Romantic' mood. His favourite adjectives are: blue—red—golden—white—black. The content is mainly hinted at, by sound and colour which are impressionistic as well as symbolic (of the beauty of autumn and man's loneliness). Death is represented as loving sleep. Pierrot himself has no name, no sex, no home, no age. He merges with landscape, and the poem ends with the swan's song in praise of Nature:

*Wo Herbstes Leier süss in Einsamkeit*
*Durch blauer Felder Sonnenschatten tönt*
*An rote Wolken, und die Wälder weit*
*Im Glanze stehn, der ihren Tod versöhnt,*

*Da küsst ihn Schlaf. Und goldener Abend träuft*
*Sein Blut auf seine Stirn im bunten Laub.*
*Schon schlummert er. Die wilde Rose häuft*
*Die Blüte seinem Grab, des Jahres Raub.*

*Ein Amselschlag in später Abendröte,*
*Wie Dämmrung zart, vom Dolch der Liebe krank,*
*So zittert fort in seiner weissen Flöte*
*Der Wind, die seiner blassen Hand entsank.*

*Und in dem Abend, wo die Wolke zieht,*
*Die zart wie goldner Hauch im Licht verrinnt,*
*Singt ihm ein weisser Schwan ein Totenlied,*
*Den langsam südwärts treibt der Abendwind.*

Oskar Loerke (1884–1941) tries to eliminate personal feeling or association from his nature-poetry completely. The key to his best nature-poems is his statement: 'Bin ein Reim zu allen Dingen.' In contrast to 'Neo-Romantic' atmosphere, to Rilke, also George, and particularly to Expressionism he lets Nature sing her own song in his verse; it is '*Gesang der Dinge*.' He does not describe his reactions to things in Nature, but he wants us to hear Pan's own music instead. The affinity of Loerke's attitude to nature-poetry to that of W. Lehmann and E. Langgässer is obvious, when we read for instance the following lines from Loerke's '*Altes Gemäuer*':

*Ein Mauerwerk zerbröckelt in das Schweigen,*
*Worein die Fugengräser sinken, steigen:*
*Das Mittelalter in ihm rührt sich nicht,*
*Das Altertum in ihm, es spürt sich nicht....*

Autumn is also the scene in '*Verlassene Küste*' by Karl Krolow (born 1915). But this poem lacks any real substance; it creates a fictitious world through images of decay and transitoriness such as breath, shadow, chalk, wind. An embarrassing riming difficulty emphasizes the unreality of this art of suggestions:

*Segelschiffe und Gelächter,*
*Das wie Gold im Barte steht,*
*Sind vergangen wie ein schlechter*
*Atem, der vom Munde geht.*

*Wie ein Schatten auf der Mauer,*
*Der den Kalk zu Staub zerfrisst.*
*Unauflöslich bleibt die Trauer,*
*Die aus schwarzem Honig ist,*

*Duftend in das Licht gehangen,*
*Feucht wie frischer Vogelkot*
*Und den heissen Ziegelwangen*
*Auferlegt als leichter Tod.*

*Kartenschlagende Matrosen*
*Sind in ihrem Fleisch allein.*
*Tabak rieselt durch die losen*
*Augenlider in sie ein.*

*Ihre Messer, die sie warfen*
*Nach dem blauen Vorhang Nacht,*
*Wurden schartig in dem scharfen*
*Wind der Ewigkeit, der wacht.*

Wolfgang Weyrauch boldly goes a step still further towards 'pure poetry' in '*Atom und Aloe*' (analysed by the poet himself in '*Mein Gedicht ist mein Messer*,' ed. by H. Bender, 1955). The highly individual use of imagery would make it almost impossible to fathom the meaning of its allusions without the writer's own comments: e.g. the word 'hebridenwärts' is connected with his love of Mendelssohn's *Hebriden—Ouvertüre*; or '*Der Kehricht küsst den Aal*' suggests that the scum of the cities attacks the animal in the sea; '*Schweisstuch*' stands for Christianity, '*Kral*' and '*Kathedrale*' represent the profane and sacred aspects in our human existence; finally '*Lotos*' (from India) and '*Schleh*' (from Europe) are joined as the progressive and the old elements in life. The poem ends in a rather unconvincing return of paradise ('*Elefantenohr und Laus*') and a brotherhood of mankind. Here are the first and the last of the twelve verses:

*Atom und Aloe*
*im letzten Areal*
*des schwarzen Ninive*
*der Hauch flieht vor der Zahl*

. . . . .

*das Kanu zieht hebridenwärts*
*Diakonie an Bord denn jetzt*
*und immer tönt die Terz:*
*das Brudersegel ist gesetzt*

The already stressed tendency towards autonomy and fragmentation of word-structure reveals not only a marked similarity of contemporary poetry to seventeenth-century lyrical devices but also an intense crisis in modern poetic expression in Europe as well as in America where Edward Estlin Cummings (born 1894), for instance in his '*Sunset*,' seeks to reduce a poem to the last and indispensable fragments or skeleton of its substance: 'stinging/gold swarms/Upon the spires/silver' . . . instead of: 'White foam and vesper wind embrace,/The salt air *stings* my dazzled face/And sunset flecks the *silvery* seas/With glints of *gold* like *swarms* of bees/And lifts tall dreaming *spires* of light/To the imaginary sight' . . . (Italics are mine). Thus E. E. Cummings endeavours to gain extreme formal intensity.

In a recent issue of the German journal: '*Zeitwende*' 6, (1959) we learn of technical oddities which go beyond those shrinking processes and which have indeed arrived in a blind alley, i.e. the mass production of word-montage as can be shown by the following two examples: the first one is called '*Love Letters*,' manufactured by the M.U.C. (Manchester University Computer), and the second one is an arbitrary combination of equally interchangeable six (Spanish) words. In both cases there is no poetic communication whatsoever, no personal vision or emotion, but simply the sensational output of a soulless artifice by an automaton. The English version of the *Liebesbriefe eines Roboters* and the six words read as follows:

Darling Sweetheart. You are my avid fellow feeling. My affection curiously clings to your passionate wish. My liking yearns for your heart. You are my wistful sympathy: my tender liking. Yours beautifully. MUC.

---

| | |
|---|---|
| avenidas<br>avenidas y flores | strassen<br>strassen und blumen |
| flores<br>flores y mujeres | blumen<br>blumen und frauen |
| avenidas<br>avenidas y mujeres | strassen<br>strassen und frauen |
| avenidas y flores y mujeres y<br>un admirador | strassen und blumen und frauen<br>und<br>ein bewunderer |

The title of Helmut Heissenbüttel's booklet of poems (1951–1954) '*Kombinationen*' is symptomatic of some latest German lyrical devices and fragmentations. In the Epilogue Hermann Kasack calls this verse collection an excursion into a terra incognita—a flight from the present, but perhaps a flight in the right direction. It may be that we *have* to go through this phase in order to gain new land, yet H. Heissenbüttel (born 1921) is not a poet but first and foremost a technician of words who is master in his laboratory of linguistic construction and abstractions. He is not concerned about human life, experience and emotion, e.g. in 'poems' such as '*Achterbahn*' (published in the '*Jahresring*,' 1959) we seem to move in a calculated system of points, lines and counter-lines. The 'verse' consists of parallel, symmetrical and asymmetrical lines, repetitions and accumulations of nouns which suggest themselves by means of association or direct contrast or by purely grammatical reference to the preceding stretches of words; others are added or joined together—apparently for the purpose of surprise; cf. also H. Heissenbüttel's '*Textbuch I*' (1960) where the word-matter is held in a mathematical relationship and where already at the very start (*Text I*) the method of contrasting and developing expressions is obvious: STEHEN–FALLEN, SCHATTEN –MORGENSONNE, BLÜHEN–TOD. In a similar way, P. Celan's '*Matière de Bretagne*' is built up on a system of co-ordination and association: the words: gelb—Eiter—Dorn—Wunde, etc., suggest a concrete image of the sinking sun, which, however, is charged with symbolic meaning. H. Heissenbüttel's fragmentary sentences have no punctuation marks, also no such archetypal vision of tragedy as we find e.g. in Celan's image of the setting sun. His technical experiments have no beginning and no end. They hang in a vacuum.

It would, however, be quite wrong to discard as mere brain-tricks or mechanical products or even irresponsible humbug many a genuine attempt by these and other German avant-garde writers to revitalize the outworn forms of lyrical utterance and to open up hitherto unknown spaces to young poets who distrust 'Nature' and consciously turn away from 'poetry' in order to be able to recreate it anew often by means of arithmetic computations of words and counter-point devices. At the moment, the stress no doubt lies on sparkling technique, cf. the abstract word-structures by E. Gomringer (born 1925), author of '*Konstellationen*', H. M. Enzensberger (born 1929), A. A. Scholl (born 1926) and others. Some of these abstractions reveal themselves as '*littérature engagée*.' Hans Magnus Enzensbergers's poem, though a masterpiece of elaborate technical invention and characteristically entitled: '*An alle fernsprechteilnehmer*' does certainly not move in a space devoid of matter and politics (see the poet's own analysis in '*Jahresring*': 1960–1961). It is an indictment of mad experiments which bring over mankind radio-active fall-out and which threaten to blot us out of existence. Yet life goes on: summer comes, the phlox blossoms—at the same time 'deadening resolutions are passed.' . . . The content of this remarkable poem is directed to us all: '*An alle*'; it is not a private concern. Its artistic form is highly sophisticated, see its sound-effects and also its metaphoric language: the navigation-metaphors = Lotse, Radar, Tanker . . . sea animals, etc. = Butt, Salm, Seestern . . ., the net-metaphors = Verstärkeramt (Telefonnetz), Spinne . . ., poison-metaphors = Blei, (Nessus)—Hemd. H. M. Enzensberger, the author of the '*Verteidigung der Wölfe*,' is an angry young writer who uses satire as his weapon against the 'sticky' dough of our mass-age: . . . *es ist etwas in der luft klebrig/und zäh. . . .*

*. . . und wir essen davon*
*und verleiben uns ein etwas zähes,*
*und schlafen im blühenden boom,*
*im fünfjahresplan, arglos*
*schlafend im brennenden hemd,*
*wie geiseln umzingelt von einem zähen,*
*farblosen, einem gedunsenen turm.*

The 'old' themes such as universe, the new man, the fatherland, (Konzentrationslager) 'K. Z. poetry' and the personal emotions do not seem to interest most word-engineers in their modern laboratories much, if at all. Not infrequently they effectively succeed in throwing a scene or gesture into 'clearer' perspective, e.g. the flash-like abstraction: '*Schwärze fällt in die säge des lachens*' in F. Achleitner's '*Warten*,' or Günter Eich's poem '*Tage mit Hähern*' which shows clear marks of the above 'distantiation.' Thus most recent German verse suggests a desire for intensification and fragmentation instead of the totality of impression. Above all, it aims at disharmony, ugliness or the deliberate deformation of the once worshipped beautiful harmony; it betrays an aversion against grandiose rhetoric or frothy verbiage in a meaningless and estranged existence, as for instance so poignantly depicted in '*Die gestundete Zeit*' (1953), by Ingeborg Bachmann (born 1926), to mention only one significant example. Many of these features of recent German verse are shared by other European literatures.

By the side of these poets with their craving for novelty and hermetic imagery, there are, as indicated above, a number of original and yet traditional writers; H. Hesse, W. Bergengruen, R. A. Schröder, F. G. Jünger, Stefan Andres, Georg von der Vring, etc., but the chief purpose of this last chapter is to introduce some extreme experiments in most recent German lyrical poetry to the reader. This modern generation in which the old Dadaist Hans Arp (born 1887) is again read and admired, goes, as we have seen, far beyond the poets of '*Menschheits—Dämmerung*' and Rilke, George and even Benn. It is conscious of living in the revolutionary 'atomic' age. Now the heliocentric conception of the universe is shattered, as was once the geocentric. But whatever '1984' may have in store for us, there is no cause for lament about the decline of the creative resources of German lyrical poetry which burst into full blossom three times: in the medieval minnesong of Walter von der Vogelweide, Heinrich von Morungen, Wolfram von Eschenbach, at the time of Goethe, Hölderlin, Eichendorff, Heine and Mörike, and in Gottfried Benn's age, mainly through Stefan George and Rainer Maria Rilke.

It is in the poet's power to give permanence to the fleeting moments of human life. He not only shapes the sensuous and intellectual chaos of our world, he also secures the continuity of man's spiritual existence. Our deeds crumble to dust. But the poet casts the stone that another threw before him till later another comes to lift it again and hurl it towards new horizons.

# ABBREVIATIONS

*AUFRISS* = *Deutsche Philologie im Aufriss*, ed. by W. Stammler, 2nd ed. 1957 ff.

*B* = F. M. Böhme's *Altdeutsches Liederbuch*. Leipzig 1877.

*DLD* = K. Bartsch's *Deutsche Liederdichter des* 12. *bis* 14. *Jahrhunderts*. 1900[4], ed. by W. Golther.

*DLL* = *Deutsches Literatur-Lexikon*. W. Kosch. Bern 1949-1958.

*DuV* = (*Dichtung und Volkstum*) Euphorion.

*DVj* = *Deutsche Vierteljahrsschrift*.

*EB* = Erk-Böhme's *Deutscher Liederhort*. 3 vols. 1893-4, ed by F. M. Böhme.

Ermatinger = *Die deutsche Lyrik seit Herder*, 3 vols. 1925[2].

*G* = Goedeke's *Grundriss zur Geschichte der deutschen Dichtung*.

*GE* = *Germanistik*, 1960 ff., ed. by H. W. Bähr and W. Gose.

*GRM* = *Germanisch-Romanische Monatsschrift*.

H = Heft.

*KDNL* = *Deutsche National-Litteratur*, ed. by J. Kürschner.

l.c. = *loco citato*.

*MF* = *Des Minnesangs Frühling*.

*MLN* = *Modern Language Notes*.

*MLR* = *Modern Language Review*.

*P* = *Palästra*.

*PBB* = *Paul-Braune Beiträge*.

*RL* = *Reallexikon der deutschen Literaturgeschichte*, edited by Merker-Stammler, new ed. by Kohlschmidt-Mohr, articles by E. Lunding, B. Markwardt, F. W. Wentzlaff-Eggebert and others.

*ZfdA* = *Zeitschrift für deutsches Altertum*.

# INDEX

DISCHARGED
DISCHARGED
DISCHARGED
DISCHARGED

FEB 21 1972
DISCHARGED
DISCHARGED
DISCHARGED
DISCHARGED
OCT 30